Critical Thinking and Writing in the Disciplines
Readings to Accompany
The Allyn & Bacon Handbook

Mary E. McGann

University of Indianapolis

Allyn and Bacon

Boston   London   Toronto   Sydney   Tokyo   Singapore

Copyright © 1992 by Allyn & Bacon
A Division of Simon & Schuster
160 Gould Street
Needham Heights, MA 02194

All rights reserved. No part of the material protected by this copyright notice may be reproduced or utilized in any form or by any means, electronic or mechanical, including photocopying, recording, or by any information storage and retrieval system, without the written permission of the copyright owner.

Executive Editor: Joseph Opiela
Production Administrator: Susan McIntyre
Editorial-Production Service: Kathy Smith
Cover Administrator: Linda Dickinson
Composition Buyer: Linda Cox
Manufacturing Buyer: Louise Richardson

Library of Congress Cataloging-in-Publication Data

Critical thinking and writing in the disciplines : readings to accompany the Allyn & Bacon handbook / [edited by]
Mary E. McGann.
    p. cm.
  Includes bibliographical references.
  ISBN 0-205-13621-4
    1. College readers. 2. English language—Rhetoric.
  3. Interdisciplinary approach in education. I. McGann, Mary

PE1417.T476 1992   91-44789
808'.0427—dc20   CIP

Printed in the United States of America

10 9 8 7 6 5 4 3 2 1   96 95 94 93 92

Credits

Page 1, Adalaide Morris, "Dick, Jane, and American Literature: Fighting with Canons," *College English*, September 1985. Copyright 1985 by the National Council of Teachers of English. Reprinted with permission. **Page 17**, Joyce R. Durham, "The City in Recent American Fiction: Listening to Black Urban Voices," *College English*, November 1990. Copyright 1990 by the National Council of Teachers of English. Reprinted with permission.

Credits are continued on page 357, which constitutes a continuation of the copyright page.

Contents

Preface   ix

1 *Readings in the Humanities*   1

Adalaide Morris, **Dick, Jane, and American Literature: Fighting with Canons**   1
An English professor proposes that literature courses should reflect true cultural and gender diversity.

Joyce R. Durham, **The City in Recent American Fiction: Listening to Black Urban Voices**   17
A scholar and teacher suggests that we can learn much about the diversity of Black life from studying the urban context of African American writings.

Brian Henderson, *The Civil War:* **"Did It Not Seem Real?"**   29
A professor of film studies examines the relationship between art and reality in the critically and popularly acclaimed documentary television series, The Civil War.

Two Critical Views of *The Handmaid's Tale*   42

Edd Doerr, **A Chilling Look at a Fundmentalist Dystopia**   43

Michael Calleri, **Another Example of How Great Novels Make Bad Films**   44
One critic responds glowingly to the film version of a feminist novel, while his colleague finds many flaws in the translation from novel to film.

Richard Welch, **Rock 'n' Roll and Social Change**   50
Writing for an educated general audience, a British writer connects the musical innovations of fifties' rock 'n roll with the movement toward civil rights for Black minorities in the United States.

Thomas Fiddick, **Beyond the Domino Theory: The Vietnam War and Metaphors of Sport**   60

An historian examines the ways in which politicians and military leaders have used the language of games and sports to discuss the war in Southeast Asia.

James Kitfield, **Total Force**   74
A writer for a government publication analyzes the ways in which the total volunteer force sent to the Persian Gulf in 1991 signals a major change for the American military.

Anthony G. Amsterdam, **Capital Punishment**   82
A noted legal scholar delineates his opposition to the death penalty.

Christopher Meyers, **Racial Bias, the Death Penalty, and Desert**   95
In a scholarly essay, a moral philosopher develops a complex argument against the death penalty.

Tracy Marschall, **An Exercise in Feminist Liberation Theology: Islam, Judaism, and Christianity**   104
A student writer seeks to reconcile a feminist theology with the tenets of the three major world religions.

Brian Handrigan, **The Way We Make Ethical Decisions: Understanding the Subjectivity of Values**   112
In examining the ideas of several famous philosophers, a philosophy student develops an argument about moral decision making.

Lisa A. Jones, **Biblical Echoes in Margaret Atwood's** *The Handmaid's Tale*   117
A literature student analyzes a pattern of Biblical images and allusions in Margaret Atwood's novel.

Further Explorations for Readings in the Humanities   123

2 *Readings in the Social Sciences*   124

B.F. Skinner, **Outlining a Science of Feeling**   124
A noted psychologist of behaviorism describes human emotions.

Elaine Hatfield and Richard Rapson, **Emotions: A Trinity**   132
Two psychologists reject Skinner's outline of feelings as too simplistic and then offer their own outline of the complex structure of human emotions.

Mary Field Belenky, Blythe McVicker Clinchy, Nancy Rule Goldberger, and Jill Mattuck Tarule, **Family Life and the Politics of Talk**   145

Four psychologists develop a picture of how young women's perceptions of themselves and the world around them have been influenced by their family upbringing.

Michael W. Tucker and Kevin E. O'Grady, **Effects of Physical Attractiveness, Intelligence, Age at Marriage, and Cohabitation on the Perception of Marital Satisfaction**   156
A professor and his student collaborate on research into college students' perceptions of what will make them happy in marriage.

Margaret A. Eisenhart, **Learning to Romance: Cultural Acquisition in College**   171
An anthropologist studies how young people learn to fit in socially at college.

Steven A. Reiss, **Sport in the Black Urban Community**   191
A social historian examines the significant role of sports and athletic games among African Americans.

Margaret Mead, **The Attitude Towards Personality**   202
An excerpt from a landmark anthropological study, Coming of Age in Samoa, *describes how people deal with personality in Samoan culture.*

Richard Feinberg, **Margaret Mead and Samoa:** *Coming of Age* **in Fact and Fiction**   206
A contemporary anthropologist analyzes and evaluates the controversy that arose in the 1980s over Mead's famous study.

Wilson Carey McWilliams, **A Republic of Couch Potatoes: The Media Shrivel the Electorate**   217
A professor of political science writes pessimistically about the American voter.

Christine F. Ridout, **The Role of Media Coverage of Iowa and New Hampshire in the 1988 Democratic Nomination**   222
A statistical study of the influence of media coverage of the presidential primary confirms that American voters do not think independently about politics.

Lori A. Rose, **Nonverbal Communication**   235
A student writer summarizes some of the major research about nonverbal communication.

Richard Shea and Daniel Zona, **A Survey of Dating Violence on a University Campus**   240
Two students develop original research in a survey of dating violence on their own campus.

Tamara S. Peters, **The Diagnosis and Treatment of** *Bulimia Nervosa*   249
A student writer examines the abnormal psychology of an eating disorder.

Further Explorations for Readings in the Social Sciences   253

3   Readings in the Sciences   255

Howard Frumkin, **Occupational and Environmental Cancer: Radical Chic and Mau-Mauing the Carcinogens**   255
A medical researcher analyzes the popular belief that environmentally caused cancers are increasing.

Scott Saleska, **Low-Level Radioactive Waste: Gamma Rays in the Garbage**   263
A scientific reporter suggests that local landfills and garbage dumps could contain a lot more than harmless residential refuse.

Ron Cowen, **Catching Some Rays: Earth-Based Detectors Hunt for Violent Stellar Events**   273
A reporter for a popular science magazine describes projects in astrophysics which seek to understand the sources of high energy rays.

Evelyn Fox Keller, **A World of Difference**   281
A scientist reflects on the maverick career of Nobel Prize winning geneticist, Barbara McClintock.

Tom Shoop, **Biology's Moon Shot: The Human Genome Project**   295
A government reporter describes a controversial federal project which will attempt to map all human cell structures.

Carole Ezzell, **Memories Might be Made of This: Closing in on the Biochemistry of Learning**   303
A report aimed at a popular audience reviews recent research in the biochemistry of memory.

Terry Crow and James Forrester, **Inhibition of Protein Synthesis Blocks Long-Term Enhancement of Generator Potentials Produced by One-Trial** *in vivo* **Conditioning in** *Hermissenda*   309
In a research report addressed to their specific colleagues, two scientists summarize one aspect of their neurobiological research into what blocks or enhances memory.

Stephen Jay Gould, **Sex, Drugs, Disasters, and the Extinction of Dinosaurs**   322

In evaluating three theories of what happened to the dinosaurs, a noted scientist discusses what makes good science.

George W. Mushrush, Douglas G. Mose, and Charles E. Chrosinak, **Indoor Radon in Northern Virginia: Seasonal Changes and Correlations with Geology** 329
Three geologists find that environmental conditions affect the measurement of radon in homes.

W.S. Fyfe, **The International Geosphere/Biosphere Programme and Global Change: An Anthropocentric or an Ecocentric Future? A Personal View** 338
A geoscientist warns that if scientists do not join forces to save the earth, everyone will lose.

Katherine Welch, **Effects, Countermeasures, and Implications of Muscle Atrophy Due to Weightlessness** 345
A student scientist surveys what space program research has discovered about muscle atrophy.

Amy Workman, **Pikas:** *Ochotona princeps* 348
A student biologist summarizes her research on a small prairie animal.

Carrie Masiello, **Marie-Sophie Germain, 18th Century Physicist** 352
A student of physics and mathematics finds that the scientific community of eighteenth century France was unprepared to admit a woman to its ranks.

Further Explorations for Readings in the Sciences 356

Preface

The term *writing across the curriculum*, or *writing across the disciplines* must be interpreted broadly to mean critical thinking and language across the curriculum, because a commitment to writing across the disciplines necessarily means that we commit ourselves to the inextricable link between thought and language. Critical thinking is impossible without language.

This reader is designed to demonstrate the connections between language and thought in a variety of disciplines. The language of the scientist is different from the language of the humanist, and those different academic languages reflect the different modes of thought which characterize each discipline.

Within each discipline there is also a range of critical thinking and writing being generated among the community of scholars, researchers, and interpreters who practice the discipline. This range is reflected in the readings selected for this book. Thus, the Social Sciences section includes examples of quantitative as well as qualitative research. There are also examples of collaboration—much more the norm in the Social Sciences and Sciences than in the Humanities.

In each section, there are essays written for public audiences and essays written for scholarly audiences, as well as hybrid forms such as Howard Frumkin's article on environmental cancer. Frumkin's article addresses a broad audience, yet he documents his argument with scholarly references.

Pairs of articles (Amsterdam and Meyers; Skinner and Hatfield and Rapson; Mead and Feinberg; McWilliams and Ridout) have been chosen to demonstrate the continuing dialogue among scholars which forms and reforms intellectual knowledge within a discipline. Our students should recognize the importance of scholars' disagreements with each other and learn to evaluate critically the positions of those scholars.

Many of the essays included in this book were suggested by my colleagues from Psychology, Sociology, Geology, Philosophy, Biology, Anthropology, History, and Literature. Several of these colleagues brought their students' papers to my attention and encouraged me to include the students' essays on a equal footing with the professional essays. I have gained some insights into the academic discourse of each discipline from these practitioners and researchers, and I must acknowledge their contribution: Victoria Bedford, John Batey, Marshall B. Gentry, O.T. Kent, Kathryn Murray, Richard Nash, Lawrence Onesti, Carolyn Panofsky, A. John Roche, Robert Schwegler, and Charlotte Templin.

A Note on the Text

If we are to help our students use language as a means of developing and refining critical thinking, we have to be prepared to recognize and accept the process by which human beings read, perceive, and come to know. That process, like writing, is recursive and fluid; it is not neat and it cannot be boxed into test questions. The questions posed before reading and during reading are guides for students who are still unfamiliar with reading academic prose. The questions after reading are not meant to be tests on the reading, but rather aids for thinking about the reading. Students and teachers should recognize that pre-reading questions do not have right or wrong answers: they are meant to encourage readers to tap prior knowledge and to prepare a preliminary context for the reading.

The ideal use of these questions and reading probes would be to have students respond to them in reading logs or journals. The more ways students rehearse their responses and ideas in generative pieces of writing such as lists, freewrites, and reactions, the more they will shape and develop a language for critical thinking.

The end of unit questions are labeled "Further Explorations," and they are meant to be just that. These questions might usefully serve as the basis for some library or ethnographic research on the part of students. The questions could also be used as paper topics, or as discussion questions for collaborative groups.

Acknowledgments

I must acknowledge the influence of the mentors who have helped me understand the nature of thinking, writing, and learning across the curriculum: James Britton, Toby Fulwiler, Elaine Maimom, and Henry Steffens.

A major acknowledgment and thanks must go to the staff of the Krannert Memorial Library at the University of Indianapolis and the staff of the Kent Cooper Periodicals Reading Room at Indiana University, Bloomington.

Joseph Opiela, Executive Editor at Allyn and Bacon, conceived of this project and gave me the support, the prodding, and the deadlines that every writer needs. Timothy J. Wiles helped me talk out ideas for this collection and responded to drafts of the questions; Linda Prince and Andy Fischer typed the students' papers; Sibyl Bedford was an excellent clerical assistant; Rose Hein McGann provided a comfortable vacation workspace; and David Wiles was patient while his Mom was busy with her work.

1

Readings in the Humanities

Dick, Jane, and American Literature: Fighting with Canons
Adalaide Morris

Adalaide Morris, a professor of English, wrote this essay for a scholarly journal which focuses on the teaching of English. Her subject is the American literary canon or the accepted body of works which compose American Literature. Morris pictures herself "fighting" with a canon that only includes white Anglo-Saxon men, excluding women and minorities. The questions she raises continue to be hotly debated by teachers of English in this country.

Before you read: FIRST THOUGHTS
                    LOOK AHEAD

1. What kinds of stories and characters do you remember from your early school reading? Are Dick and Jane familiar to you?
2. What associations do you make with the following words: *canon, canonize, canonization*?
3. Read paragraphs 1–3. Write a reaction to Leslie Silko's early experience with Dick and Jane and their family.

During reading: REACT
                      QUESTION
                      SUMMARIZE

1. What do you think Morris perceives as the most damaging result of establishing an exclusive canon of works of literature? Do you agree or disagree with her?

2. Morris summarizes three stages she perceives in the rethinking of the canon of American literature so that it includes the experience of women and ethnic minorities. Explain these stages in your own words.

THE VERY FIRST BOOK I remember reading had bold pictures and clean, brisk words. "See Spot run," I read, sliding a stubby finger along the line. "See Puff play." It was the story of Dick and Jane, the boy and girl who lived with their dog and cat, Mother and Father, and baby sister Sally in a little house with a red door, a curving walk, and a bright green lawn with bushy trees. Father was tall and wore a suit, Mother was shorter and wore an apron, and baby Sally crawled and cried making us feel proud to be grown-up first-graders reading books. This was my world, and I recognized its every striped ball, spotless pinafore, and smiling postman.

At about the same time I was seeing Spot run, another American girl was also reading *Dick and Jane*. The Native American writer Leslie Silko grew up on the Laguna Pueblo in the Southwest. To her the father with his briefcase, the mother with her cookie pans, the children cavorting on the lawn must have seemed strange creatures. What worried her, however, was the robins. Dick and Jane (and children in the Chicago suburbs) know when winter comes robins fly south. What, then, was the matter with the Pueblo robins? Why didn't they leave? (67)

Toni Morrison's first novel, *The Bluest Eye*, starts with Dick and Jane: "Here is the house. It is green and white. It has a red door. It is very pretty. Here is the family. Mother, Father, Dick, and Jane live in the green-and-white house. They are very happy." Her second paragraph runs the sentences together without breaks ("Here is the house it is green and white it has a red door"), and the third drops the spaces between the words ("Hereisthehouseitisgreenandwhite") (7–8). The stately, reassuring rhythms of Dick and Jane undergo nightmare acceleration, and the words fuse into a monolithic chunk of type, a block as heavy as a tablet of commandments. Chips from this block introduce Morrison's chapters about a poor black family: Cholly Breedlove, Mrs. Breedlove, Sammy, and Pecola, who live in an abandoned store underneath the headquarters of three whores named China, Poland, and the Maginot Line. Cholly drinks and beats his wife, Sammy runs away, and each night Pecola prays for blue eyes. She, like her mother, like the girls at school, like all of us first graders, knew that if she resembled Jane she would be all right. Like Silko's robins, however, by any standard we recognized, she was not all right. Out of his own tenderness and agony, her father rapes her, goes to jail, and dies; she bears a dead baby and goes mad. The ironic interplay between the chapterheads ("fatherwillyouplaywithjanesmilefathersmile") and the chapter contents indicts a whitewashed world so sure of itself it has no space between its words for little black girls in abandoned stores.

No one told us, perhaps no one in my early fifties school system *could* have told us, that Dick and Jane were a special case, a small minority of suburban, white, middle-class children of Anglo-Saxon parentage and Protestant heritage. We thought, and our parents thought, and Native American, Black, Jewish, and Asian-American children were urged to think that when the robins left for us, they should leave for all.

When many of us reached college in the early sixties and studied what was now called "American literature," Jane and baby Sally fell away, but we continued to read about Dick. Now Dick becomes Franklin's Poor Richard who knows that *God helps them that help themselves* or Horatio Alger's Ragged Dick the Match Boy who rises from rags to riches to become, in Fitzgerald's mythic rewriting, The Great Gatsby. Or he becomes Nick, Hemingway's Nick Adams making his separate peace in the Michigan woods, or Ike, Isaac McCaslin in Faulkner's "The Bear" who earns his manhood in the Mississippi wilderness. These two great paradigms of American literature—the success story and the story of rugged individualism—are our primers. Like *Dick and Jane*, they are training tales, stories that tell us how to live, what to do. They are the stories that we have institutionalized as the "American literary canon."

Like the schools in which it is taught, like the church, like the legal system, what we call "American literature" is an institution: an authoritative organization of principles and precepts. The canon is its charter: an official designation of membership and a certification of rights and privileges. As all first graders once read *Dick and Jane*, college students now read Emerson, Thoreau, Melville, Whitman, and Twain. We like to think of literature as a representation of experience, but the question Silko and Morrison ask is blunt: *whose* experience? How have Ahab, Walt, Huck, Nick, and Ike come to stand for *the* "American" experience? Who made Injun Joe and Nigger Jim? And where in the world is Jane?

I'd like to approach these questions by rethinking a word central to the problem: the word *canon*. This is a mighty word, a word that decrees, regulates, codifies, and constitutes. With others of its family, however, it starts from a slim and supple source: the Greek word *kanna*, meaning a hollow tube or reed. If we use this reed to measure things, it becomes a canon: a general rule, formula, or table. Mounted on the parapets of a fort, it becomes the *cannon* we shoot at those who are unlucky enough to live outside or disobey our rules. If long enough and strong enough, this reed becomes a *cane* which can support us or flog others. Unlike a reed, which may be swayed or woven or even whistled through, the canon, cannons, and canes have fixed functions, They don't invite rethinking. It seems to be no accident that *canon* sounds so much like *cannot*.

In our profession, the literary canon not only regulates, defends, and supports us: it seems to sanctify us. In the precise sense we appropriate from ecclesiastical parlance, the canon is an authoritative list of books accepted as holy scripture. Our canon is the "great books," the Modern Library list of classics, or, most pertinently here, the Library of America volumes now emerging in a uniform format, each printed on Oxford style onion paper and bound, like a bible, with a grosgrain ribbon placemarker.[1] These books are the basis for the lists academics live by (course lists, M.A. Exam lists, Ph.D. Comprehensive Examination lists, the

---

[1] For an astute account of this series, see Wayne Franklin.

list of "books I want to read" or "books I'll never admit I haven't read" or "books I swear I'll read next summer"). Lined down the page, these texts become the table of contents for anthologies, the schedule of sessions at conventions, and the subjects of scrutiny in our favorite professional journals. When we as students and teachers try to understand what we're doing in this world, the canon seems to offer a center for all our peripheries. It is, in another ecclesiastical borrowing, our mission or missal: a catalogue of saints, a liturgical sequence, an annual or customary payment or tribute.

And it should be. The canon is for us what the epic was for the Greeks: an encyclopedia of culture, a compendium of what we know, a background against which forms the figure of what we read and what we write. "Masterpieces are never single and solitary births. They are," as Virginia Woolf has reminded us, "the outcome of many years of thinking in common, of thinking by the body of the people, so that the experience of the mass is behind the single voice" (68–9). Reading any text is necessarily listening to a voice in conversation with other voices. No writer, no artist of any art, has his or her complete meaning alone. To understand the soliloquist, we need also to listen to the chorus.

The problem arises when the canon becomes a cane by which we yank the soliloquist off the stage or a piece of artillery we use to hurl her or him into the outer darkness. The problem arises when, to alter the metaphor slightly, the chorus rises and says to the soliloquist something like "you're not the best that has been thought and said," a formula inevitably followed by adjectives like "propagandist," "second-rate," "narrow," "partial," "distorted," or "subjective." At this moment it is hard not to notice that the chorus consists almost entirely of white gentlemen of the middle or upper classes and that they're toting signs emblazoned with the words "universal," "timeless," "natural," and "self-evident."

The fact of canonization puts any work beyond questions of establishing its merit and, instead, invites us to offer only increasingly more ingenious readings and interpretations, the purpose of which is to validate labels like "great" or "universal" (Kolodny, 1980, 8). The general effect of canonization, as it became evident in the sixties, is threefold:

1. to propagandize the world view of canonized works, which tends to be almost entirely the world view of relatively privileged social classes in societies actively engaged in conquering and ruling other peoples
2. to reinforce our own authority and position as students and professors of literature who possess valuable knowledge, social usefulness, and, above all, superior taste, and
3. to substitute a tiny part for the whole, demeaning as subliterary almost the entire body of literature, especially popular literature, folk literature, oral literature, literature based on the experience of work, and almost all literature by nonwhite, nonmale peoples.[2]

---

[2] For an extended discussion of these points, formulated by H. Bruce Franklin, see "English as an Institution."

Much has happened since the sixties: we have grown suspicious of words like "timeless" and "self-evident"; we have understood the canon as, among other things, a political document, and we have begun to admit some women, a few Blacks, and here and there a Native American.

Fish can't see the water because they are in it. Students and teachers frequently fail to see the canon because they are of it. Like ideology, the canon is the medium in which we move. It is that which we assume, that which is repeated, public opinion, the mind of the majority, the voice of reason, all that we know without knowing quite how we came to know it. For this reason, it is important to step back a moment and consider the formation of the American canon. How did we come to know that Hawthorne, Faulkner, and Mailer belong, but Sarah Orne Jewett, Eudora Welty, and Toni Morrison don't?

It is jolting to remember that only some seventy years ago American literature itself was noncanonical. American writing was just the tip of a twig on the great tree that sprang from Homer, only a minor sprout on a limb that grew from *Beowulf* and *The Canterbury Tales*. It was not part of what Matthew Arnold called "the best that is known and thought in the world"; it was not in what F. R. Leavis called *The Great Tradition*. It was popular reading, that which one could work up on one's own, say on rainy Sunday afternoons.

In fact, only two hundred years ago the term "American literature" was itself tentative, more a boast than an actuality. It became common after the 1783 Treaty of Paris (Golding 281), But in the next hundred years few agreed on what it meant. Did it include the Puritans, geographically American but politically English? Was it descriptive, specifying a historical or territorial range, or was it prescriptive, honoring as "American" only those writings that met some criterion of moral purity, political ideology, or national character?

If we understand the "American literary canon" to be that set of authors and books generally included in introductory American literature courses and discussed in standard works of literary history and criticism, it is possible to mark who's in and who's out by checking the contents of teaching anthologies. The first thing we notice about these anthologies, of course, is that, try as they might, they can't be merely descriptive. They are to the whole body of literature produced in the United States as the *Social Register* is to the Philadelphia phonebook. The second thing we notice is that, like the *Social Register*, they record surges of fashion as fixed certainties. The anthologist is generally an eminent critic, someone who has written one or more of the standard texts of literary history and criticism, and he (for it is almost invariably "he") magisterially assumes an undefined community of readers who concur with his judgment. What's interesting, however, is the way that across time the powerful decline and poor cousins prevail. As Longfellow, the only American fixed in stone in the Poet's Corner of Westminster Abbey, fades away, wicked Walt Whitman strides in.

Let me take two pairs of anthologies, one of poetry, one of prose, to illustrate this process.[3] The first pair is two successive editions of *The Oxford Book of American*

---

[3] I am indebted for the examples here to two excellent essays on the canon-shaping force of teaching anthologies: Golding's "A History of American Poetry Anthologies" and Lauter's "Race and Gender in the Shaping of the American Literary Canon."

Verse. In 1927, Bliss Carmen's anthology gave more pages to Longfellow than to Whitman and Dickinson combined; it granted ample space to the poems of Bryant, Whittier, Holmes, and James Russell Lowell, "productions of an earlier age 'which no gentleman's library should be without,' " but it included only those twentieth-century poets who represented what Carmen felt to be the "valiant and joyous spirit" of the age (Preface iv-v) and admitted no black poets beyond the token Paul Dunbar. In 1950, F. O. Matthiessen dismantled Carmen's canon. He cut 147 poets (including Dunbar) from the register and added 28, among them Anne Bradstreet, Jones Very, Melville, Eliot, Williams, Crane, H.D., Stevens, and cummings. He smashed the plaster busts of Longfellow and his circle and elevated Emerson, Thoreau, Poe, Whitman, and Dickinson, the nineteenth-century writers on whom he had centered *The American Renaissance*. And, finally, he understood the twentieth century not as an age of valor and joy but as the terrain of the waste land, of Mr. Eugenides, Hugh Selwyn Mauberley, and the Equilibrists. Where Carmen included in his anthology only one poem by Pound, Matthiessen not only amply represented Pound but selected work by other poets that executed Pound's command to cut the cackle. We are now fish swimming in the pool constructed by Matthiessen.

The second pair of anthologies provides an even sharper juxtaposition. Both were assembled by the great critic Norman Foerster, both were introduced with the same composed certainty of judgment, and yet they disagree radically. In the preface to his 1916 volume, *The Chief American Prose Writers*, Foerster observes that "the nine writers represented in this volume have become, by general consensus, the American prose classics." In the 1963 introduction to his *Eight American Writers*, he reiterates, "In the consensus of our time eight writers . . . constitute our 'American classics' " (qtd. in Lauter "Race and Gender" 436). Only Poe, Emerson, and Hawthorne are common to both lists. "Our American classics," it appears, are as wobbly as the consensus that constitutes them. The constants are not the texts themselves but the tone and vocabulary that canonize them, that and the amazing fact that none of them are by women, Blacks, or Native Americans.[4]

Canon formation is the ache of ambitious critics. Magisterial readers like Samuel Johnson, Matthew Arnold, F. R. Leavis, Cleanth Brooks, T. S. Eliot, Northrop Frye, and Harold Bloom not only set the terms of criticism but dictate the texts to be honored or harrassed by our judgments. I entered college during the reign of T. S. Eliot. Imagining myself to be contemplating the best that has been thought and said—for that is what we do in college—I memorized the definitions

---

[4] As Krupat points out, "only in the past thirty years or so has philological and, in particular, structural analysis of Indian literatures begun to establish their formal principles on anything like a scientific basis" (311). Native American texts, however, have been available since nineteenth-century historians and ethnographers began to transcribe and translate them. Dorris stresses the folly of clumping an extremely diverse and difficult body of texts into something neatly termed "Indian literature" and then teaching it without a sharp sense of its various contexts and intents. Nevertheless, by the time of Matthiessen's and Foerster's anthologies, it was possible to acknowledge these texts as important "American" productions and to begin to appreciate their ecosystemic wisdom and their performative poetics.

of "objective correlative" and "dissociation of sensibility" and set about applying them to Dryden, Donne, and Jules Laforgue. Scorning Tennyson's watery sentimentality, I tried to savor the bitter tang of Jacobean drama. If its double-dealing poisoners were repellent, we nonetheless knew that they were crucial to the story of great literature.

When we go beyond anthologies to the critical texts that precede and determine them, we can see a fact obscured by the largely unadorned enumerations of anthologies. Canons are not simply lists: they are narratives, stories that assemble and activate the figures on the roster. To shift the metaphor a little, canons are not simply catalogues of stars; they are constellations, patterns pieced out by the observing eye. The hunter and his prey, the reunited twins, the big dipper scooping the milky way: these formations tell more about us and our dramas than about the fiery distances they purport to describe.

The stories that form the current canon of American literature were written by men working in the first half of the twentieth century, each constrained by his own particular heritage and history, each centering his narrative on a master metaphor. D. H. Lawrence's battle between the Puritans and the Redskins, Oscar Cargill's "ideas on the march," F. O. Matthiessen's "American Renaissance," Henry Nash Smith's "virgin land," R. W. B. Lewis's "American Adam": these are our canon-founding constellations. Each compels because each, in its way, is deeply motivated. To take just one example, D. H. Lawrence's *Studies in Classic American Literature*, published in the era of Foerster's prose and Carmen's poetic canons, radically readjusts the concept of the American classic, excoriating Old Daddy Franklin and Gentleman Cooper and exalting the fierceness of Melville and Whitman. The book was written in the grim years of World War I out of Lawrence's fury with what he considered England's pother and bosh. In it Lawrence uses American literature to pound the first nail into the tires of Clifford Chatterley's wheelchair.

In the fifteen years since I left the American literature surveys of graduate school, post-structuralist theory has joined with the social movements of the sixties in exposing the cultural ambitions of the canon. If for feminist, Black, and Native American critics, the theme of canonization is power, the power by which white Anglo-Saxon Protestant patriarchs protect their interests, post-structuralist literary theorists mount a more general attack. If I can borrow for a moment their pleasure in punning, they go after not just the wasps but the bees; all our humanist reifications of being. For these critics, the canon is the privileged site of the humanist ideals of transcendence, endurance, and universality, a construction that, like all manifestations of the desire for mastery, must be demystified and dismantled.

A demystified canon is, of course, as post-structuralist critics recognize, still a canon. Its wheelbase may be disconnected from its firing chamber, but it remains, nonetheless, the monument on our courthouse lawns. We go on and will go on teaching courses called "American Literary Classics," reading journals entitled *American Literature* or *American Literary Quarterly*, and perusing histories of American literary production. In the liberal, pluralistic seventies, the main response to critical pressure on the canon has been to "open" or "expand" it: to admit, as I suggested earlier, some Blacks, a few women, and here and there a Native American. Updating the *Norton Anthology of Poetry* from 1970 to 1975, for example, the editors self-consciously claim "four new black poets [who] amplify the presentation of that tradition" and "twice as many women poets as before" (Allison, et al., eds. Preface xlv).[5] What is the effect of such an expansion? Have we, in fact, changed the canon's firepower or, as one disillusioned student suggested, merely enlarged its bore size?

I'd like to approach this problem by returning to an earlier question: whatever happened to Jane and baby Sally? Supposing that Jane and Sally, like Silko and Morrison, grow up to write superb poems and stories, what place will they claim in our literary curricula? There are two possibilities, one liberal and one radical, and both, I will argue, have significant drawbacks.

Women writers have been active in America since the earliest colonial days, but at least up until the mid-1970s, the canon of American literature contained no women novelists, no women dramatists, no women short story writers, and only two women poets: Anne Bradstreet and Emily Dickinson. The recent addition of women's texts to the American canon is a gain. To read "twice as many women poets as before" or to teach Kate Chopin's *The Awakening,* Charlotte Perkins Gilman's *The Yellow Wallpaper,* or Zora Neale Hurston's *Their Eyes Were Watching God* as American classics stretches our sense of both "America" and "classics." One marker of the change in the curriculum is the recent appearance of a Monarch Notes pamphlet entitled *Twentieth-Century American Women Authors: A Feminist Approach.* Like most such enterprises, it is filled with slippery shortcuts, but it suggests that women writers and feminist critics have grown respectable. Like *Walden* and *Moby Dick* we are sufficiently part of the American canon to be officially distorted for desperate students (Diamond 149).

In expanding the canon, we accomplish the goal of what might be called the liberal stage of a feminist rethinking of American literature, a stage equivalent to—but fortunately more successful than—the push for the Equal Rights Amendment. The premise of the Equal Rights Amendment is, of course, that we live in a reasonably democratic system, a system whose assumptions and methods need not be radically reformed. The notion behind canon expansion is similarly benign: having admitted women authors to our courses and comps lists, we ought now to be able to begin equal application of our assumptions, methods, and theories. This *might* work—but only if we can find novels with the following plots:

1. A young girl in Minnesota finds her womanhood by killing a bear.
2. Believing she has murdered her drunken Ma, a young scamp runs for the river where she joins up with an escaped black woman. They meander downriver, rafting by night and adventuring by day. Soon after foiling two tricksters masquerading as the Queen and the Duchess, our heroine, hiking up her skirts, lights out for the territories.

---

[5]I am indebted to Golding for this example.

3. A maniacal, peg-legged captain drives her whaling ship with its crew of rag-tag women on a doomed chase of the famed white whale, Moby Jane.[6]

Why are these plots so funny, so odd, so deeply unthinkable? Surely it is because the methods and mythology of American literary study have presupposed a world that is all but exclusively male.

As Nina Baym has argued, American literary critics from the beginning searched for a cultural essence, something "truly American" to distinguish our literature from continental or English writing. They found it in a number of stories about men, most typically, perhaps, in the story of the American Adam encountering the promise of a new land. In this mythology, the wilderness is the terrain upon which the individual inscribes his own destiny, but only if he successfully escapes an entrammeling society. The sexual or gendered character of the myth is evident in its metaphoric structure: the protagonist is the individualistic, active male who eludes a society of Widow Douglases and embraces the virgin land. In the American tradition, Jane has signified, on the one hand, gentility, conformity, and mawkish morality, and, on the other, the fresh green breast of an all-nurturing, all-passive wilderness (Baym "Melodramas" 131–136).[7]

How can a woman writer inhabit this mythology? A central part of it is the journey west, but as Leslie Fiedler has pointed out, "westering, in America, means leaving the domain of the female" (60)—something a woman, obviously, cannot do. The journey culminates in the drama Annette Kolodny has called *The Lay of the Land*, the ravishing of a receptive mother-earth—again, of course, a plot unavailable to women. Our concepts of periodization, the plots we develop to sequence our literature, are no more easily applicable to women's writing. The Renaissance F. O. Matthiessen charts, to give just one example, was not a renaissance for women.

If our methods, mythology, and periodization do not fit women's texts, it is because there is something fundamentally different about these texts. The efforts of the more radical stage of a feminist rethinking of the American canon have been devoted to speculation about this difference. This effort has returned to circulation works previously lost or ignored, reinterpreted known works, and investigated the possibility that women have developed a related or even unique tradition of their own.[8]

The recovery of so-called "lost" women's writing has brought to us not only the work of Chopin, Gilman, and Hurston but texts like Rebecca Harding Davis's

---

[6]For the first of these plots and a fine analysis of the impossibilities of such gender reversal, see Russ.

[7]Judith Fetterley's argument that the works of American fiction execute a series of designs on the female reader forcefully elaborates these problems. See her "self-defense survival manual for the woman reader lost in 'the masculine wilderness of the American novel'" in *The Resisting Reader* (viii).

[8]It is telling that the early arguments positing a powerfully separate tradition of women's writing concentrated largely on British writers. See Spacks, Moer, Showalter's *A Literature of Their Own*, and Gilbert and Gubar's *The Madwoman in the Attic*. Showalter's important essay "Feminist Criticism in the Wilderness" elaborates the tasks such gynocentric criticism must undertake.

Life in the Iron Mills, Mary E. Wilkins Freeman's "Revolt of Mother," Agnes Smedley's *Daughter of the Earth*, and Edith Summers Kelley's *Weeds*, spotted in a second-hand bookstore by Matthew J. Bruccoli. Paul Lauter has catalogued the literature of working-class women ("Working-Class Women's Literature"), and Henry Louis Gates, Jr.'s painstaking research has restored to us *Our Nig*, thought to be the first novel in America by a woman of Afro-American descent. Rich and fascinating sourcebooks of statements by and about lost writers include Tillie Olsen's *Silences*, the many new feminist anthologies of women's fiction, drama, and poetry, and, most fortunately, the publishing lists of the Feminist Press in New York.[9]

In this search-and-restore mission, many known writers have been found again. Anne Bradstreet has been understood as a poet of radical intellectual force; Edith Wharton and Willa Cather have acquired fuller, racier lives; and Emily Dickinson, our Spinster-Recluse, has finally been seen as the tough and powerful poet who, in Adrienne Rich's words, "chose to have it out at last/on [her] own premises" (" 'I Am in Danger—Sir—' " 33).[10] One of the most exciting projects has been a rereading of the sentimental novelists, Hawthorne's "damned mob of scribbling women" who snivelled their way into bestsellerdom and, in one critic's view, all but "feminized" nineteenth-century America (Douglas). When we take the premises of these novels seriously, as Nina Baym has done, it is clear that most of them are, in fact, quite unsentimental. Their plots "repeatedly identify immersion in feeling as one of the great temptations and dangers" for a disenfranchised and property-deprived woman negotiating her limited social possibilities. The real issue, as Baym argues, is power and how to live without it. "If critics ever permit the woman's novel to join the main body of 'American Literature,' " Baym concludes, "then all our theories about American fiction, from Richard Chase's 'romance' to Richard Poirier's 'world elsewhere' to Carolyn Heilbrun's 'masculine wilderness,' will have to be radically revised" (*Women's Fiction* 25, 36–37).

The tasks of the second stage of a feminist rethinking of the canon intersect here in the charting of a separate tradition of women's writing and the use of that tradition to challenge the assumptions and methods behind what we've called the American canon. The supposedly "pure" literary criteria employed to identify "the best American works" have resulted in a literature which, in Baym's sharp summary, privileges the whaling ship over the sewing circle as a symbol of human community, satirizes domineering mothers and shrewish wives rather than tyrannical fathers and abusive husbands, and displays exquisite compassion for the crises of the adolescent male while dismissing the parallel turmoil of the female (*Women's Fiction* 14).

At the end of the second stage, we have, in effect, two canons: one of hunters, one of quilters. If the danger of the first stage was a kind of tokenism, the danger of the second is a kind of ghettoizing: instead of one or two women in an

---

[9] See especially here Gilbert and Gubar, *The Norton Anthology of Literature by Women*; Green; and Stetson. The Feminist Press has recently published two canon-revising documents: Williamson's *New Feminist Scholarship* and Lauter's *Reconstructing American Literature*.

[10] See also Rich's revisionary essay, "Vesuvius at Home: The Power of Emily Dickinson."

unreconstructed male course, we will have separate courses examining separate traditions. The old canon will man the fort labelled "basics," while the new canon rusts on the outskirts. In a time when many march under the banner "back to basics," this is especially problematic.[11]

I would like, in closing, to examine a possible third stage, one which would probe the causes and effects of sexual differentiation by setting male and female texts into dialogue. As Myra Jehlen has argued, to speak about the female writer as a figure separate from the male writer is inevitable in a culture that has made much of sexual difference; to speak of them together might prepare a ground for possible cultural reconstruction. It makes no sense for women to disclaim the continuing seriousness and value of the "great tradition" or to try to reclaim it as, after all, somehow an expression of our own viewpoint; nor does it make sense for men to denigrate the richness of a women's tradition or to appropriate it as an expression of their viewpoint. To set the two traditions into conversation demonstrates the contingency of both and allows us to hear each other, and ourselves, anew.

Jehlen's excellent essay, "Archimedes and the Paradox of Feminist Criticism," introduces and explores a method she terms "radical comparativism." This method juxtaposes writings that have overlapping contexts, conditions of production, or plot paradigms in order to search for the borders which light up the outer parameters of both worlds. The focus here would be on "the relations between situations rather than on the situations themselves," and the process would illuminate the philosophical and linguistic grounds of the two traditions, traditions that otherwise might seem absolute and unimpeachable (578, 585–87).

This method turns the intertextual into the intersexual. A course constructed along these lines might be team-taught by a man and a woman. The reading list might juxtapose, for example, male and female wilderness journals and captivity narratives, Ralph Waldo Emerson and Margaret Fuller on self-reliance, Melville's *Moby Dick* and Arnow's *Hunter's Horn*, James' *Portrait of a Lady* and Wharton's *House of Mirth*, Wright's *Black Boy* and Marshall's *Brown Girl, Brownstones*, or Bradley's *The Chaneysville Incident* and Morrison's *The Song of Solomon*—there are many possible combinations. Discussions of such texts would highlight not only their mutual concerns but their radically different assumptions and approaches, their contrasting linguistic and imagistic patterns, and the complementary blindnesses and insights which form them.

Ed Folsom and I have taught such a course at the University of Iowa. By pairing Whitman and Dickinson, Pound and H.D., Merwin and Rich, we wanted to investigate three lines of force: the male mainstream tradition linking Whitman, Pound, and Merwin; a female tradition joining Dickinson, H.D., and Rich: and a larger rhythm of response and exchange between the sexes. While we knew this exchange would involve contradiction, we assumed we would also find areas in

---

[11]William Bennett's roster of thirty texts all high school students should be required to read is a prime example of this tendency. For the titles of these books and reaction from the National Council of Teachers of English, see Savage.

which the male and female traditions refreshed and renewed each other, the sort of terrain from which a new canon might emerge.

In its most utopian formulation, our ideal for the course suggests yet another meaning to the word *canon*, a meaning that presupposes such mutual response and exchange. There is a dance called the *canon dance* in which the male and female dancers follow patterns set by others, then switch to new patterns, followed by others, who then, in their turn, create new patterns. This play of imitation and inventiveness is, of course, the way literary traditions evolve, and as a model for the interactions between male and female writers, it is an ideal that still engages and entices me. What we found in the course, however, is that such elegant interchange must be preceded by harsher, less harmonious stumblings.

The simplest part of the semester, of course, was delineating the patterns created by the male dancers. We fell upon Whitman, Pound, and Merwin as old friends whose insistences, irritations, and inventions were, if complex, nonetheless familiar. The women students felt comfortable speaking about the male poets, since, like Blacks and Native Americans, women have been schooled in the methodologies that make mainstream writing available. Few of us, however, had a ready formulation of the patterns danced by the women poets. The traditions of women's writing—its mythic and linguistic strategies, its characteristic themes and tones—are only just being delineated in the remarkable efflorescence of feminist criticism, criticism few male professors and fewer male or female students have perused.

As for interactions between the poets, we found many subtle lines of connection between Whitman, Pound, and Merwin and between Dickinson, H.D., and Rich, but the interchange between male and female dancers was stopped and sterile, stopped, that is, for the men and sterile for the women. Whitman and Dickinson, of course, remained unaware of each other; Pound never listened to Dickinson and felt free to turn H.D. into a muse—"You are a poem," he told her, "though your poem's naught" (12); and Merwin, though at one point Rich's close friend and confidante, fell away when she started to speak, deliberately and defiantly, as a woman. For the women poets, the pairings of the course illustrated the difficult necessity of writing across the structures of male texts. H.D., after all, learned first from Pound, and Rich found breadth and courage in Whitman, but both, ultimately, wrote their finest poems in confronting directly the constraints of patriarchal power.

Perhaps because they recognized long suppressed animosities, the overtly political poems of Dickinson, H.D., and Rich were exhilarating to teach. "My Life had stood—a Loaded Gun—/In Corners—till a Day/The Owner passed—identified—/And carried Me away—": this poem by Emily Dickinson, a poem neither Carmen, nor Matthiessen, nor Perkins, Bradley, Beatty, and Long anthologize, tells about a life packed with a potential that the self was not empowered to activate. Whitman took himself seriously, he assumed himself, but in the gender system our society has constructed women have waited in corners until they were "carried away" and "identified"—given an identity—by a suitor, a master, a husband. Adrienne Rich's first feminist poem, "Snapshots of a Daughter-in-Law," a poem that took her two years to compose, returns to Dickinson "reading while waiting for the iron to heat, writing, *My Life had stood—a Loaded Gun—*/in that Amherst pantry while the jellies boil and scum."[12] Rich's daughter-in-law is "nervy, glowering," ready to strike when the iron is hot. As daughters, fiancees, and daughters-in-law, women have not been equal partners in the dance. As they come into speech, their words are sharp as knives and what we have is less a dance than a fight.

Poems like these open wounds, but they also open dialogue. In this course, it was no longer possible to see Dick's point of view as hegemonic, as we do when we read the American classics as an all but exclusive male tradition, nor was it possible to hear only the cries and whispers of Jane, as I frequently do in attending primarily to the female literary tradition. At our best, we entered into the fray, taking shots from both sides; at our worst, we retreated into defensive edginess, the men when they felt accused and sometimes guilty, the women when they felt confused, ashamed, and sometimes angry.

Just as interactions within a family replicate interactions in the larger social structure, interactions among students in a course frequently become symptomatic of an interplay between the texts. If our problem, the problem of the texts, and the problem of the culture was polarization, our symptom was excessive politeness, the kind of politeness I remember experiencing at those sixth grade dances when the boys huddled on one side and the girls on the other, while a few desperate couples struggled like strangers not to tread on each other's feet.

This politeness speaks not only to the force with which the male and female canons contest and elude each other but also to our desire to find a resolution. In the fifteen weeks of that semester, we and our students accomplished many things, but we did not, at least in any significant way, refashion the canon of American poetry. Though we recognized the power of Dickinson, H.D., and Rich, we did not develop a unifying narrative to assimilate them into a list of accepted American classics. Nor did we find a rhythm of reciprocal response and exchange between our writers. There was no canon dance. By the end of the course, in fact, these ideals seemed happy but hollow formulations.

The metaphors of "opening" or "expanding" the canon impute an elasticity to something that is, by definition, rigid. Given the structures of power in this country, an open canon is like a Pepsi ad or, more pertinently, like the primers that have replaced *Dick and Jane*: in them, there are a few black faces and, perhaps, a girl holding a hammer, but the basic stereotypes remain. Differences are homogenized: conflict is masked; and cooptation removes any chance for real communication and change.

Politeness is a way of negotiating conflict; in agreeing to mute our differences, we agree not to listen, not to care. Conflict is contact: we enter each other's terrain, we step on each other's feet, we hear each other's most intimate and uneasy words. What we found in our course was that to read any text well was not to push

---

[12]Both poems are anthologized in Gilbert and Gubar, *The Norton Anthology of Literature by Women*, 860 and 2026–29.

toward resolution but to enlist in two sorts of struggle, in the poet's struggle with either the male or female canons or both and in our own struggle as readers and writers to see and name, identify and empower ourselves anew.

Despite our discomfort, what we were doing, finally, was fighting. Canons are, after all, instruments of war; they define and protect zones of contention. American literature has always been an arena of competition—between men and women, Native Americans and "Transplant Americans," Blacks and whites, northerners and southerners, workers and bosses. It may be that we do not need a larger canon. Instead we need to do the legwork to find and the reference work to value the multiple and conflicting canons that we have always had.

This is a rigorous ideal. What it means is that when we read Leslie Silko's novel *Ceremony*, we make ourselves responsible for knowing not only the white mainstream canon of the American novel but also something about the oral traditions of the Pueblo people and something about the rich interconnections among contemporary Native American women writers. It means that when we read Morrison's *The Bluest Eye* we recognize not only our own Dick and Jane but also the traditions of Afro-American storytelling from the folktales, spirituals, blues, and slave narratives to the work of Richard Wright, Zora Neale Hurston, and Alice Walker. It means, finally, that we commit money to Black Studies, Native American Studies, and Women's Studies Programs, that we work to keep the writings from these traditions in cheap paperback editions and thick American anthologies, and that we require ourselves and our students to become literate in a number of the many traditions of American writing.

Defenders of the expanded canon argue that if we are to be a community we must discover or create a common intellectual heritage, a heritage that would bind us into an understanding of our enterprise as Americans. The problem with this, of course, is that it results in one of two formulations: either what a colleague of mine calls the "pale male" canon, the familiar story of Walt, Huck, Nick, Ike, and Old Ez, or its bland liberal replacement, a canon so diversified and disorganized we cannot locate a narrative to unify it.

Traditionally a canon is defined as that which is shared. For Americans, however, it is the battle that is shared, not the canons that fight it. Our common heritage is struggle. We are not and never have been a mono-cultural people; we haven't even been a monolinguistic people. American literature is a clash of contending canons, a vital argument about how to live, what to do. There is no center, except as we enter and momentarily inhabit a writer's consciousness. We don't need to remain entrenched, but we do need to perceive and protect our differences. Fighting with canons can open a way to see not only Dick but also Jane and baby Sally, Pecola Breedlove, and Leslie Silko's stubbornly persisting robins.

Works Cited

Allison, Alexander W., Herbert Barrows, Caesar R. Blake, Arthur J. Carr, Arthur M. Eastman, and Hubert M. English, Jr., eds. *The Norton Anthology of Poetry*. Rev. Ed. New York: Norton, 1975.

BAYM, NINA. "Melodramas of Beset Manhood: How Theories of American Fiction Exclude Women Authors." *American Quarterly* 33 (1981): 123–39.

———. *Women's Fiction: A Guide to Novels by and about Women in America, 1820–1870.* Ithaca: Cornell UP, 1978.

CARMEN, BLISS. Preface. *The Oxford Book of American Verse.* New York: Oxford UP, 1927. iii–v.

DIAMOND, ARLYN. "Practicing Feminist Literary Criticism." *Women's Studies International Quarterly* 1 (1978): 149–52.

DORRIS, MICHAEL. "Native American Literature in an Ethnohistorical Context." *College English* 41 (1979): 147–62.

DOUGLAS, ANN. *The Feminization of American Culture.* New York: Knopf, 1977.

FETTERLEY, JUDITH. *The Resisting Reader: A Feminist Approach to American Fiction.* Bloomington: Indiana UP, 1977.

FIEDLER, LESLIE A. *The Return of the Vanishing American.* New York: Stein and Day, 1968.

FIEDLER, LESLIE A., and HOUSTON A. BAKER, JR. eds., *English Literature: Opening up the Canon.* Selected Papers from the English Institute, 1979, n.s. 4 Baltimore: Johns Hopkins, 1981.

FRANKLIN, H. BRUCE. "English as an Institution: The Role of Class." Fiedler and Baker 92–106.

FRANKLIN, WAYNE. "The 'Library of America' and the Welter of American Books." Forthcoming in *The Iowa Review.*

GATES, HENRY LOUIS, JR. Introduction. *Our Nig; or, Sketches from the Life of a Free Black, In A Two-Story White House, North.* By Harriet E. Wilson. New York: Vintage, 1983. xi–lv.

GILBERT, SANDRA M., and SUSAN GUBAR. *The Madwoman in the Attic: The Woman Writer and the Nineteenth-Century Literary Imagination.* New Haven: Yale UP, 1979.

———, eds. *The Norton Anthology of Literature by Women.* New York: Norton, 1985.

GOLDING, ALAN C. "A History of American Poetry Anthologies." von Hallberg 279–307.

GREEN, RAYNA, ed. *That's What She Said: Contemporary Poetry and Fiction by Native American Women.* Bloomington: Indiana UP, 1984.

H. D. *End to Torment: A Memoir of Ezra Pound.* New York: New Directions, 1979.

JEHLEN, MYRA. "Archimedes and the Paradox of Feminist Criticism." *Signs* 6 (1981): 575–601.

KOLODNY, ANNETTE. *The Lay of the Land: Metaphor as Experience and History in American Life and Letters.* Chapel Hill: U of North Carolina P, 1975.

———. "Dancing Through the Minefield: Some Observations on the Theory, Practice and Politics of a Feminist Literary Criticism." *Feminist Studies* 6 (1980): 1–25.

KRUPAT, ARNOLD. "Native American Literature and the Canon." von Hallberg 309–335.

LAUTER, PAUL. "Race and Gender in the Shaping of the American Literary Canon: A Case Study from the Twenties." *Feminist Studies* 9 (1983): 435–63.

———, ed. *Reconstructing American Literature: Courses, Syllabi, Issues.* Old Westbury, NY: Feminist Press, 1983.

———. "Working-Class Woman's Literature—An Introduction to Study." *Radical Teacher*, no. 15 (March 1980): 16–26.

MOER, ELLEN. *Literary Women: The Great Writers.* Garden City, NY: Doubleday, 1976.

Morrison, Toni. *The Bluest Eye.* New York: Washington Square, 1972.

Rich, Adrienne. " 'I Am in Danger—Sir—,' " *Necessities of Life: Poems, 1962–65.* New York: Norton, 1966.

———. "Vesuvius at Home: The Power of Emily Dickinson," *On Lies, Secrets, and Silence: Selected Prose, 1966–1978.* New York: Norton, 1979. 157–83.

Russ, Joanna. "What Can A Heroine Do? or Why Women Can't Write," *Images of Women in Fiction: Feminist Perspectives.* Ed. Susan Koppelman Common. Bowling Green, OH: Bowling Green U Popular P, 1972. 3–20.

Savage, David G. "The Top 30 Books for Pupils? List Draws Fire." *Los Angeles Times* 12 Aug. 1984, part 1, 3 +.

Showalter, Elaine. "Feminist Criticism in the Wilderness." Rpt. in *Writing and Sexual Difference.* Ed. Elizabeth Abel. Chicago: U of Chicago P, 1982. 9–35.

———. *A Literature of Their Own: British Women Novelists from Bronte to Lessing.* Princeton: Princeton UP, 1977.

Silko, Leslie Marmon. "Language and Literature from a Pueblo Indian Perspective. " Fiedler and Baker. 54–72.

Spacks, Patricia Meyer. *The Female Imagination.* New York: Knopf, 1976.

Stetson, Erlene, ed. *Black Sister: Poetry by Black American Women.* Bloomington: Indiana UP, 1981.

Von Hallberg, Robert, ed. *Canons.* Chicago: U of Chicago P, 1984.

Williamson, Jane, ed. *New Feminist Scholarship: A Guide to Bibliographies.* Old Westbury, NY: Feminist Press, 1979.

Woolf, Virginia. *A Room of One's Own.* New York: Harcourt, 1957.

After Reading: CONSOLIDATE INFORMATION

1. How does Morris's description of her own experience with reading literature, first in elementary school where she encountered Dick and Jane, and later in college where she read American literature, compare with your experiences of reading in school?
2. Morris commits herself to a certain interpretation of what it means to have a canon of agreed on works of literature. Do you think that she supports her claims? How?
3. Morris's article was written primarily for an audience of English teachers. What do you think its main purpose is?

The City in Recent American Fiction: Listening to Black Urban Voices
Joyce R. Durham

Joyce Durham is a professor of English. In this scholarly essay, written for other English teachers, she argues for teachers and critics of English to broaden their view of the American city by examining Black or African-American writing about urban life.

Before you read: FIRST THOUGHTS
                LOOK AHEAD

1. When you think of the city and what it stands for in American life, what images come to your mind?
2. What is your first reaction to Durham's title?
3. Why do you think Durham focuses on literature about living in cities written by Black Americans?

During reading: REACT
               QUESTION
               SUMMARIZE

1. Durham points out that many studies have examined the role of the city in literature, but that most of these studies have neglected Black American writers' portrayal of the city. What do you think are possible reasons for that neglect?
2. What do you think Durham means when she writes that "it is now clear that Black *urban* life has become a fact of American consciousness"?

    AT A CONFERENCE in 1980 which brought together an ethnically diverse group of literary artists to discuss the relationships between literature and the urban experience, Joyce Carol Oates asked an important question: "If the City is a text, how shall we read it?" Limiting her analysis to white American authors, she traced the transformation of the twentieth-century fictional city from a place of qualified hope to a "species of hell" (11). Oates went on to cite the consummate city novelist, Saul Bellow, as being "obsessed with the riddle of what it means to be an urban man in a secular, mass-market culture . . . without a coherent sense of history or tradition" (12). Yet at that same conference, Amiri Baraka pronounced, "The history and culture of black people in this country are steeped in pain and suffering, exploitation and oppressing"—a description of hell itself, it would seem (139). Also addressing the question of history was Toni Morrison, who claimed that what is missing in city fiction is the black writer's own history, the presence of the ancestor (39–40).

Removing these few scattered comments from their individual contexts is not an attempt to force a common framework by which to read the textual cities of black and white fiction writers, for our urban history and our literary history alike tell us that these experiences are too divergently complex to subject to any such simplistic approach. Morrison, in fact, emphasized at the conference that the emotion of the black writer defies comparison with the white "because its sources are not the same" (37). These evident disparities, however, as well as the common themes of alienation from and hostility to the urban environment, all give added urgency for the reader of modern American fiction to view the city from as many vantage points as the fiction will allow. For if, as David Weimer states in his valuable study, *The City as Metaphor*, "There are as many cities as there are imaginations" (6); if, as LeRoi Jones/Amiri Baraka writes in "City of Harlem," "There are . . . contained within the central mythology of Harlem, almost as many versions of its glamour, and its despair, as there are places with people to make them up" (qtd. in Lee 62); and if we are to get some kind of meaningful grasp of what American writers' visions of the urban landscape have been, then we must tap these diverse imaginations; we cannot skip entire portions in our reading of the text.

Morrison has suggested that the life of a city is best represented by the "dispossessed," the "disenfranchised" (35). She says, "It may be that the positive and negative aspects of urbanism can best be articulated by those who know it, but who have no vested political, cultural, or philosophical interests in supporting or rejecting it as it presently exists" (37). Perhaps, perhaps not. Nonetheless, to travel alternate paths through these fictional cities can only help us enlarge our own visions and hone our perceptions of our environments.

Many good studies have been written about the city in the American imagination; however, with a few exceptions, these ignore black American writers, presumably sending a message that the American imagination has not often encompassed the ghettos and black belts of our urban centers. Notwithstanding the slight, the record of the city in black fiction, the novel specifically, is there and is beginning to be interpreted in various ways, primarily by black scholars and critics.

A kind of record exists in Robert A. Bone's earlier general survey of black fiction, *The Negro Novel in America*, making it relatively easy to trace black novels of the city historically and relegate them to tidy categories: "The Talented Tenth," "The Harlem School," "The Rear Guard." With this historical approach, it becomes a reasonable thesis that black accounts of the city have roughly paralleled those of white authors, even while city life itself lagged behind for a number of years. Indeed Paul Laurence Dunbar and James Weldon Johnson were conceiving of their characters as powerless figures in an amoral world (the "big city") quite as convincingly as Crane, Dreiser, and Norris. For example, in one of the first fictional records of black experience in the city, *The Sport of the Gods* (1902), Dunbar, reminiscent of Dreiser's rendering of those "forces" on Sister Carrie, reiterates the effect of the "wicked city" on the provincial:

> [t]he stream of young negro life would continue to flow up from the South, dashing itself against the hard necessities of the city and breaking like waves against a rock—that, until the gods grew tired of their cruel sport, there must still be sacrifices to false ideals and unreal ambitions. (213–14)

Likewise in 1912, the protagonist in Johnson's *The Autobiography of an Ex-Colored Man*, expresses an ambivalence reflected earlier by Dunbar and echoed in almost every subsequent novel of the black in the city when he compares the "fatally fascinating" New York City to a "great witch at the gate of the country" with victims that she "at once crushes beneath her cruel feet"; even the ones she favors are not spared, for "with a sudden breath she blows the bubbles out and laughs mockingly as she watches them fall" (442).

Obviously these views provide access to early black writers' perceptions of their relationships to the city, but that environment now seems primarily a world of chance dictated by limited sensibilities, stereotypical reactions, and commonly shared metaphors. In *Being & Race*, Charles Johnson, author recently turned literary critic, confesses that much of his own early fictional failures rested on their being partially grounded in naturalism which, he learned, "concealed a reductionistic model of human psychology, of what motivates men and women" (6). He finally discovered, he says, that writing must create, not just record experience (5–6).

Another kind of record, A. Robert Lee's essay, "Harlem on My Mind: Fictions of a Black Metropolis," stands as an important catalogue of responses to that mythical "city-within-a-city." This essay, which has secured a place in an edited collection of essays about the American city, offers a variety of literary and cultural perspectives in its inclusion of fictional responses to Harlem.

But it seems to me that a more important kind of study has surfaced which speaks not only to the cultural and historical but also to the artistic trends in black literature. Melvin Dixon's recent book, *Ride Out the Wilderness: Geography and Identity in Afro-American Literature*, attempts to impose some order on the uses of environment in black American literature. Across the decades of fiction from early slave songs and narratives to the latest novels by Toni Morrison, he traces how black writers "have used language to create alternative landscapes where black culture and identity can flourish apart from any marginal, prescribed 'place' " (2). Ordering the fiction around images of the wilderness, underground, and mountain, he analyzes these recurring images in both the religious culture and the black literary tradition, claiming that these writers have analyzed and identified with spaces and environments which have helped them sustain their individual identities. Although the categories seem arbitrary at times and not altogether relevant to the city perspective discussed here, Dixon provides valuable insights into the mythologies and assumptions of black American fiction so neglected by most urban studies.

One returns, then, to the question of how to approach the city as a text. Certainly most would not dispute that 1940 was the year that Richard Wright took all the elements of the urban scene and translated them into the highly successful and artistic *Native Son*. Charles Johnson, in fact, credits it as being "one of our most phenomenologically successful novels, a nightmare as frightening, in its own way, as George Orwell's *1984*" (13). Stepping outside a daunting body of critics who view Wright's portrayal of the black ghetto as a predictable piece of victim literature, Johnson lauds Wright's "construction of a consistent, coherent, and complete racial universe—[South Side] Chicago" (14), one in which readers immerse themselves completely and suffer with the character.

Additionally, when the master of city fiction, Saul Bellow, has Augie March begin his story in 1953, "I am an American . . . and go at things as I have taught myself, free-style, and will make the record in my own way" (5), it may be that those who thoroughly understand the existential theme are those who had accompanied Ralph Ellison's unnamed protagonist on his quest for identity in 1952 only to hear him cry from the bowels of New York at the end of the journey but the beginning of the story: "I am an invisible man" (7). Augie defends his individuality in the Chicago urban sprawl against people who try to define his reality for him, but only after Ellison's character had lamented: "I was pulled this way and that for longer than I can remember. And my problem was that I always tried to go in everyone's way but my own" (496). No doubt Wright's and Ellison's renderings of the city—in which environment and story are virtually inseparable—will remain high in the tradition of black urban voices. However, in 1960, Blyden Jackson was noting that like the ghetto itself, which severely limited behavior and stunted possibilities even more, the majority of black fiction had illustrated "a world in which the distinctive cosmic process is not change, but a holding action" ("Negro's Image" 630). If perceived this way, Jackson feels, the ghetto at the end of *Native Son* is no different from the beginning; the urban environment of the invisible man, for all his hopes of gaining his individuality, his identity, remains static. One of Jackson's criticisms about the fictional universe is this quality of "stasis," which, he feels, relegates black fiction to a "literature of protest" ("Negro's Image" 630).

Yet despite Jackson's apparent despair about the "unchanging backdrop" of black fiction and despite the continued success of authors in Robert A. Bone's "Wright School" such as Ann Petry and Willard Motley, something was happening in American cities during the 50s and 60s that altered the way blacks lived in, thought about, and then created the urban environment in their fiction. That phenomenon was the possibility of change. It was an era that saw the emphasis shift from civil rights legislation to Black Power, from the NAACP to the SNCC, from revolution in the minds to revolution in the streets. Another resulting shift, one of the most important phenomena to occur in the 60s and 70s, was the Black Aesthetic Movement, an affirmation of racial pride and dignity emanating from the black community. In his lecture/essay called "Black Literature and the Afro-American Nation: The Urban Voice," Baraka comments on the literary trends of that time:

But clearly, the urban voice of black literature was a revolutionary nationalist one—a voice that wanted to openly combine its politics and its aesthetics, that reflected the still intensifying militancy of the Black Liberation Movement. (156)

It is difficult to categorize these black urban voices of the 60s and 70s, for even though they share a certain revolutionary stance toward their environments, their politics, and their literary materials, they are as different from each other in their portrayal of city life as they are from their white contemporaries. However, the critic who seeks to assess the city accurately in American fiction needs to include Nathan Heard's and Robert Pharr's attempts to give an authentic representation of black street life; Ronald Fair's and Louise Meriwether's personal autobiographies; Charles Wright's existential themes and surrealistic views of New York City; John A. Williams' fiction which, like that of Baldwin, chronicles the decade of the 60s and whose work culminates in the novel of militancy; Sam Greenlee's exploitation of the militant novel to the fullest degree; Chester Himes' Harlem detective thrillers; and indeed, Clarence Major's, Ishmael Reed's, and LeRoi Jones' experiments with subject matter and form.

One important way, then, to view the city in the black imagination and tradition—a starting point—is to begin assessing fiction that captures the spirit of the change, fiction that has laid the groundwork for the outpouring of literature that celebrates blackness. A particular writer quickly comes to mind. From the 50s through the 60s and 70s, James Baldwin became the literary spokesman for blacks in general and for Harlem in particular. His succession of novels tracks his urban protagonists from John Grimes, who accepts his segregated existence governed by white values, to Leo Proudhammer, who doesn't, through a view of the city as black on white to black and white, a gigantic leap to a time when the fiction becomes in other black writers, according to Reginald Martin, "a type of writing that pled for simple justice and threatened social upheaval and violence if that plea went unanswered" (374). Because he has produced a body of fiction that frequently makes the city itself a character and has written articulately about cities in his fictionalized essays, Baldwin acts not only as that starting point, but also as a bridge to understanding the changing attitudes toward the urban environment in the black imagination.

Baldwin articulates his obsession with his own identity as a man, a black, and a homosexual throughout his writings, but he best defines for us what our history tells us about the black man's and woman's Procrustean roles in American society in "The Black Boy Looks at the White Boy": "one had to make oneself up as one went along" (183). In *After Alienation*, Marcus Klein assesses Baldwin's attitude toward identity as "something to be attained or achieved, especially in America, especially by a Negro, and that is to imply that 'identity' is dynamic and progressive" (150). The Negro's past, he quotes Baldwin as saying, is an "endless struggle to achieve and reveal and confirm a human identity" (150). Baldwin's whole ethos rests on tensions created by this possibility of change, so it follows that much can be learned from this black urban voice.

The calling forth of his Harlem youth has become a trademark for Baldwin the writer. He reaches back to his own past to illuminate his creative present or, as he puts it in "Autobiographical Notes," "to recreate out of the disorder of life that order which is art" (5). Baldwin's rendering of the city landscape that he knew so well, from his first novel in which a black youth makes his peace with the ghetto to his later fiction which disallows that possibility, is the change that merits attention. For if Ellison's city novel symbolically traces the migration of black Americans from south to north, to a world of social and economic immobility, Baldwin's work represents, in part, the fictional history that black writers have captured in recent literature, particularly in novels about city life—the journey from reluctant acceptance to rejection of that immobility.

In 1953 with Baldwin's first novel, *Go Tell It on the Mountain*, the ghetto offers John Grimes no more choices than did that of Bigger Thomas or the invisible man. But through Baldwin's juxtaposing views of a real and a created city, he illustrates what it means to a seeker of identity.

Harlem, the community of the oppressed, emerges immediately as a carefully constructed background for the equally oppressive drama of the Grimes family. Throughout the novel, John's religious doubts and ultimate conversion act as a filter through which the reader views New York. Baldwin artistically uses the black store-front church as a moral center for his young protagonist and John's conversion itself as a center from which he later explores not only the past history of the Grimes family but also the history of the black race. The physical details of ghetto life become metaphors for what Dixon calls the "moral pollution" in the family (128): "Dirt was in the walls and the floorboards.... Dirt was in every corner, angle, crevice of the monstrous stove, and lived behind it in delirious communion with the corrupted wall" (21–22). Baldwin then expands his imagery of dirt and squalor to reflect John's spiritual crisis: "For was it not he, in his false pride and his evil imagination, who was filthy?" (22). Finally, at a higher level of abstraction, the entire history of blacks is linked to the image of the family deliberately named Grimes and the filth that cannot be diminished: "It became in his imagination his impossible, lifelong task, his hard trial" (26). John's trial becomes a metaphor for the black condition. Melvin Dixon perceptively comments, "The perspective of religion enables the author to have better control over his material, his past, and his use of environment or metaphorical space" (124); it is, he feels, what liberated Baldwin from the naturalistic influences of Richard Wright. And that control over his environment is also one of the reasons that Baldwin's first novel is one of the most powerful and artistic examples of the city in the American imagination.

The city in this story also functions as an extension of fantasy, one in which the black man dreams of gaining control over his environment, but also one in which he sees the futility of this dream. On an excursion to Central Park, John retreats from the squalor to a hill from which he has often viewed the distant skyline of New York. On this hill John confronts the enigma of his own attitude toward the city below. He runs up the hill like a madman "willing to throw himself headlong into the city that glowed before him" (33). Burton Pike, in *The Image of the City in Modern Literature*, reflects upon archetypal meanings created by this perspective of the city. From above, he maintains, the character removes himself from the possibility of involvement, which "greatly diminishes the city in size and its activity in importance in relation to the emptiness and silence of the spaces around it" (34). Because of this chasm between city and narrator, John Grimes' consciousness, then, creates the city for the reader. From this distance, the hill acts as a forum for John's hopes and "a pinnacle of self acceptance for which John yearns" (Dixon 126).

At the top, John imagines that he is "a giant who might crumble this city ... a tyrant who might crush this city beneath his heel" (33). Yet he is not deceived by the specious attractions of the city. His dilemma is that, although he knows its promise for the black man is only illusory, the lure of the city is strong. Dismissing the "glories of eternity" as unimaginable and the city as real, he plunges into that other world thinking, "I can climb back up. If it's wrong, I can always climb back up" (34).

John's journey to that "other side" is real enough: "Niggers did not live on these streets where John now walked; it was forbidden" (36). Yet the account is not of these streets but of John's continued journey through a city in his fantasy. The white city through which he walks becomes a mere touchstone for his flight from reality and a means for the reader to learn of the duelling forces in John's mind. He vacillates between sympathy and hatred for these white people who controlled his image of himself. He sees the contrast between the white world of prosperity and the black world of poverty and servility. While Baldwin does not ignore the relationships between blacks and whites in the story, he does make less conscious use of cityscape to reflect those relationships than he does in his later fiction.

Part Two of the novel, which dramatizes the cultural shock of John's aunt, mother, and father, presents the harsh, realistic elements of Harlem life. While the city in this section reflects the psychological imprisonment of ghetto life, these episodes also explain the profound influence of families' lives on the new generation, which is destined to reenact similar tragedies.

Part Three reveals not only John's acceptance of his family's religious beliefs but also his own imprisonment within the confines of the ghetto as well. At his conversion John again recreates his fantasy city, that city from the top of the hill, "way in the middle of the air ... a city out of time, not made with hands, but eternal in the heavens" (204). John's image of Harlem reflects his recent conversion; now that his crisis is over, "the avenue, like any landscape that has endured a story, lay changed under Heaven, exhausted and clean, and new. Not again, forever, could it return to the avenue it once had been" (215). However, even though John has purportedly changed, Harlem has not, and Baldwin makes this very clear: "the houses were there, as they had been; the windows, like a thousand, blinded eyes, stared outward at the morning ... that was the same for them as the mornings of John's innocence, and the mornings before his birth" (216).

Despite the apparent exaltation and relief in John's religious conversion, *Go Tell It on the Mountain* is still a story of despair, a story of limited choices, but one which nonetheless contains Baldwin's dynamic views of the continued search for new identity. Klein summarizes, "The novel creates in its protagonist an intimate version, not of what it is to be, but what it is to become a Negro in America, what it is to accept the conditions that create that identity" (178).

From the time of that first novel to the third, *Another Country*, Baldwin, temporarily abandoned the American scene. When he returned in 1957, it was to Greenwich Village, not Harlem. Before he returned to the treatment of the black urban environment in fiction, Baldwin left a personal record of the city in his collections of essays which, in fact, are often difficult to distinguish from his fiction. In "Fifth Avenue, Uptown: A Letter from Harlem," Baldwin conveys, in descriptive, literary prose, the bleakness engendered by the environment: city trees "snarling," people "struggling in the fishhooks, the barbed wire, of this avenue," "the unrehabilitated houses, bowed down, it would seem, under the great weight of frustration and bitterness they contain ... the ominous school houses from which the child may emerge maimed, blinded, hooked, or enraged for life" (55, 60).

Just as Baldwin's appraisal of the city becomes angry and prophetic in his essays, so his translation of urban blacks undergoes a radical change in subsequent novels. It is a long way in 1962 from the suffering acceptance of ghetto life in his first novel nearly ten years before. From the confines of Harlem and the defeated, martyred John Grimes, Baldwin expands his stage to encompass the whole of Manhattan Island and a cast of angry blacks and whites alike. The environment in his earlier novel is subdued and metaphorically manipulated to put the drama of his character in high relief. However, like his contemporaries in city fiction—Saul Bellow, Norman Mailer, and Charles Wright, specifically, who are treating their own themes of personal dislocation and indicting the urban environment just as bitterly—Baldwin deliberately elevates the city in *Another Country* to the status of a villainous major character. Undoubtedly influenced by the working out of Baldwin's attitudes in the essays and undoubtedly reflecting the changing attitudes of urban blacks in general, *Another Country* becomes a candid, sexually explicit, and occasionally sensational social commentary which uses the New York setting to narrate three variations on the theme of isolation: the suffering of all twentieth-century urban dwellers, the futility of black-white relationships, and the alienation of the homosexual.

The opening of *Another Country* creates a portrait of New York beyond the boundaries of Harlem. Rufus Scott, an unemployed jazz musician, is wandering down Seventh Avenue at Times Square, broke, homeless, and painfully black. Beneath the great phallic buildings of New York City, the metaphors expand to include Rufus as one of the undifferentiated masses who are inevitable victims of a dying civilization: "one of the fallen—for the weight of this city was murderous—one of those who had been crushed on the day, which was every day, these towers fell. Entirely alone, and dying of it, he was part of an unprecedented multitude" (10). The city here becomes an amorphous organism in time rather than space, an ambivalent way of thinking about a city in terms of its transitory qualities, which tends to produce clear results: "The instability of our spatial surroundings seems not so much a fact in itself as evidence of a temporal process of decline and decay" (Pike 135). The chapter, which begins by describing the character and his environment in images of death and decay, ends with the suicide of Rufus Scott, who then becomes more of an influence than a character throughout the remainder of the novel.

Vivaldo, writer and liberal white friend of Rufus, experiences a similar estrangement from the city. Baldwin makes Vivaldo one of the most city-conscious of the characters, perhaps because as a sensitive although unsuccessful writer, he perceives more vividly the environment's unyielding power over its people.

Vivaldo reflects on his own loneliness: "He felt totally estranged from the city in which he had been born" (*Another* 55). He remembers the nightmares his loneliness has driven him to and wonders "where such a violent emptiness might drive an entire city" (56). Exploring a different kind of relationship in this story, Baldwin also shows the effects of reverse discrimination and the alienation of his white character in a black world. Vivaldo remembers entering a bar in Harlem where, ironically, he becomes the invisible man: "[n]o one made any effort to talk to him and an almost imperceptible glaze came over their eyes whenever they looked in his direction" (57).

Throughout the remaining chapters Baldwin continues to explore the relationships between blacks and whites in America, a theme that had become a vital issue in American cities. The impending doom of Rufus's relationship with the southern white Leona and his inevitable death are foreshadowed through a self-conscious use of the environment. Rufus meets Leona at a large party where an enormous silver ball reflects light in the room, making "its own unloving comment on the people in it" (18). Into that room the "brutal sounds of the city began their invasion," as Rufus glances upward at the ball, "always just failing to find himself and Leona reflected there" (20). Here is a symbolic and prophetic rendering of the hostility that Leona and Rufus will encounter from a society which does not approve of the liaison, a relationship which even a simple, reflective, inanimate object does not acknowledge.

However, a theme hinted at in his first novel and treated fully in his second provides the most consciously bitter indictment of the city in this story—the alienation of the homosexual in the urban environment. Seeking a theatrical career in New York and awaiting the arrival of his French lover Yves, Eric gives a perspective on the city that surely rings of Baldwin's own return to America. Before leaving Paris, Eric warns Yves that, however misunderstood they have been in Paris, it would be worse in New York. His homosexuality and his exile from New York have given him a cynical view of the city: "So superbly was it in the present that it seemed to have nothing to do with the passage of time: time might have dismissed it as thoroughly as it had dismissed Carthage and Pompeii . . . it became, at last, the most despairingly private of cities" (195). Here again the city is cast in metaphors of time and out of time, full of paradox and mythical allusions. Robert Bone entertains the possibility that for Baldwin, "homosexuality becomes a metaphor of the modem condition . . . the homosexual becomes emblematic of existential man" (234). However Eric is viewed, the city threatens to be destructive to even the only apparently successful relationship in the novel. Although the concluding sentence of the novel reflects Yves' optimism and guile as he views "that city which the people from heaven had made their home" (366), the impression we are left with is that Yves, too, will join the forces of Baldwin's wandering aliens.

There is little about Baldwin's city in this novel that lends itself to anything but an oppressive atmosphere. The city offers no relief to its characters in the bitter cold winters or the stifling hot summers: "It was a city without oases, run entirely, insofar, at least, as human perceptions could tell, for money; and its citizens seemed to have lost entirely any sense of their right to renew themselves" (267). None of the characters in this novel is able to find a common ground in the existing city, so all are seeking "another country," which may exist only in their own minds.

However, in his creation of black city life, black city themes, and black city history, Baldwin has traveled a great distance to that country.

In *Tell Me How Long the Train's Been Gone* (1968), Baldwin's story of a black actor who struggles to the top of a competitive talent jungle in search of the good life, his treatment of the city becomes perhaps not less honest but far more militant than in his previous fiction. Like his hero, Leo Proudhammer, Baldwin rejects the impotent social system within which he has previously worked and leans to the revolutionary. As one critic notes, "he now assumes a hipster stance, contemptuous of the 'square' world, by which is meant everything that has to do with the white man's assumptions" (Long 769). At the close of *Another Country*, the reader is aware of Baldwin's despair over the irreconcilable differences between his whites and blacks, the redemptive power of love notwithstanding. He progresses from that philosophical position to a definite political stance on the subject in this novel, from the emotionally spent Vivaldo Moore to the committed Leo Proudhammer.

The Rufus device in *Another Country* gives way to the Leo Proudhammer device here, which Baldwin uses as another sounding board for his increasingly hostile views. Although the setting for this novel is San Francisco, the book is about Harlem, for everything Leo is now he sees as having begun on those streets. In *Tell Me How Long the Train's Been Gone*, Baldwin resumes his use of the past to explain the present, incorporating the flashback extensively.

Leo Proudhammer, successful actor, example of the black Horatio Alger story, or "fat cat" as the young militant Christopher calls him, has had a heart attack in San Francisco. During his convalescence, he stops to examine what he has been and what he must become. Scenes from the past move freely in time, as Baldwin presents New York City through the bittersweet reminiscences of a middle-aged black revolutionary.

Some of the best passages in this novel, although they are colored with indignation and cynicism, are descriptions of the city's people. Leo says, "There is probably no more vivid rendering of silence and no more definitive image of attention, than that presented by Harlem windows, some Sunday afternoons" (167). Although it appears that old men and women and young children are uncaring dreamers, a sensitive viewer can feel the rage, the sadness, as those "dreamers" watch the debris in the street being blown by the wind. Projecting an eerily prophetic statement about the late 60s, Baldwin writes, "Everything is happening and nothing is happening, and everything is still, like thunder" (168).

In Leo Proudhammer, Baldwin creates the awakening of a black boy's sensibility to his limited alternatives, a boy who "hit the streets" to explore all those alternatives. Later in his life, Leo and his fellow struggling actors and actresses in the Village steal books and barter their bodies for food. There, also among all their intimacies, Leo realizes the crucial difference between himself and the white, southern Barbara. Her exile is self-imposed, but he has no choices: "The world in which we lived threatened, every hour, to close on the rest of us forever. We had no equipment with which to break out—and I, least of all. But she could walk out of it at any instant that she chose" (58). His anger grows and, remembering his brother Caleb's misuse at the hands of whites, Leo vows to nurture his hate: "I would keep it healthy, I would make it strong, and I would find a use for it one day" (184).

The epigraph to Book III is part of a traditional black song which hints at a possible reconciliation between blacks and the city: "Mother, take your daughter,/father, take your son!/You better run to the city of refuge,/you better run!" (235). At the chapter's end, the city has acted instead as another irony in the black man's history. Leo utters a bitter indictment of the city, which is not out of character for him, but appears more to capture the spirit of the militant city black dweller of the time:

> I really can't bear any of the American cities I know . . . most of them seem very harsh and hostile, and they are exceedingly ugly. . . . All of the American cities seem boiling in a kind of blood pudding, thick, sticky, foul, and pungent, and it can make you very sad to walk through, say, New Orleans and ask yourself just why a city with no unconquerable physical handicaps, after all, should yet be so relentlessly uninhabitable. (250)

Leo contemplates joining forces with Christopher after he realizes that he has failed to affect the generation of the young militant: "not all of my endeavor, not all of the endeavor of so many for so long, had lessened his danger in any degree" (255). At the close of the novel, a metaphor of the city is called up to illustrate Leo's despair about his own successes: "Indeed, I had conquered the city: but the city was stricken with the plague" (366). The passage also indicates Baldwin's own despair about blacks finding the city a just place to live. The last chapter of the book unites the wavering moderate Leo with the young black revolutionary Christopher, who is himself conspiring to conquer the white man's city with force. The crisis of blacks, which is like the crisis of the city to Leo, has reached epidemic proportions, and the reader leaves him committed to Christopher's cure. He has no doubt found a use for his hate.

There is also no doubt that rage becomes the conquering emotion as Baldwin ends the 60s with the strident tone of *Tell Me How Long the Train's Been Gone*. A less impassioned comment on his career might be that during this time he moves from the private to the social, and in the movement, he has provided many insights into the work of other black writers who have made the city a subject for their art. Although he has the young Leo Proudhammer, in a moment of introspection, lament, "My life, in effect, had not yet happened in anybody's consciousness," it is now clear that black urban life has become a fact of the American consciousness (124). Blyden Jackson tells us that the black novel has almost always been a city novel and that this city novel "has thereby afforded us a picture of the Negro mind which reflects both a permanent cast of Negro thought and the sensitivity of that cast to changes in the Negro's immediate environment" ("The Ghetto" 183). To understand the influences of this thought on the American consciousness, we must then review these perceptions of black city life and explore fictional models which correspond to black urban reality. Only then can we achieve a balanced critical appraisal of the city in the American imagination.

Works Cited

BALDWIN, JAMES. *Another Country.* New York: Dell, 1962.

———. "Autobiographical Notes." *Notes of a Native Son.* Boston: Bantam, 1955.

———. "The Black Boy Looks at the White Boy." *Nobody Knows My Name.* New York: Dell, 1961.

———. "Fifth Avenue, Uptown: A Letter from Harlem." *Nobody Knows My Name.* New York: Dell, 1961.

———. *Go Tell It on the Mountain.* New York: Dell, 1953.

———. *Tell Me How Long the Train's Been Gone.* New York: Dell, 1968.

BARAKA, AMIRI. "Black Literature and the Afro-American Nation: The Urban Voice." Jaye and Watts 139–59.

BELLOW, SAUL. *The Adventures of Augie March.* Greenwich: Fawcett, 1953.

BONE, ROBERT A. *The Negro Novel in America.* New Haven: Yale UP, 1965.

DIXON, MELVIN. *Ride Out the Wilderness: Geography and Identity in Afro-American Literature.* Chicago: U of Illinois P, 1987.

DUNBAR, PAUL LAURENCE. *The Sport of the Gods.* New York: Dodd, 1902.

ELLISON, RALPH. *Invisible Man.* New York: NAL, 1952.

JACKSON, BLYDEN. "The Ghetto of the Negro Novel: A Theme with Variations." *The Waiting Years: Essays on American Negro Literature.* Baton Rouge: Louisiana State UP, 1976. 179–88.

———. "The Negro's Image of the Universe as Reflected in His Fiction." *Black Voices.* Ed. Abraham Chapman. New York: NAL, 1968. 622–31.

JAYE, MICHAEL C., and ANN CHALMERS WATTS, eds. *Literature and the Urban Experience.* New Brunswick: Rutgers UP, 1981.

JOHNSON, CHARLES. *Being & Race: Black Writing Since 1970.* Bloomington: Indiana UP, 1988.

JOHNSON, JAMES WELDON. *The Autobiography of an Ex-Colored Man. Three Negro Classics.* New York: Avon, 1965.

KLEIN, MARCUS. *After Alienation.* New York: World, 1965.

LEE, A. ROBERT. "Harlem on My Mind: Fictions of a Black Metropolis." *The American City: Literary and Cultural Perspectives.* Ed. Graham Clarke. New York: St. Martin's, 1988. 62–85.

LONG, ROBERT EMNET. Rev. of *Another Country,* by James Baldwin. *Nation* June 1968: 769.

MARTIN, REGINALD. "The New Black Aesthetic Critics and Their Exclusion from American 'Mainstream' Criticism." *College English* 50 (1988): 373–82.

MORRISON, TONI. "City Limits, Village Values: Concepts of the Neighborhood in Black Fiction." Jaye and Watts 35–43.

OATES, JOYCE CAROL. "Imaginary Cities: America." Jaye and Watts 11–33.

PIKE, BURTON. *The Image of the City in Modern Literature.* Princeton: Princeton UP, 1981.

WEIMER, DAVID R. *The City as Metaphor.* New York: Random, 1966.

After reading: CONSOLIDATE INFORMATION

1. Durham cites novelist and critic Joyce Carol Oates as tracing the way in which the American city has become a "species of hell." What in your knowledge and experience of city life supports or contradicts Oates's description?
2. Summarize Durham's analysis of the ways in which Black American accounts of city life have changed from early writers like Ralph Ellison and Richard Wright to James Baldwin.
3. After reading Durham's analysis of James Baldwin's fiction and nonfiction writings, how would you explain her choice of Baldwin as a representative Black urban voice?

The Civil War: "Did It Not Seem Real?"
Brian Henderson

In the past twenty-five years television and films have become the subject of scholarly analysis. Brian Henderson wrote this essay for Film Quarterly, *a scholarly journal of film studies. In his analysis Henderson assumes that every film, even one which documents something that actually happened, is shaped by a director who wants to communicate certain ideas, opinions, or arguments.*

Before you read: FIRST THOUGHTS
                  LOOK AHEAD

1. What do you know about Ken Burns's documentary television series *The Civil War?* Even if you are completely unfamiliar with Burns's film series, what do you think a documentary film about the Civil War would do?
2. When you think of the American Civil War (1861–65), what images and popular conceptions come to your mind?
3. What do you think a documentary film has as its main purpose?

During reading: REACT
                 QUESTION
               SUMMARIZE

1. What is your first reaction to Henderson's description of the series?

2. Henderson writes of the series' "ideological project" as "the rewriting of popular memory." What do you think he means by that phrase?

———●✦●———

THE CIVIL WAR (1990), a series of films made by Ken Burns and a large number of collaborators, was seen by more viewers than any other program in the history of the Public Broadcasting System. Thirty-nine million Americans watched the 11-hour series on five consecutive nights in September 1990. Since that time the series has been rebroadcast in its entirety on a weekly basis and an additional rebroadcast has been scheduled for spring 1991; an album of the music used in the series has been released; a book based on the series has been published; and, since January 1991, all nine of the series' episodes have been available for purchase or rent on the home video market. Critically, *The Civil War* has been widely hailed as the television event of the year. Indeed, it has probably been more ardently and universally praised than anything in the history of public television. (*Roots*, one recalls with some difficulty, was produced for and shown on network television.)

The PBS program guide observes, accurately as far as it goes: "The series uses archival photographs, period paintings, footage of battle sites, interviews with historians and a chorus of voices reading from diaries, letters, speeches and newspapers of the era." To this list should be added music, sound effects (battle cries, firearm sounds, wind and rain sounds), and graphics (maps, battle diagrams, episode and section titles, etc.).

These constituent elements of *The Civil War* are of considerable interest in themselves. But what is truly extraordinary, in my view, are the ways in which these elements are interwoven in the text of the series as a whole. A preliminary survey of that text is attempted in what follows. Begun here, although not completed, is an argument that *The Civil War* constitutes a new kind of textuality, involving new kinds of arrangements, or dispositions, of sounds and images. Understanding the textual operation of *The Civil War* in this sense is not a necessary preliminary to other studies—the film's rewriting of popular memory, its "ideological project," etc.—but it may contribute to such studies.

Fundamental to the complex textuality of *The Civil War* are the ways in which its photographs, voices, music, and sound effects interact with its three levels of organization. These comprise: (1) 11 episodes, titled by year and by verbal designation, more or less metaphoric; (2) section headings within each episode, variable in number and in manner of reference to the subject of the episode; and (3) an overall division, cutting across the other two levels, between chronicle (Gettysburg: The First Day; Gettysburg: The Second Day; Gettysburg: The Third Day) and topics not dependent on chronological placement: the role of women in the war; food and drink in the war; the firearms used in the war; etc. On a qualitative basis, somewhat nebulously perhaps, one might also identify a number of "set-pieces," in which images and sounds are more closely related than in the vast bulk of the series, and in which an aesthetic ambition is more than usually discernible. The

The overall episode break-down is as follows:

Episode One:	1861—The Cause	(99 min.)
Episode Two:	1862—A Very Bloody Affair	(69 min.)
Episode Three:	1862—Forever Free	(76 min.)
Episode Four:	1863—Simply Murder	(62 min.)
Episode Five:	1863—The Universe of Battle	(95 min.)
Episode Six:	1864—Valley of the Shadow of Death	(70 min.)
Episode Seven:	1864—Most Hallowed Ground	(72 min.)
Episode Eight:	1865—War is All Hell	(69 min.)
Episode Nine:	1865—The Better Angels of Our Nature	(68 min.)

The section-headings of the nine episodes are as follows:

1861—The Cause
All Night Forever
Are We Free?
A House Divided
The Meteor
Gun Men
Manassas
A Thousand Mile Front
Honorable Manhood

1862—A Very Bloody Affair
Politics
Ironclads
Lincolnites
The Peninsula
Our Boy
Shiloh
The Arts of Death
Republics
On to Richmond

1862—Forever Free
Stonewall
The Beast
The Seven Days
kiss Daniel for me
Saving the Union
Antietam
The Higher Object

1863—Simply Murder
Northern Lights
Oh! Be Joyful
The Kingdom of Jones
Under the Shade of the Trees
A Dust Covered Man

1863—The Universe of Battle
Gettysburg: The 1st Day
Gettysburg: The 2nd Day
Gettysburg: The 3rd Day
She Ranks Me
Vicksburg
Bottom Rail on Top
The River of Death
A New Birth of Freedom

1864—Valley of the Shadow of Death
Grant
Lee
In the Wilderness
Move by the Left Flank
Now, Fix Me
The Remedy

1864—Most Hallowed Ground
a warm place in the field
Nathan Bedford Forrest
Summer, 1864
Spies
The Crater
Headquarters, U.S.A.
The Promised Land
The Age of Shoddy
Can these be men?
The People's Resolution
Most Hallowed Ground

1865—War is All Hell
Sherman's March
The Breath of Emancipation
December 25, 1864
Died of a Theory
I Want to See Richmond
Appomattox

1865—The Better Angels of Our Nature
Assassination
Useless, Useless
The Picklocks of Biographers
Was it Not Real?

set-pieces come most often at the end of an episode and are rarely more than a few minutes in duration; they include the reading of the letter of Sullivan Ballou (in Episode One), the death of Stonewall Jackson (Four), and the reading of Lincoln's Gettysburg Address (Five).

The photographs used in the series—16,000 of them were filmed—are perhaps what most astonished and bewitched most viewers. For that reason, and to displace the tyranny of the visual, I will begin with the series' voices. To displace in turn the logocentric privileging of speech, or at least to postpone it for a brief time, I will begin with a few words about *The Civil War's* music.

With one or two exceptions, all the series' music comes from the Civil War period. This is not surprising; nineteenth-century romantic composers made the use of folk songs and other native materials obligatory in celebrating a nation or region—their own or a patron's. The classical Hollywood composers, many of them displaced Europeans, used this approach as a matter of course, and used it also as a shortcut to finish the vast amount of work they were asked to do. Even a modernist like Virgil Thompson orchestrated cowboy songs and regional songs—with wit, dissonance, and trenchant commentary—in his scores for *The Plow that Broke the Plains* (1936) and *The River* (1937), both by Pare Lorentz. *The Civil War* made the decision *not* to orchestrate, but to use its Civil War songs individually, and separately, as artifacts. The series went much further than this, however, by avoiding the traditional arrangements of the songs it uses, and with them any attempt to reproduce what people of the Civil War era actually heard. It subjects the songs instead to its own severe, evocative stylization, involving, first of all, an instrumental minimalism. Thus the "Battle Cry of Freedom," heard again and again throughout the series, is played on a solo piano by Jacqueline Schwab. So are "Flag of Columbia," "All Quiet on the Potomac," and one of two versions of "Marching Through Georgia"—the other version is played by two fiddles, a guitar, and a banjo. "Lorena" is played by two fiddles and a guitar. "Shenandoah" is played by a cello and a piano. "Dixie" is played by Bobbie Horton on solo guitar, and so on. Resorting neither to orchestration nor traditional settings, the series' approach to its Civil War songs is to turn them into chamber music.

We do not know what 16,000 Civil War photographs are supposed to look like on film; we do not know what voices reading Civil War texts should sound like; we do not know indeed what an 11-hour reconstruction or evocation of the Civil War is supposed to look and sound like. But we do have some idea what the most familiar Civil War songs are supposed to sound like. The series' music tells us that the series as a whole is a chamber work for solo voices and instruments. The longest, most expensive, most elaborately researched work in the history of American public television, which concerns some of the most large-scale, epic events in American history, itself severely avoids both epic and largeness of scale.

A second point about the music, distinct from but related to the first, is that many, if not most of the songs, including those mentioned, are played in a sad, contemplative, funereal, and/or dirge-like way. Sometimes this is topical—an upbeat "Marching Through Georgia" is played when the Northern perspective of Sherman's March is presented, the solo piano version, called a "lament" in the sound-track recording credits, when the Southern perspective is explored. There is a brass-band version of "Dixie" in the South's glory days and both solo guitar and solo piano dirges later when the Confederacy is falling apart. Many other songs, such as "Battle Cry of Freedom," have no upbeat versions—Schwab's sad, hesitant, ruminative version is the farthest thing from either a battle cry or a rally 'round the flag. Here too the music sets the tone for the series as a whole. Many of the voices, certainly the countless photographs of the dead, the dying, the maimed and the buried, and the series as a whole have a chastened, quietly grieving quality. Reviewing the series for *The Nation*, Robert Cole asks, "Is melancholy the only emotion the producers could associate with this revolution?" It is a good question and the answer seems to be, in the terms posed, yes. Emotionally speaking, melancholy may well be the most important product of the series. Of course this has to do with the wholesale slaughter that we see and hear about throughout the series, but it has also to do with what historian Barbara J. Fields calls in several places the "higher purpose"—the liberation of the slaves—which she says emerged after the war had begun as its chief goal. But Fields, in one of the last commentaries in the series, asks who in fact won the war—since many basic rights of citizenship were systematically denied blacks for a hundred years after it.

The songs of the series are rarely played whole, but almost always fragmented into phrases and sections. These fragments—sometimes the same fragment, sometimes different ones—are then recycled through the series as a whole. Many of them recur dozens of times, creating an effect of evocative repetition that is a major feature of the series' textuality. Such fragmentation is also necessary for interweaving the music closely with other elements of the text. Sometimes a musical phrase accompanies a speech of no more than a few sentences; other musical passages bridge several photos and/or a shift from one topic to another in the narration. It is not surprising that Ken Burns lists himself as one of the series' two musical directors—he helped choose the musical selections and also worked with the musicians to achieve the tonal and mood variations he wanted for different passages in the text.

The music is so carefully integrated into the text that one might disagree with this or that selection as one would disagree with an argument. Passages from "Lorena," an 1857 song of romantic loss and remembrance popular with troops on both sides, are played frequently in the series. (This is the song that Max Steiner uses for the opening scene of *The Searchers*, masterfully adapting it to the rhythm of Ethan's slow approach on horseback.) It seems to me inappropriate that the series plays "Lorena" when it discusses the hard-working women of the war, nurses and others, who faced horror, and sometimes danger, on a daily basis. But "Lorena" is also played in the wake of Lincoln's assassination, brilliantly suggesting that, reviled on many sides while alive, Lincoln became a lost romantic object in death.

An exception to the series' practice of fragmenting its songs is "Ashokan Farewell," a 1984 composition by Jay Ungar that sounds more like a Civil War song than many of the genuine article. (It is performed by three fiddles, including Ungar's, and two guitars.) This piece, which is played more often than any other in the series except, possibly, "The Battle Cry of Freedom," appears most often at the beginnings and ends of episodes. Because of its crucial placements, and because it is usually played whole, "Ashokan Farewell" has come to seem, more than any other, the musical emblem of *The Civil War*. It is the series' chief lament-anthem of farewell in a number of senses—which will have to be explored elsewhere.

Like many of its musical arrangements, *The Civil War*'s voices are all solos. They may be subdivided into an overall narrational voice (David McCullough), representing no particular person, and a number of voices representing individual persons. The latter includes well-known historical figures as well as unknown or little-known people who kept diaries or wrote letters that the series draws on. The historical figures, and the people—unseen—who read them, are as follows:

Abraham Lincoln	Sam Waterston
Ulysses S. Grant	Jason Robards
Frederick Douglass	Morgan Freeman
Joshua L. Chamberlain	Paul Roebling
Walt Whitman	Garrison Keillor
Robert E. Lee	George Black
William T. Sherman	Arthur Miller
Jefferson Davis	Horton Foote
Horace Greeley	Philip Bosco
George McClellan	Terry Courier
Stonewall Jackson	Jody Powell
Benjamin F. Butler	Studs Terkel

The most important lesser-known figures are:

Mary Chestnut	Julie Harris
Pvt. Elisha Hunt Rhodes	Chris Murney
Pvt. Sam Watkins	Charley McDowell
George Templeton Strong	George Plimpton

The four lesser-known voices, all diarists, fall—rather too neatly perhaps—into a North/South, high-born/low-born schema. On the high end, George Templeton Strong was a wealthy, conservative lawyer and civic leader in New York City; Mary Chestnut had access to the highest levels of the Confederacy—her husband, a former senator from South Carolina, was a member of the Davis cabinet. On the low end, Elisha Hunt Rhodes was a private in the 2nd Rhode Island Volunteers and Sam Watkins was a private in Company H of the 1st Tennessee. Some background of the well-known figures is provided when they first appear, in the nature of facts, especially about their early lives, that viewers might not know. The four diarists, whom only specialists will know, are very pointedly introduced—as individuals and as diarists—in the series' first episode. Their writings are returned to again and again throughout the series.

In *The Civil War*, it is worth noting, the historical figures, great and small, and the voices that speak their words become virtually indistinguishable. This puts pressure on the speakers in the series, both the actors—Harris, Waterston, Robards, Freeman, Bosco—and the non-actors—Miller, Foote, Powell, McDowell. (Terkel,

Keillor, and Plimpton are non-actors but celebrities—their performing voices are well known to us.) "The act of love is a confession," said Camus. "Selfishness screams aloud, vanity shows off, or else true generosity reveals itself." Where Camus writes of self-revelation, we would write of presentation of self or role-playing. Even in these terms, one is tempted to say, the act of love is nothing compared to the naked human voice held up to the grave issues of the Civil War. *The Civil War's* speakers achieve, almost uniformly, a restrained, often melancholy tonality that meshes remarkably with the other elements of the text. (A partial exception may be Garrison Keillor, who, reading Whitman and others, seems to try too hard to be expressive.)

Frederick Douglass and Lincoln were orators but the readings of Freeman and Waterston assiduously avoid the orational, or any public style; each seems to speak, quietly, to a friend, or to himself. Morgan Freeman holds back from "acting" Frederick Douglass; he uses the remarkable instrument of his voice—low, grave, thrilling—as simply as possible. This allows Douglass's words to reach the viewer with maximum clarity and emotional power. In an 1863 speech, Douglass urged black people to "fly to arms" and to smite to death "the power that would bury the Government and your liberty in the same hopeless grave"; he concludes, "This is your golden opportunity." The temptation for an actor to wrap his voice around the last phrase is powerful, but Freeman resists it. He speaks it as flatly and tonelessly as his musical voice permits and instead of an actor we are aware of hundreds of years of oppression that can be overthrown in a moment. (Freeman's melancholy sound suggests, beyond Douglass's words, the oppression and suffering that were not ended in that moment.) Waterston continually displaces us as a speaker for Lincoln—this is not the voice we expect. But we pay closer attention to Lincoln's words as a result; and Waterston's reading of the Gettysburg address cuts against decades of tradition: not *of* the people, *by* the people, *for* the people but "government of the *people*, by the *people*, for the *people*, shall not perish from the earth." Even at the end of the series we may not accept Waterston's voice as Lincoln's, but there will be no going back to the intonements of Raymond Massey either.

The amateurs were perhaps more typecast for voice than the professionals—not what a figure sounded like but how he or she "should" sound. We see pictures of Jefferson Davis and hear Horton Foote's voice and are convinced without thinking about it that this is how Davis should sound. After the Battle of Bull Run, called Manassas in the South, we hear a number of Northern voices describing and bemoaning the rout and its implications. There is then a switch to a jubilant Davis, "My fellow citizens, your little Army, derided for its want of arms, derided for its lack of all the essential material of war, has met the grand army of the enemy, routed it at every point..." The jaunty music of "Bonnie Blue Flag" accompanies the speech, but there is music in Foote's voice also. There is no ordinary music in Arthur Miller's Sherman, and should not be. Miller's gravelly voice, cutting through the nonsense to the blunt, disturbing truth of a subject puts Sherman—our idea of him—before us. George Black is soft-voiced and recessive as Robert E. Lee; a voice that seems to convey sentiment openly but to hide the person beneath. The undefeated South seems to rasp in Jody Powell's reading of Stonewall Jackson and a number of other Southerners.

Important aspects of *The Civil War* have to do with the overall narrator and with interactions between the overall narrator and the other voices of the text. The overall narrator is unidentified in the series whereas each of the other voices is identified not only initially but also, with rare exceptions, at the end of every speech. Thus virtually every speech except the overall narrator's is vocally signed—"Mary Chestnut," "Frederick Douglass," "Abraham Lincoln," etc. All of the voices of the series except that of the overall narrator say what the signers said or wrote—the series merely quotes them. The words of the overall narrator, on the other hand, are not quoted; they are written by the film-makers to be spoken by the narrator. The narrator is by no means a spokesman for the film-makers or their views, however—his is as much a voice located in the text as the various levels of voice and narration that critics of the fiction have proposed. The figure of the overall narrator is constructed, and one of the guidelines for constructing it was suggested by Ken Burns in a filmed interview.

> So many people start a documentary film with the idea that they know the answer, that the documentary is merely a means of expression. For us it is a process of discovery; we don't know what it's going to be about. We are as curious, we hope, as the viewer is about what happened and use the process of making a documentary film as an exploration.

A finished text cannot itself embody the discovery or exploration process involved in its making; it can only represent it. Such representation can be a very effective rhetorical strategy, however, as *The Civil War* shows. It is crucial to such a strategy that the overall narrator not speak retrospectively. He cannot speak from the standpoint of the end of the war, that is, with full knowledge of what is to transpire. He sometimes anticipates a later event, or hints at it, but this most often occurs in the preview-like passages that begin many of the episodes—Episode Five, for example:

> Now, to draw federal troops away from Vicksburg, Lee led his army onto Northern soil again, looking for the right moment to attack. When it came, on the morning of July 1st, 1863, it would be in the most ordinary of places. For three days, 150,000 men would make war on the gentle farmland of southern Pennsylvania. When the third day was over, it would prove to have been the most crucial day of the entire war.

The narration, mainly by Geoffrey C. Ward, is not written omnisciently and retrospectively, but certain speakers might have made it sound that way—Gregory Peck or James Earl Jones, for instance. McCullough's voice, neither ringing nor booming, sounds unrhetorical; it is a pragmatic-sounding voice, brightly interested in each of the carloads of facts, names, ironies, and events it speaks, giving each its due, its proper intonation and emphasis, but never becoming moved or fascinated, always, after nicely judged pauses, moving along. His voice also has another quality essential to an 11-hour series—it wears well; it seems able to go anywhere, to treat any subject, person, or emotion, and never tire us or strike a false note.

There is a division of function between the overall narrator and the other voices of the text, but it is not a hard and fast one. The signed voices speak out of their own experience, even when they are philosophizing or fantasizing. At the same time, the overall narrator speaks of strategic and statistical matters that the participants could not know; like the signed voices and the historians, however, he sometimes tells anecdotes and sometimes makes interpretations. The overall narrator's voice, unimposing in itself, never overwhelms the other voices and never intrudes upon or competes with the interviews with historians that are spread throughout the text. A rare, perhaps unique exception occurs in Episode Eight. Miller as Sherman has just spoken the second of two Sherman quotes in close succession, whereupon the narrator begins his next passage with yet another Sherman quote. Sherman said so many pungent things about the war that everyone gets into the act.

A more typical instance of interaction between the overall narrator and the other voices of the text occurs during the Battle of Bull Run/Manassas. The presentation of the battle alternates between the narrator's description of battle movements, North and South, and the testimony of a number of witnesses and other commentators on the event and its aftermath, including a number of English and French observers. The nonretrospective narration reinforces, and is reinforced by, the standpoint of the contemporary witnesses, who did not know what was going to happen. North and South both believed the war would be short-lived, indeed that the first large battle would be decisive. Rather than state this fact through the overall narrator, the series builds up a sense of it through a very large number of voices, quite differently positioned, each stating its viewpoint. Thus the results of the battle, when they come, have some of the shock to viewers that they had to the disillusioned witnesses—pictures of amputations, including a pile of severed limbs; Union troops running, walking, dragging all night long until they saw the spires of Washington, DC. The narrator's overall description of the battle, never anticipating or prejudging what will happen next, provides context for the witnesses' testimonies without undermining them.

The visual material of the series may be divided into the photographic, the filmic, and the graphic—the film's episode and section titles, its credits, etc. The photographic material consists of 16,000 photographs, paintings, lithographs, broadsides, and newspapers of the Civil War period. The filmic materials consist of present-day footage of battle sites of the Civil War, synch-sound discussions by present-day historians, and archival footage, some of it silent, some with original voice-over, of several reunions of Civil War veterans.

Civil War-era photographs make up the vast bulk of the series; at least they seem to do so—they are what viewers remember and critics most prize. The gathering and selection of these photos, enough to fill out much of the series' 11 hours, was a prodigious feat of research. The film-makers visited more than 80 museums and libraries, including not only well-known ones, but state and regional archives and historical societies as well. The film-makers include works by celebrated photographers—the Matthew Brady studio, Alexander Gardner, and Timothy O'Sullivan, for example; but they draw much more extensively upon anonymous newspaper photographers, portrait and souvenir photos (many sold to soldiers by photographers in camp and on campaign), the records of regiments and other combat units, family albums, and chillingly medical photographs of the wounded, maimed, starved, and dead.

Seeing the assembled Civil War photos in the series, however, is a very far thing from seeing them in an archive or a book of photographs. The photographic images of the series are time-bound, which means that the time of the viewer's perception of each, and the arrangement of successive images in time, is indeed bound, not free. There is also, of course, the work of the camera, which sometimes begins with the whole of a photograph then moves in—by either a cut or a camera movement—to a detail or series of details. Sometimes the camera starts with a detail and moves out gradually to encompass either the whole photograph or a larger section of it. Sometimes a photograph is returned to later in the series, either for the same view and/or for different ones, creating a sense that the text is not through with the photo, that it has to come back to explore it further, in some cases again and again, as though seeking its elusive meaning.

One of these photos is reproduced in the series book, which describes it as showing an "airy ward in the Armory Square Hospital [in Washington, DC] (that) appears to be decorated either for the Fourth of July or perhaps for the end of the war." The series' text seems as fascinated with this photograph as Roland Barthes's *Camera Lucida* is with its photos. Perhaps it is the very deep space of the photo, whose centrally located vanishing point is interrupted by a young man with an amputated leg sitting in a wheel chair with his head tilted back and his eyes on the camera; perhaps it is the festive flags hanging high up on rafters in the foreground, contrasting with the sad scene of convalescents, some of them amputees, beneath; or perhaps it is the sort of half-banner with stars, apparently hanging from a rafter deeper in space than the flags, but impossible to read, either because it is semi-transparent and partially reveals deeper space behind it or because it is itself stamped with a trompe l'oeil design, or both.

The viewer's perception of the series' photographs is conditioned, in addition to the factors discussed above, by the various linguistic components and levels of the text. But this conditioning is by no means reducible to Roland Barthes's notion of *anchrage*, the idea that photographs almost always appear with linguistic messages that tell us how to read them, limiting the virtually unlimited number of interpretations that a photograph itself might sustain. *The Civil War* limits the readable potential of the photos it displays, if only by cutting down the time of reading and, sometimes, by offering only a detail of the photo for viewing; but it makes little if any use of linguistic *anchrage*, opting instead for a non-*anchrage* or even, since it seems to be a methodological principle, anti-*anchrage*.

Never does the overall narrator or anyone else in the series address us about the photos shown: to tell us how to look at them, to take particular note of one rather than another, or to notice some aspect or detail of any one of them. Rarely does a speaker even refer to a photo; only twice, that I can recall, in 11 hours. At the beginning of Episode Five, we see a photograph of three Confederate soldiers captured at Gettysburg and hear historian Shelby Foote tell us that he is very fond of the photo and why he is; at the end of the same episode, the overall narrator explains, as we look at it, that the only photo of Lincoln at Gettysburg shows him sitting down after his speech—expecting a longer address, the photographer took his time focussing. If the voices of the text do not, with two exceptions, refer to the photos, neither do the photos illustrate specific points of narration. The two unravel independently, linked only very generally by a common topic. A category of partial exception seems necessary when a photo of a particular historical figure accompanies a commentary about him. The same few photos of Grant and Sherman, among others, tend to be used again and again throughout the series, and coincide with a wide variety of narrational situations and contexts. Indeed, their very frequency and multi-function make such photos a general, not specific, support for any particular piece of narration. The matter is different, however, when the camera moves slowly into a detail of the subject's face, or even of his eyes, while the narration probes his character. There the photo, pinned like a butterfly by the camera, is impressed into the narration's specific service, if only for a moment.

The kind of text that results from this anti-*anchrage* policy is strange and extraordinarily interesting. Generalization takes us only so far, however—*The Civil War* is enormously varied and the relations of photos and voices vary accordingly. I will look closely at the final section of Episode One, "Honorable Manhood," which presents a reading of Sullivan Ballou's letter to his wife. One of the best-known passages in the series, it is reproduced in toto in a filmed interview with Ken Burns and is included in audio form on the sound-track recording; also, some photos from the passage and the text of the letter are reproduced in the series book. The placement of the section, outside Episode One's chronology, sets it off significantly from the rest of the episode, and in some respects from the rest of the series as a whole. The preceding section, "A Thousand Mile Front" took up the series' chronicle from the Battle of Bull Run in July 1861 to the appointment of General McClellan as commander of the Union army five days later to his training of the army in August and September 1861. Then McClellan formulated a grand Union strategy with offensives on Richmond in the east, into Tennessee in the center, and along the Mississippi in the west; but for the balance of 1861 he did nothing. The episode concludes with a remark by George Templeton Strong on December 31st, in which he looks forward to an 1862 no better than the year just ending. This should end an episode called "1861" but it doesn't; another heading appears on the screen—"Honorable Manhood"—which concerns a letter written July 14, 1861.

A very close reading of "Honorable Manhood," which lasts 3 1/2 minutes, would take many pages. A shot of a Union camp begins the episode—rows of white tents with officers and men in formation in front of them; on the sound track we hear the sounds of drill—a distanced-sounding "column left," etc. At the same time the narrator tells us that a week before the Battle of Bull Run, Sullivan Ballou, a major in the 2nd Rhode Island Volunteers, wrote home to his wife in Smithfield. We continue to hear drill sounds over the beginning of the letter, even after the shot changes to the photo of what seems to be an officer's quarters inside a white tent—through which outside sounds could no doubt be heard. While we continue to hear Ballou's letter, the camera moves slowly around the photo of the room, coming to rest first on a white hammock chair, then on the crude table next to it, then on an unlit candle placed on the table. The camera seems to be trying to imagine the physical circumstances under which the letter was written. At some point in the camera's movement the drill sounds recede and we hear the start of "Akoshan Farewell," which is played without interruption until its conclusion. The camera focuses on a strange reproduction of a painting, or photo, pinned on the wall of the room, perhaps of an orator giving an impassioned speech.

As Ballou begins to talk about his love for his wife, we see a formal photo of a handsome man and his wife looking into the camera—is this Sullivan and Sarah Ballou? The photo is followed, however, by photos of four Civil War–era couples, two of them beginning with a shot of hands touching tenderly and moving up and back to the photo as a whole. When Ballou speaks of his regretting not living and loving more and not seeing their two sons grow up to honorable manhood, we see a photo of a couple and two boys. Is this Ballou and his family? It seems not likely since the man has a corporal's stripes on his arm and Ballou was a major even before the war's first big battle. As Ballou speaks of the dead coming back to earth, we see several film shots in color of a battle field at dawn or twilight, with a single cannon in silhouette on the horizon—perhaps the very battlefield he died on. When Ballou writes that he will be there when the soft breeze fans his wife's cheek, we see a closer shot of the cannon with the grass beneath it blowing in the breeze and a chain loop from the cannon hanging prominently in the foreground. Ballou had spoken earlier of his being bound to his wife "with mighty cables that nothing but Omnipotence can break" but also of his love of country coming over him like a strong wind that "bears me irresistibly with all these chains to the battle field." Does the shot suggest that the chains prevailed over the cables?

As the letter concludes, the images again show a tent interior, this time a different one, and come back finally to a different photo of the tents and drill formations seen at the beginning of the section. The narrator informs us, just as the music ends, that Ballou was killed a week later at the first battle of Bull Run.

The photos of the Union camp that begin and end the "Honorable Manhood" section actually show the 5th Vermont at Camp Griffin, Virginia, not the 2nd Rhode Island Volunteers, Ballou's unit, which was camped at Washington, DC. We know this because a two-page reproduction of the 5th Vermont photo appears on the title pages of the series book—the left half of the photo is the first photo of the "Honorable Manhood" series; the right side is its last.

It seems likely that not one of the photographs in the passage has anything literally to do with Sullivan Ballou. The film-makers used the photographs they had not for a referential function but to build a metaphoric series suggested by Ballou's letter and what they imagined to be its likely circumstances of composition. (The shots of the couples are a metaphoric series within a series.) They also perused adjacent details within several of the photographs with the camera—a metonymic series (within a metaphoric whole), used not for realism but to imagine the composition of Ballou's writing in a different way. Some will say the film-makers did what they did because, lacking photos of Ballou and other subjects, they had no choice. In fact, there *is* a photo of Ballou's unit, the 2nd Rhode Island Infantry, shown drilling in the summer of 1861 in a camp near Washington, DC—it is reproduced in the front endpapers of the series book. But it is a far less evocative photo [than] the ones used, and it has no tents behind the troops for (imagined) metonymic displacement from exterior to interior. (The sounds effects of drill, metonymic to both spaces, provide another bridge between them.)

What the film-makers did in the Sullivan Ballou section is far more interesting than an assembly of Ballou photos would have been—far more interesting, far more innovative, far more "creative" by any standard. And what the film-makers did in this section they also did—to borrow the narration's words for the war's farflung theater of operations—at 10,000 other places in the text. Each of these sites is different and each poses a distinct challenge for the analyst.

Ken Burns addressed some of the issues discussed above in a filmed interview about the making of the series. "*The Civil War* was a logistical nightmare," he says

> to keep all of the film footage, and all the first-person quotes, and all the music, the sound effects, and the writing all straight. We really wanted with the writing and the shooting to not worry about whether there were images to fit the particular writing or whether there was writing to fit the images. We would go off and film what we wanted to film, go off and write about what we wanted to write and not worry about that. Later on that made editing incredibly difficult. But we were able really to explore the war ... So the writing is independent, the shooting is independent, all of the stuff is. And then when we get into editing and begin a really long difficult process of horsetrading between these two sides, seemingly disparate sides, to make it all work out to tell our story, our his-tory, to our best ability.

Burns reveals perhaps more than he realized when he speaks of independent writing and independent shooting, followed by "a really long difficult process of horsetrading between the two sides." "The two sides": that is, narration and photographs, words and pictures, are themselves engaged in a kind of civil war. That war, like the Civil War, took place not globally, one supposes, but in 10,000 places. The metaphor of horsetrading for working out an accommodation between narration and photographs—"to make it all work out, to tell our story, our his-tory"—is interesting also. The word probably refers to highminded debates among colleagues all seeking the best series: what to include, what to exclude, how best to match these photos and these narrations. But horsetrading in American terminology and legend is also par excellence a situation of dishonesty, of fudging, of making appearance pass as reality, of discounts and short shrifts, of fooling the eye and therefore the mind, of making the viewer buy what he thinks he sees, but does not. In works such as Faulkner's "Spotted Horses" (in *The Hamlet* [1940]), John Ford's *Wagonmaster* (1950), and many others, there is also a specific discrepancy between what one sees—wild or painted or broken-down horses—and what one hears—the lies, the explanations, the glossings over of a persuasive seller. The listener, who always swallows the deal, does not discover the truth until after the fact, when it's too late; he is always complicit in the swindle, however; he has seen what he wanted to see.

The Civil War's makers seem untroubled by the horsetrading between sounds and images that went on in its making—and they should be. It is the text itself that points to the matter in a number of ways and places, bearing traces of its making but perhaps doing more than that. No pointing is more notable than the last passage spoken in the entire series, particularly its last two sentences, which may be read as applying to the series itself, as well as the matter at hand. Over photos of the 50th Anniversary Reunion at Gettysburg, we hear the voice of Shelby Foote:

> In time even death itself might be abolished. Sgt. Barry Benson, a South Carolina veteran . . . of the war from before Fort Sumter to Appomattox saw it so when he got around to composing the reminiscences he hoped "would go down among my descendants for a long time." Reliving the war in words he began to wish he could relive it in fact; and he came to believe that he and his fellow soldiers, gray and blue, might one day be able to do just that, if not here on earth then afterwards in Valhalla. "Who knows," he asked, as his narrative drew toward its close, "but it may be given us after this life to meet again in the old quarters, to play chess and draughts and get up soon to answer the morning roll call, to fall in at the tap of a drum to drill and dress parade, and again to hastily don our war gear while the monotonous patter of a long roll summons to battle. Who knows but again the old flags, ragged and torn, snapping in the wind, may face each other in a flutter of pursuing and pursued, while the cries of victory fill a summer day. And after the battle then the slain and wounded will arise and all will be together under the two flags, all sound and well, and there will be talking and laughter and cheers. And all will say, 'Did it not seem real? Was it not as in the old days?'"

After reading: CONSOLIDATE INFORMATION

1. Summarize Henderson's main argument about the television series, *The Civil War*.
2. How does Henderson evaluate Burns's epic documentary series?
3. Why do you think Henderson discusses the music and the spoken text of the series first, before he analyzes the visual images?

Two Critical Views of *The Handmaid's Tale*
Edd Doerr and Michael Calleri

The following two responses to the film The Handmaid's Tale *were written for a popular audience. Edd Doerr's short piece is more an appreciation than a review; he reflects his own and his readers' fears and concerns that a totalitarian society like the one portrayed in Margaret Atwood's novel and the film could occur in our lifetime.*

Michael Calleri makes a more complex argument than does Doerr; he raises questions about whether novels can be successfully translated into films.

Before you read: FIRST THOUGHTS
       LOOK AHEAD

1. Write a short reaction to Doerr's title, "A Chilling Look at a Fundamentalist Dystopia."
2. What do you think the word *dystopia* means? If you are not sure, make some guesses and then look it up in a dictionary.
3. What can you predict about Michael Calleri's evaluation of the film, based on the title of his essay?

During reading: REACT
       QUESTION
       SUMMARIZE

1. Does Doerr give you much evidence for his conclusion, which equates the film and the novel and states that both "deserve the highest praise and the largest audience"?
2. React to Calleri's implied judgment that most films do not achieve intellectual depth and merely provide superficial entertainment.

A Chilling Look at a Fundamentalist Dystopia
Edd Doerr

MARGARET ATWOOD, the eminent Canadian novelist-poet and 1987 Humanist of the Year, gave us a chilling look at a possible American fundamentalist dystopia in her best-selling 1986 novel, *The Handmaid's Tale*. The novel depicted a United States taken over in the near future by racist hyperconservative fundamentalists and renamed the Republic of Gilead, in which women have no rights. Following an environmental-ecological disaster which has left most women sterile, those capable of reproduction are assigned to government and military officials for breeding purposes.

  The Handmaid's Tale has been expertly and faithfully translated to film by screenwriter Harold Pinter (*Betrayal*) and director Volker Schlondorff (*The Tin Drum*). From the opening credits to the final fadeout, the film fully captures the horror of a "moral majoritarian" dictatorship lacking the most elemental civil liberties, a puritanical yet hypocritical dystopia based upon the most brutal interpretations of the Old Testament. Yet, the film is no mere tract but alive with very nuanced, believable characters and a credible plot.

Heading the excellent cast are Natasha Richardson (daughter of Vanessa Redgrave and director Tony Richardson), Robert Duvall, Faye Dunaway, Aidan Quinn, Elizabeth McGovern, and Victoria Tennant, whose sensitive performances perfectly fit the tone of Atwood's novel.

Scenes depicting public executions ("particicutions"), the deportation of blacks, the roundup of fertile women, and the isolation and degradation of the "handmaids" are shocking—like the Holocaust or the hanging of Quakers in seventeenth-century Boston—but realistic and not at all overdone.

Technically, *The Handmaid's Tale* (both film and novel) belongs to the science-fiction genre, but at the very upper end. All too much of what is called science fiction is fantasy, juvenilia, or Hollywood westerns with rockets and space suits. Atwood, Pinter, and Schlondorff anchor their story in the unpleasant realities of past and present: Ceaucescu's dictatorship outlawing birth control and abortion in Romania, Nazi genocide, Iranian public executions and compulsory chador-wearing, South African apartheid, and the all-too-abundant examples of censorship and book-burning. The theme of surrogate mothers (the film's "handmaids") comes straight from the Bible (Genesis 30), where Jacob's wife Rachel, unable to conceive, turns her maid over to her husband: "Here is my maidservant Bilhah as a consort, and Jacob had intercourse with her. When Bilhah conceived and bore a son, Rachel said, 'God has vindicated me; indeed he has heeded my plea and given me a son!'"

The fundamentalist dystopia that Atwood has created in *The Handmaid's Tale* is both more credible and more likely than George Orwell's Oceania in *1984*. Both the novel and the film versions of *The Handmaid's Tale* deserve the highest praise and the largest audiences.

Another Example of How Great Novels Make Bad Films
Michael Calleri

IMPORTANT NOVELS rarely become important films. Alfred Hitchcock often commented that well-crafted fiction was much harder to film than second-rate writing. Great novels—those multidimensional works which explore the interior life of their characters and offer gripping emotional development—are extremely difficult to transfer to the screen. Contrast this with popular fiction, such as the gothic romance, from which entertaining movies can be made because the audience reacts on a visceral level. A good example would be Daphne du Maurier's *Rebecca*, expertly filmed by Hitchcock.

The challenge of adapting novels to the screen lies not merely in the writing of the script but also in the selection of the novel itself. It is virtually impossible to turn some books into movies that do them justice. Directors and screenwriters can be as faithful to the book as they desire, even slavishly so. They can, and often do, aim high. But if the novel is centered around thought and mood rather than deed and action, the battle usually is already half lost.

The battlefield becomes even more treacherous if the novel presents some vision of the future. Many directors and screenwriters—both good and bad—have failed in their attempts to capture the essence of books about the shape of things to come, especially when the novel's tone is intellectual. Too many films based upon books forecasting a gloomy, totalitarian future end up being labored and pedantic. It's almost as if the very nature of fascism—and all the evil the word signifies—prevents humanistically inclined writers and directors from completely capturing the heart of their angry intent. These creative people know the who, what, and why of the enemy, but they cannot make their vision work on the screen.

This failure is often the result of their taking on a novel that is profoundly difficult (in the good sense). Movies, whether one likes it or not, are primarily entertainment—"pieces of time," as filmmaker Peter Bogdanovich once wrote, which are supposed to move, jolt, or scare an audience. Box office hits are generally comedies and slam-bang action films; edification is seldom on the credit side of the profit ledger.

This certainly does not mean that films cannot be edifying as well as entertaining. In the crap shoot that is the motion picture business, the dice are loaded against intellectual achievement, but occasionally movies set in the future manage to provoke as well as entertain. Peter Watkins's *The War Game* and *Punishment Park*, Stanley Kubrick's *A Clockwork Orange*, Ridley Scott's *Blade Runner*, George Miller's *The Road Warrior*, James Cameron's *The Terminator*, Lindsay Anderson's . . . *if*, and Kevin Brownlow's *It Happened Here* are all examples of movies that successfully attack fascism, examine societies in decline, expose the dehumanization of technology, condemn censorship, and reveal the means by which lunatics can control human beings and maintain their own illegitimate authority.

There is little doubt that Margaret Atwood's *The Handmaid's Tale* is an important novel. Its sweeping indictment of a nation suffering under the doctrinaire dementia of well-armed religious fundamentalists made it a *cause célèbre* when it was first published, during the heyday of militant right-wing Christian fundamentalism. Of course, this was before the desire of some ministers to satisfy their below-the-belt propensities or concoct bizarre money-raising schemes rendered much of the movement laughable instead of truly dangerous, before these political biblicists were scattered by a whirlwind of condemnation.

Unfortunately, the power of Atwood's novel stems from its ideas and language—two qualities that transfer badly to the screen. The protagonist in *The Handmaid's Tale* is Kate, a young woman whose life in the fundamentalist Republic of Gilead is a nightmare of oppression and state-sanctioned rape, and her journey through the stained looking-glass is a mournful testament of both horror and hope. In Atwood's novel, Kate is both crafty and resilient. She's not a fool, but she can play the fool when her survival depends upon it. Unfortunately, German filmmaker Volker Schlondorff's screen version of *The Handmaid's Tale* gives us a Kate who seems both naive and even a bit vacuous. The movie's failure to capture the Kate of the novel lies at the center of what's wrong with Schlondorff's beautiful but boring film of Atwood's masterpiece.

The most telling example of Schlondorff's and screenwriter Harold Pinter's colossal misinterpretation of the seriousness of the novel comes at the very beginning of the film. A verdant setting appears, followed by a shockingly silly title: "Once upon a time . . . in the recent future . . . a country went wrong . . . called the Republic of Gilead." It's the use of the phrase *once upon a time* that is so far off the mark. Schlondorff seems to be taking a page from the works of his long-departed countrymen, the Brothers Grimm; the use of that phrase places the film safely in the realm of fantasy. But Atwood has not written merely a *fable* about the future; she's written a dynamic study of people, richly drawn characters caught up in the maelstrom of fundamentalist mania. These fundamentalists exist, their ideas are a familiar feature of the North American political and cultural landscape, and the power of Atwood's book derives from its depiction of the human toll of a total fundamentalist revolution. There's no happy ending, no Aesopian moral by which we're expected to live, and that's precisely the kind of ending the phrase *once upon a time* promises. Its use diminishes the novel and makes one question exactly why Schlondorff (a German) and Pinter (a Brit) wanted to make this film. Did they see it as an opportunity to satirize the United States, condemn the Reagan-Bush agenda, or mock fundamentalism? It's difficult to tell.

In any event, the movie's simple-mindedness is so unengaging and its villainy so obvious that we nearly lose sight of the fact that Atwood's novel is so textured and surreal. It's hard to believe that this film was directed by the same man who turned Gunter Grass's extraordinarily complex novel *The Tin Drum* into a cinematic masterpiece. It's apparent in *The Handmaid's Tale* that Schlondorff and Pinter loathe fundamentalists and fascism, but we need a little more energy and substance than we're given. Okay, guys, we know your politics, but give us a motion picture that does something more than rehash twenty-five years of feminist writing in so cartoonish a fashion. Kate Millett wasn't in the fairy tale business.

That goofy *once upon a time* is symptomatic of the film's failure to capture the tone of Atwood's lyrical prose. Again, we find ourselves facing that all-too-familiar dilemma of how to turn a great book into a great movie. Pinter hasn't done much to dramatize the detailed discourse that Kate provides in the novel. Reportedly, early versions of the screenplay contained large chunks of narration, and Kate's monologues were shortened, then lengthened, then shortened again as the film was being shot. Somewhere down the line, Schlondorff and Pinter made the wrong choice, and so we end up with a main character who spends most of her time reacting to people and events. Their decision to make Kate so passive throws everything out of whack; by the time she does something about her situation, at film's end, it's as if she's been offered a ride home from the mall. "Hey, Kate, we're planning to escape tonight, wanna come?" "Yeah, sure, why not?" We never get a sense of what Kate is thinking—or if in fact she's thinking *anything* at all.

Pinter's screenplay has other problems as well. He writes action scenes badly, so a lot of the horrors of Gilead are shown in passing: quick scenes and odd flashes occurring at random in the movie, many of them shot from a distance and most of them unexplained. Pinter has always been a writer who distances himself from emotion, but *The Handmaid's Tale* needs expressive writing and an ability to *show* on-screen what's related in the novel. To capture the full horror of Atwood's vision, the movie needs a more visual screenwriter.

Structural coherence is also not among Pinter's strong suits. The film's continuity is seriously flawed, especially when we're trying to follow the activities of two important characters: Serena Joy, the Commander's wife (played by Faye Dunaway in her best benevolent bitch style), and Aunt Lydia, a sadistic headmistress at the handmaids' training school (played by Victoria Tennant). For much of the movie, Serena Joy spends her time gardening and moseying in and out of scenes, delivering such Joan Crawfordesque lines as, "I get trouble, I give trouble." (Kate, of course, doesn't react at all to the line, but the audience gets a big laugh out of it.) Suddenly, Serena Joy disappears—not because anything has happened to her, and not for any reasons of plot, either. She just leaves the movie, and, after a while, she returns (no explanation given) and resumes her gardening and moseying.

Aunt Lydia's disappearance is even more bizarre. She's a monster right out of some schlocky women's prison picture; give *her* trouble and she'll have you hung (in long shot, of course), with handmaids pulling the rope. You don't want to mess with Aunt Lydia; she catches plotters against the state faster than cats catch mice. One such plotter is Moira, played by Elizabeth McGovern. She's guilty of "gender treachery"—she's a lesbian and she wants out of Gilead. So, one night she rouses the unsuspecting Kate from her sleep and gets her to lure Aunt Lydia into the unused men's room of their large dormitory, where Moira proceeds to strip Aunt Lydia and tie her to a urinal. Kate is fascinated by Moira's action; we know she's in awe because her blank look has a hint of admiration in it. Moira and Kate leave Aunt Lydia tugging at the bonds that lash her to the porcelain male trough (make of *that* what you will—it's just one more of those simplistic touches in which Schlondorff revels). Moira escapes the compound—actually, she rather implausibly *ambles* past the guards, who don't seem to recognize her even though they've seen her many times in the past—and Kate returns to bed, leaving Aunt Lydia to remain a prisoner in the men's room for what we assume will be the duration of the movie. Since no men are allowed in the dormitory—men only enter the compound itself to serve as guards or to be beaten to death by angry handmaids—Moira figures that no one will ever go into the lavatory and free Aunt Lydia. But Auntie somehow manages to liberate herself, because half a reel later she returns to the movie to oversee the hanging of a handmaid (not Moira, incidentally). Aunt Lydia's minor excursion in bondage has left her none the worse for wear, and—in one of those unaccountable lapses in logic that mar Pinter's screenplay—she seems strangely untroubled by this humiliating challenge to her authority. She never sounds an alarm, she never seeks the women out, she never rails at the assembled handmaids, and she never (as far as we know) even *mentions* it to anyone. The scene amounts to just another poorly handled plot twist in Pinter's screenplay—nothing more.

Moira is eventually recaptured (we never see that happen, either), and she's forced to work as a prostitute in a brothel, a hangout for corrupt male fascists who want to spend some quality time away from their wives. The place is supposed to be a den of debauchery, but it's nothing more than a nicely decorated bar—all shiny furniture and soft lighting—where the guys can meet the whores, drink some scotch, sneak in their favorite handmaid, and dance a little. The place is so tame that you wonder if Schlondorff and Pinter have ever gone out for a night on the town. Haven't these two ever been to Berlin or even seen a Fassbinder film? Again, the director and screenwriter expect the audience to recoil at the idea of unpleasant things; they haven't made anything (except the costumes and set design) extraordinarily visual.

The brothel scene is so dull and draggy that the movie really begins to unravel, and we are constantly wondering what the focus is supposed to be. Are we being shown the innate venality of men, the duplicity and hypocrisy of fundamentalists (both men and women), or merely the fact that religious moralists wouldn't know a good time if one sat on their laps? Do the men hate their wives, or are they just being "men" (you know, rutting little piggies)? You really can't blame them, though. All the rulling-class women wear the same loopy little hat, the same strand of pearls, and the same blue dress (fashion magazines are collectors' items, by the way) and spend a lot of time at garden parties stiffly strolling around, like characters who have wandered in from a Jacques Tati movie. But Tati meant that stuff to be funny, whereas Schlondorff and Pinter are being very serious. There's a lot of talk about making disobedient handmaids clean up toxic waste, and you assume that all of these women are sterile because of nuclear fallout or toxic pollution, but the script is no help in this regard. Time and again in *The Handmaid's Tale*, Pinter perversely withholds such vital information.

Atwood's novel touches on the relationships between men and women, sexually transmitted diseases, militarism, male domination, the feminist movement, the environment, and a myriad other themes, all of them filtered through the consciousness of a strong and cunning Kate. Not so with the film. The movie even manages to botch one of the book's most celebrated scenes: Kate's rape by the Commander (played in the film by Robert Duvall)—the central metaphor in Atwood's novel, drawn from the Old Testament story of the trials of Rachel (and her handmaid Bilhah). The scene as filmed is static and flat, without tension or horror or any sense of Kate's rage; it just lays there, like Kate, a trio of one-dimensional ciphers fornicating. The scene recurs later in the film, with much the same effect (or lack thereof); the Commander actually does get red in the face this time and grunts a little, but it's not much of an improvement.

Full blame for the weaknesses of *The Handmaid's Tale* rests squarely with Schlondorff and Pinter. They've failed to correctly interpret Atwood, and the film will be virtually unintelligible to anyone who hasn't read the novel. In the past, Schlondorff has shown himself capable of providing sweep and depicting paranoia in his work. His *The Lost Honor of Katharina Blum* is a brilliant study of persecution and political repression. The big problem with the screen version of *The Handmaid's Tale* is that Pinter is too insular a writer for the job. He doesn't build dramatic tension from scene to scene. The movie is the outline of a terrific book—a cinematic Cliff Notes, if you will.

However, not everything in the film is a disappointment. Faye Dunaway, Elizabeth McGovern, and Robert Duvall give superb performances, providing just the touch of edge that the entire film needs to be successful. Natasha Richardson sleepwalks through her role, though this is Schlondorff's fault. I guess he assumes that Kate is a regimented zombie; he must have been reading a different novel. Or maybe Schlondorff chose Richardson because of her somewhat similar performance in the title role of Paul Schrader's film *Patty Hearst*, in which case his selection becomes a truly lazy choice.

Visually, the film is stunning, thanks to American artist Jennifer Bartlett (credited as conceptual adviser) and costumer Coleen Atwood, whose use of primary colors—including the handmaids' vibrant red—is extraordinary. Not enough good can be said about Ryuichi Sakamoto's music, which provides the movie with some much-needed emotional shading. Igor Luther's photography is crisp, albeit too claustrophobic, which is another of Schlondorff's mistakes: Gilead, being the United States, is a huge place, but the camera never pulls back enough to give you an adequate sense of period and place.

Watching Schlondorff's film, I was reminded of another, better movie about a repressive, regimented future society in which sex is forbidden and everyone looks the same: George Lucas's *THX-1138*. The opportunity certainly existed to turn *The Handmaid's Tale* into an equally powerful and convincing vision of a totalitarian future. Atwood's religious fanatics are chilling characters; they bring to mind George Bernard Shaw's observation about zealots who wear the cloak of religious conviction—that what these people want is not morality but conformity. And great movies have been made about fundamentalists—Richard Brooks's *Elmer Gantry* and John Huston's *Wise Blood*, for example.

So, what ultimately went wrong? To be successful, movies set in some nightmarish apocalyptic future have to strike a balance between the seriousness of their ideas and the stylistic daring of their presentation. Many people—including a number of those who liked the novel when it first came out—now argue that recent events have made Atwood's vision of the future unlikely. But this is not the point. The future probably won't look like *Blade Runner* or *The Road Warrior* either, but their energy and visual hyperbole certainly sucked you into their polemics. As the saying goes, "In the land of the deaf, you have to scream to be heard." But in *The Handmaid's Tale*, Schlondorff and Pinter prove themselves incapable of such a balancing act. Instead, they opt for a grim and deadly earnestness, and so they've wound up with a movie that takes itself too seriously and is unintentionally funny to boot, like bad propaganda. Schlondorff and Pinter shake a stern and schoolmarmish finger at you, when they should be scaring the hell out of you with their screams.

After reading: CONSOLIDATE INFORMATION

1. Compare the two articles: do Doerr and Calleri have adequate evidence for the claims they make?

2. The film, *The Handmaid's Tale*, is widely available for video rental; view the film and evaluate it. Do you agree with Calleri about the film's flaws and its strengths? Alternatively, go to the library and find other reviews of the film; compare these reviews with Calleri's evaluation.
3. Reread the two opinion pieces. What is Doerr's primary focus? How does Doerr's focus differ from that of Calleri? Summarize the similarities and the differences between the two pieces.

Rock 'n' Roll and Social Change
Richard Welch

Writing for a popular audience in a British publication, History Today, *Richard Welch argues that there is a close relationship between American popular music of the 1950s and 1960s and the enormous social changes that took place in American life at the same time.*

Before you read: FIRST THOUGHTS
LOOK AHEAD

1. What is your initial reaction to the title?
2. When you think of the 1950s in America, what images come to your mind?
3. Read the first paragraph and make a list of the reactions or questions you have while reading.

During reading: REACT
QUESTION
SUMMARIZE

1. How does Welch make clear the connections between the popular film images created by Tony Curtis, Marlon Brando, and James Dean and the revolution created by popular musicians of rock 'n' roll?
2. How did you react to Welch's use of the term *revolution* to describe what happened to American society in the late fifties and early sixties?

REVOLUTIONS ARE NOT DELICATE OPERATIONS. People experiencing them usually realise they are passing through tumultuous times. The changes are noted and recorded. Both casual observers and scholars can detect remote and immediate causes. The focal points of the revolutions are located and the results analysed. Yet one of the most profound cultural changes in American history is seldom credited for what it was and did. In the mid-1950s this enormous cultural revolution swept aside prevailing notions of American popular music, blended black and white musical traditions and integrated black performers into the pantheon of musical superstars in an unprecedented fashion. In such a way, this revolution both presaged and encouraged the desegregation movement of the 1956–64 period. More generally, this revolution created a music which became the common property not only of two generations of Americans, but millions throughout the world, creating the most ubiquitous, and perhaps, most influential form of American popular culture. The revolution was rock 'n' roll.

The startling success of rock 'n' roll in transforming American popular music and culture owed much to the phenomenon of the mass-market adolescent subculture. While adolescence is normally a time of some rebellion against adult authority and mores, nothing seen before in history was quite as dramatic as the transformation of adolescents from an age group to a virtual class after the Second World War. To some degree this was a consequence of the increasingly large number of teenagers, especially in the United States. By 1970 half the population of the United States would be twenty-five or under. Additionally, post-1945 American teenagers enjoyed an unprecedented level of affluence. Their taste in film, music, literature and entertainment was backed up by enormous purchasing power which record producers and film-makers were quick to satisfy.

By 1950 there were growing signs that American teenagers were rejecting, consciously or not, the quasi-official popular culture which had flourished during the Depression and war years. With some significant exceptions, the purveyors of popular culture and entertainment during the 1930s and 1940s prescribed a highly idealised, romanticised picture of family and national life. Once television became common, it too projected a monochromatic, self-congratulatory depiction of America. This sterile version of American life was increasingly scorned by teenagers seeking to deal with an increasingly atomised family life and domestic and international tensions. Some idea of the growing alienation of American adolescents could be gauged by the almost instantaneous popularity they gave J.D. Salinger's unrelentingly anti-adult *Catcher in the Rye*.

Additionally, American teenagers sought alternative explanations to their questions about American life from beyond the mainstream. They began to seek satisfaction for their longings for something new and different in the various subcultures which had always been present in the United States. One of these, the criminal, had long been a staple of folk myth in American popular culture. In the 1930s, Hollywood increased the reach and impact of mythic gangsters and outlaws, especially when they were played by attractive actors capable of projecting a sense of integrity and honour. In the 1950s three films which depicted youthful outlaws as alienated loners shaped and furthered the adolescent consciousness of themselves as a separate culture group and greatly influenced the look, if not the sound, of rock 'n' roll.

The first of these formative films was *City Across the River* (1951) which dealt with youth gangs in Brooklyn. Tony Curtis' characterisation of a hard but honest youth created an adolescent archetype. Moreover, his perfectly sculpted, swept-back, teetering pompadour 'duck's ass' hair style would start a major trend among teenage boys after it was flaunted by Elvis Presley in 1955. The second movie, *The Wild One*, about motorcycle gangs in California, featured Marlon Brando as the laconic, distant, rebellious, but ultimately honourable gang leader. Brando's motorcycle anti-hero came across as infinitely more attractive than the ignorant, wishy-washy or brutal adults with whom he dealt. The last movie, *Rebel Without A Cause*, starring the still legendary James Dean, focused not on an outlaw, but a troubled, alienated young man trying to find his own truth in a world where adults provide little guidance. Dean's performance electrified the nation, especially teenagers. Certainly, Dean's portrayal of teenage anomie fed off the same impulses which were simultaneously creating rock 'n' roll. Underlining the interrelationship between Dean and rock 'n' roll, Nicholas Ray, the director of *Rebel Without A Cause*, remembered that when he first met Elvis Presley in Hollywood '. . . [Elvis] knew I was a friend of Jimmy's so he got down on his knees before me and began to recite whole passages from the script. Elvis must have seen *Rebel* a dozen times by then and he remembered every one of Jimmy's lines'.

In addition to the criminal, outlaw and social fringe groups, American teenagers increasingly turned to the black sub-culture as an alternative to homogenised America. Black slang, and to a lesser degree, clothing styles, became increasingly common among American teenagers after 1950. Some whites had registered their dissatisfaction with the then current mass culture by becoming jazz cultists in the 1930s and 1940s. While some whites continued in this direction after 1950, the black music which found the largest audience among young whites was the hard driving, visceral rhythm and blues whose typical twelve-bar structure became rock 'n' roll's most common format.

By 1953, the growing fascination of young whites with black music came to the attention of a Cleveland, Ohio, disc jockey. Allen Freed, who certainly popularised the term 'rock 'n' roll' though he did not invent it, was alerted to the phenomenon by a record-shop owner. He had been doing a classical music programme, but asked to do a rock'n'roll segment after his usual stint. The new programme caught on and Freed quickly became the most popular disc jockey in Cleveland. In March, 1953, he organised a stage show featuring black rhythm-and-blues acts. Two-thirds of the 30,000 who showed up were white. The inter-racial attraction of the music was apparent and the implications of growing numbers of young whites appreciating black music and attending integrated performances were enormous. Ruth Brown, a rhythm-and-blues vocalist, remembered that when performing in the still segregated South in the 1950s a rope was strung down the centre of the theatres to keep the races apart. Brown also recalled that by the time the show was over the rope was frequently gone and the audiences mixing freely. The effect of the increasing integration of musical tastes and resulting racial mixing is difficult to gauge. It seems likely that such developments predisposed at least a majority of young whites to accept the Supreme Court's outlawing of legal segregation in 1954.

Two other musical sub-cultures lured young whites. The first was folk music, generally derived from British and Irish sources, which had survived in the Appalachian areas of the country. The 'folk movement' however, did not become powerful until 1960, and its practitioners and adherents were initially hostile to rock 'n' roll. After the mid-1960s, performers such as Bob Dylan and The Byrds grafted folk onto existing rock 'n' roll styles producing yet another rock variant. Far more popular, but originally more geographically confined was country and western music. This music was derived from Anglo-American ballad and dance music though black influences were also present. Country was primarily popular in the South and Southwest among working- and lower-middle-class whites. Whites higher up the social scale often denigrated it as 'hillbilly music'. After the late 1940s, maverick country singers, most especially Hank Williams, gave country music a harder, driving sound, and an edge which in some ways paralleled the emotions blacks were putting into rhythm and blues. Clearly, a music which could combine elements of black rhythm and blues and white country—musical styles distinct but alike in their choice of primitive power and raw emotion over sophistication, musical styles which were scorned by mainstream culture pundits, musical traditions conceived from the point of view of a disadvantaged outsiders—would prove very attractive to the American teenager.

The music which resulted from the combination of the two racial musical traditions, rock 'n' roll, emerged in different places and in somewhat different styles. Not surprisingly, however, many of its pioneer practitioners came from the margins of society where the major subcultures existed side by side in uneasy love-hate relationships. Consequently, much of what became rock 'n' roll appeared first in the American South, and few places proved so fertile to the development of the new music as Memphis, Tennessee, where the Sun Record Company unleashed the singer who came to epitomise everything people loved or hated about the new music.

Sun Records was founded by Sam Phillips whose experiments in musical hybridisation are now legendary. Phillips, a former radio engineer from Florence, Alabama, started his company in 1950. Originally, he recorded black bluesmen such as Howlin' Wolf and BB King. Phillips understood that young, white people were dissatisfied with the popular music of the time, typified by songs like *How Much is That Doggie in the Window?* Like Freed and a few other independent producers, Phillips became convinced that the restless, white youth market could be tapped by someone with a black-based musical style. Not many people in the record industry believed him. Nevertheless, Phillips persevered in his convictions, realising that if he were to win the young white record buyers his fortune would be made. Phillips also seemed to have a genuine personal commitment towards the discovery of artists who could seize the best of white and black musical styles. 'I was in it to record something I loved, something I thought other people ought to hear' is the way he later explained it. In the summer of 1954 Phillips found what he was looking for.

The man whom Phillips used to start the revolution was an unlikely candidate. Elvis Aaron Presley came from decidedly humble origins. His father had done time for forgery and the family lived much of the time in public housing. When he first came to Sun the man whose swagger, leer, and exuberant sexuality would delight and dismay in near equal numbers was remembered by Phillips as 'the most introverted person that came into that studio'. Presley was a loner, heavily attached to his mother and had few real friends. He compensated for his isolation by listening to everything that came out of the radio. He was, in fact, a repository for almost every musical form in America, white country, black blues, black and white gospel and Tin Pan alley crooning. After his career took off he described how two of the influences affected him.

> I'd play along with the radio or phonograph. We were a religious family going around to sing together at camp meetings and revivals, and I'd take my guitar with us when I could. I also dug the real, low-down Mississippi singers, mostly Big Bill Broozy and Big Boy Crudup, although they would scold me at times for listening to them. 'Sinful music' the townfolk in Memphis said it was. Which never bothered me I guess.

At the time of his first meeting with Phillips, Presley was a truck driver. He came to the studio ostensibly to make a record for his mother's birthday. He might actually have been looking for a way to audition. However shy, lonely and isolated Presley might have been, his ambition was enormous. Phillips was impressed by what he heard.

> I knew he had the fundamentals of what I wanted. He was the first one I had seen who had that potential. He had a different type of voice. And this boy had listened to a lot of different music . . .

Before he left the studio, Presley agreed to return if Phillips found a song he thought suitable for him.

In the meantime, Phillips began assembling the back-up band which became an essential part of Elvis' early sound. The pivotal instrument was the electric guitar which was the cutting edge of both blues and country music. For Presley's lead guitar player Phillips chose Scotty Moore, a veteran of country swing bands. Moore's clean, sharp, and sometimes haunting solos helped define the early Presley sound, and rock 'n' roll guitar playing in general. Bill Black, 'the best slap bass player in the city' originally provided the rhythm along with Elvis' acoustic guitar. Later D.J. Fontana introduced drums, and the archetypical rock 'n' roll combo was created.

In August, 1954, Phillips came up with a song called *Without Love* which he thought might suit Presley's style. Moore, Black and Presley worked through the night trying to get a satisfactory take, but nothing seemed to jell. Taking a break from their frustrations, Presley and the two back-up players went into a blues number. *That's Allright Mama*. Phillips heard the song in the recording booth. He had found his singer.

What the 'damned thing' was was something no one had ever quite heard before. In fact, it was so bizarre for the time that many had trouble knowing how to react to it. Like most early rock 'n' roll, *That's Allright Mama* was based on a blues pattern, though not the standard twelve-bar variety. This led, and still leads, some to contend that Presley was simply a white man singing black blues. If he were just the first white man to do this successfully, he would still be notable. However, Presley and the Sun sound, and the best of rock 'n' roll in general, were much more.

That's Allright Mama was originally written and sung by black bluesman Arthur 'Big Boy' Crudup. Even a quick listening of the two versions reveals the difference between blues and rock 'n' roll. Presley took the song, and the strong rhythmic element in it, but kicked it out of the heavy, almost ponderous groove, Crudup used. What Presley succeeded in doing was injecting the blues with an abandoned hillbilly attitude characteristic of what Southerners sometimes indelicately refer to as 'shit kickin' music'. The result was a musical hybrid, destined to prove more exciting than either its blues or country parents, while retaining elements of both. While Black and Moore were certainly important in the new music, the emerging style owed the most to Presley's own creative intuitions. And he knew it. 'I don't sing like nobody', the young singer once explained to Phillips.

Some recognised the revolutionary quality of the new music almost immediately. Marion Keisker, Phillips secretary, decided it was '... like a giant wedding ceremony. It was like two feuding clans who had been brought together by marriage'. When Presley first began exciting his growing audiences at live performances, his fans saw a white man, playing black-based music with clear country influences. What else could he be but the 'Hillbilly Cat' the sobriquet used on his early tours. And while all the emerging black-influenced music was being called rock 'n' roll, Sun records became the home of a distinctive sub-genre—rockabilly. And Presley was its prophet. The record appeared first on WDAI, the most influential black station in the South, then began its climb into the charts, crossing over from blues to country and then into the pop categories.

The year after August 1954 was perhaps the most creative in Elvis Presley's career. *Good Rockin' Tonight, Baby Let's Play House, Milkcow Blues Boogie* and the near-atavistic *Mystery Train* were all products of this dazzling year. The legend of the Hillbilly Cat spread throughout the South and rumours of his dynamic, charismatic performances were being heard in the North. Those with an eye and an ear for musical trends and markets began to take notice. Most significantly, American teenagers found in the music and Presley's public persona precisely what they had been looking for. Embracing the new music as their own, teenagers made rock 'n' roll a badge of their identity and distinctiveness from the adults who generally hated it. In one year, 1955–56, American popular music was transformed by dollar-propelled teenage musical preferences. Post-1955 record charts were, and remain, dominated by rock 'n' roll and rock influenced music.

Teenage enjoyment of rock 'n' roll was greatly enhanced by the condemnations heaped upon it by the adult population, especially the guardians of conventional popular culture. To many, rock 'n' roll was too loud, too raucous, too sexual, or too black. The earthiness of many of the lyrics, the pounding back-beat rhythm, not to mention Presley's leering sensuality, rendered the music objectionable to many. This dislike was most pronounced among the more fundamentalist churches in the South. Ministers railed against rock'n'roll as obscene, and sometimes branded Presley as an agent of the devil. Television critic John Crosby denounced Presley as an 'unspeakably untalented, vulgar young entertainer ... Where do you go from Elvis Presley short of obscenity—which is against the law'. In early 1956, the *New York Times* reported that a white Southern church group wanted rock 'n' roll suppressed, claiming it was a plot by the National Association of

Colored People to corrupt white youth. All in all the furore was wonderful publicity. '... now if I hadn't affected people like that I might have been in trouble' was Sam Phillips' wry appraisal of the anti rock 'n' roll movement.

Elvis Presley's burgeoning popularity attracted the attention of RCA Victor. They contacted Phillips who, despite the success of Presley's records, was having financial difficulties. The end result was that Phillips sold Presley's contract to RCA for $35,000, plus $4–5,000 that Phillips owed the singer.

Even before Elvis had left, Phillips signed a young man from Jackson, Tennessee, whose first hit put Sun solidly in the black. Carl Perkins, next in line of Sun's major artists, came from a background more impoverished and racially mixed than Presley's:

> I was raised on a plantation in the flatlands of Lake County, Tennessee, and we were the only white people on it ... The night I was born my mom lay in a bed with no doctor but a granny lady named Mary. My daddy had double pneumonia on the next bed and almost died. He was always in bad health after that, later had a lung removed. They wouldn't give him good land on account of his health but he did all he could.

Like Presley, Perkins was exposed to heavy doses of black music, along with the white country traditionally available to young southern whites.

> The man who taught me guitar was an old colored man. I can see him now sitting on his porch... I'd ask him in the field 'Uncle John, you gonna play tonight? Maybe, if my back ain't too tired', he'd say. My daddy'd let me go over for an hour. Uncle John'd get his old guitar out and fill a pot with oily rags to keep the mosquitos away. John Westbrook was his name, the champion cotton picker on the plantation. He taught me to pick cotton too. I could pick 300 pounds a day and, man that's grabbin' ...

Things picked up somewhat for the Perkins family when they left Lake County for Jackson. A few years later when he first attempted to get a Sun contract, Phillips, who seemed to believe Presley had a monopoly on rock 'n' roll, was not overly interested. He finally signed Perkins, but had him do a different type of music from the rockabilly style he had developed. After Presley left, Perkins told him he had written a song called *Blue Suede Shoes*.

> The easiest song I ever wrote, got up at 3.00 a.m. to write it when my wife Valda and me were living in a project. Had the idea in my head seeing kids by the bandstand so proud of their new city shoes—you gotta be real poor to care about new shoes like I did—and that morning I went downstairs and wrote out the words on a potato sack ...

Potato sack or no, *Blue Suede Shoes* became Perkins' first hit, transcending racial lines by running up the charts in blues, country and pop categories.

Perkins, who, unlike Presley, wrote his own material, was not a one-shot hit maker. *Boppin' the Blues*, *Your True Love* and *Matchbox* (with Jerry Lee Lewis on the piano), all sold well and had enormous influence on the young musicians learning from his records. Yet Perkins never quite became a superstar. Elvis was already king, and Perkins lacked Presley's charisma and physical presence. Being married also distanced him from young female fans whose record-buying habits did much to determine who the next stars would be. Worse, at the height of his own popularity, Perkins was in a serious accident which put him out of commission for months. In 1959, Perkins left Sun for Columbia which totally misunderstood his music, pushing him away from his infectious rockabilly and casting him into the role of a hard rocker for which he was unsuited.

Perkins' career at Sun overlaps with the third giant in Phillips stable, the wildest of them all, and the man Phillips himself described as the most talented person he ever knew. Jerry Lee Lewis had looks, a pounding roadhouse piano style and a sense of theatricality exceeding even Presley. Lewis grew up on a farm in Ferriday, Louisiana, and turned to music at an early age. He learned a little guitar from his father, but turned to piano which proved natural for him. Lewis once said he didn't see how anyone influenced him. 'God, man, I just got with it, you know, I created my own style'. Nevertheless, he was exposed to the same multiple influences as Presley and Perkins, particularly the country-blues combination.

Like the other two Sun artists, what he did with these influences was highly individual and he sounded as distinctive from them as they did from each other. Lewis' background was more religious than most of the other Sun singers. He was an active member of the Holiness Church, Meeting of God Assembly, and even went to the South West Bible School. Consequently, Lewis also did a large amount of gospel singing. 'We sang it with a beat . . . we always sang it with a beat'. That did not stop him from frequenting less spiritual establishments where he found earthier sources of inspiration. 'Well, I used to hang around Haney's Big House', he recollected in 1971. 'That was a colored establishment where they had dances and stuff . . . Haney was this little colored fellow and we was just kids, we wasn't allowed in. So we'd slip around to the back and sneak in whenever we could. I saw a lot of 'em there, all those blues players . . .' Lewis' attempts to begin a recording career were rocky at first. He'd been rejected by every label in Louisiana when he sold all the eggs on his father's farm to pay for a trip to Memphis.

As soon as he heard Lewis, Phillips did not hesitate. Lewis' first Sun release, *Crazy Arms* became a medium hit and *Whole Lotta Shakin' Goin On* took the country by storm. Follow up records like *Great Balls of Fire*, *Breathless* and *High School Confidential* turned Lewis into a major rock'n'roll star, a rival to Elvis himself. And while Elvis' originality was being eroded by fame and suffocating management, Lewis' manic, leering vocalisations, exuding a primordial joie de vivre served to remind everyone what rock'n'roll was all about.

And then it stopped. In 1958, with three monster hits behind him, Lewis married a thirteen-year-old cousin. Many fans, disc jockeys and much of the media turned on him. For three years he wandered in an entertainment wilderness, his marriage the mark of Cain. When he began to re-emerge the decisive moment had passed for him, too.

The golden age of Sun records lasted about four years, from Elvis' first records to Jerry Lee's personal debacle. Sun continued to have the occasional hit with singers such as Charlie Rich, but Phillips, who did not personally produce a record after 1963, seemed to grow tired of the game. Apprehensive about the way the record giants were buying talent away from the independent labels, Phillips came to believe the majors 'would eat me alive'. Though he could have been a producer with one of the megacompanies, Phillips had no desire to work for another company. He sold Sun in 1969.

More than any other group of rock pioneers the Sun artists created not only some of the best rock 'n' roll records, but the very image of rock 'n' roll itself—the abandoned, somewhat frenzied guitar slinger 'letting it all loose' about women and fast times. This image, made irreversible by Presley, became fixed in the public mind. The basic rock 'n' roll band unit of singer, lead and rhythm guitars, bass and drums became standard to a large degree because of Sun rockers. And the risqué, sometimes overtly sexual nature of the music, which has proved a perennial source of controversy, was there from the beginning as well. Not that the Sun singers did it all themselves. Even within rockabilly, distinctive versions could soon be heard from Gene Vincent in Virginia, Buddy Holly in Texas and lesser groups from almost everywhere.

A permanent legacy of the Sun rockabillies and their colleagues was the injection of black musical influences into mainstream American music in an unprecedented fashion. Certainly, black rock artists played their part in the development, but equally clearly the use of black musical idiom by Presley, Perkins and Lewis greatly enhanced the prospects for black performers. The merged black and white musical traditions of the early white rock 'n' rollers, most especially Presley, introduced the entire nation to elements of black music. Storming through the gap blasted by Presley and his compatriots, seminal black artists such as Chuck Berry, Little Richard and Fats Domino achieved great success and financial remuneration. Certainly, several black rockers and bluesmen realised the role white audiences played in elevating them to a stardom that would otherwise have been impossible.

Thinking back on this period black rock 'n' roll pioneer Chuck Berry, whose distinctive style incorporated elements of country music, remarked 'it seems to me that the white teenagers of the forties and fifties helped launch black artists in to mainline of popular music'. Many, if not most, of the whites credited by Berry with opening the door to black rockers were themselves first drawn to the new black influenced music by Presley and his compatriots. It is difficult not to give some credit to rock 'n' roll for the growing white appreciation of both black culture and black grievances in a segregated society.

Certainly, the rise of rock 'n' roll as the predominant form of popular music overlaps with the appearance of the black civil rights movement as a major force in American society and politics. By the time the Southern Christian Leadership Conference initiated its 'Freedom Rides', voter registration drives and lunch-counter boycotts, young whites had experienced five years of musical integration via rock 'n' roll. The increased mixing in music seems to have anticipated, indeed, sometimes initiated, greater contacts between the races. On an early tour in the South in 1956, Chuck Berry saw ropes used to divide theatres into black and white sections. Nevertheless, he also witnessed more whites than blacks coming up on stage after a show to talk with black performers.

The stunning rise of rock 'n' roll as America's predominant popular music not only transformed the nation's prevailing musical norms, but signalled the triumph of the emerging youth culture. Despite the opposition and antagonism of the entrenched leaders of the music and entertainment industries, not to mention the desultory efforts at suppression by some religious and parental groups, American teenagers had imposed their will on the nation's airwaves, record stores and concert halls, The hitherto inchoate alienation of American adolescents coalesced to weld two cultural forms of 'outsider' groups.

Borrowing heavily from the musical traditions of blacks and white southerners, the rock 'n' roll pioneers of the mid-fifties fused elements of both to create a music which consciously rejected the conventions of the time and yet proved successful beyond the wildest dreams of its creators. The powerful black element in the music heralded new possibilities in interracial relations. Certainly rock 'n' roll made possible greater acceptance, appreciation, and a wider audience for black culture. But ultimately the triumph of rock 'n' roll signalled the coming of age of a new generation, one whose norms, culturally, intellectually and politically, often stood in sharp contrast to those of the generation immediately preceding it. The strength of the rock 'n' roll generation's break with previous attitudes, which first manifested itself musically, would reach full fruition in the social and political upheavals of the sixties.

After reading: CONSOLIDATE INFORMATION

1. Summarize what Welch means by the phrase "social change" in his title.
2. Evaluate Welch's argument and his supporting evidence. Does he provide you with enough evidence to support his claim that the popular music of the fifties helped cause social changes in race relations and civil rights?
3. Think back to your initial reaction (or if you wrote a reaction, review it) to the title and the mental images you associated with the 1950s. How did reading Welch's article confirm or contradict those preconceptions?

Beyond the Domino Theory: The Vietnam War and Metaphors of Sport

Thomas Fiddick

Thomas Fiddick wrote the following essay for scholars and teachers who are interested in American popular culture and the way it reflects historical and social realities.

Before reading: FIRST THOUGHTS
                       LOOK AHEAD

1. What do you know about the Domino Theory? What is the source of the term?
2. As you read Fiddick's title, what sports do you think he will use as comparisons with the notion of war?
3. What do you remember having read or having heard about the wars in Southeast Asia, usually referred to as the Vietnam War?

During reading: REACT
                     QUESTION
                     SUMMARIZE

1. Why do you think Fiddick concentrates on the metaphors of football, boxing, and poker?
2. What is the effect of Fiddick's using game terms to describe war or actions associated with war?

    THE AMERICAN COMMITMENT to support the anti-communist side in Vietnam's civil war was once justified by a famous metaphor used by President Eisenhower in a press conference on April 7, 1954. Comparing the nations of S.E. Asia to a "row of dominoes," he warned that, if Indochina "fell," the rest would "go over very quickly."[1] While this "Domino Theory" has been hotly debated as to its prophetic accuracy, what has largely gone unobserved by historians of the United States' involvement is the use of other metaphors which U.S. leaders invoked when escalating that conflict during the next decade. Historians of Popular Culture, who spotlight the importance of leisure-time activities and their impact on nations or societies, help us to understand that such seemingly insignificant or trivial matters as, for instance, games which people play or watch, unconsciously influence such life-and-death matters as the wars which people fight. Such historians should thus not be surprised to discover that the American escalation of its commitment of young men to a combat role, along with a bombing campaign against North Vietnam, in the mid-1960s, became compared to such all-male games and contests as football, poker-playing and boxing.[2]

One writer who analyzed the relationship of war to metaphor was "think tank" intellectual, Herman Kahn. In his book, *On Escalation: Metaphors and Scenarios* published just as the war was intensifying in 1965, Kahn suggested that one analogy which contributes to war is the comparison of such conflict to the adolescent game of "chicken," which he described as "played by two drivers on a road" who "drive toward each other at top speed. The first driver to lose his nerve and swerve . . . is 'chicken'—an object of contempt and scorn—and he loses the game," which is played "for prestige, for girls, for leadership of a gang."[3]

There is one passage in Lyndon Johnson's memoirs that seems to suggest that he saw the approaching collision with Ho Chi Minh as similar to such a game of chicken. He wrote that "Hanoi was pushing the throttle," while assuring his readers that "we were trying to put on the brake."[4] But aside from this self-serving description, there are few if any references in the statements of American leaders which would support Kahn's thesis as it pertains to the Vietnam War. His model would seem to have been taken from the Cuban Missile Crisis, in which Khrushchev did appear to "swerve" to avert a military clash. But Dean Rusk's famous statement that they were "eyeball to eyeball" and that "the other guy just blinked" conjures up the adolescent, if less lethal, game of "stare-down." Moreover, the film which best dramatized the game of "chicken," or a variation of it, was *Rebel Without a Cause*, and it demonstrated the deadly stupidity of such a contest, as two cars went hurtling over a cliff. The villain became a victim to be pitied, while the hero, James Dean, won the girl by "bailing out" in time. The moral of the story was that it was better to be a live "chicken" than a dead daredevil.

Contra Kahn, there are other, more popular games in America that lend themselves to warlike metaphorical use better than the passing fad of "chicken." George Carlin, the comedian, is much more observant about American culture, especially in his famous comic bit which compares football and baseball. The use of "helmets" (as opposed to "caps") and such terms as "the bomb" and "the blitz," makes football ideal as a central metaphor of war. In his masterful account of his Vietnam experience, *A Rumor of War*, Philip Caputo perceived the parallel perfectly: "The months of blank-cartridge scrimmaging were behind them; they were going to play the Big Game. . . . Huddled around me," their platoon leader, "like a football team around a quarterback, helmets held under their arms. . . . Their old fellowship had an adolescent quality to it; it was like the cliquishness of a football team or a fraternity."[5]

John F. Kennedy enjoyed playing touch football with family and friends, but he rarely if ever compared the serious business of war, which he had experienced with near-fatal results in WW II, to football or any other sport. He was often criticized for only sending "advisers" to Vietnam rather than combat troops. And at least one pundit chided him by employing the analogy to football. James Reston of the *N.Y. Times*, writing in June, 1963, said of him: "He is a tactician but not a teacher. He plays touch government. He seems to touch everything and tackle nothing."[6]

When L.B.J. succeeded him in the role of the nation's "quarterback," he may have been reacting to this kind of criticism. During a press conference in which he was trying to justify his war policy, Johnson claimed that the "American people, when we get into a contest of any kind . . . want it decided and decided quickly . . . whether it's in a war, or an election or a football game."[7] Not having any combat medals himself, being unathletic and from the state of Texas, which glorified heroics on both the battlefield and the gridiron, he may have felt somewhat inferior. One of the popular songs of the day asserted: "You've got to be a football hero to get along with the beautiful girls." This may help account for his telling reporters who were criticizing his strategy in Vietnam: "All I want is for you to give me a little running room. I want to make a touchdown for you if you'll let me."[8] As though addressing that absurd parallel drawn by the Commander-in-Chief, John DiFusco concluded Act I of his highly acclaimed play, *Tracers*, by having a character say: "It's my team against his. And a kill is just a touchdown."[9]

Richard Nixon's relationship with football was much more intimate. George Allen, coach of the Washington Redskins, observed: "The President looks at football as a way of life. He is a competitor. One of the things I admire about him is not that he came back and won, but that he came back after being beaten twice." And his old football coach, "Chief" Wallace Newman, had this to say about his famous bench-jockey:[10]

> Dick was very serious about football. I never knew anyone so determined. There was a bulldog tenacity about him. . . . He was so light, he'd take an awful beating in scrimmage. But what an inspiration he was to the team! Weeks would go by and he wouldn't even play a minute, but he almost never missed practice. . . . He was wonderful for morale. Here was this second-string kid on the bench encouraging the other guys and telling them how well they played. . . . It isn't easy to sit it out for four years.

Whether or not he had bottled-up resentments and frustrated ambitions as a result of this experience I will leave to the psychohistorians. But he may well have been thinking of himself when he wrote that "potentially creative people must not stay on the sidelines. They must play their part. . . ." As President he was able to play his part by blitzing North Vietnam even more than his predecessor, and the name of one of his bombing campaigns, in 1972, was termed Operation Linebacker.[11]

But Nixon was even more intrigued by another analogy taken from the world of games, namely, the comparison between international affairs and poker. Perhaps this was because he was far more successful in that game, having acquired a reputation during World War II as quite a cardsharp. In a passage from his book, *Six Crises*, he explained that Nikita Khrushchev, being Russian, may have been a good "chess player," but he, Nixon, recognized his Soviet adversary as a fellow poker player.

> I do not know chess, but I do know poker.... Khrushchev would have made a superb poker player. First he is out to win. Second, like any good poker player he plans ahead so that he can win the big pots. He likes to bluff, but he knows that if you bluff on small pots and fail consistently to produce the cards, you must expect your opponent to call your bluff on the big pots.... Khrushchev ... has caught us bluffing on some small pots. (173)

By continuing the metaphor with relish, Nixon made it clear that *he* was thinking of international relations as a poker game, and merely projected onto Khrushchev his own penchant. Referring to the "poker game of world politics," he prided himself on being a member of the Eisenhower team, saying its policies were based on "the principle that we should stand ready to call international Communism's bluff on any pots, large or small"—either when "the stakes are small" or "when the stakes are higher." (173)

Nixon was not alone in seeing world politics as a poker game. When France was faced with defeat at Dienbienphu, and had to negotiate a withdrawal at Geneva in 1954, Georges Bidault arrived at the talks lamenting that he was only holding a "two of clubs and a three of diamonds." Later President Johnson would reject an offer to negotiate at a neutral site because he feared that "the deck would be stacked against us."[12] Although Vietnam was supposed to be re-unified in 1956, the American Friends of Viet-Nam sponsored a conference of its own that year in Washington, D.C.; urging that the U.S. support a continued division of that nation, they called their conference "America's Stake in Viet-Nam"—suggestive of a large pot to win at poker. During the debate in the Johnson Administration over whether or not to bomb North Vietnam, Roger Hilsman opposed raising "the ante by bombing" because the North would send more troops southward, and thus "we would be paying the international political cost for nothing." William Bundy argued that Kennedy had already "decided to raise the ante" by sending more advisers, thus increasing "the stakes of the conflict," while "Hanoi preferred to conceal its hand."[13] His brother, McGeorge, National Security Adviser, saw the bombing as leading to some kind of card game: "We want to trade these cards for just as much as possible" in order to "mesh our high cards against Communist concessions."[14] General Maxwell Taylor, Chairman of the Joint Chiefs and later Ambassador to Saigon, titled one chapter of his memoirs "Playing a Losing Game." But the kind of game he had in mind was indicated in subsequent chapters, wherein he spoke of the "blue chips which each side would bring to the table." The American bets consisted of "our use of blue chips, particularly our bombing of North Vietnam." Although "our most valuable chip" was the bombing, there "were other blue chips in our bag."[15] Johnson phrased it somewhat differently, saying we ought not "to throw in our hand," and "not ... rule out playing our bombing card."[16]

It is of course common to speak of "bargaining chips" or playing one's "China card" when referring to diplomacy. But to use these poker expressions to refer to *bombing* is to anesthetize oneself as to the destructive consequences of one's actions. It is somewhat similar to what Ronald Reagan did when he said all he was trying to do in Nicaragua was make the Sandinista government say "uncle." That expression comes right out of the world of American adolescence, conjuring up images of playgrounds where young boys engage in rites of passage—ritualistic contests aimed at comparing one another's fighting skill, or strength of will. Such agonistic displays feature wrestling, boxing, or some combination of both, and they end when one of the combatants says "uncle"—meaning "I've had enough." Game's over; you win. As Johnson phrased it shortly after becoming president, the war in Vietnam was "first and foremost a contest," although admittedly a "dangerous game." By a "semaphore system of diplomacy" he hoped "Uncle Ho" would signal "uncle."[17]

In his memoirs, General William Westmoreland described the thought processes which led to the decision to begin bombing North Vietnam in 1964–5. "Ambassador Taylor and some civilian officials in Washington were also tending to think of bombing in terms of . . . twisting the enemy's arm with more and more pressure until, eventually, so the theory had it, the North Vietnamese leaders would cry 'uncle.' " This comparison between bombing and "arm-twisting," as though the war was some kind of wrestling match, was a misleading metaphor, to say the least. And it made little sense militarily, for, instead of making Hanoi cry "uncle," it merely reinforced the North's determination. Instead of surrendering, it sent even more troops to the South to strike back at the Saigon regime and its American supporters. Westmoreland himself realized this would occur:

> Only days after I reached Vietnam in early 1964, the United States Joint Chiefs of Staff proposed striking . . . North Vietnam. Had I been consulted on the proposal, I would have disagreed . . . why take provocative actions that might prompt increased North Vietnamese participation? I was particularly concerned lest the North Vietnamese respond to bombing by committing major troop units in the South.

Westmoreland's concerns proved tragically prescient, for, three years after the bombing campaign began, the Tet Offensive took place. Communist forces were strong enough to seize most of the urban centers in the South—something they had been unable to do before the decision to take the war to the North. But in his memoirs, Westy shifted his criticisms of the bombing strategy. Instead of pointing out how the Tet Offensive proved the validity of his earlier predictions, he condemned the bombing *pauses* which the Johnson Administration had periodically ordered between 1965–1968: "Bomb a little, stop it awhile to give the enemy a chance to cry uncle, then bomb a little bit more. . . . That was no way to win."

As is well known, after the Viet Cong forces were driven out of the cities in the wake of the Tet Offensive, Westmoreland requested some 200,000 more troops, which would have brought the total number of U.S. forces to about 750,000. This request was turned down and Johnson made his momentous decision to "choose not to run" for re-election. He also decided to scale down and then to cease the bombing campaign, since Hanoi was refusing to negotiate while its nation was being bombed. But Westmoreland justified his request for more troops and interpreted the result of the Tet Offensive as a U.S. victory, maintaining that Washington had "surrendered" when it should have pressed the issue; and in arguing his case the general used the following metaphor: "It was like two boxers in the ring, one having the other on the ropes, close to a knock-out, when the apparent winner's second inexplicably throws in the towel."[18]

This analogy, appearing in his 1976 memoirs, was not simply used for literary effect. For a book published three years earlier contained an interview with Westmoreland, who was apparently intrigued by the metaphor. The war, he told the writer, was "like two boxers in a ring. If you have your opponent on the ropes, that's the time to bore in. It's not the time to throw in the towel."[19] And the general may well have lit upon this comparison between war and boxing by communicating with his Commander-in-Chief, who seems to have shared this view. As early as 1961, after returning from a trip to Asia, Vice President Johnson summarized the dilemma which he felt the U.S. faced—and which he himself eventually faced. In May of that year he wrote that we must "face the challenge of Communist expansion now in S.E. Asia . . . or throw in the towel."[20] (The 1979 film *Main Event* ends with Barbra Streisand, the fight manager for Ryan O'Neal, tossing in the towel just as he is winning. The plot may well have been suggested by Westmoreland's metaphor.)

It might be argued that comparing war to another activity, such as boxing, which is also brutal, is normal and to be expected. On the other hand, it might be recalled that Franklin Roosevelt, when the U.S. finally entered World War II, tried to strike a pose as one who heals rather than one who wreaks havoc. He styled himself "Dr. Win-the-War." Johnson, who admired FDR in many respects, seems to have tried to emulate him at one point by portraying himself as a doctor trying to take care of a sickly little nation, South Vietnam. But he also seems to have seen himself as a fight promoter, and this confusion of images gave rise to the craziest mixed metaphor, saying that he did not want to "enter the patient in a 10-round bout, when he was in no shape to hold out for one round. We should get him ready to face 3 or 4 rounds at least."[21]

This capacity to see life-and-death struggles as though they were comparable to staged sporting events was apparent in LBJ as early as 1951. When a Senator from Texas he stated: "We can go on fighting in Korea. We can probably handle another war in Indochina," where the French were battling the Viet Minh, with American aid. "We may even be able to take on a *bout* in Iran or Yugoslavia."[22] It is little wonder that one of his aides once told a reporter: "Working for Johnson is like managing Joe Louis when he was in his prime."[23]

If Joe Louis was the Brown Bomber, Lyndon Johnson would be the White Bomber, employing the U.S. Air Force rather than his fists, of course. As he told the NSC in July, 1965: "We can bring the enemy to his knees by using our Strategic Air Command." Earlier, shortly after the Tonkin Gulf incident, Johnson justified his air strikes against the North by saying "we are not going to take it lying down."[24] Stripped of its figurative features, Johnson was implying that North Vietnam, a tiny agrarian nation on the other side of the world, could pin the most powerful nation in the world to the canvas—by firing some torpedoes which actually missed their mark.

As the war escalated, a kind of group fantasy seemed to envelop Johnson and his advisers. Assistant Secretary of Defense, John McNaughton, advised the government to keep "slugging away."[25] CIA Director John McCone urged Johnson to "hit the North harder and inflict greater damage," even though many CIA analysts were warning that this might actually strengthen the North's morale.[26] One of LBJ's staunchest defenders of his bombing campaign, Senator Thomas Dodd of Connecticut, stated that "a dozen nations might soon throw in the sponge" if the United States, "as the champion of freedom ... can be laid in the dust by a few thousand primitive guerrillas."[27] Another solid supporter and adviser, Walt W. Rostow, assured Johnson that he did not believe the Communists would be able to deliver their "Sunday punch."[28] (This was before the Tet Offensive.)

The self-image which Johnson and his supporters seemed to have of the United States was that of a veritable Rocky Marciano, an undefeated world champion holding forth in an international arena filled with communist challengers threatening to take away its title. In his psychological study of the war, published in 1968, Ralph White interviewed several policy makers and noted that "the image of a tough, victorious fighter breaks through. We must clobber the North, or break the back of the Viet Cong. Refraining from more intensive bombing of the North is described by Representative Hale Boggs as expecting our men to 'fight with one hand tied behind their back.' "[29] And Johnson himself said in justification of his bombing policy: "I can't ask our American soldiers out there to fight with one hand tied behind their backs."[30]

This phrase has become a cliché used by many chauvinists who are frustrated over the constraints they believe were placed on the American side during both the Korean and Vietnam Wars. Although literally quite facetious—no G.I.s were ever sent into battle with one arm tied behind their backs—figuratively the metaphor implies that the U.S. was "pulling its punches," or, in the words of Charles Roberts, "fighting at a crippling disadvantage." Roberts, a correspondent for *Newsweek*, wrote an insider's account in 1965, entitled *LBJ's Inner Circle*. He revealed that Johnson had decided during the 1964 presidential campaign that he would carry the air war to the North, even though he was saying in public that "we are not going north and drop bombs at this stage of the game." Without seeing the irony in the use of the word "game," Roberts explained: "Under the old rules, the U.S. was a muscle-bound giant fighting at a crippling disadvantage."[31]

The notion that the Americans were fighting the Vietnam War with one hand tied down is the underlying assumption behind the question which John Rambo posed: "Do we get to win this time?" The popular fantasy of war as boxing match helps explain the ease with which Stallone's character, Rocky, could turn in his boxing gloves for the more phallic rocket-launching rifle, becoming a muscle-bound giant able to win over crippling disadvantages. The fantasy also helps to hide the ugly reality, namely, that a technologically advanced superpower, using napalm, defoliants, anti-personnel bombs, etc. was wreaking devastation on a far smaller, backward nation. As Ralph White explained it, "a virile self-image" tended to make us "blind to the figure we cut in the eyes of ... the rest of the world, beating our breast and proclaiming our courage in a situation that they perceive as a very strong nation beating up a very weak one."[32]

The ability to see ourselves as others see us is very rare, and almost impossible for those who share the group fantasy of America as undisputed champion of the free world. For instance, Senator Dodd, in his speech to the Senate shortly after Johnson began Operation Rolling Thunder against North Vietnam, asserted that, from the time the United States passed the Lend-Lease Act to aid England in

1941, "we assumed the burden and the glory of being the champion and defender of man's highest aspirations."[33] For such a super patriot it would have been outright heresy to suggest that the American blitz over Indochina had more in common with the Nazi blitz over England than with FDR's Lend-Lease aid. Once a nation is crowned "champion" its actions defend its "title."

It has been argued that the reason why the United States lost the war in Vietnam was because journalists developed a critical, or adversarial, attitude toward the American government and its war. But a good case could be made for the opposite argument, namely, that certain members of the fourth estate helped further the myth, or fantasy, that the war was like a boxing match, a drama rather than a trauma. For example, in 1962 *The Saturday Evening Post* came out with an article about North Vietnam's legendary General Giap; it was entitled: "Master of the Red Jab." In 1966, a distinguished Washington journalist continued the analogy describing Johnson's policy as one of "jabbing" North Vietnam in order to "deter Hanoi" from allegedly threatening America's "exposed jugular."[34] By portraying the war as a personal fight between leaders who were just engaged in "jabbing" each other, the gore is ignored and the glory or excitement is misleadingly magnified.

Another journalist who contributed to the notion that Lyndon Johnson was a gifted fighter, who might be able to take on the "Master of the Red Jab," was Leonard Baker. A conservative columnist for the *St. Louis Globe Democrat*, Baker published a flattering biography of LBJ which portrayed him as a verifiable Rocky in the art of pugilistic politics. As Majority Leader of the Senate, Johnson "had not hesitated to flex his political muscles to produce votes." If necessary he "strong armed" his fellow Senators. In describing the "in-fighting" between him and the liberals, who sought to strip him of his power over committee appointment, he used this analogy:

> It was Round One, and the northern liberals had lost. It had been a brief skirmish. ... If the significance of those first two rounds in 1959 and 1960 had been understood as signs of growing revolt against Lyndon Johnson, the third round in 1961 might never have happened.

Assuring his readers that LBJ "did not use his power viciously," the reporter asserted that the "liberals ... wanted to slap his face in public. ... This was Round Three and the liberals wanted to draw blood." After fending off all these attacks from Northern liberals, this political biographer concluded, Johnson was "now the leading *contender* for his party's Presidential nomination."[35]

Of course this particular prediction by a columnist proved wrong, since the Northern liberals took on the contender that the Republican Party threw up, Richard M. Nixon. Reminiscing about the 1960 debates between the two, one of Kennedy's aides told an interviewer that JFK entered the verbal arena "like a well-conditioned fighter brought to the peak of his fighting ability."[36] But to outsiders Kennedy did not seem like such a battler. In discussing his "weaknesses as a public leader," Walter Lippmann concluded: "I think a public leader ... has to get into struggles where somebody gets a bloody nose."[37] And less than a week before JFK was assassinated he was condemned by Nelson Rockefeller for being appeasement-minded. Said Rocky, who was a contender for the Presidential nomination: "No wonder Khrushchev came to the conclusion" that " 'the United States is too liberal to fight.' " (*New York Times*, November 17, 1963, from a speech given in St. Louis)

When he became President, Johnson may have felt vulnerable to such criticism which, for a Southerner, implied that he would be the "coward of the county," or the whole country, if he ran away from a fight. In foreign policy he seems to have feared that any attempt at compromise would be construed as cowardice, as a desire to "cut and run." His memoirs repeatedly revealed such fears. He wrote that the American people "knew Lyndon Johnson was not going to pull up stakes and run" from the "contest" in Vietnam. While assuring his readers that he (and we) "were determined not to be provocative," he quickly added: "nor were we going to run away." And, while summing up his years in the White House, he proudly stated that his "service was over, and it had ended without my having to haul down the flag, compromise my principles, or run out on our obligations."[38] And at the time he was making the decisions which proved disastrous, he would say "we are not about to start another war, and we're not going to run away." Questions of war and peace were seen not as a matter of life and death but as if they were tests of his personal courage or his will to face danger:[39]

> As long as this nation endures we are going to be engaged in the affairs of the world. I welcome this involvement.... It may bring danger but... there is really no escape from problems. You can't run away from them.

When Senator Eugene McCarthy challenged Johnson's Vietnam policy by entering the primaries in 1968 it put the tall Texan in a dilemma: in the Far East he was engaged in what Bernard Fall had called a "slugging match" which Johnson vowed he would never quit fighting.[40] (America, he kept insisting, was undefeated and he did not want that record broken.) But now he had to defend his war in New Hampshire against a contender who championed peace. He expressed his dilemma this way to reporters: "Do you walk off" from the war, "leave it all and *slug it out* in New Hampshire?"[41]

War, said the military theorist, von Clausewitz, is a continuation of politics. Johnson's phrase about "slugging it out" with peace candidate, McCarthy, adds a new dimension to the Clausewitz dictum, or perhaps reverses it. For men like Johnson politics was an extension of war, only fought in the domestic battlefield. He was not alone in this view. Richard Nixon wrote in his memoirs that "combat is the essence of politics."[42] And that was not a conclusion that came to him reluctantly, or after calm reflection in retirement. As early as 1952 he told his running mate, Dwight Eisenhower:[43]

> This is just like a war, General. Our opponents are losing. They mounted a massive attack against me and have taken a bad beating. It will take them time to regroup, but when they start fighting back, they will be desperate.

Such a view of politics is quite different from the time-honored Anglo-Saxon notion of the "art of compromise," based on reasonable give and take, and arrived at by debates between honorable members of the same House. It is also alien to the concept of politics as a pluralistic marketplace, where interests are pursued by such unheroic means as lobbying, log-rolling and mutual back-scratching. Nixon, like Johnson, would seem to fall into that category of political leader which Robert Tucker calls "the warfare personality."[44] Their type of leadership tended to "militarize" politics, and in this sense the war in Vietnam was a political war.

When Nixon became the nation's champ he still considered himself at War against domestic opponents. His use of an "enemies' list" and such tactics as spying, infiltration and sabotage against political opposition were all methods more appropriate to warfare than to traditional politics. What tended to justify the use of those tactics, in his own eyes and those of his fans, was the image he liked to project of a "fighter." In 1952 he had promised Ike a "rocking, socking campaign." According to his psychobiographer, Fawn Brodie, Nixon's idealized self-image was partly derived from the view he had of his father as a "natural fighter ... a scrapper ... a hard man to down."[45] He also liked to project the image of an underdog, a "come-back kid," which appeals to many Americans. As Jonathan Schell observed while writing about Nixon, "the public often sympathizes with an underdog, but it wants to see him fight back." And as President he used his Vice President, Spiro Agnew, to play the role which he once played for Eisenhower. Although critics might call such a role that of hatchet-man or mud-slinger, Agnew himself preferred to say: "It's time to take my gloves off"—meaning he was no longer going to use kid gloves but bare knuckles."[46]

In his study of "symbolic leaders," Orrin Klapp wrote that the American public was "impressed" by Nixon's "sudden emergence as a fighting senator," and went on to write, with some exaggeration:

> An ideal hero looks upon life as a contest, a chance to try his powers.... the candidate should remember that a hero's basic obligation is to knock out his opponents and promise victory without exposing his followers to unnecessary risk.... They share his glory vicariously; as their champion, he is their protector as well as their protagonist.... Their motto is: 'Let's you and him fight.'

Klapp concluded that most people want "a safe ringside seat."[47]

These observations were partly derived from an examination of Nixon's book, *Six Crises*, published two years before Klapp's study. The self-image of a never-say-die political in-fighter was cleverly cultivated in his chapter dealing with the so-called "Kitchen Debates" which he, as Vice President, had with Khrushchev. Actually the first of the two "debates," which were more like a series of verbal pokes than formal debates, took place in a model television studio, with Nixon extolling the advances in American color TV. In his own account of the confrontation, which Klapp referred to as Round One, Nixon complained that he had to walk "on eggs" because of negotiations going on in Geneva at the time. Thus he had to use "finesse" and could "only defend," rather than counterattack.

Employing the cliché so beloved in some circles, he explained: "I had to counter him like a fighter with one hand tied behind his back."

In describing "round two," Nixon tried to counter the impression he had given of a Republican Betty Furness bragging about the newest kitchen appliances. (Indeed, during his debates with Nixon, JFK chided Nixon for dwelling on consumer goods while Khrushchev was boasting of Soviet advances in "rocket thrust.") Thus Nixon opened his chapter with a quotation from Eisenhower to the effect that "intensive planning is . . . essential to avoid being knocked off balance." But, despite his own advance planning, which consisted of long talks with experts on the Kremlin, after his first meeting with the Soviet Premier newscaster Bob Considine wrote that Nixon was not only knocked off balance but through the ropes.

Citing that reporter's colorful analogy, Nixon admitted that it was like "the first round of the Dempsey-Firpo fight. Khrushchev had started the encounter by knocking me out of the ring." But, he assured his readers, he immediately "climbed back in to fight again." And by the end of the "bout" they were "going at it toe to toe." But Nixon was not content to leave the metaphor at that, returning to it while describing a leisurely sight-seeing tour. "For seven hours," he asserted with typical hyperbole, "beginning on our ride down the river, and continuing through the long luncheon, I had been engaged in virtual hand-to-hand combat with Khrushchev."[48]

Like most fantasies, which have an air of dream-like unreality, the fantasy of politician-as-boxer is emotionally satisfying, a wish-fulfillment, until reality intrudes. If Richard Nixon, the narrow-shouldered lawyer, had actually, literally, been engaged in "hand-to-hand combat" with the burly ex-miner, Khrushchev, the result would have been ludicrous in the extreme, and probably humiliating for the American side. But it is the magical power of metaphor and group fantasy which encourages a suspension of disbelief and masks ugly realities. And when the fantasy extends to war and compares mortal combat to a boxing match, consequences for world peace can be quite dangerous and destructive.

In his study of the psychological aspects of bombing and war, Irving Janis discovered that some people, faced with their fear of nuclear war, arrived at this simplistic solution: "Probably the only thing we can do is hit them first, hit them real hard," referring to the Russians. "We might be able to knock them out first."[49] In a similar vein, Lyndon Johnson said during the Korean War: "We are ready to face a showdown. . . . I am sure we will use the atomic bomb . . . if and when we can use it to stem the tide of aggression." Like a schoolboy who draws a line in the dirt and dares another boy to cross it, Johnson urged the Truman Administration to give an ultimatum to the Soviets, saying "the first step you take over your boundary, we will smash you . . . and it will be a crushing blow." Speaking about the "inevitability of a showdown" in 1952, as if war was a shoot-out at the OK Corral, or a championship bout, he said "we should unleash all the power at our command upon the vitals of the Soviet Union."[50] He seems to have had in mind a good swift left hook to the Russian bear's solar plexus.

Nixon, too, seems to have seen war in such simplistic terms. In his memoirs he refers four times on one page to the idea of a "knock-out blow," which he felt could be delivered to North Vietnam in the form of bombing its dikes or using "tactical" nuclear bombs.[51] By using the term "knock-out blow," the deaths of perhaps millions of peasants could be more easily contemplated, since it was not much different from rendering an opponent temporarily unconscious. Later, in his book, *No More Vietnams*, he maintained that public opinion, when he assumed office in 1969, "favored a military victory in Vietnam—but only a victory won by delivering a knock-out blow." Like so much else Mr. Nixon has said and written, there is no support given for such an assertion, which is belied by the fact that his opponent, Hubert Humphrey, began to rise in the polls when his President, Johnson, finally ordered a bombing halt in late 1968. And Nixon himself admits that it was not moral qualms which prevented him from delivering a "knock-out blow" by bombing dikes or using "nukes"; it was because such actions would cause an "uproar" of opposition, at home as well as abroad.[52]

The greatest uproar of opposition which confronted his first administration took place after he ordered the "incursion" into Cambodia. Massive demonstrations took place, leading to the deaths of students at Kent State and Jackson State Universities. Calling it "Operation Total Victory," the incursion aimed at taking out the so-called "privileged sanctuaries" along the Cambodian-Vietnamese border, which he had been bombing secretly for more than a year. Far from being a "total victory," the invasion of Cambodia just drove the Communists deeper into that country, where they began organizing even more recruits for the struggle against the new pro-American regime of Lon Nol. In retrospect, Nixon tragically miscalculated the effects of his "incursion," and one reason why he did may have been because he confused war with a boxing match. For his orders to his generals concerning the "sanctuaries" were simple, and simplistic: "Knock them all out."[51] His inspiration for this order seems to have been General George Patton, whose portrayal by George C. Scott Nixon had recently seen; if similar orders were to be given today, they would obviously be more inspired by Rocky and Rambo, as portrayed by Sylvester Stallone.

In summary, it can be seen that games which are popular in American culture—at least among American males—influenced the way American leaders, and others as well, viewed the Vietnam War. Football and poker were used as metaphors for the decisions that escalated the conflict, but wrestling and boxing were even more important as operative analogies—more so than the image of falling dominoes. Long before the films featuring Rocky and Rambo, boxing exercised a fascination over popular American culture. For instance, in 1947 a film entitled *Boomerang* and starring Dana Andrews as a battling prosecutor had one character say: "A good politician, like a good boxer, never quits fighting until the final bell." Several years later John Foster Dulles told the UN that the "Communist-dominated armies in Indo-China have no shadow of a claim to be . . . the champions of an independence movement."[54] As a popular song put it many years later: "We are the champions, my friend; and we'll keep on fighting to the end; we are the champions, we are the champions of the world."

Notes

1. George C. Herring, *America's Longest War: The United States and Vietnam, 1950–1975* (New York: John Wiley & Sons, 1979) 33; for numerous other references to "dominoes," see William G. Effros, *Quotations Vietnam: 1945–1970* (New York: Random House, 1970) 46–52.

2. Addressing the importance of metaphor as it affects the psyche of soldiers who engage in war, as opposed to how it reflects a nation's values, Harry Halloway and Robert Ursano concluded that the "role of metaphor in the recall of traumatic events requires further study." See their article, "The Vietnam Veteran: Memory, Social Context, and Metaphor," *Psychiatry* 47.2 (May, 1984) 107. This author believes that metaphor is a key to understanding the causes as well as the results of war, and the Vietnam War in particular.

3. Herman Kahn, *On Escalation: Metaphors and Scenarios* (New York: Frederick A. Praeger, 1965) 10.

4. Lyndon B. Johnson, *Vantage Point: Perspectives of the Presidency, 1963–1969* (London: Weidenfield and Nicholson, 1971) 67.

5. Philip Caputo, *A Rumor of War* (New York: Ballantine Books, 1977) 206; 60; 128.

6. Orrin E. Klapp, *Symbolic Leaders: Public Dramas and Public Men* (Chicago: Aldine Publishing, 1964) 67fn.

7. See the television documentary, *The Ten Thousand Day War*, Part I, based on the book of that title by Michael Maclear, subtitled, *Vietnam: 1945–1975* (New York: St. Martin's Press, 1981).

8. Frank Cormier, *LBJ: The Way He Was* (Garden City: Doubleday and Company, 1971) 186.

9. John DiFusco, *Tracers* (New York: Hill and Wang, 1986) 55.

10. Henry D. Spalding, *The Nixon Nobody Knows* (New York: Jonathan David Publishers, 1972) 88; 92.

11. Richard M. Nixon, *Six Crises* (Garden City: Doubleday and Company, 1962) 289; Herring 243.

12. Herring 36; 207.

13. Hilsman's words are cited in John R. Boettiger, ed., *Vietnam and American Foreign Policy* (Boston: D.C. Heath & Company, 1968) 27; see also Gerald Kurland, ed., *Misjudgment or Defense of Freedom: The United States in Vietnam* (New York: Simon & Schuster, 1975) 66–76.

14. Larry Berman, *Planning a Tragedy: The Americanization of the War in Vietnam* (New York: W.W. Norton, 1982) 56.

15. M. Taylor, *Swords and Plowshares* (New York: W.W. Norton, 1972) 352–3; 371.

16. Lyndon Johnson, *Vantage Point* 600; he was replying to a proposal from McNamara suggesting a bombing pause in 1967.

17. John R. Boettiger, ed. 33.

18. William C. Westmoreland, *A Soldier Reports* (Garden City: Doubleday and Company, 1976) 112; 105; 410.

19. Herbert Y. Schandler, *The Unmaking of a President: Lyndon Johnson and Vietnam* (Princeton: Princeton UP, 1973) 345fn.

20. Johnson 54.

21. Herring 124.

22. Ronnie Dugger, *The Politician: The Life and Times of Lyndon Johnson* (New York: W.W. Norton, 1982) 370–1.

23. Charles Roberts, *LBJ's Inner Circle* (New York: Delacourt Press, 1965) 126. Roberts also points out the odd coincidence that the aircraft carrier which Johnson dispatched to the Dominican Republic was the *Boxer*. (200)

24. Johnson 149; 116.

25. Herring 129; the Pentagon debated whether to apply a "slow squeeze" or a "fast squeeze," as though in a wrestling match. (125)

26. Johnson 140.

27. David L. Bender, ed., *The Vietnam War: Opposing Viewpoints* (St. Paul: Greenhaven Press, 1984) 29–30.

28. Schandler 307.

29. Ralph White, *Nobody Wanted War: Misperception in Vietnam and Other Wars* (Garden City: Doubleday and Company, 1968) 189.
30. Johnson 125.
31. Roberts 21.
32. White 191.
33. Bender 30.
34. Philip Geylin. *Lyndon B. Johnson and the World* (New York: Frederick A. Praeger, 1966) 204, cited in Boettiger, 33.
35. Leonard Baker, *The Johnson Eclipse: A President's Vice Presidency* (New York: Macmillan & Co., 1966) 22–27; 98.
36. "America Remembers J.F.K." (WGN, November 17, 1983).
37. Orrin Klapp 67fn.
38. Johnson 68; 113; 567.
39. Boettiger 37.
40. "Vietnam Blitz," *The New Republic* (October, 1965) 21.
41. Cormier 264.
42. *RN: The Memoirs of Richard Nixon*, I (New York: Warner Books, 1978) 350.
43. Fawn Brodie, *Richard Nixon: The Shaping of His Character* (New York: W.W. Norton, 1981) 288.
44. Robert C. Tucker, *The Soviet Political Mind* (New York: W.W. Norton, 1971) 40.
45. Brodie 52; 251.
46. Jonathan Schell, *The Time of Illusion* (New York: Alfred A. Knopf, 1976) 252; 130.
47. Klapp 228–9.
48. *Six Crises* 235–71.
49. *Air War and Emotional Stress: Psychological Studies of Bombing and Civilian Defense* (New York: McGraw-Hill, 1951) 239
50. Dugger 365–71.
51. Nixon, *RN* 430.
52. Richard M. Nixon, *No More Vietnams* (New York: Arbor House, 1985) 101–2.
53. *Ibid.*, 120.
54. Dwight D. Eisenhower, *The White House Years: Mandate for Change, 1953–1956* (New York: New American Library, 1963) 218.

After reading: CONSOLIDATE INFORMATION

1. Summarize the main points of Fiddick's argument.
2. Evaluate Fiddick's argument. Did he convince you—why or why not?
3. Some critics of American culture have argued that sports and violence are closely linked in the American national culture and that this link has led to an increasingly violent society; evaluate and respond to this criticism.

Total Force
James Kitfield

This essay was written as a report in a publication that is read primarily by government managers and executives. Kitfield raises questions that link current historical events with government policy.

Before you read: FIRST THOUGHTS
LOOK AHEAD

1. To what does the term "Total Force" refer?
2. What do you remember about the Persian Gulf War of 1991?
3. How was your life or the lives of those around you affected by the Persian Gulf War of 1991?

During reading: REACT
QUESTION
SUMMARIZE

1. Read the first three paragraphs and stop for a moment. What point do you think Kitfield wants to make with the stories he tells about people who comprised the military force in the Persian Gulf War?
2. What do the following subheadings tell you about Kitfield's argument? Make some notes about each on a piece of paper or a page in your reading log/journal:
    Establishing Total Force
    "Round-Out" Controversy
    Retreat from Total Force?
    A Burden for Blacks
    Women at War

For Cathy Stokoe, the realization that the Navy has truly changed hit home with the announcement of a Tupperware party. She might have expected the party, since the Family Services Center she helps run at the Norfolk Naval Base was encouraging worried spouses to form such informal support groups. Still, she had to smile when she learned the party was being hosted by a man whose wife had left to fight in Saudi Arabia.

Rep. Beverly Byron, D-Md., experienced a similar epiphany on a flight apron at Rhein Main Airbase in Germany. A reserve sergeant who looked surprisingly old next to his younger charges relaxed against a pile of duffel bags, while the young reservists whooped it up on an obvious adrenaline high.

"I'm just letting them tire themselves out so they'll be nice and manageable when I get them in-country," the wily sergeant told her before slipping his cap back over his eyes. The key role the experienced reservist plays in today's armed services was suddenly clearer to Byron, who chairs the House Armed Services Subcommittee on Military Personnel and Compensation. Then, as if to drive the point home, her son was called up.

In Atlanta, Rep. John Lewis, D-Ga., came to a similar understanding that today's is a different type of military. He was looking over the congregation at Ebenezer Baptist Church, the former pulpit of Rev. Martin Luther King Jr. and cradle of the civil rights movement. No fewer than 18 members of the mostly black congregation were absent, filling ranks in a Saudi Arabian desert rather than church pews at home. In one case, a father and his son had both deployed.

The myriad images of mobilization and war that have mesmerized the country during Desert Shield and Desert Storm—the wrenching parting of families, the sight of women wearing desert fatigues and packing M-16 rifles, the anxious faces of both young enlistees and gray-haired reservists aglow in the hot furnace of battle—all reflect a new U.S. military, unlike any force this country has sent to war in its history.

The thread that binds U.S. troops in the Persian Gulf is that they are all volunteers; it's the first time this century that a purely volunteer American force has gone to war in such numbers.

"Obviously, if you asked them if they would rather be in the Middle East or at home with their families, they'd rather be at home. But I think the overall quality of this force is directly attributable to the fact that they are all volunteers," says Christopher Jehn, assistant secretary of Defense for force management and personnel. Besides reducing morale and disciplinary problems, he says, an all-volunteer force saves the services the effort and expense of training soldiers, sailors and airmen who would rather be someplace else.

With 94 percent of enlistees having completed high school, and nearly all officers having finished college, no one disputes that today's is the most well-educated military force the United States has fielded in modern times. Compared to earlier U.S. military forces it is also older (26.4 years for the average enlistee and 33.4 for officers); more likely to be married (53 percent); more heavily black (20.8 percent) and female (11 percent); and more reliant on the reserve "citizen soldier."

What is very much in dispute, however, are the social and political ramifications of sending such a force into battle. Because there has been no major war to spark serious debate about the make-up of the military since the draft was abolished following Vietnam, the public has yet to fully come to grips with a number of key issues.

"Suddenly people seem amazed that we're sending women to war, that a disproportionate number of blacks may be casualties and that we had to rely on a reserve callup to support even our rapid-deployment forces," says Lawrence Korb, an analyst with the Brookings Institution, who served as assistant secretary of

Defense for manpower and reserve affairs from 1981–85. "If you look at its performance so far in Desert Storm, I don't think there's any doubt that the all-volunteer force is good for the military. The question we now have to answer is whether the all-volunteer force is good for the country."

Establishing "Total Force"

Certainly when the draft was abolished in 1973, the idea of an all-volunteer force was a balm to a country lacerated by the wounds of Vietnam. As far as the public was concerned, almost any experiment seemed worthwhile if it meant an end to the draft. "America was weary of the war, weary of the military and weary of the draft," says Martin Binkin, a manpower and reserve expert and author at Brookings. "So the debate was never really engaged at a high level."

For their part, military leaders were bitter that throughout much of the war, President Lyndon Johnson had steadfastly resisted mobilizing the reserves, in order to avoid the contentious public and congressional debate such a move would surely have provoked. That forced the Army to draw down dangerously on its active force structure from Europe and other areas of responsibility and to fight a war for which it had little public support. It also made the reserves popular havens for some who wanted to avoid the draft.

Stung by the episode, Army leaders in 1973 settled on a "Total Force" policy, partly as a way to force a reserve call-up much earlier in any future conflict. Key support and even combat responsibilities were shifted into the reserve components, allowing the Army to maintain the same 18 active divisions while decreasing its active strength from more than 1 million soldiers in the early 1970s to roughly 750,000 today.

According to the General Accounting Office, 50 percent of the Army's total personnel strength now resides in the reserves, along with 70 percent of its combat service support. Because so many key support roles such as strategic lift, water purification and chemical decontamination are weighted heavily toward reserve units, many reservists were needed on the first day of the Desert Shield mobilization.

That heavy dependence on early reserve support had long concerned many experts, who warned that any hesitation by the political leadership to call up the reserves in an emergency could leave the military seriously hamstrung. "For years, force planners said we can't rely on the reserves because the civilian leadership would never call them up in time," says Stephen Duncan, assistant secretary of Defense for reserve affairs. "However, since 1973 no military department actually recommended that we needed a call-up, so there was no reason to leap to that conclusion. And I hope President Bush's quick call-up for Desert Shield has finally put that myth to rest."

"Round-Out" Controversy

If it assuaged some concerns about a quick reserve call-up, Desert Shield did nothing to dispel doubts about the Total Force's "round-out" concept. Under the plan, National Guard combat brigades are supposed to train, deploy and fight alongside several of the Army's active combat divisions. When the 24th Mechanized Division and 1st Cavalry Division deployed for Saudi Arabia, however, both left their National Guard brigades behind.

DoD officials say the six-month limit (90 days, with a 90-day extension) on the initial reserve call-up did not leave them enough time to give round-out brigades additional training and then deploy them to the Persian Gulf. Congress responded by doubling the time the Pentagon could activate the round-out brigades to one year. "We've heard a number of reasons for not sending reserve combat units, but they're about as solid as sand," said Rep. Les Aspin, D-Wis., chairman of the House Armed Services Committee, in a release last year. "I suspect the most important factor is the active force prejudice against using reserve forces."

The Pentagon responded to continued congressional pressure last November by finally activating the combat round-out brigades, which are some of the best-equipped and most ready in the reserves. Rather than send them to the gulf, however, it scheduled further training for them at the National Training Center in California. According to National Guard officials, none of the round-out brigades is likely to deploy before the end of March.

"When all this is over, I think we're going to have to go back and redress the whole round-out concept," says Gen. Karl Brantley, commander of the 155th Mississippi National Guard brigade, which was supposed to round out the 1st Cavalry Division. "I understand DoD's rationale, but the fact is we didn't go with the unit that we trained with, and we felt we were ready."

By leaving the round-out brigades behind in their first real test, DoD seemed to support those experts, both inside and outside the Pentagon, who had long argued that the concept was seriously flawed. Many active-duty Army officers believe front-line infantry combat troops require a degree of technical proficiency, synchronization and physical fitness that is difficult, if not impossible, for a part-timer to maintain. Their argument was bolstered by reports that the 48th Infantry Brigade (Mechanized), the first National Guard round-out brigade sent to the National Training Center to prepare for deployment, was woefully unready.

Air Force leaders, by contrast, seem to feel that the reserve attributes of experience and maturity lend themselves well to air missions. Air National Guard pilots frequently top their active-duty counterparts in head-to-head competitions. Indeed, two National Guard fighter squadrons have helped wage the air war over Kuwait and Iraq. The Marine Corps has also deployed several reserve combat units to the Gulf.

Others say it is not the round-out concept that is wrong, but rather the timing. Reserve combat brigades, in their view, should never have been assigned to divisions that would deploy so early in a contingency. "If you ask Army planners privately why a round-out division was assigned to Central Command, they will tell you that during the Cold War, when everyone's attention was on Europe, no one gave a damn about Centcom and the Middle East," says Binkin.

In light of Desert Storm, DoD planners concede they are taking a fresh look at the entire structure of Total Force. "Given the rapidly changing strategic environment, I'll be the first to say that we can't do business around here the way it's been done in the past," says Duncan. DoD planners are now looking at whether the divisions to which the round-out brigades were assigned deployed too early to allow the round-out brigades time to get ready, and whether perhaps a brigade-sized unit is too large a configuration for roundout.

"I think at the individual-soldier and small-unit levels, those round-out brigades were ready," says Duncan. "But as you get into larger sized reserve configurations, it becomes increasingly difficult to keep those complex manuever skills current."

Retreat from Total Force?

What most concerns reserve proponents, however, is that the apparent snubbing of the round-out brigades was just the latest in a series of moves that seem to signal a retreat from DoD's commitment to a large reserve role in the Total Force. For instance, chief of staff Gen. Carl Vuono called the Army's commitment to the reserves into question when he mandated a 1989 study that determined that the Army could fight a three- to five-division war without relying on reserve units. His concerns were bolstered by a 1989 GAO study that found numerous deficiencies among some National Guard units, including inadequate training and a lack of critical equipment. DoD's 1991 budget request asked for massive reductions in both reserve budgets and troop strengths, including a cut of about 20,000 Army reservists. Congress refused to go along with the cuts.

Most recently, a Total Force Policy Report released by the Pentagon to Congress at the beginning of this year outlined four basic military theaters—strategic, contingency, Pacific and Atlantic. Only the Atlantic force, with its focus on what many consider the very unlikely scenario of a major land war in Europe, mentioned heavy participation by the reserves. Internal DoD documents obtained by *Government Executive* reveal that the shift away from the reserves was far from unintentional.

Commenting on an early draft of the report, Lewis Libby, principal deputy undersecretary of Defense for policy, complained, "The paper still exhibits the general reserve-favorable "tilt" of the previous draft.... Clearly the primary role in forward presence and rapid crisis response, and combat force structure generally, is and will remain the active components."

Says one National Guard official who asked that his name not be used, "We understand that the services need a contingency force that can go anywhere for a short time without having to rely on us. The way we read this study, however, it espouses a new philosophy that unless we get into a very long-term, global conflict—read European scenario—then the National Guard and reserves won't play much of a role. That raises the old question of whether this country can afford to become inextricably involved in a conflict without gauging the will of the American people, which is what a reserve call-up does."

A number of experts caution that before Pentagon planners decide how big a role the reserves should play in future force structure, they had better wait and see how many stay in the reserves given their experience with Desert Shield and Desert Storm. Already, Defense Secretary Dick Cheney has said publicly that he may ask for authorization to extend reserve tours to as long as two years. In their first activation in more than 20 years, many "citizen soldiers" are finding themselves unexpectedly ripped from work-a-day lives for many months, to risk their lives. Many have also taken significant cuts in pay in shifting to active military duty, and some have lost clients and seen their small businesses threatened.

"I think it's fair to expect that this experience will affect reserve recruiting and retention, but to what extent I just don't know," says DoD's Jehn. "Certainly if there were any lingering doubts among reservists about how seriously we take their role in today's military, the past six months should have dispelled them."

In the early stages of Desert Shield, active-duty recruiting for the Army dipped an average of 30 percent compared to the previous year and then picked up. According to official DoD figures, all the services met or exceeded their recruitment goals for the quarter ending Dec. 31, 1990, though recruitment figures for the individual reserve components were not available.

A Burden for Blacks

In a January *New York Times*/CBS News poll that questioned whether 3,002 adults favored starting military action or continuing the use of economic sanctions, the 250 blacks polled split about evenly, while whites favored military action by a 4-to-1 margin. Equally as telling, all the black Democrats in Congress voted against the measure authorizing force in the Gulf.

Black leaders say the apparent schism between blacks and whites in support for the war reflects the feeling among blacks that they will shoulder a disproportionate share of its burden. Indeed, while representing 12 percent of American society at large, blacks account for more than 20 percent of the armed services and almost 30 percent of all Army troops.

In significant ways, however, the debate about the role of blacks in Desert Storm today differs from complaints heard during the Vietnam War that the country was drafting an army of minorities and the dispossessed to do its dirty work. The all-volunteer force is viewed as a powerful catalyst for upward mobility, especially for minorities and rural youth, who may have fewer opportunities.

Indeed, when the Army last summer announced a plan to recruit nearly 30,000 fewer enlistees in 1990, it drew criticism for squeezing shut a key avenue of advancement for blacks, who because of their tendency to enlist in greater numbers would be disproportionately affected. With the United States now at war, however, those arguments have been turned on their head.

"DoD is being criticized from both sides, and that comes from the basic paradox that during peacetime military service is seen as a benefit, and in wartime it's a burden," says Binkin. He points out, however, that the presidential commission that initially studied the concept of the all-volunteer force back in 1973 did assure the public that it would not lead to a military that was lopsided with minorities.

"And they were wrong. So you can argue that there is a sort of economic conscription going on," he says. "The fact is, however, that the armed services have led society by a couple of decades in giving minorities and women a fair shake."

The contention that blacks believe the armed services are serious about equal opportunity is perhaps best supported by re-enlistment rates. All minorities in the Army re-enlist at a higher rate than their white counterparts, and fully 63 percent of eligible black soldiers sign on for a second tour (compared to 37.6 percent of eligible whites). "People tend to vote with their right arm by re-enlisting, and I think you can pretty much sum up race relations in the Army by our retention rate among blacks," says Maj. Dean Plumer, chief of the Army's Equal Opportunity branch.

What blacks find in the services that they don't find back home is sometimes hard to quantify. Sgt. Major Jerome Tettis, the senior non-commissioned officer in the Army's Equal Opportunity branch, believes community support is a big factor. "Whenever my friends back home talk about problems they're having, I often find myself saying, 'Gee, in the military that's not a real problem, because here's where you go to get that fixed,'" he says.

While he is concerned about the war robbing black communities of some of their brightest young people, Rep. Lewis says he felt that sense of fraternity among men and women in uniform while visiting troops in the Persian Gulf. "I believe many young African-Americans find a greater degree of significant integration, more interracial cooperation and a greater sense of community and family in the military than they do in American society," he says.

DoD officials also contend that the racial composition of the force does not argue that the United States is sending a dispossessed underclass to fight its wars. High enlistment rates have allowed DoD to become increasingly selective over the past decade, and nearly all new recruits are high-school graduates. In fact, according to a 1989 Congressional Budget Office study, based on 1987 statistics, 45 percent of active-duty recruits come from areas of above-average incomes.

"It's simply not true that today's service member comes from a lower socioeconomic strata than if we randomly selected from the civilian sector," says DoD's Jehn. "Most come from two-parent families who own their own homes and have the same ambitions for themselves and their children as the rest of middle America."

Regardless, abolishing the all-volunteer force and reinstating the draft would hardly guarantee a truly representative military force or proportionate combat casualties in a war. Children of the affluent found ways to avoid previous drafts, and higher educated draftees would probably not be steered toward combat jobs. The Pentagon also recruits fewer than 300,000 people annually, so only about 1 family in 10 stands to have a child in the armed services.

"If you want a truly representative force, you either have to increase the size of the military dramatically and still allow qualified young blacks to enlist, or else you have to tell them they can't join because we want to draft Donald Trump's son," says Binkin. "I don't think that will fly."

Women at War

When Rep. Byron ducked into a women's shower room at a forward military airbase in Saudi Arabia, she was confronted with still other implications of the composition of today's armed services. Five young female service members were enjoying their first shower in more than a week. Interspersed with their talk about the long hours and the danger of enemy missile attacks, the women spoke of children they had left behind. One was a single parent who had to send her child away to a Catholic school. (In the Army alone, there are more than 12,000 single female parents.) Another of the women had a two-month old infant, and was worried about missing a critical period of bonding with her baby.

Byron knows that those women have now come under bombardment by Iraqi Scud missiles. "When you talk about women under fire, mothers who will leave young infants behind if they become casualties, that definitely adds another dimension. For that reason, I still feel strongly that we don't need women in front-line combat," she says.

However, modern warfare in general—and Scud missiles in particular—have seriously blurred the lines between the front and rear in a combat zone. Certainly no one denies that Desert Storm has drawn more women (roughly 27,000 U.S. servicewomen have deployed to the Persian Gulf) closer to combat than any war in our history. "We have women in combat in the Persian Gulf right now, just as we had women in combat in Panama," says Maj. Marcene Etchieson, a spokeswoman for women in the Army. "What our policy of excluding them from front-line combat units is designed to do is limit the number of women who become casualties."

As the number of women in the armed services has grown, the issue of women in combat has become increasingly contentious. In Vietnam, women made up only 1.5 percent of the Army. In today's all-volunteer Army, more than 11 percent of soldiers are female. Though they are prohibited from serving in ground combat units, warships or attack planes, women in uniform may be found standing armed guard at Persian Gulf installations, ferrying supplies as pilots and driving ammunition trucks.

Because promotions in the armed services are traditionally bound to rotations through combat units, many women in uniform bridle at the combat restrictions. They point out that in 1989, for instance, women comprised 12 percent of Air Force officers but only 4 percent of the service's lieutenant colonels, 2 percent of its colonels and 1 percent of its brigadier generals. In an August 1989 *Government Executive* survey of the 941 highest-ranking women in the services, 58 percent said they favored repeal of the combat-exclusion statute.

"In wartime, women are just as much in harm's way as men, because the first things that tend to be hit are command and supply centers where they work," says Rep. Pat Schroeder, D-Colo. As a member of the House Armed Services Committee, Schroeder introduced an unsuccessful bill last year to allow Army women to join combat units on an experimental basis. The idea was backed by the Defense Advisory Committee on Women in the Services, a Pentagon-sponsored organization that proposed just such a four-year Army experiment. Under federal law, the Air Force and Navy are forbidden from allowing women into combat units.

"Some Members of Congress are running for cover on this issue too, but the only thing DoD is protecting women from is promotions," says Schroeder. "And if women become casualties in Desert Storm, that will blow this cover they're using that this is all designed to keep women safe."

According to Army officials, women have actually been selected for command opportunities, across the spectrum of jobs, at rates higher than men. Female casualties in Desert Storm could also work against those who propose allowing them into front-line combat units. "We've seen a lot of moms going away to this war, and once the stark reality sets in that these women can die, people may come to the conclusion that it's enough that they're serving in the Gulf," says Binkin. "This push for women in combat may prove more of a peacetime phenomenon."

Manpower experts both inside and outside the Pentagon know that the entire all-volunteer force has been a peacetime phenomenon, a social experiment interrupted only briefly by operations like Grenada and Panama. Thus, the months ahead will find that force undergoing its closest scrutiny in more than 20 years. If the image that emerges as we peer anxiously through the smoke of war disturbs us as a country—if it is too old, too racially unbalanced, too full of single-mothers, citizen soldiers or next-door neighbors—then we should at least find the faces familiar. We have seen the all-volunteer army, and it is us.

After reading: CONSOLIDATE INFORMATION

1. Kitfield's article was originally published in April, 1991, but it was written before the military action in the Persian Gulf was ended. How does your knowledge of how the conflict actually ended, the actual numbers of casualties, and the reaction of the American public compare with Kitfield's speculations and analysis?
2. How do you interpret Kitfield's stance on the totally volunteer military? Do you think he believes that such a military force will continue to be feasible?
3. What reasons would you give to either support or deny the practicality of a totally volunteer military force?

Capital Punishment
Anthony G. Amsterdam

Anthony G. Amsterdam, a lawyer and professor of law, is one of the foremost legal experts on capital punishment. He wrote the following essay (which he adapted from a speech he gave) for an popular audience. He develops his argument concerning capital punishment from a philosophical analysis of the concepts of retribution and deterrence.

Before you read: FIRST THOUGHTS
LOOK AHEAD

1. What emotional reaction do you have to the title?
2. Write a short response to the words *retribution* and *deterrence*.
3. Read Amsterdam's first paragraph. What clues does it give you to his position about capital punishment?

During reading: REACT
QUESTION
SUMMARIZE

1. What is the effect of the two things Armstrong asks his readers to remember when they are exposed to descriptions of terrifying murders?
2. How do you react when Armstrong equates the two words, *execution* and *murder*?

My Discussion of Capital Punishment will proceed in three stages.

First, I would like to set forth certain basic factual realities about capital punishment, like the fact that capital punishment is a fancy phrase for legally killing people. Please forgive me for beginning with such obvious and ugly facts. Much of our political and philosophical debate about the death penalty is carried on in language calculated to conceal these realities and their implications. The implications, I will suggest, are that capital punishment is a great evil—surely the greatest evil except for war that our society can intentionally choose to commit.

This does not mean that we should do away with capital punishment. Some evils, like war, are occasionally necessary, and perhaps capital punishment is one of them. But the fact that it is a great evil means that we should not choose to do it without some very good and solid reason of which we are satisfactorily convinced upon sufficient evidence. The conclusion of my first point simply is that the burden of proof upon the question of capital punishment rightly rests on those who are asking us to use our laws to kill people with, and that this is a very heavy burden.

Second, I want to review the justifications that have been advanced to support capital punishment. I want to explore with you concepts such as retribution and deterrence, and some of the assumptions and evidence about them. The conclusion of my second point will be that none of these reasons which we like to give ourselves for executing criminals can begin to sustain the burden of proof that rightfully rests upon them.

Third, I would like to say a word about history—about the slow but absolutely certain progress of maturing civilization that will bring an inevitable end to punishment by death. That history does not give us the choice between perpetuating and abolishing capital punishment, because we could not perpetuate it if we wanted to. A generation or two within a single nation can retard but not reverse a long-term, worldwide evolution of this magnitude. Our choice is narrower although it is not unimportant: whether we shall be numbered among the last generations to put legal killing aside. I will end by asking you to cast your choice for life instead of death. But, first, let me begin with some basic facts about the death penalty.

I. The most basic fact, of course, is that capital punishment means taking living, breathing men and women, stuffing them into a chair, strapping them down, pulling a lever, and exterminating them. We have almost forgotten this fact because there have been no executions in this country for more than ten years, except for Gary Gilmore whose combined suicide and circus were so wildly extravagant as to seem unreal. For many people, capital punishment has become a sanitized and symbolic issue: Do you or do you not support your local police? Do you or do you not care enough about crime to get tough with criminals? These abstractions were never what capital punishment was about, although it was possible to think so during the ten-year moratorium on executions caused by constitutional challenges to the death penalty in the courts. That is no longer possible. The courts have now said that we can start up executions again, if we want to. Today, a vote for capital punishment is a vote to kill real, live people.

What this means is, first, that we bring men or women into court and put them through a trial for their lives. They are expected to sit back quietly and observe decent courtroom decorum throughout a proceeding whose purpose is systematically and deliberately to decide whether they should be killed. The jury hears evidence and votes; and you can always tell when a jury has voted for death because they come back into court and they will not look the defendant or defense counsel in the eyes. The judge pronounces sentence and the defendant is taken away to be held in a cell for two to six years, hoping that his appeals will succeed, not really knowing what they are all about, but knowing that if they fail, he will be taken out and cinched down and put to death. Most of the people in prison are reasonably nice to him, and even a little apologetic; but he realizes every day for that 700 or 2,100 days that they are holding him there helpless for the approaching slaughter; and that, once the final order is given, they will truss him up and kill him, and that nobody in that vast surrounding machinery of public officials and servants of the law will raise a finger to save him. This is why Camus once wrote that an execution

> ... is not simply death. It is just as different ... from the privation of life as a concentration camp is from prison ... It adds to death a rule, a public premeditation known to the future victim, an organization ... which is itself a source of moral sufferings more terrible than death ... [Capital punishment] is ... the most premeditated of murders, to which no criminal's deed, however calculated ... can be compared. ... For there to be an equivalency, the death penalty would have to punish a criminal who had warned his victim of the date at which he would inflict a horrible death on him and who, from that moment onward, had confined him at his mercy for months. Such a monster is not encountered in private life.

I will spare you descriptions of the execution itself. Apologists for capital punishment commonly excite their readers with descriptions of extremely gruesome, gory murders. All murders are horrible things, and executions are usually a lot cleaner physically—although, like Camus, I have never heard of a murderer who held his victim captive for two or more years waiting as the minutes and hours ticked away toward his preannounced death. The clinical details of an execution are as unimaginable to me as they are to most of you. We have not permitted public executions in this country for over 40 years. The law in every state forbids more than a few people to watch the deed done behind prison walls. In January of 1977, a federal judge in Texas ruled that executions could be photographed for television, but the attorneys general of 25 states asked the federal Court of Appeals to set aside that ruling, and it did. I can only leave to your imagination what they are trying so very hard to hide from us. Oh, of course, executions are too hideous to put on television; we all know that. But let us not forget that it is the same hideous thing, done in secret, which we are discussing under abstract labels like "capital punishment" that permit us to talk about the subject in after-dinner conversation instead of spitting up.

In any event, the advocates of capital punishment can and do accentuate their arguments with descriptions of the awful physical details of such hideous murders as that of poor Sharon Tate. All of us naturally and rightly respond to these atrocities with shock and horror. You can read descriptions of executions that would also horrify you (for example, in Byron Eshelman's 1962 book, *Death Row Chaplain*, particularly pages 160–61), but I prefer not to insult your intelligence by playing "can you top this" with issues of life and death. I ask you only to remember two things, if and when you are exposed to descriptions of terrifying murders.

First, the murders being described are not murders that are being done by us, or in our name, or with our approval; and our power to stop them is exceedingly limited even under the most exaggerated suppositions of deterrence, which I shall shortly return to question. Every execution, on the other hand, is done by our paid servants, in our collective name, and we can stop them all. Please do not be bamboozled into thinking that people who are against executions are in favor of murders. If we had the individual or the collective power to stop murders, we would stop them all—and for the same basic reason that we want to stop executions. Murders and executions are both ugly, vicious things, because they destroy the same sacred and mysterious gift of life which we do not understand and can never restore.

Second, please remember therefore that descriptions of murders are relevant to the subject of capital punishment only on the theory that two wrongs make a right, or that killing murderers can assuage their victims' sufferings or bring them back to life, or that capital punishment is the best deterrent to murder. The first two propositions are absurd, and the third is debatable—although, as I shall later show, the evidence is overwhelmingly against it. My present point is only that deterrence *is* debatable, whereas we *know* that persons whom we execute are dead beyond recall, no matter how the debate about deterrence comes out. That is a sufficient reason, I believe, why the burden of proof on the issue of deterrence should be placed squarely upon the executioners.

There are other reasons too. Let me try to state them briefly.

Capital punishment not merely kills people, it also kills some of them in error, and these are errors which we can never correct. When I speak about legal error, I do not mean only the question whether "they got the right man" or killed somebody who "didn't do it." Errors of that sort do occur: Timothy Evans, for example, an innocent man whose execution was among the reasons for the abolition of the death penalty in Great Britain. If you read Anthony Scaduto's recent book, *Scapegoat*, you will come away with unanswerable doubts whether Bruno Richard Hauptmann was really guilty of the kidnaping of the Lindbergh infant for which he was executed, or whether we killed Hauptmann, too, for a crime he did not commit.

In 1975, the Florida Cabinet pardoned two black men, Freddie Lee Pitts and Wilbert Lee, who were twice tried and sentenced to death and spent 12 years apiece on death row for a murder committed by somebody else. This one, I am usually glibly told, "does not count," because Pitts and Lee were never actually put to death. Take comfort if you will but I cannot, for I know that only the general constitutional attack which we were then mounting upon the death penalty in Florida kept Pitts and Lee alive long enough to permit discovery of the evidence of their innocence. Our constitutional attack is now dead, and so would Pitts and Lee be if they were tried tomorrow. Sure, we catch some errors. But we often catch them by extremely lucky breaks that could as easily not have happened. I represented a young man in North Carolina who came within a hair's breadth of being the Gary Gilmore of his day. Like Gilmore, he became so depressed under a death sentence that he tried to dismiss his appeal. He was barely talked out of it, his conviction was reversed, and on retrial a jury acquitted him in 11 minutes.

We do not know how many "wrong men" have been executed. We think and pray that they are rare—although we can't be sure because, after a man is dead, people seldom continue to investigate the possibility that he was innocent. But that is not the biggest source of error anyway.

What about *legal* error? In 1968, the Supreme Court of the United States held that it was unconstitutional to exclude citizens from capital trial juries simply because they had general conscientious or religious objections to the death penalty. That decision was held retroactive; and I represented 60 or 70 men whose death sentences were subsequently set aside for constitutional errors in jury selection. While researching their cases, I found the cases of at least as many more men who had already been executed on the basis of trials infected with identical errors. On June 29, 1977, we finally won a decision from the Supreme Court of the United States that the death penalty is excessively harsh and therefore unconstitutional for the crime of rape. Fine, but it comes too late for the 455 men executed for rape in this country since 1930–405 of them black.

In 1975, the Supreme Court held that the constitutional presumption of innocence forbids a trial judge to tell the jury that the burden of proof is on a homicide defendant to show provocation which reduces murder to manslaughter. On June 17, 1977, the Court held that this decision was also retroactive. Jury charges of precisely that kind were standard forms for more than a century in many American states that punished murder with death. Can we even begin to guess how many people were unconstitutionally executed under this so-called retroactive decision?

Now what about errors of fact that go to the degree of culpability of a crime? In almost every state, the difference between first- and second-degree murder—or between capital and noncapital murder—depends on whether the defendant acted with something called "premeditation" as distinguished from intent to kill. Premeditation means intent formed beforehand, but no particular amount of time is required. Courts tell juries that premeditation "may be as instantaneous as successive thoughts in the mind." Mr. Justice Cardozo wrote that *he* did not understand the concept of premeditation after several decades of studying and trying to apply it as a judge. Yet this is the kind of question to which a jury's answer spells out life or death in a capital trial—this, and the questions whether the defendant had "malice aforethought," or "provocation and passion," or "insanity," or the "reasonableness" necessary for killing in self-defense.

I think of another black client, Johnny Coleman, whose conviction and death sentence for killing a white truck driver named "Screwdriver" Johnson we twice got reversed by the Supreme Court of the United States. On retrial a jury acquitted him on the grounds of self-defense upon exactly the same evidence that an earlier jury had had when it sentenced him to die. When ungraspable legal standards are thus applied to intangible mental states, there is not merely the possibility but the actuarial certainty that juries deciding substantial volumes of cases are going to be wrong in an absolutely large number of them. If you accept capital punishment, you must accept the reality—not the risk, but the reality—that we shall kill people whom the law says that it is not proper to kill. No other outcome is possible when we presume to administer an infallible punishment through a fallible system.

You will notice that I have taken examples of black defendants as some of my cases of legal error. There is every reason to believe that discrimination on grounds of race and poverty fatally infect the administration of capital justice in this country. Since 1930, an almost equal number of white and black defendants has been executed for the crime of murder, although blacks constituted only about a tenth of the nation's population during this period. No sufficiently careful studies have been done of these cases, controlling variables other than race, so as to determine exactly what part race played in the outcome. But when that kind of systematic study *was* done in rape cases, it showed beyond the statistical possibility of a doubt that black men who raped white women were disproportionately sentenced to die on the basis of race alone. Are you prepared to believe that juries which succumbed to conscious or unconscious racial prejudices in rape cases were or are able to put those prejudices wholly aside where the crime charged is murder? Is it not much more plausible to believe that even the most conscientious juror—or judge, or prosecuting attorney—will be slower to want to inflict the death penalty on a defendant with whom he can identify as a human being; and that the process of identification in our society is going to be very seriously affected by racial identity?

I should mention that there have been a couple of studies—one by the *Stanford Law Review* and the other by the Texas Judicial Council—which found no racial discrimination in capital sentencing in certain murder cases. But both of these studies had methodological problems and limitations; and both of them also found death-sentencing discrimination against the economically poor, who come disproportionately from racial minorities. The sum of the evidence still stands where the National Crime Commission found it ten years ago, when it described the following discriminatory patterns. "The death sentence," said the Commission, "is disproportionately imposed and carried out on the poor, the Negro, and members of unpopular groups."

Apart from discrimination, there is a haphazard, crazy-quilt character about the administration of capital punishment that every knowledgeable lawyer or observer can decribe but none can rationally explain. Some juries are hanging juries, some counties are hanging counties, some years are hanging years; and men live or die depending on these flukes.

However atrocious the crime may have been for which a particular defendant is sentenced to die, "[e]xperienced wardens know many prisoners serving life or less whose crimes were equally, or more atrocious." That is a quotation, by the way, from former Attorney General Ramsey Clark's statement to a congressional subcommittee; and wardens Lewis Lawes, Clinton Duffy, and others have said the same thing.

With it I come to the end of my first point. I submit that the deliberate judicial extinction of human life is intrinsically so final and so terrible an act as to cast the burden of proof for its justification upon those who want us to do it. But certainly when the act is executed through a fallible system which assures that we kill some people wrongly, others because they are black or poor or personally unattractive or socially unacceptable, and all of them quite freakishly in the sense that whether a man lives or dies for any particular crime is a matter of luck and happenstance, *then*, at the least, the burden of justifying capital punishment lies fully and heavily on its proponents.

II. Let us consider those justifications. The first and the oldest is the concept of *retribution:* an eye for an eye, a life for a life. You may or may not believe in this kind of retribution, but I will not waste your time debating it because it cannot honestly be used to justify the only form of capital punishment that this country has accepted for the past half-century. Even before the judicial moratorium, executions in the United States had dwindled to an average of about 30 a year. Only a rare, sparse handful of convicted murderers was being sentenced to die or executed for the selfsame crimes for which many, many times as many murderers were sent away to prison. Obviously, as Professor Herbert Wechsler said a generation ago, the issue of capital punishment is no longer "whether it is fair or just that one who takes another person's life should lose his own.... [W]e do not and cannot act upon ... [that proposition] generally in the administration of the penal law. The problem rather is whether a small and highly random sample of people who commit murder.... ought to be despatched, while most of those convicted of ... [identical] crimes are dealt with by imprisonment."

Sometimes the concept of retribution is modernized a little with a notion called *moral reinforcement*—the ideal that we should punish very serious crimes very severely in order to demonstrate how much we abhor them. The trouble with *this* justification for capital punishment, of course, is that it completely begs the question, which is *how severely* we ought to punish any particular crime to show appropriate abhorrence for it. The answer can hardly be found in a literal application of the eye-for-an-eye formula. We do not burn down arsonists' houses or cheat back at bunco artists. But if we ought not punish all crimes exactly according to their kind, then what is the fit moral reinforcement for murder? You might as well say burning at the stake or boiling in oil as simple gassing or electrocution.

Or is it not more plausible—if what we really want to say is that the killing of a human being is wrong and ought to be condemned as clearly as we can—that we should choose the punishment of prison as the fitting means to make this point? So far as moral reinforcement goes, the difference between life imprisonment and capital punishment is precisely that imprisonment continues to respect the value of human life. The plain message of capital punishment, on the other hand, is that life ceases to be sacred whenever someone with the power to take it away decides that there is a sufficiently compelling pragmatic reason to do so.

But there is still another theory of a retributive sort which is often advanced to support the death penalty, particularly in recent years. This is the argument that *we*—that is, the person making the argument—we no longer believe in the outworn concept of retribution, but the *public*—they believe in retribution, and so we must let them have their prey or they will lose respect for law. Watch for this argument because it is the surest sign of demogagic depravity. It is disgusting in its patronizing attribution to "the public" of a primitive, uneducable bloodthirstiness which the speaker is unprepared to defend but is prepared to exploit as a means of sidestepping the rational and moral limitations of a *just* theory of retribution. It out-pilates Pilate in its abnegation of governmental responsibility to respond to popular misinformation with enlightenment, instead of seizing on it as a pretext for atrocity. This argument asserts that the proper way to deal with a lynch mob is to string its victim up before the mob does.

I don't think "the public" is a lynch mob or should be treated as one. People today are troubled and frightened by crime, and legitimately so. Much of the apparent increase of violent crime in our times is the product of intensified statistics keeping, massive and instantaneous and graphic news reporting, and manipulation of figures by law enforcement agencies which must compete with other sectors of the public economy for budget allocations. But part of the increase is also real, and very disturbing. Murders ought to disturb us all, whether or not they are increasing. Each and every murder is a terrible human tragedy. Nevertheless, it is irresponsible for public officials—particularly law enforcement officials whom the public views as experts—first to exacerbate and channel legitimate public concern about crime into public support for capital punishment by advertising unsupportable claims that capital punishment is an answer to the crime problem, and then to turn around and cite public support for capital punishment as justification when all other justifications are shown to be unsupportable. Politicians do this all the time, for excellent political reasons. It is much easier to advocate simplistic and illusory solutions to the crime problem than to find real and effective solutions. Most politicians are understandably afraid to admit that our society knows frighteningly little about the causes or cure of crime, and will have to spend large amounts of taxpayers' money even to begin to find out. The facile politics of crime do much to explain our national acceptance of capital punishment, but nothing to justify it.

Another supposed justification for capital punishment that deserves equally brief treatment is the notion of *isolation* or *specific deterrence*—the idea that we must kill a murderer to prevent him from murdering ever again. The usual forms that this argument takes are that a life sentence does not mean a life sentence—it means parole after 7, or 12, or 25 years; and that, within prisons themselves, guards and other prisoners are in constant jeopardy of death at the hands of convicted but unexecuted murderers.

It amazes me that these arguments can be made or taken seriously. Are we really going to kill a human being because we do not trust other people—the people whom we have chosen to serve on our own parole boards—to make a proper judgment in his case at some future time? We trust this same parole board to make far more numerous, difficult, and dangerous decisions: hardly a week passes when they do not consider the cases of armed robbers, for example, although armed robbers are much, much more likely statistically to commit future murders than any murderer is to repeat his crime. But if we really do distrust the public agencies of law—if we fear that they may make mistakes—then surely that is a powerful argument *against* capital punishment. Courts which hand out death sentences because they predict that a man will still be criminally dangerous 7 or 25 years in the future cannot conceivably make fewer mistakes than parole boards who release a prisoner after 7 or 25 years of close observation in prison have convinced them that he is reformed and no longer dangerous.

But pass this point. If we refuse to trust the parole system, then let us provide by law that the murderers whose release we fear shall be given sentences of life imprisonment without parole which *do* mean life imprisonment without parole. I myself would be against that, but it is far more humane than capital punishment, and equally safe.

As for killings inside prisons, if you examine them you will find that they are very rarely done by convicted murderers, but are almost always done by people imprisoned for crimes that no one would think of making punishable by death. Warden Lawes of Sing Sing and Governor Wallace of Alabama, among others, regularly employed murder convicts as house servants because they were among the very safest of prisoners. There are exceptions, of course; but these can be handled by adequate prison security. You cannot tell me or believe that a society which is capable of putting a man on the moon is incapable of putting a man in prison, keeping him there, and keeping him from killing while he is there. And if anyone says that this is costly, and that we should kill people in order to reduce government expenditures, I can only reply that the cost of housing a man for life in the most physically secure conditions imaginable is considerably less than the cost of putting the same man through all of the extraordinary legal proceedings necessary to kill him.

That brings me to the last supposed justification for the death penalty: *deterrence*. This is the subject that you most frequently hear debated, and many people who talk about capital punishment talk about nothing else. I have done otherwise here, partly for completeness, partly because it is vital to approach the subject of deterrence knowing precisely what question you want to ask and have answered. I have suggested that the proper question is *whether there is sufficiently convincing evidence that the death penalty deters murder better than does life imprisonment so that you are willing to accept responsibility for doing the known evil act of killing human beings—with all of the attending ugliness that I have described—on the faith of your conviction in the superior deterrent efficacy of capital punishment.*

If this is the question, then I submit that there is only one fair and reasonable answer. When the Supreme Court of the United States reviewed the evidence in 1976, it described that evidence as "inconclusive." Do not let anybody tell you—as death-penalty advocates are fond of doing—that the Supreme Court held the death penalty justifiable as a deterrent. What the Court's plurality opinion said, exactly, was that "there is no convincing evidence *either supporting or refuting* . . . [the] view" that "the death penalty may not function is a significantly greater deterrent than lesser penalties." *Because* the evidence was inconclusive, the Court held that the Constitution did not forbid judgment either way. But if the evidence is inconclusive, is it *your* judgment that we should conclusively kill people on a factual theory that the evidence does not conclusively sustain?

I hope not. But let us examine the evidence more carefully because—even though it is not conclusive—it is very, very substantial; and the overwhelming weight of it refutes the claims of those who say that capital punishment is a better deterrent than life imprisonment for murder.

For more than 40 years, criminologists have studied this question by a variety of means. They have compared homicide rates in countries and states that did and did not have capital punishment, or that actually executed people more and less frequently. Some of these studies compared large aggregates of abolitionist and retentionist states; others compared geographically adjacent pairs or triads of states, or states that were chosen because they were comparable in other socioeconomic factors that might affect homicide. Other studies compared homicide rates in the same country or state before and after the abolition or reinstatement of capital punishment, or they compared homicide rates for the same geographic area during periods preceding and following well publicized executions. Special comparative studies were done relating to police killings and prison killings. All in all, there were dozens of studies. Without a single exception, *none* of them found that the death penalty had any statistically significant effect upon the rate of homicide or murder. Often I have heard advocates of capital punishment explain away its failures by likening it to a great lighthouse: "We count the ships that crash," they say, "but we never know how many saw the light and were saved." What these studies show, however, is that coastlines of the same shape and depth and tidal structure, with and without lighthouses, invariably have the same number of shipwrecks per year. On that evidence, would you invest your money in a lighthouse, or would you buy a sonar if you really wanted to save lives?

In 1975, the first purportedly scientific study ever to find that capital punishment *did* deter homicides was published. This was done by Isaac Ehrlich of Chicago, who is not a criminologist but an economist. Using regression analysis involving an elaborate mathematical model, Ehrlich reported that every execution deterred something like eight murders. Naturally, supporters of capital punishment hurriedly clambered on the Ehrlich bandwagon.

Unhappily, for them, the wagon was a factory reject. Several distinguished econometricians—including a team headed by Lawrence Klein, president of the American Economic Association—reviewed Ehrlich's work and found it fatally flawed with numerous methodological errors. Some of these were technical: it appeared, for example, that Ehrlich had produced his results by the unjustified and unexplained use of a logarithmic form of regression equation instead of the more conventional linear form—which made his findings of deterrence vanish. Equally important, it was shown that Ehrlich's findings depended entirely on data from the post-1962 period, when executions declined and the homicide rate rose *as a part of a general rise, in the overall crime rate that Ehrlich incredibly failed to consider.*

Incidentally, the nonscientific proponents of capital punishment are also fond of suggesting that the rise in homicide rates in the 1960s and the 1970s, when executions were halted, proves that executions used to deter homicides. This is ridiculous when you consider that crime as a whole has increased during this period; that homicide rates have increased about *half* as much as the rates for all other FBI Index crimes; and that whatever factors are affecting the rise of most noncapital crimes (which *cannot* include cessation of executions) almost certainly affect the homicide-rate rise also.

In any event, Ehrlich's study was discredited and a second, methodologically inferior study by a fellow named Yunker is not even worth criticizing here. These are the only two scientific studies in 40 years, I repeat, which have ever purported to find deterrence. On the other hand, several recent studies have been completed by researchers who adopted Ehrlich's basic regression-analysis approach but corrected its defects. Peter Passell did such a study finding no deterrence. Kenneth Avio did such a study finding no deterrence. Brian Forst did such a study finding no deterrence. If you want to review all of these studies yourselves, you may find them discussed and cited in an excellent article in the 1976 *Supreme Court Review* by Hans Zeisel, at page 317. The conclusion you will have to draw is that—during 40 years and today—the scientific community has looked and looked and looked for any reliable evidence that capital punishment deters homicide better than does life imprisonment, and it has found no such evidence at all.

Proponents of capital punishment frequently cite a different kind of study, one that was done by the Los Angeles Police Department. Police officers asked arrested robbers who did not carry guns, or did not use them, *why* they did not; and the answers, supposedly, were frequently that the robber "did not want to get the death penalty." It is noteworthy that the Los Angeles Police Department has consistently refused to furnish copies of this study and its underlying data to professional scholars, apparently for fear of criticism. I finally obtained a copy of the study from a legislative source, and I can tell you that it shows two things. First, an arrested person will tell a police officer anything that he thinks the officer wants to hear. Second, police officers, like all other human beings, hear what they want to hear. When a robber tries to say that he did not carry or use a gun because he did not wish to risk the penalties for homicide, he will describe those penalties in terms of whatever the law happens to be at the time and place. In Minnesota, which has no death penilty, he will say, "I didn't want to get life imprisonment." In Los Angeles, he will say, "I didn't want to get the death penalty."

Both responses mean the same thing; neither tells you that death is a superior deterrent to life imprisonment.

The real mainstay of deterrence thesis, however, is not evidence but intuition. You and I ask ourselves: Are we not afraid to die? Of course! Would the threat of death, then, not intimidate us to forbear from a criminal act? Certainly! *Therefore*, capital punishment must be a deterrent. The trouble with this intuition is that the people who are doing the reasoning and the people who are doing the murdering are not the same people. You and I do not commit murder for a lot of reasons other than the death penalty. The death penalty might perhaps also deter us from murdering—but altogether needlessly, since we would not murder with it or without it. Those who are sufficiently dissocialized to murder and are not responding to the world in the way that we are, and we simply cannot "intuit" their thinking processes from ours.

Consider, for example, the well-documented cases of persons who kill *because* there is a death penalty. One of these was Pamela Watkins, a babysitter in San Jose who had made several unsuccessful suicide attempts and was frightened to try again. She finally strangled two children so that the state of California would execute her. In various bizarre forms, this "suicide-murder" syndrome is reported by psychiatrists again and again. (Parenthetically, Gary Gilmore was probably such a case.) If you intuit that somewhere, sometime, the death penalty *does* deter some potential murders, are you also prepared to intuit that their numbers mathematically exceed the numbers of these wretched people who are actually induced to murder by the existence of capital punishment?

Here, I suggest, our intuition does—or should—fail, just as the evidence certainly does fail, to establish a deterrent justification for the death penalty. There is simply no credible evidence, and there is no rational way of reasoning about the real facts once you know them, which can sustain this or any other justification with the degree of confidence that should be demanded before a civilized society deliberately extinguishes human life.

III. I have only a little space for my final point, but it is sufficient because the point is perfectly plain. Capital punishment is a dying institution in this last quarter of the twentieth century. It has already been abandoned in law or in fact throughout most of the civilized world. England, Canada, the Scandinavian countries, virtually all of Western Europe except for France and Spain have abolished the death penalty. The vast majority of countries in the Western Hemisphere have abolished it. Its last strongholds in the world—apart from the United States—are in Asia and Africa, particularly South Africa. Even the countries which maintain capital punishment on the books have almost totally ceased to use it in fact. In the United States, considering only the last half century, executions have plummeted from 199 in 1935 to approximately 29 a year during the decade before 1967, when the ten-year judicial moratorium began.

Do you doubt that this development will continue? Do you doubt that it will continue because it is the path of civilization—the path up out of fear and terror and the barbarism that terror breeds, into self-confidence and decency in the administration of justice? The road, like any other built by men, has its detours, but over many generations it has run true, and will run true. And there will therefore come a time—perhaps in 20 years, perhaps in 50 or 100, but very surely and very shortly as the lifetime of nations is measured—when our children will look back at us in horror and unbelief because of what we did in their names and for their supposed safety, just as we look back in horror and unbelief at the thousands of crucifixions and beheadings and live disembowelments that our ancestors practiced for the supposed purpose of making our world safe from murderers and robbers, thieves, shoplifters, and pickpockets.

All of these kinds of criminals are still with us, and will be with our children—although we can certainly decrease their numbers and their damage, and protect ourselves from them a lot better, if we insist that our politicians stop pounding on the whipping boy of capital punishment and start coming up with some real solutions to the real problems of crime. Our children will cease to execute murderers for the same reason that we have ceased to string up pickpockets and shoplifters at the public crossroads, although there are still plenty of them around. Our children will cease to execute murderers because executions are a self-deluding, self-defeating, self-degrading, futile, and entirely stupid means of dealing with the crime of murder, and because our children will prefer to be something better than murderers themselves. Should we not—can we not—make the same choice now?

After reading: CONSOLIDATE INFORMATION

1. Evaluate Amsterdam's argument that capital punishment does not deter crime. Does he convince you? Why or why not?
2. In the last section of his essay, Amsterdam states that capital punishment is a "dying institution." Yet, many states have reinstated capital punishment. Why do you think the United States remains one of the few modern nations to execute criminals?
3. Amsterdam wrote this essay in 1977 and it contains the basic philosophical arguments which opponents of the death penalty still use. In the years since, news stories of terrible crimes, many of them serial killings involving atrocities committed against victims, as well as actual executions in states that have reinstated the death penalty, have kept the debate about capital punishment alive. Do you think the basic assumption that Amsterdam makes, that killing human beings is wrong no matter how or why it is done, is still valid?

Racial Bias, the Death Penalty, and Desert

Christopher Meyers

Professor Meyers wrote this essay for a scholarly audience of philosophers and teachers. His analysis focuses on a philosophical argument which draws on Anthony Amsterdam's discussion of the moral and ethical grounds for opposing capital punishment.

Before reading: FIRST THOUGHTS
                     LOOK AHEAD

1. Respond to Meyers's title. What do you think the concept of *desert* means?
2. From Meyers's use of the phrases "racial bias" and "death penalty" together in the title, what do you think he will be discussing?
3. Read Meyers's first four paragraphs. In the fourth paragraph he forecasts what his argument will be, as well as his position concerning capital punishment. Based on what he writes here, what do you think you can expect from the rest of the article?

During reading: REACT
                     QUESTION
                     SUMMARIZE

1. In discussing the McCleskey case, what does Meyers write about the Supreme Court's understanding of the nature of racial bias and prejudice?
2. Why does Meyers use the analogy of two men applying for the same retirement benefits? What is the effect of such an analogy?

ONLY ONE TIME in U.S. history has the Supreme Court ruled that capital punishment is unconstitutional—the landmark 1972 case of *Furman v. Georgia*. Although sharply divided on the case (five separate majority opinions were written), the Court did find that bias, in particular bias against blacks, resulted in the death penalty being applied in a "capricious" and thus unconstitutional manner. Importantly, however, the Court did *not* rule that a sentence of death is in and of itself "cruel and unusual"; its concern in *Furman* was solely with a *just application* of the penalty. Thus when states were later able to convince the court that bias was no longer present in sentencing procedures (*Gregg v. Georgia*, 1976), the Court again made execution a legal form of punishment.

It was with this history in mind that opponents of the death penalty eagerly awaited the Court's ruling in the 1987 case of *McCleskey v. Kemp*. This, like *Furman*, was a case in which irrefutable evidence was provided that the penalty was being applied in an arbitrary manner, based upon racial bias. The defense argued that McCleskey was the victim of a proven pattern of racial discrimination that made it much more likely that black defendants or killers of whites would receive a death sentence than would whites or killers of blacks. Surely, abolitionists believed, the Court would rely upon the same reasoning used in *Furman* and ban capital punishment, at least in those states in which this pattern of racial bias was present.

However, a bitterly divided Court rejected McCleskey's appeal, 5–4. In this paper, I will argue that although the Court displayed a disturbingly inadequate understanding of prejudice and discrimination, its decision in *McCleskey* was nonetheless just, *assuming that only* application, *and not* retribution, *was at issue.*

I defend this view from a position of strong opposition both to the death penalty and to the kind of racial bias made evident in McCleskey's defense. However, I hope to show that arguments against capital punishment must be addressed first and foremost to revealing that retribution is not a sound moral principle. As I will argue below, if one starts with the presupposition that retribution *is* a just basis for punishment, that a person's actions sometimes warrant her death, then concerns over equitable application are relevant only if it can be shown that the defendant has received *more* than she deserves.

I will also argue that this conclusion suggests that abolitionists should alter their strategy. Rarely do defendants claim that they have received a greater penalty than the law establishes for their crime, and since the Court seems steadfast in its belief that retributive executions do not violate constitutional protections against cruel and unusual punishment, the goal must be to convince state legislators that a civilized society cannot tolerate the state-sanctioned killing of its citizens.

Discrimination and the Death Penalty

Any number of studies have shown that discrimination based on race has permeated U.S. capital trial procedures throughout this century.[1] But it is sometimes argued that this bias *no longer* exists, that it is an unfortunate part of our past but not of our present, that rulings like *Furman* and *Gregg* have designed processes that effectively eliminate the kinds of discretion through which discrimination is expressed. Both the facts presented in *McCleskey* and the Court's reaction to them prove otherwise.

Relying upon the Baldus Study, which surveyed sentencing procedures in Georgia (Baldus et al. 1983), McCleskey's attorneys showed that racial bias still plays a powerful role in determinations of who is sentenced to death. The study provides conclusive evidence that black defendants, especially when the victim is white, continue to stand a much greater chance of receiving the death sentence than would whites convicted of similar crimes.

The Case

Warren McCleskey, a black man, was convicted in 1978 on two counts of armed robbery and one count of murder. According to evidence presented at the trial court, he and three accomplices robbed a furniture store at gunpoint. During the robbery a white police officer, entering the store in response to a silent alarm, was struck by two bullets. One of these bullets was traced to the revolver McCleskey was said to be carrying. Two witnesses also testified that McCleskey admitted to the shooting.

McCleskey was convicted of murder, and during the penalty phase, the jury deemed that the crime satisfied Georgia's criteria for aggravating circumstances. (Two aggravating circumstances were found—murder committed during the course of an armed robbery and murder committed upon a peace officer engaged in the performance of his duties.) After exhausting all appeals at the state level, McCleskey turned to the Federal Courts, basing his case on Fourteenth Amendment, Equal Protection, considerations.

It is important that at this stage of the appeals process McCleskey no longer claimed innocence; he appealed only for a reduction of his death sentence to one of life imprisonment without possibility of parole. That is, McCleskey did not claim he did not deserve to be punished, only that it was unfair that he be given death as punishment. Further, McCleskey did not challenge Georgia's criteria of "aggravating circumstances." These were accepted as valid, and thus so was the principle that, *in a system that treated all defendants equally*, any who satisfied the criteria deserved to die.

McCleskey's challenge, of course. was that the system did *not* treat all defendants equally—that the criteria were being applied in a racially biased manner. He argued that had he been white, and/or especially had his victim been black, the chances of his receiving the death penalty would have been significantly reduced. Summarizing the major conclusion of the Baldus Study (and the cornerstone of McCleskey's defense), Anthony Amsterdam, one of McCleskey's attorneys in the Supreme Court appeal, points out that "death sentences were being imposed in Georgia murder cases in a clear, consistent pattern that reflected the race of the victim and the race of the defendant and could not be explained by any non-racial factor" (Amsterdam 1988, 84). This represented a clear violation of the Equal Protection Clause, McCleskey advanced, thereby invalidating the assessment of the death penalty in his case.

The Baldus Study

Baldus and his colleagues analyzed 2,484 Georgia homicide cases between 1973 and 1979. Through a sophisticated process of multiple-regression analyses, they were able to factor out all considerations other than race. The study, "uniformly praised by social scientists as the best study of any aspect of criminal sentencing ever conducted" (Amsterdam 1988, 84), concludes that black defendants, regardless of the color of the victim, are 1.1 times as likely to receive a sentence of death. Furthermore, when the victim is white, defendants are 4.3 times as likely to receive death. When these statistics are combined, a clear case emerges that blacks convicted of killing whites stand the greatest chance of being sentenced to death (Baldus 1983, 708–10).[2]

Although the study was criticized at the District level, both the Appeals Court and the Supreme Court assumed its validity. However, the Supreme Court ruled 5–4 that the study did not provide sufficient evidence that Georgia sentencing procedures represented a violation of either the Eighth or Fourteenth Amendments. McCleskey's appeal was therefore denied.[3]

A close look at the reasoning behind the denial, however, reveals that the Court maintains a disturbingly superficial and antiquated understanding of the complex nature of racial bias.[4]

Racial Bias as "Malicious Intent"

In rejecting McCleskey's appeal to Equal Protection, the Court argued: "For this claim to prevail, McCleskey would have to prove that the Georgia Legislature enacted or maintained the death penalty statute *because of* an anticipated racially discriminatory effect . . . not merely in spite of its adverse effects upon an identifiable group" (107 S.Ct. 1756, 1987, 1761). In other words, if a person does not *consciously intend* malicious racial bias, the Court ruled, it is not a violation of constitutional protections; it is not enough that actions taken serve merely to perpetuate racial prejudice.

But of course most racial prejudice is unintended. If prejudice were always, or even commonly, intentionally malicious, it would be much easier to devise methods to counter it. It is the *underlying* mentality that proves most insidious. Whether Georgia jurors or legislators *want* blacks to be harmed is irrelevant. Similarly, whether they are even *aware* that racial bias is present in their system is also irrelevant. The fact is that blacks in Georgia do suffer from the effects of racial bias.

The Supreme Court must no doubt balance its disapproval of this bias with its other legal and social obligations, e.g., the maintenance of an effective criminal justice system made possible, in great part, by a process of discretionary punishment:

> Petitioner's claim, taken to its logical conclusion, throws into serious question the principles that underlie the entire criminal justice system. His claim easily could be extended to apply to other types of penalties and to claims based on unexplained discrepancies correlating to membership in other minority groups and even gender (107 S.Ct, 1756. 1987, 1761).

Discretion *is* a crucial component of our system of criminal justice. However, preserving discretion and criticizing racial bias need not be mutually exclusive. Indeed, *McCleskey* provided an ideal opportunity for the Court to condemn such bias; it could have rejected the appeal on constitutional grounds (the lack of evidence of malicious intent directed against McCleskey personally), while also voicing disdain for the type of prejudice that brought the case before it. The Court did not do this; indeed, it did not even seem to understand fully the manner in which prejudice works.

Noting this lack of understanding on the Court's part, however, does not provide grounds for accepting McCleskey's appeal. The just response to prejudice in criminal proceedings, ironically, is stated by Amsterdam: "There can be no justice in a system which treats people of color differently from white people, or treats crimes against people of color differently from crimes against white people" (Amsterdam 1988, 86). When this clearly correct principle of justice is combined with an acceptance of retribution as a sound basis for punishment, then the appropriate response would not be to reduce the penalties of blacks (or killers of whites), but to guarantee that *all* those who deserve capital punishment receive it.[5]

Discrimination and Desert

Recall Amsterdam's words, quoted earlier: "Death sentences were being imposed in Georgia murder cases in a clear, consistent pattern that reflected the race of the victim and the race of the defendant and could not be explained by any non-racial factor." Amsterdam is correct, but in a misleading way.

The *pattern* of sentencing reflected racial bias and could not be explained by any non-racial factor. But of course there was also a non-racial factor present in the case—McCleskey was found guilty of first-degree murder. Further, it was determined that his crime satisfied the criteria for "aggravating circumstances" under Georgia law. Given an acceptance of these criteria as valid, the only just response of the Court was to uphold McCleskey's sentence. Remember, McCleskey was not claiming that he did not deserve punishment, only that he was being treated in an unequal fashion. Given this, Amsterdam in essence sentences his client to death when he grants to the state "powers of imprisonment and death" in order to help accomplish the "vital work" of controlling crime (Amsterdam 1988, 86).[6] Once it is accepted that persons sometimes deserve to die, that valid criteria can be formulated to determine when persons' actions warrant their deaths at the hands of the state, then evidence of racial bias in the judicial process is in important ways irrelevant.

Receiving One's Just Reward

Take another, hypothetical, example. The state of Georgia has developed certain criteria for qualifying for retirement benefits. Wilson, a black man, has fulfilled all those criteria and upon turning 65, appeals to the state retirement board for his benefits. After careful evaluation (including judicial review) the board deems that Wilson has indeed satisfied the criteria and judges him deserving of full benefits.

Smith, a white man, also applies for benefits upon turning 65. By purely objective standards, he too satisfies the criteria. These criteria are plainly set forth and clear, but of course as with any system of evaluation, they allow for some discretionary judgment. And it turns out that in Smith's case there are a few areas where the facts are somewhat obscure and thus the board's discretion becomes crucial.

Unfortunately for Smith, most members of the board and of the judicial review team harbor prejudice against whites. They are not, on the whole, aware of these biases and they hold nothing against Smith personally. Rather, it is simply part of their cultural approach to, and understanding of, the world. Thus on those matters where discretion plays the key role, Smith ends up suffering the brunt of this systematic prejudice, though, again, none of the jurists is prejudiced against Smith per se. As a result, the board determines that he does not deserve full benefits.

Now it would be most odd if at this point Wilson appealed the decision in his case, claiming that he received his benefits only because race (and no other factor) played a decisive role. On the contrary, he received his benefits because he *deserved* them, based upon the criteria established by the Georgia legislature.

Similarly, were Smith to appeal and win, no one would argue that in order to redress the inequity, Wilson's rightful benefits should be withdrawn. Wilson's benefits are his due, just as are Smith's. The only morally sound way of reversing the effects of the discrimination would be to intervene so as to make sure that *both* receive their just rewards.

The analogy to McCleskey's case should be apparent. As per the criteria established by the Georgia legislature and implicitly approved by both the Georgia citizenry and the U.S. Supreme Court (through *Furman* and *Gregg*), McCleskey deserves to die for his actions. It is his just reward, his due. It may also be the just reward of others (murderous whites and killers of blacks), but they have been "cheated out" of their due by a system which includes racial bias. But then it is *they* who have a claim of discrimination, not McCleskey.

Nor is it relevant that in McCleskey's case, as opposed to the one in the fictional example, the "just reward" is undesirable. If the reward is something the recipient truly deserves, it is immaterial whether that reward is good or bad.

Thus the correct response would not be to overturn McCleskey's penalty, but rather to attempt to make certain that murderous whites and killers of blacks *also* are sentenced to death. McCleskey was not discriminated against; he got what he "deserved." It was those who did not receive their due (white murderers and killers of blacks) who have grounds for complaint under Equal Protection. In fact, the Court broadly hinted at this when it said, "petitioner cannot prove a constitutional violation by demonstrating that other defendants who may be similarly situated did *not* receive the death penalty" (107 S.Ct. 1756, 1987, 1761).

It needs to be stressed at this point that these arguments are not intended as a toleration of racial bias. Amsterdam is absolutely correct in his criticism of the Supreme Court's countenancing of Georgia's discriminatory practices and in his general indictment of criminal justice in the United States.

However, the arguments do show that evidence of racial bias alone cannot warrant reducing a justly deserved sentence of death. For such a sentence reduction to be justified on grounds of discrimination, the defendant would have to demonstrate that the discrimination resulted in her receiving *more* than what was deserved. That is, it would have to be shown that either the criteria for determining death over life imprisonment (i.e., the state's list of aggravating circumstances) or the judgment of guilt reflected racial bias. Georgia's criteria clearly are racially neutral and McCleskey did not challenge the determination of guilt. Thus although he may well have been the victim of racial prejudice, according to these arguments McCleskey was not the victim of discrimination.[7] Hence the Supreme Court was correct in denying his appeal on those grounds. As per the defense's tacit admission, he was guilty and deserved to be punished, regardless of whether a similarly situated white defendant would be punished in the same manner. According to Georgia's legal criteria, again tacitly accepted by the defense, the punishment McCleskey deserved was death.

Opposing Capital Punishment

This conclusion—given an acceptance of Georgia's criteria for special circumstances, McCleskey deserved to die—should serve to motivate a change in strategy on the part of abolitionists. For it rests upon a premise that abolitionists in recent years seem, mistakenly, to have granted—i.e., that execution is a morally defensible form of punishment. Opponents of capital punishment appear to have conceded this issue and have extended little effort to convince state legislatures to abolish the penalty. Instead, they have directed their attention to the judiciary, attempting, as in *McCleskey*, to halt executions in those states where there was a proven pattern of arbitrary application. Although this strategy proved temporarily successful in *Furman*, it is in the long run misguided.[8]

It is misguided because first, it mistakenly assumes that if not all those who deserve death receive it, none should; second, it can produce only limited success (in only those states where the pattern has been proved and only until the pattern has been eliminated); and third, it grants a false assumption—that executions are morally justified. It is time to take this last concern back to the public, to convince them and their state representatives that a civilized society cannot tolerate the state-sanctioned killing of its citizens.

Strategy here should include at least the following: Reminding the public that the intentional killing of another person is *prima facie* wrong[9]; providing the public with information about other less repugnant (and less expensive[10]) ways of removing violent individuals from society; informing the public that capital punishment likely does not serve as a deterrent[11]; and convincing them that retribution is not a sound moral principle.

Clearly the last task will be the most difficult. Polls consistently reveal strong public support for the death penalty and for the "eye for an eye" sense of justice upon which it rests. However, the Supreme Court last year may have provided abolitionists with their most effective weapon when it upheld the death sentence in cases where the defendant is a minor or mentally retarded. This ruling has upset even moderates on this issue,[12] and will likely produce serious questioning of what retribution entails and whether it can be morally justified. In fact, this reaction seems to be a confirmation of Hugo Adam Bedau's prediction—that carrying retribution to its logical conclusion (all who kill, regardless of race, income, or intelligence, will in turn be killed), will result in a socially intolerable bloodbath (Bedau 1980, 178). Abolitionists would do well to respond to this reaction, the first sign in years that the U.S. population has hesitations about retribution. It may provide just the opening needed for the beginnings of a nation-wide change in sentiment.[13]

Notes

1. See, for example, Johnson 1941, and Wolfgang and Reidel 1973.

2. As this paper was being prepared, the General Accounting Office released a "letter report" confirming at least part of the Baldus Study on a nation-wide scale. Summarizing 28 different studies on capital sentencing procedures, the report concludes that "those who murdered whites were found to be more likely to be sentenced to death than those who murdered blacks. This finding was remarkably consistent across data sets, states, data collection methods, and analytic techniques" (GAO 1990, 5). However, the report reaches no final judgment on how the race of the defendant influences the process: "The evidence for the influence of the race of defendant on death penalty outcomes was equivocal. Although more than half of the studies found that race of defendant influenced the likelihood of being charged with a capital crime or receiving the death penalty, the relationship between race of defendant and outcome varied across studies" (GAO 1990, 6).

3. Following this denial, McCleskey's case took a somewhat bizarre twist. According to Patsy Morris of the Georgia Resource Center, McCleskey received a stay of conviction in late 1987 when it was discovered that the state had placed a "snitch" in the cell next to him in order to obtain incriminating information. Georgia is currently appealing this stay (personal communication, July 1989).

4. Amsterdam addresses other problems with the ruling (Amsterdam 1988, 84–85), but, for reasons that should become apparent in what follows, this is the most telling.

5. Ernest van den Haag makes a similar argument (van den Haag 1982), and later defends the position against rebuttal (van den Haag 1983). However, he uses the argument as part of a general defense of capital punishment. My claim is merely that evidence of unequal application of the penalty does not provide sufficient justification for abolishing it.

6. This point would seem inconsistent with some of Amsterdam's earlier writing in which he generally rejects the death penalty. (See, for example, his "Capital Punishment" [Amsterdam 1977]). At best, the current willingness to grant such powers to the state represents a change in philosophical position; at worst it provides further evidence of the overreliance on procedural concerns at the expense of a direct moral challenge to state-sanctioned execution.

7. Stephen Nathanson argues that the very nature of "guided discretion" will produce discriminatory applications of the penalty. He worries that in a discretionary process, even racially neutral criteria cannot be translated into just laws that effectively distinguish those deserving of death from those who are not (Nathanson 1985, 153–54). However, if objective criteria are applied in a manner that protects against the mistaken conviction of innocents, they will assuredly pick out at least some of those who, on this standard, deserve to die. And thus although some will receive less than they deserve, no one will receive more. In a more recent work, Nathanson continues to defend the concept of retribution, but argues that it is impossible to determine when someone deserves *to die*. That is, he now seems to reject the possibility of establishing a coherent set of criteria that determine what kinds of criminal behavior should result in the defendant's execution (Nathanson 1987, 69–95).

8. David Dolinko reaches a similar conclusion in his "Foreword: How to Criticize the Death Penalty" (Dolinko 1986).

9. The burden of proof has somehow been reversed in the death penalty debate. Rather than having to provide justified grounds for intentionally killing, abolitionists find themselves having to argue why convicted murderers should *not* be killed.

10. Current statistics for New York reveal that it costs approximately $602,000 to imprison someone for forty years but approximately $1.8 million to carry out an execution. Figures vary for other states and even within states, but the three to one ratio is fairly standard (Leigh Dingerson, National Coalition Against the Death Penalty, personal communication, July 1989).

11. Archer et al. (1983) and Forst (1983) are among the many researchers to reach this conclusion. In a more recent study, Bailey and Peterson determine that an increase of one *highly publicized* execution per month would result in one and one-half one-hundredths of a person decline in the murder rate. That is, it would require an increase of sixty highly publicized executions per month to reduce the murder rate by one person, a reduction surely not justified by the moral costs (probability of error, effect upon the moral tone of the community, etc.) (Bailey and Peterson 1989, 739).

12. For example, the Rev. Thom White Wolf Fassett, head of the United Methodist Board of Church and Society, called the ruling "an outrage . . . reprehensible to·people of faith." The American Jewish Committee "is appalled" by the ruling, noting that the execution of the young and the retarded makes a "mockery of justice" (Cornell 1989).

13. Support for this project was provided by the Kegley Institute of Ethics, California State University, Bakersfield. I also wish to thank Bruce Jones, Gary Kessler, Jacquelyn Kegley, Robert Rafalko, and Tamara Taylor for their help in revising the paper.

Works Cited

AMSTERDAM, ANTHONY, "The Death Penalty." *Stanford Magazine*, Vol. 5 (1977): 42–47.

———. "Race and the Death Penalty." *Criminal Justice Ethics*, Vol. 7 (1988): 2, 84–86.

ARCHER, DANE, et al. "Homicide and the Death Penalty: A Cross-National Test of a Deterrence Hypothesis." *Journal of Criminal Law and Criminology*, Vol. 74 (1983): 991–1032.

BAILEY, WILLIAM C., and RUTH D. PETERSON. "Murder and Capital Punishment: A Monthly Time-Series Analysis of Execution Publicity." *American Sociological Review*, Vol. 54 (1989): 722–43.

BALDUS, DAVID C., CHARLES PULASKI, and GEORGE WOODWORTH. "Comparative Review of Death Sentences: An Empirical Study of the Georgia Experience." *Journal of Criminal Law and Criminology*, Vol. 74 (1983): 661–753.

BEDAU, HUGO ADAM. "Capital Punishment." In Tom Regan, ed., *Matters of Life and Death: New Introductory Essays in Moral Philosophy*. New York: Random House, 1980, 148–82.

CORNELL, GEORGE. "Religion Today." *The Bakersfield Californian*, July 15, 1989, D-5.

DINGERSON, LEIGH, National Coalition Against the Death Penalty, personal communication, July 1989.

DOLINKO, DAVID. "Foreword: How to Criticize the Death Penalty." *Journal of Criminal Law and Criminology*, Vol. 77 (1986): 546–601.

FORST, BRIAN. "Capital Punishment and Deterrence: Conflicting Evidence?" *Journal of Criminal Law and Criminology*, Vol. 74 (1983): 927–42.

GENERAL ACCOUNTING OFFICE. "Death Penalty Sentencing: Research Indicates Pattern of Racial Disparities." GAO/GGD-90-57, February 1990.

JOHNSON, GUY B. "The Negro and Crime." *The Annals of the American Academy of Political and Social Science*, Vol. 217 (1941): 93–104.

MORRIS, PATSY, Georgia Resource Center, personal communication, July 1989.

NATHANSON, STEPHEN, "Does It Matter if the Death Penalty Is Arbitrarily Administered?" *Philosophy and Public Affairs*, Vol. 14 (1985): 149–64.

———. *An Eye for an Eye*. Totowa, New Jersey: Rowman and Littlefield, 1987, 69–95.

JUSTICE POWELL, majority opinion, "McCleskey v. Kemp," 107 S.Ct. 1756 (1987): 1756–1806.

VAN DEN HAAG, ERNEST. "In Defense of the Death Penalty: A Practical and Moral Analysis." In Bedau, Hugo Adam, ed., *The Death Penalty in America*. New York: Oxford University Press, 1982, 323–33.

———. "Refuting Reiman and Nathanson." *Philosophy and Public Affairs*, Vol. 14 (1983): 165–76.

WOLFGANG, MARVIN E., and MARC REIDEL. "Race, Judicial Discretion and the Death Penalty." *The Annals of the American Academy of Political and Social Science*, Vol. 407 (1973): 119–33.

After reading: CONSOLIDATE INFORMATION

1. How does Meyers demonstrate the perspective of a philosopher in this discussion of the concept of *desert*?
2. At one point Meyers cites Anthony Amsterdam and suggests that Amsterdam has changed his position since 1977. What evidence does Meyers use to support that suggestion?
3. Summarize the position Meyers believes that those opposing the death penalty should take.

An Exercise in Feminist Liberation Theology: Islam, Judaism, and Christianity

Tracy Marschall

Tracy Marschall, a English major with a minor in Philosophy and Religion at the University of Indianapolis, wrote the following paper in a World Religions course.

TRACY MARSCHALL / *An Exercise in Feminist Liberation Theology*

Before reading: FIRST THOUGHTS
                       LOOK AHEAD

1. What do you think the phrase *feminist liberation theology* means?
2. Choose the religious denomination to which you belong or one you know something about and write a short freewrite on the attitudes you think that religion has toward women.

During reading: REACT
                      QUESTION
                      SUMMARIZE

1. How do you react to Marschall's introduction?
2. What stance does Marschall take toward the three religions she examines?

THE LITERATURE OF A RELIGION is very important in that it generally not only records history, but that it also provides insight, defines boundaries, and proscribes behaviors. That it is oft considered divinely inspired lends credence to its authority and a responsibility to those who attempt to proclaim and interpret it. This responsibility demands a sincere commitment on the part of the interpreter to remain as true to the spirit of the Scripture as possible, taking into consideration the limitations of the interpreter's natural bias. An interpreter's bias can develop out of attitudes rooted in social, cultural, and national differences, to name a few, as well as attitudes related to personal experience and factors intrinsic to the "normative" climate that surrounds him or her. For example, the foundations of three major religions: Islam, Judaism, and Christianity, were laid within a society where patriarchal authority was the normative climate. It is only natural that the interpretation of prophesy and extant literature would reflect this important aspect of culture. The problem develops, however, when this interpretation is used to legitimize the subordination of women in present-day society where the factors that made a patriarchal society appear necessary are no longer present. The ideal solution would be to appeal to the ultimate authority, the Divinity, for an explanation; however, considering the difficulty in obtaining any rationale, especially a controversial one, that is accepted by all members of the faith community as truth, our most favorable alternative would be to examine the literature of the community of believers.

The most basic problem that must be considered when studying a religion is the difference between what can be termed the "real" and the "ideal." The "ideal" can be defined as the way the founder, either human or divine, sets up the system of belief and how he or she expects it to be executed. The "real" consists of the actual or practical way the belief system is internalized and applied. There seem to be two occasions where the gap between the two can occur. The first exists in the transmission between the Divinity and the prophet or oracle. For example, the Divinity could have intended for men and women to exist as equals, but because of the prophet's natural bias, namely that women in authority or even in a position of equality was an unfamiliar concept, this intent was never recorded in Scripture or relayed to the populace by the prophets. The second opportunity for digression from the ideal can occur between the recording of the revelation and the practical application. For example, the Scripture may suggest that men and women should exist on an equal plane, but because of cultural conditions, a subordinate role is emphasized and rationalized. Clearly, very little can be done to establish how far off a prophet's perspective of the revelation is in comparison to the intent of the Divine. We can, however, examine the scripture in light of its historical and cultural conditions for the existence of a bias that predisposes the literature to discriminate against a group of people. The purpose of this paper is to justify the use of a feminist theological interpretation of Scripture in the Islamic, Judaic, and Christian traditions to expose the practice of using Scripture to reinforce the submission of women to a patriarchal authority.

As Elisabeth Schussler-Fiorenza states in her book *Bread Not Stone*, "a feminist critical theology of liberation . . . seeks to evaluate *all* biblical texts, interpretations, and the contemporary uses of the Bible [and other Scripture] for their contribution to the religious legitimization of patriarchy as well as for their stand toward patriarchal oppression" (Fiorenza xvi). She continues by explaining that this patriarchal expression is not identical with androcentrism or sexism, but instead is a *"sociopolitical and social structure of graded subjugations and oppressions"* [emphasis mine] (Fiorenza 5). This structure, which is often viewed as a "hierarchal system of male dominance," is the primary obstacle when we consider Biblical texts, and the reason why "a feminist theology of liberation must remain first and foremost a critical theology of liberation as long as women suffer the injustice and oppression" (Fiorenza 6). Our necessary starting point is with a "hermeneutic of suspicion" which takes the assumption that "[Scriptures] and their interpretations are androcentric and serve patriarchal functions" (Fiorenza 15). The task of the interpreter, then, is to identify the bias and its effects on any meaning which is to be extracted. In the following sections we shall examine specific Scripture from the three traditions and their relationship to the legitimization of patriarchal oppression.

According to Darlene May, "the traditional Islamic view of woman is . . . rooted in the two basic sources of Islamic theology: the Quran, which Muslims hold to be the Word of God exactly as it was revealed to the Prophet Muhammed; and the Sunnah, the collection of Hadiths, or inspired sayings uttered by the Prophet, as well as the actions performed by him" (May 371). The Hadith tells us that both man and woman are essential for life and that both stand equally before God. According to the creation account in the Quran, both Adam and Eve were held accountable for their actions against God equally. Womankind was not singled out and made to suffer unnecessarily with the reproductive processes because of her participation in the disobedience; rather, her discomfort was merely a natural biological phenomenon experienced by all mammals created by God (May 372). Ruthven adds that the "act of disobedience [eating the forbidden fruit] is . . . not dwelt upon." There is no "strong sense of disgrace" as in the biblical version. The fruit is "an allegory of the limits which the Creator has set to mankind's [sic] desire and actions" (Ruthven 125). The Quran also tells us that man and woman alike were created by God as full and equal partners in the process of procreation (Quran IV:1). According to the Quran's record of revelation, the ideal, it appears that women were meant to enjoy the status of equality with men. As we consider the effects of the Quran on its believers, we can see that the Quran did improve the status immensely, but the most basic is "the fact that the woman was given a full-fledged personality" (Rahman 35). According to Scripture, "the spouses are declared to be each other's 'garments': the woman has been granted the same rights over man as man has over his wife, except that man, being the earning partner, is a degree higher" (Rahman 35). Taking into consideration the social conditions of the time, this is not entirely offensive. Now, however, that women are quite capable of being and often are earning partners as well, it could be argued that the corollary attached to the basic premise of equality should be dropped. In fact, the early Muslim modernists took up this challenge and "argued for the 'equality' of the sexes on Islamic grounds [and] advocated and effected the education of women" (Rahman 285). This movement was followed by a conservative trend. While the modernists assert "an absolute parity of the sexes on the basis of the Quran" appealing to the above-mentioned verse according to which "women possess rights over against men just as men possess rights over against women," conservatives accused the modernists of "ignoring the subsequent words of the Quran: but men are a degree higher (II,29)" (Rahman 286). I would argue that these conservatives have also erred. If we must not overlook the stipulation that men are higher than women, we must also not overlook the reasoning behind it. If the reasoning is no longer valid or pertinent, then neither is the stipulation. The conflict is that the convenience of the patriarchal society seems to be considered inherently more valuable than the intrinsic value of a woman's right to equal status and her potential contribution to the community of faith. And, once again, "divine writ" [and its interpreters] appears to insist that women's subordinate economic status is an unalterable fact of existence, rather than the result of time-bound circumstance (Ruthven 166).

During the time of the Prophet, several changes took place within the Islamic patriarchal system that improved the woman's position. One such change includes the payment of the *mahr*, or "bride-price" to the bride herself instead of to her father. The *mahr* generally consisted of "a sum of money or goods" and was awarded then to the wife in the event that her husband should divorce her. In this way, women were assured economic rights as individuals (Ruthven 164). In addition to Quranic legislation, during Mohammed's time women were also allowed to pray alongside men and, as far we know, they took an active part in the affairs of the community. An interesting bit of oral tradition tells us that a woman of the first Islamic community asked the Prophet why Allah only addressed men. Realizing the justice of her complaint, God from then on addressed the faithful of both sexes within revelation (Ruthven 165). Thus, Allah, through Mohammed, the Prophet, made provisions for women and did not desire for one half of the human race to be at the mercy of the other half. The Quran tells us that Allah "created from you mates from yourselves that ye might find rest in them, and he ordained between you love and mercy" (XXX:21).

Most interpretations of the Quran emphasize that man and woman can enjoy the same status and perform the same functions. However, they also stipulate that this is possible only in situations where one's sexual characteristics do not affect one's status and function (May 373). For example, the Quran also says "men are in charge of women, because God has made the one of them to excel the other, and because they spend of their property (for the support of women). So good women are obedient..." (IV:34). How can one explain this conclusion in light of the preceding conclusion? Some attempt to utilize the same argument as do many evangelical Christians, that this does not imply that the wife is inferior, just that the man has been entrusted with some responsibilities and rights that "do not pertain to women" and vice versa (May 374). The argument states that because man has more responsibilities in certain areas of life, he should be awarded additional authority over family matters. Woman, on the other hand, has supposedly been exempted from certain obligations in order to compensate for her having to submit to man's authority. This is said to develop a "complimentary and reciprocal" relationship (May 374). From the perspective of the feminist theologian, this is clearly unacceptable. A parasitic relationship is not what God had in mind if humans were created equal. Reciprocity is not equality. There are very few things that women are incapable of accomplishing. Of these, the majority are related to physical limitations. In no way are they credible evidence of woman's inferiority to man. Thus, there is no reason why responsibilities should be delegated according to some criteria that supposedly judges one partner to be more suitable for specific functions according to his or her gender. This is merely an attempt to rationalize away the cycle of patriarchal oppression. This clearly illustrates the distinct differences between the "real" and the "ideal." Ruthven concludes by asserting: "outside matters of ritual, the area in which the Shari'a ["the path to a waterhole"; a name given to the sacred law of Islam which governs all aspects of a Muslim's life] has been most consistently applied has been in marriage and family law. Here again, however, the Quranic Spirit gradually succumbed to the suffocating and restrictive practices sanctioned by the *fiqu* ["understanding"; the system of jurisprudence based on the Quran, the sunnah (custom sanctioned by tradition), and analogical deduction]. The centuries following the coming of Islam saw a progressive deterioration in the status and education of Muslim women" (Ruthven 164).

Perhaps the most telling Scriptures concerning women in the Judaic faith are the creation accounts and their surrounding tradition. In Genesis 1, man and woman are created equal. In Genesis 2, woman is created out of man's rib. These seemingly contradictory elements led to the development of the Lilith myth. Lilith was said to be Adam's first wife, created by God out of the earth as was Adam. Because they were both of the same origin, she considered herself to be his equal and refused to obey him. They quarreled and she flew away from him and vanished into thin air (Priesand 3).

The account above indicates several attitudes toward the equality of women. Lilith was punished for her independence. "Her desire was to be Adam's equal, but this did not coincide with the scheme of things" (Priesand 4). It was Eve, over whom God commanded Adam to rule [according to Scripture] who would find a place in official Jewish history. The Lilith myth serves two important purposes: it tells us something about the society in which it was written, and it sets standards of behavior (Priesand 5). Women are taught to be submissive like Eve. Women are expected to avoid the characteristics of Lilith: independence, aggression, self-assertion, and strength. They are expected to live vicariously through their husbands, abandoning their own desires in favor of obedience. Furthermore, the character Eve as a prototype is somewhat less than desirable as well. Eve has been traditionally associated with evil because she is believed to be the first to surrender to temptation and violate God's law. According to Nehama Aschkenasy, "Her story is thus seen as a parable of the moral weakness and the strong proclivity for evil that characterize the female of the human species" (Aschkenasy 39).

Another example of the early Judaic tradition that starkly illustrates the psychology that contributes to the discrimination of women can be found in the early Mishnaic period. A widely known rabbinic saying called the "three-fold daily prayer" can still be found in many Jewish prayer books. It reads like this: "Praised be God that he has not created me a gentile! Praised be God that he has not created me a woman! Praised be God that he has not created me an ignoramus!" Subsequent lines include "justification" for each line. Supposedly the believer is to thank God that he has not been created a woman because "she is not obliged to fulfill the commandments" (Swidler 80).

It is understandable that a patriarchal society would breed a community of believers with a similar perspective. Unfortunately, this belief, that women are somehow inferior on theological as well as physical grounds, persists. According to Blu Greenberg, "What was a sociological truth about women in all previous generations—that they were the 'second sex'—was codified in many minute ways into Halakhah [the body of Jewish religious law] as religioethical concepts, binding upon future generations as well" (Greenberg 5).

In the New Testament, the foundation of the Christian tradition, one can see the attitude towards women in one passage, Ephesians 5:22–33. This passage deals with the husband-wife relationship in one of the several household codes to be found in the New Testament. The central theme of this passage is the christological justification of patriarchal authority. Women are instructed to submit to their husbands "in everything" in order to follow the example of the church submitting to its head, Christ. Husbands are not instructed to submit to their wives in this passage, and it is clear that this was not an oversight on the part of the author. While some of the other passages do contain that phrase, the theme and its illustrations prohibit such reasoning here. The relationship between Christ and the church is clearly not a relationship between equals since "the church-bride is totally dependent and subject to her head, or bridegroom" (Fiorenza 1983 267ff.). As the church is subordinated to Christ, the wife is expected to subject herself to her husband. Verse 5:22 insists that the submission of the wife is a natural demand of her on the basis of "her religious submission to Christ, the Lord" (Fiorenza 1983 267). This command clearly reinforces the custom of patriarchal authority in marriage and justifies it christologically. As Fiorenza summarizes, "the relationship of wife and husband in patriarchal marriage combines the traditional household code form with the church-body theology and the Pauline bride-bridegroom notion found in 2 Corinthians 11:3. The relationship between Christ and the church expressed in the metaphors of head and body, as well as of bridegroom and bride, becomes the paradigm for Christian marriage and vice versa" (Fiorenza 1983 268).

In v. 25 we see Christ's holy love for the church held up as an example to men as the way they ought to love their wives, sacrificing for her benefit. It is here that the passage seems to take an unusual twist. The idea of patriarchal domination is questioned. This self-sacrificing attitude does not seem to reinforce the idea of absolute, unquestionable patriarchal authority. The next section, however reverts back to a male-dominant perspective as men are instructed to treat women as they would their own bodies and take care of them with that in mind. It is because of this androcentric filter that men must be instructed how to treat women in terms of themselves. It is not enough, apparently, to treat them appropriately because of their own value. As Fiorenza states: "patriarchy as a male pyramid of graded subordinations and exploitations specifies women's oppression in terms of the class, race, and country or religion of the men to whom we 'belong' " (Fiorenza xiv). Rosemary Reuther adds that "the androcentric bias of male interpreters of the tradition" reveals their belief that "maleness" is "normative" humanity (Reuther 113). Unfortunately, v. 25–29 do not have the power to unseat the patriarchal pattern of the household, even with its "christological modification of the husband's patriarchal position and duties" (Fiorenza 1983 270). Instead, Ephesians christologically cements the inferior position of the wife in the marriage relationship.

The next section alludes to the Genesis 2:24 passage with the stipulation that it is meant in the New Testament to define or describe Christ's relationship to the church, rather than the marriage relationship common to the Old Testament. This appears odd in that the passage appears to be focusing on the marital relationship. Why take a passage that is usually used to refer to the matter at hand and specify its meaning to be something else? Verse 32 seems to indicate that there is a possibility that the emphasis of the Ephesians passage is **not** the power structure of the marriage, but **rather** the unity of Christ and the church. If this is true, it could be that the marital relationships of the time were supposed to serve as an illustration of the relationship of Christ and the church. It could be further argued that these "instructions" are not commands to change behavior at all, but rather are a retelling of the accepted order **as it existed.** This would follow as the sociocultural condition of the time indicates the existence of patriarchal dominance. Aristotle insisted that the discussion of political ethics and household management begin with marriage defined as "the union of natural ruler and subject." The studies of the social world of early Christianity suggest that the patriarchal ethic of the household expresses the ethos of the early Christian mission (Fiorenza 73). This is one explanation that I believe might account for some of the confusion. However the passage is virtually impossible to separate from its tradition, and its context firmly anchors it in a patriarchal society. Therefore it must be interpreted as an illustration of oppression and an attempt to justify it. The passage is concluded with an injunction to the woman to fear or to respect her husband (v. 33) in the name of Christian service and duty. What the author forgets, however, is that Jesus' call to service in the gospels is targeted for those in power, not to those who are least (Fiorenza 90).

To summarize, we have established that Ephesians 5:21–33 is instrumental in re-establishing patriarchal dominance insofar as it takes over the household code pattern and "reasserts the submission of the wife to her husband as a religious Christian duty" (Fiorenza 1983 269). It modifies the patriarchal code by replacing patriarchal super-ordination and domination with the Christian command of love to be lived according to the example of Christ, but it is not successful in "christianizing" the code because the "cultural-social structures of domination are theologized and thereby reinforced" (Fiorenza 1983 270).

In conclusion, as I reflect upon the interpretation of the above passages, I am reassured of the validity and necessity of this approach. "All people are equally loved, judged and accepted by God. This belief has been promoted by the [Christian] church and has its roots in the Judeo-Christian tradition. [Similarly, Islam states "all people are equal, as equal as the teeth of a comb. There is no claim of merit of an Arab over a non-Arab, or of a white over a black, or of a male over a female. Only God-fearing people merit a preference with God" (May 372]. Young and old, **male** and **female,** and persons of every racial, cultural and national background are included in the faith community. Basic to a sense of equality and inclusiveness is the recognition that God by nature transcends all categories (*An Inclusive Language Lectionary* 5). This God spoken of here, as I see it, cannot conceivably support a hierarchy of power that exploits a vital half of humanity. Therefore as we all are "God's chosen people," our only option is to develop, assist, and utilize this feminist theology of liberation. There is no longer room for oppression, even in its most subtle form.

Works Cited

Aschkenasy, Nehama. *Eve's Journey: Feminine Images in Hebraic Literacy Tradition.* Philadelphia: Univ. of Penn Press, 1986.

Greenberg, Blu. *On Women and Judaism: a View from Tradition.* Philadelphia: The Jewish Publication Society of America, 1981.

Inclusive Language Lectionary: "Readings for the Year B", 1987.

May, Darlene. "Women in Islam: Yesterday and Today" Pullapilly, Cyriac K., ed. *Islam in the Contemporary World.* Notre Dame: CrossRoads Books, 1980.

Priesand, Rabbi Sally. *Judaism and the New Woman.* New York: Behrman House, Inc., 1975.

Rahman, Fazler. *Islam.* New York: Doubleday and Co., 1966.

Russell, Letty M. *Feminist Interpretation of the Bible.* Philadelphia: Westminster Press, 1985.

Russell, Letty M. *The Liberating Word: A Guide to Nonsexist Interpretation of the Bible.* Philadelphia: Westminster Press, 1976.

Ruthven, Malise. *Islam in the World.* New York: Oxford Univ. Press, 1984.

Schussler-Fiorenza, Elisabeth. *In Memory of Her.* New York: Crossroads, 1983.

Schussler-Fiorenza, Elisabeth. *Bread Not Stone.* Boston: Beacon Press, 1984.

Swidler, Leonard. *Women In Judaism: The Status of Women in Formative Judaism.* New York: Scarecrow Press, Inc., 1976.

After reading: CONSOLIDATE INFORMATION

1. Summarize Marschall's analysis of the role of women in Islam.
2. As she analyzes each religious system, what are Marschall's basic assumptions about women and their place in the social structure?
3. Evaluate Marschall's conclusion.

The Way We Make Ethical Decisions: Understanding the Subjectivity of Values
Brian Handrigan

Brian Handrigan, a student at Rhode Island College, wrote the following paper for a 200-level course in Philosophy. In his writing, he attempts to synthesize the ideas of four philosophers who wrote about moral values.

Before reading: FIRST THOUGHTS
                LOOK AHEAD

1. How do you think people develop a sense of right and wrong?
2. What do you think shapes our morality or our belief in what is right and wrong?
3. What do you think Brian Handrigan means in his subtitle "Understanding the Subjectivity of Values?"

During reading: REACT
                QUESTION
                SUMMARIZE

1. How does Handrigan define subjectivity of value?
2. What are the differences in the positions on ethical choice taken by Hume, Kierkegaard, Sartre, and Ayer?

How Do We Make Ethical Decisions? Are we born with *á priori* knowledge that influences us? Is it a matter of inscribed social instructions that create standards for living? Is it purely instinctual, thus devoid of reason, consisting of impulses of calm and violent passions that we are helpless to control; or are we left to make decisions based on our life experiences? While there is no clear answer to this confusion, examining the different analyses of philosophers such as Hume, Kierkegaard, Sartre, and Ayer can help us to understand where we stand.

The first thing to do is define what is meant by subjectivity of value. The subjectivity of value is the importance and influence that we place on any object, action or situation as it relates, in this essay, to ethical behavior. Many people say that "stealing is wrong," but how do we know that it is "wrong" to steal? If we can understand the criteria used for determining the "wrongness" in stealing, we will be able to understand the subjectivity of value for that particular set of circumstances. If something is subjective, it is concerned with individual responses to a situation or stimuli. In this essay, we will examine the responses of four philosophers to the issue of subjectivity of value.

To simplify things, we will use the same action, stealing, as our point of reference. The question that is raised is "How do we know that it is wrong to steal?" The four philosophers that have been chosen have different views on this matter which range from *á priori* knowledge to assumptions that right and wrong are only expressions of emotion. While we cannot agree with all of their opinions, they will make us think and even question our own beliefs and probably modify them.

David Hume does not believe that people make any decisions to act because of reason, but passion. There is no way that reason can cause a person to act. There has to be a powerful desire in order to provoke action, where reason's function is to inform an individual not to influence him. He suggests that individuals act in order to fill desires, and a passion can never be right or wrong. Instead, he says that either the means that the individual chooses to take to achieve the object of desire are flawed or the object is inadequate to fulfill the passion. The role of reason in Hume's realm is to clarify the individual's passion. He may believe that he desires X but after careful reasoning he realizes that what he really desires is Y. The individual still has his passion, but has modified the object of his desire to more accurately satisfy it.

Hume states that all passions are not the same, and distinguishes them as being either calm or violent. He says that violent passions are the strongest possible motivating forces, but they are also the most dangerous. He uses anger as an example of a violent passion, because the individual can become blinded to the consequences of obtaining the object of desire. Calm passions are said to be more sedate, and "though they be real passions, produce little emotion in the mind, . . . [and] are readily taken for determinations of reason" (Hume 171). Examples of these calm passions are aversion to evil, and a love of life. Hume says that some of these passions are developed during one's lifetime, but those used in making ethical decisions are originally implanted in us and therefore can be considered *á priori* emotions.

These calm passions regulate an individual's ethical behavior. Hume would say that it is wrong to steal because stealing is an evil act. Since all people are implanted with an aversion to evil, they would choose not to steal because it goes against their calm passion. Hume says that a man is not able to control his actions over his passions, but if a violent passion were to supersede the calm passion then the individual could make himself steal. Without the influence of the violent passion, the person would not be able to steal because any justification he had for stealing would be useless against aversion to evil, because reason never supersedes passion.

Hume presents a very clear argument, but I do not agree with him, while I do believe that there is *á priori* knowledge, I believe it affects the individual's intellectual reasoning abilities rather than his passions. Passions can be strong and influence people's behavior, but it is not the sole motivating force for a person. Hume's argument that reason only guides, never controls passion is interesting but flawed. A hungry man may have a strong desire to eat, and perhaps steal, but if he has a strong moral character he can rationalize why he should not steal and control that passion while considering his other possibilities. While I do not agree with the specifics of argument, I like the hierarchy of passions that he uses. I found his approach interesting, if not convincing.

Looking at the issue in a similar manner is Kierkegaard. His contention is that if an individual takes the time to think about the moral implications of an act he can do nothing but choose the right thing to do. This is similar to Hume's theory in that the individual does not think about his actions, but is motivated by passion thus releasing the individual from responsibility. The major difference between Hume and Kierkegaard is that Kierkegaard gives the individual the option to think about his situation; then he removes all but one possible choice. It is Kierkegaard's contention that if a man were to think about the moral implications of an action, he would never choose to do the wrong or evil action. In doing the wrong action, the man would understand that he would be eternally damned for his action. Considering all of this, Kierkegaard said that the man would never choose eternal damnation over a pleasant afterlife, thus he could never make a conscious decision to do wrong, a decision which would guarantee an after-life in Hell.

> I should like to say that in making a choice it is not so much a question of choosing the right as of the energy, the earnestness, the pathos with which one chooses.... Therefore, even if a man were to choose the wrong, he would discover, precisely by reason of the energy with which he chose, that he had chosen the wrong [and was responsible for that choice.] (Kierkegaard 225).

Taking this stance in relation to our example of stealing, the main factor in Kierkegaard's reasoning is whether or not the individual thought about his action before he did it. If he were to steal something suddenly, without thought, then there is no basis to examine the subjectivity of his decision. His action was more of an impulse or fruition of a passion, and therefore there is no cerebral component of his action. On the other hand, if the individual took the time to think about what he was going to do, then Kierkegaard would say that he could not choose to steal. In making that choice, the individual is able to also consider all of the consequences from his choice, including eternal damnation, and he believes that no rational being would consciously choose eternal hell and therefore if he thinks about choosing between right and wrong, he can only choose right.

Of all of the theories, this is the one that I would most like to see in existence. However, it is an impossibility. The idea of considering all possibilities when one is in the process of making an ethical decision is novel, but impractical. People cannot and will not take the necessary time to consider all possibilities when making an ethical decision. Sometimes it is not possible to think of all the possible effects, but one should not be damned forever because of this. As well, one cannot be excused of responsibility because they did not think at all about a decision. All people have to take responsibility for their actions, but all cases have different circumstances which Kierkegaard cannot account for in his theory. While it appears to be encompassing at first glance, the limitations that he puts on the individual once he chooses to think actually eliminates all choices but one. Kierkegaard's theory is self-destructing because it chooses for the individual rather than letting him decide for himself.

In opposition to Kierkegaard's contention that the individual only chooses to act on his own behalf, there is Jean-Paul Sartre's idea that men possess absolute freedom. Sartre's idea of freedom does not include the right to do whatever one wants to do whenever he wants to do it. Instead, it places absolute responsibility on the individual for not only his own actions, but the actions of all men. Sartre does not look at freedom as the pleasant thing people have, but rather as a thing which damns us with the responsibility of absolute freedom. With the right to do anything, there also comes the responsibility to use this power appropriately. A person must not only act in a way that he would like to act, but as an example of how he believes all men should act.

Considering the action of stealing in Sartre's world is rather an easy act. If a person said that they stole, but it was all right because not all men stole, there would be a problem for Sartre. He would argue that the fact that one man stole, was an example that was telling all men that it is proper to steal. Regardless of the circumstances, Sartre would argue that the act itself is wrong, and cannot be permitted. The individual who defended his action by saying that his stealing did not affect anyone else would be wrong because his actions influence not only his own likelihood of stealing again, but it may taint the dispositions of his victims and youngsters around him. This is important to consider because Sartre believes that man creates his own existence. "Before you come alive, life is nothing; it's up to you to give it a meaning, and value is nothing else but the meaning that you choose" (Sartre 396).

Sartre makes a noteworthy attempt to create an ideal world but falls short. All of his ideas would make the world a better place if they were in effect, but that is the impossibility. There is no way that an individual can be expected to act in the interest of all people when it is in his nature to act in his own best interest. If there were ever a conflict between the two, it can be assumed that at least half would act in their own best interest. Even with a modest figure of 50%, Sartre's theory fails any standard of widespread acceptability.

A.J. Ayer takes a position that is radically different than all of the philosophers that have been examined so far. Ayer is a Logical Positivist and believes that an assumption must be able to be proved scientifically if it is to be accepted as having validity. Unfortunately, he does not believe that moral distinctions can be proved. In that a person's opinion about the rightness and wrongness of the same action can change according to the circumstances illustrates the flaw. Therefore, no action can either be right or wrong, and labeling them as such is only equivalent to placing punctuation marks around them or an inflection of one's voice.

According to Ayer, saying that stealing is wrong only expresses an individual's emotional feeling towards that act, and does not make it right or wrong.

> [If I say] "Stealing money is wrong," I produce a sentence which has no factual meaning—that is, expresses no proposition which can either be true or false. It is as if I had written "Stealing money!!"—where the shape and thickness of the exclamation marks show, by a suitable convention, that a special sort of moral disapproval is the feeling which is being expressed. It is clear that there is nothing being said here which can be true or false (Ayer 377).

The purpose is to affect other people's emotional responses to the action enough to keep them from performing the action. Ayer states that it is impossible to make a judgement about an action because the criteria is so arbitrary that one cannot define any logical procedure for evaluation.

While there is a great emotional value within the realm of moral decisions, I do not believe that value judgements of right and wrong are totally arbitrary. Ayer eloquently bridges the gap between human emotions and reason, but he renders this distinction useless by his belief that value judgements are totally unrelated to fact. A person may perceive the action of stealing as right, but without proper substantiation they would be unable to prove their belief in the light of the facts that exist proving stealing to be dangerous and not right. As with Kierkegaard, Ayer's theory deconstructs itself under close examination. Ayer offers many interesting insights, but is unable to convince me of their absolute value.

All of these philosophers work to enlighten us to some of the many different options that exist for determining subjective values. While it is by no means an easy distinction to make, reading various educated views helps us to define and re-define our own ideas. Which answer is right? They all are; it is just a matter of the individual's perspective in relation to the question. Answering the question of finding subjective value is also a subjective one.

Works Cited

AYER, A. J. *Language, Truth and Logic*. ETHICS: *Selections from Classical and Contemporary Writers*. Ed. Oliver A. Johnson. Fort Worth: Holt, Rinehart and Winston, 1989. 372–381.

HUME, DAVID. *A Treatise of Human Nature*. ETHICS: *Selections from Classical and Contemporary Writers*. Ed. Oliver A. Johnson. Fort Worth: Holt, Rinehart and Winston, 1989. 167–182.

KIERKEGAARD, SØREN. *The Journals, Either/Or, and Fear and Trembling*. ETHICS: *Selections from Classical and Contemporary Writers*. Ed. Oliver A. Johnson. Fort Worth: Holt, Rinehart and Winston, 1989. 222–234.

SARTRE, JEAN-PAUL. *Existentialism* ETHICS: *Selections from Classical and Contemporary Writers*. Ed. Oliver A. Johnson. Fort Worth: Holt, Rinehart and Winston, 1989. 390–397.

After reading: CONSOLIDATE INFORMATION

1. Summarize Handrigan's analysis of Hume's ethical system.
2. How does Sartre's idea of absolute freedom place absolute responsibility on the individual?
3. How does Ayer differ from the other three philosophers discussed here?

Biblical Echoes in Margaret Atwood's *The Handmaid's Tale*
Lisa A. Jones

Lisa Jones noticed a pattern in biblical imagery that Margaret Atwood used to construct the atmosphere in her novel A Handmaid's Tale. *Lisa analyzed that imagery in the following essay which she wrote for a class on Literature by Women at the University of Indianapolis.*

Before reading: FIRST THOUGHTS
          LOOK AHEAD

1. Read Jones's first paragraph. What can you predict about her paper from her introduction?
2. Do you think that fiction writers consciously choose images to broaden the meaning of their stories?

During reading: REACT
          QUESTION
          SUMMARIZE

1. React to the title of Atwood's novel, *The Handmaid's Tale*.
2. Why do you think Jones is so disturbed by the use and misuse of examples from the Bible by those in power in the fictional Gilead? From what she writes, do you think that that effect (disturbance and discomfort) is justified?

MARGARET ATWOOD, in her *The Handmaid's Tale*, creates for the reader a society gone awry. Set somewhere in the twenty-first century, she shows us a society controlled by a handful of right-wing extremists who use biblical imagery and language to mask the reality of their regime. The narrator, Offred, is one of the victims of this male-dominated society and reveals to the reader the contradictions and the ironies lurking beneath the religious facade.

Offred, because of her "sins" against the Republic's "ideals" of marriage and family, chose to become a handmaid rather than clean up toxic waste in a place known as the Colonies. As unpleasant as sweeping up toxic waste sounds, the role of the handmaid is not much better we find as Offred describes her duties, status, regulations, and uniform. The handmaids are women from all walks of life who are guilty of such "sins" as adultery, divorce, lesbianism, abortion, etc. Even nuns are victimized because of their celibacy, which the governing powers insist they give up for the sake of the "common good" of boosting the population (p. 284). It is the handmaid's duty to provide to a childless Commander and his Wife a child sired by the Commander.

Also in a Commander's household are the Guardians and the Marthas. The Guardians of the Faith perform routine policing duties and various menial tasks such as heavy gardening jobs and basic car maintenance (p. 27). Their name and their presence suggest a guardian angel role. The Marthas are the female domestic help. "Martha" comes from an incident in Luke 10:39–42. Jesus was staying in the home she shared with her brother Lazarus and her sister Mary. Martha was making the household preparations for His stay while Mary sat at the Lord's feet to listen to His words. Martha wanted Mary to help her instead. The Commanders would have sent poor Mary straight to the kitchen, if not straight to the Colonies. Recalling Jesus's response, the nature of this regime becomes more evident.

Because of their duties and privileges, the Angels are aptly named. They are soldiers, acting at the command of leaders as messengers like in Genesis 32:1, 24, destroyers of the enemy as in Exodus 12:23, informers as in Job 1:6, and assistants as in II Thessalonians 1:7. What the Angels say is law, for it is the word of their leaders (Hebrews 2:2), but they will always be servants (Hebrews 1:7). The Angels are considered privileged in that they get to marry the Commanders' daughters. What is really ironic is the appearance of the Angels of Light on page 106. It brings to mind II Corinthians 11:14—". . . for Satan himself masquerades as an angel of light" (NIV).

The intelligence agents of this society are called the Eyes. Anyone could be an Eye, provided the person is a male. A couple of appropriate references were mentioned in the book:

1. On page 119, II Chronicles 16:9—"For the eyes of the Lord run to and fro throughout the whole earth, to shew Himself strong in the behalf of them whose heart is perfect toward Him . . ." (KJV).
2. On page 250, Proverbs 15:3—"The eyes of the Lord are everywhere, keeping watch on the wicked and on the good" (NIV).

That pretty much describes the nature of the Eyes' work.

One of the more interesting names was the one assigned the mostly black population of Detroit: The Children of Ham. Ham, one of the sons of Noah, discovered his father one day drunk and naked. Instead of quietly covering Noah up and leaving the rest none the wiser, he ran to tell his brothers before anyone else got the chance. His brothers remedied the situation, and Ham's descendants were cursed through his son Canaan in Genesis 9:25: ". . . Cursed be Canaan! The lowest of slaves will he be to his brother." Because of the reference to slavery, this phrase has too long been associated with those of African descent and the scripture that is its source has been used as a justification for black slavery. However, the Canaanites were Caucasian, so this assumption is unfounded. The use of "the children of Ham" in such a manner reveals more than a shadow of racism in the Republic of Gilead.

The names of places are also interesting to pull apart and inspect. The name Gilead in the Bible refers to a region southeast of the Sea of Galilee. It is a hilly region, relatively fertile, providing many agriculture opportunities. It has long been associated with spice and medicinal herbs. While "the balm of Gilead" may not actually have been produced in Gilead, trade of such things occurred there, and Gilead was where the surrounding areas got such items. In a way one might say that Gilead was a land of healing. Atwood's Gilead is obviously not a fertile or healing land. Offred speaks of the low quality and low quantity of the food. The leaders of Gilead are not interested in healing wounds—they are too busy tearing apart families and weeding out undesirables.

What stores that do remain are assigned names that suggest scripture passages and can be represented in pictures. Milk and Honey plays on Exodus 3:8—". . . a land flowing with milk and honey." Exodus 3:8 was the Lord's announcement of a promised land for His people who were enslaved in Egypt. Gilead is no promised land.

Lilies of the Field, the clothing shop, is linked with Matthew 6:28–29:

> And why take ye thought of raiment? Consider the lilies of the field, how they grow: they toil not, neither do they spin: And yet I say unto you, that even Solomon in all his glory was not arrayed like one of these. (KJV)

The clothing that the people receive from that shop is a mockery of the scripture behind the name. All Flesh, the meat shop, really has no direct scriptural reference, but the connotation behind the word flesh usually takes on an earthly aspect as opposed to spiritual aspects. Daily Bread takes its name from the line in the Lord's Prayer, "give us today our daily bread." This is also contradictory. Offred tells us that she only gets bread there when the supply is short at the Commander's house (p. 212). Daily bread is made at home. Loaves and Fishes brings to mind the account of Jesus feeding the five thousand men and uncounted women and children in Luke 14. Jesus took five loaves and two fish and ended up with a well-fed crowd and several baskets of leftovers. In Gilead, Loaves and Fishes sells no loaves and rarely has any fish—and there are never baskets of food leftover when everyone is satisfied.

One of the more revealing pictures in Gilead is that of the Soul Scrolls. The whole process is self-contained. It requires no outside resources or divine intervention, it is all mechanical, it is all activity and "busy-ness," and it produces nothing. It is Gilead in miniature.

Then there is Jezebel's. The biblical Jezebel was evil. She promoted idol worship, killed the Lord's prophets, and had a man killed so her husband could have his vineyard. In II Kings 9, she came to a violent end; she was pushed out of a tower window, hit the ground so hard the blood splattered up the side of the tower, and was left in the street where she was trampled by horses. What was left was eaten up by dogs. Jezebel was wickedness personified. The women at Jezebel's are there because there's no place left for them to go. It is a brothel of women considered wicked under the Gilead regime. There is no hope there; it is the very pit of despair.

Not only places, but things like cars have "religious" labels. The high class car, the Whirlwind, is the automobile of luxury. Perhaps the Commanders fantasize about being taken to heaven in a whirlwind like the great prophet Elijah in II Kings 2:11-12. The Chariot is probably the mid-sized economy model for those who wish to ride around like a high-ranking Roman official. Last of all is the Behemoth which must be like the family station wagon or mini-van. The Behemoth mentioned in Job 40 was a massive land animal, possibly a dinosaur of some sort.

The book is just riddled with phrases with biblical connotations:

1. Page 62—"Forgive them, for they know not what they do." (Luke 23:34)
2. Page 120—"A mist of Lily of the Valley surrounds us . . ." (Song of Songs 2:1)
3. Page 196—". . . Whatever is silenced will clamor to be heard . . ." (Luke 19:40)
4. Page 259—". . . Sons of Jacob . . ." (Genesis 30-50)
5. Page 292—"We were waiting, always, for the incarnation. That word, made flesh." (John 1:14)
6. Page 367—"She has died that I may live." (John 15:13)

The abuse and misuse of biblical passages by the leadership to indoctrinate the Gilead society is most disturbing. They use partial accounts of Old Testament incidents as examples for their victims and twist other passages to justify what they are doing. The Rachel and Leah story from Genesis 20-30 is used to justify the handmaid system. Leah could have children, and Rachel could not, so Leah flaunted it in Rachel's face. Driven by jealousy, Rachel gave Jacob her servant girl to have children for her. There was only more envy and jealousy as Leah hands over her servant girl too. The tension only mounts between the wives, like it does for the handmaids and wives in Atwood's book. The leadership institutes this policy to "be fruitful and increase in number and fill the earth" (Genesis 9:1). The Gilead regime have taken to heart this command God gave to Noah after the flood so they can stop the decrease in population they are experiencing.

Another justification for the handmaid system credited to the apostle Paul in the book of Acts is actually a corruption of a Marxist slogan: "From each according to her ability, to each according to his needs" (p. 151). The closest anything in Acts is in chapter 2, verses 44-45 (NIV): "All the believers were together and had everything in common. Selling their possessions and goods, they gave to anyone as he had need."

The parable of the sower (Luke 8:1–15) is also twisted into propaganda to use on the handmaids. Instead of the seed representing the Word of God, it was used to represent the sexual ability of the handmaid and how quickly she could become pregnant. Aunt Lydia smoothly takes the parable and turns it to her advantage (p. 25).

Offred was right about the inclusions and deletions in the Beatitudes that the Aunts wanted the handmaid trainees to learn. There is no "blessed are the silent." Most of the time the handmaids' beatitudes were full of who were to be considered blessed, but left off the blessings. After all, in Gilead there is no mercy for the merciful, no inheritance for the meek, no righteousness for those who seek it, no peace for the peacemakers, and no joy for the persecuted.

The Gilead leadership also uses Bible verses to enforce headcoverings for the women (I Corinthians 11:5–6), as seen on page 82. They use them on page 146 to justify withholding anesthetics from women in childbirth (Genesis 3:16). Proverbs 31:15 is a vague reference to the wife being in charge of the female servants. This is backed up with Sarah's example in Genesis 16 of her treatment of Hagar. Abraham her husband left the servant's welfare to Sarah; he wanted no part of it. On page 44 Offred tells the reader that doctors who once performed abortions or are suspected of still doing them are sentenced with death. This would be loosely based on Exodus 21:22 where injuring a pregnant woman so that her baby dies is punishable by death. Then there is the requirement of two witnesses for any misdeed, which can be referenced to Deuteronomy 19:15:

> One witness is not enough to convict a man accused of any crime or offense he may have committed. A matter must be established by the testimony of two or three witnesses. (NIV)

Really, the only scripture passage quoted correctly in the whole book is a passage out of the King James Version of the first book of Timothy. Here it is in the New International Version for a clearer understanding:

> I also want women to dress modestly, with decency and propriety, not with braided hair or gold or pearls or expensive clothes, but with good deeds, appropriate for women who profess to worship God.
>
> A woman should learn in quietness and full submission. I do not permit a woman to teach or to have authority over a man; she must be silent. For Adam was formed first, then Eve. And Adam was not the one deceived; it was the woman who was deceived and became a sinner. But women will be saved through childbearing—if they continue in faith, love, and holiness with propriety.

This passage, I Timothy 2:9–15 is quoted on page 286 of Atwood's book. It has become a sort of thorn in the flesh for the modern young Christian woman. Here the male leadership has taken this piece of scripture and bludgeoned the women over the head with it in Gilead to establish all male authority. Scripture should not be used as a weapon for heavy handed tyranny, nor should it be waved away with a few excuses about its being dated. Nobody knows what to make of it, so it is often misused, as here, by the Gilead regime.

Another thought encouraged by people like the Aunts is that all flesh was weak and that it was the woman's duty to set the boundaries. It sounds as if only the men are considered flesh. What are the women then if they aren't flesh? Wood? Stone? What?

The biblical echoes throughout Margaret Atwood's book give a more haunting nature to the book, as well as allusions to the events going on around us in the world today. Putting it all in the first person makes it all the more real. Offred is not a Christian, so while she is caught in the crossfire of the ironies, she is not fully aware of what they are. She is concerned with survival. She isn't horrified by what's being said because there are worse things happening to her that she has to deal with. That's what makes her story more believable; she is more concerned with coming out alive than upholding some principle or ideal. But still, the manipulation of words and ideas is a scary thought when we live in a place where we are allowed the expression of our individual thought.

Works Consulted

ATWOOD, MARGARET. *The Handmaid's Tale*. New York: Ballantine Books, 1985.

The NIV Study Bible. Grand Rapids, Michigan: Zondervan Corporation, 1985.

The Holy Bible. King James Version.

ELWELL, WALTER A. ed. *Baker Encyclopedia of the Bible*, Vol. 1. Grand Rapids, Michigan: Baker Book House, 1988.

After reading: CONSOLIDATE INFORMATION

1. Summarize Jones's argument about the way imagery functions in Atwood's novel.
2. Compare Jones's response to Atwood's novel with Edd Doerr's review of the novel and the film based on the novel. What similarities do you see?
3. Toward the end of her essay, Jones point out that the only passage quoted correctly from the New Testament in *A Handmaid's Tale* is a passage from I Timothy 2: 9–15. Jones goes on to say that this passage "has become a thorn in the flesh for the modern young Christian woman," but does not address the feminist implications of a male-dominated, extremist government (such as the one in Atwood's Gilead) citing such a passage. From what you know of Atwood's novel from Jones, Edd Doerr, and Michael Calleri, why do you think Atwood uses this passage?

Further Explorations for Readings in the Humanities

1. Adalaide Morris, Joyce Durham, and Brian Henderson seem to share certain assumptions about the role literature and art play in human life. By analyzing and evaluating these assumptions, how can you define the ideal role the arts should play in the life of a society?
2. Brian Henderson and Thomas Fiddick examine popular or public perceptions about two wars in American life (the American Civil War and the Vietnam War). Looking at these essays together, what answers do you think these writers give to the questions "In what relation do we stand to the past?" and "What do we owe future generations?"
3. Writing in the Humanities almost invariably focuses on texts, but these texts are not always single printed documents; some of the essays in this section examine film as text (Henderson, Doerr, Calleri), an entire literary canon as text (Morris), and the city as text (Durham). How has your concept of text changed in reading these essays? Can you think of texts other than print to which you might apply a humanistic perspective?
4. In their philosophical essays, Anthony Amsterdam and Christopher Meyers assume certain human values. What are these values and how do they compare with what you assume to be basic American values about human life?
5. Compare the tone, vocabulary, and structure of Richard Welch's article with Thomas Fiddick's essay on the Vietnam War. Based on this comparison, how would you describe the differences in the audiences each is addressing?
6. How does Lisa Jones echo the same reactions to *The Handmaid's Tale* as Doerr and Calleri?
7. Adalaide Morris and Tracy Marschall both develop arguments about traditional texts (Morris in literature, Marschall in religious studies) which support and legitimize male dominance and what Marschall terms "patriarchal oppression." Evaluate Morris's and Marschall's positions and the evidence they use to support their positions.

2

Readings in the Social Sciences

Outlining a Science of Feeling
B. F. Skinner

B. F. Skinner (1904–1990) was a world renowned psychologist and a major proponent of a school of research into human behavior known as operant conditioning. *This essay was written for a British publication,* The Times Literary Supplement, *which publishes reviews and articles about general intellectual and cultural issues for a well-educated, non-specialist audience.*

Before reading: FIRST THOUGHTS
           LOOK AHEAD

1. How do you react to the linking of the two words, *science* and *feeling*?
2. What does the word *verisimilitude* mean to you? Check your own meaning against the one you find in a dictionary. What does the term mean here?
3. How are behavior and emotions linked?

During reading: REACT
           QUESTION
           SUMMARIZE

1. Think about something that makes you feel anxiety or fear. Does your experience with these emotions confirm Skinner's analysis?

2. What, according to Skinner, do the following have to do with emotions or feelings: outside stimuli, environment, and other people?

A Review of Gerald Zuriff's *Behaviorism: A conceptual reconstruction* in the *TLS* of July 19, 1985, begins with a story about two behaviourists. They make love, and then one of them says, "That was fine for you. How was it for me?" The reviewer, P. N. Johnson-Laird, insists that there is a "verisimilitude" with behaviourist theory. Behaviourists are not supposed to have feelings, or at least to admit that they have them. Of the many ways in which behaviourism has been misunderstood for so many years, that is perhaps the commonest.

A possibly excessive concern for "objectivity" may have caused the trouble. Methodological behaviourists, like logical positivists, argued that science must confine itself to events that can be observed by two or more people; truth must be truth by agreement. What one sees through introspection does not qualify. There is a private world of feelings and states of mind, but it is out of reach of a second person and hence of science. That was not a very satisfactory position, of course. How people feel is often as important as what they do.

Radical behaviourism has never taken that line. Feeling is a kind of sensory action, like seeing or hearing. We see a tweed jacket, for example, and we also feel it. That is not quite like feeling depressed, of course. We know something about the organs with which we feel the jacket but little, if anything, about those with which we feel depressed. We can also feel *of* the jacket by running our fingers over the cloth to increase the stimulation, but there does not seem to be any way to feel *of* depression. We have other ways of sensing the jacket, and we do various things with it. In other words, we have other ways of knowing what we are feeling. But what are we feeling when we feel depressed?

William James anticipated the behaviorist's answer: what we feel is a condition of our body. We do not cry because we are sad, said James, we are sad because we cry. That was fudging a little, of course, because we do much more than cry when we feel sad, and we can feel sad when we are not crying, but it was pointing in the right direction: what we feel is bodily conditions. Physiologists will eventually observe them in another way, as they observe any other part of the body. Walter B. Cannon's *Bodily Changes in Pain, Hunger, Fear, and Rage* (1929) was an early study of a few conditions often felt. Meanwhile, we ourselves can respond to them directly. We do so in two different ways. For example, we respond to stimuli from our joints and muscles in one way when we move about and in a different way when we say that we feel relaxed or lame. We respond to an empty stomach in one way when we eat and in a different way when we say that we are hungry.

The verbal responses in those examples are the products of special contingencies of reinforcement. They are arranged by listeners, and they are especially hard to arrange when what is being talked about is out of the listener's reach, as it usually is when it is within the speaker's skin. The very privacy which suggests that we ought to know our own bodies especially well is a severe handicap for those who must teach us to know them. We can teach a child to name an object, for example, by presenting or pointing to the object, pronouncing its name, and reinforcing a similar response by the child, but we cannot do that with a bodily state. We cannot present or point to a pain, for example. Instead, we infer the presence of the pain from some public accompaniment. We may see the child take a hard fall, for example, and say, "That must have hurt," or we see the child wince and ask, "Does something hurt?" We can respond only to the blow or the wince, but the child also feels a private stimulus and may say "hurt" when it occurs again without a public accompaniment. Since public and private events seldom coincide exactly, words for feelings have never been taught as successfully as words for objects. Perhaps that is why philosophers and psychologists so seldom agree when talking about feelings and states of mind, and why there is no acceptable science of feeling.

For centuries, of course, it has been said that we behave in given ways because of our feelings. We eat because we feel hungry, strike because we feel angry, and in general do what we feel like doing. If that were true, our faulty knowledge of feelings would be disastrous. No science of behaviour would be possible. But what is felt is not an initial or initiating cause. William James was quite wrong about his "becauses." We do not cry *because* we are sad or feel sad *because* we cry; we cry *and* feel sad because something has happened. (Perhaps someone we loved has died.) It is easy to mistake what we feel as a cause because we feel it while we are behaving (or even before we behave), but the events which are actually responsible for what we do (and hence what we feel) lie in the possibly distant past. The experimental analysis of behaviour advances our understanding of feelings by clarifying the roles of both past and present environments. Here are three examples.

LOVE. A critic has said that for a behaviorist "I love you" means "You reinforce me." Good behaviorists would say "You reinforce my behavior" rather than "You reinforce me," because it is behavior, not the behaving person, that is being reinforced, in the sense of strengthened; but they would say much more. There is no doubt a reinforcing element in loving. Everything lovers do that brings them closer together or keeps them from being separated is reinforced by those consequences, and that is why they spend as much time together as they can. We describe the private effect of a reinforcer when we say that it "pleases us" or "makes us feel good," and in that sense "I love you" means "You please me or make me feel good." But the contingencies responsible for what is felt must be analyzed further.

The Greeks had three words for love, and they are still useful. Mentalistic psychologists may try to distinguish among them by looking at how love feels but much more can be learned from the relevant contingencies of selection, both natural selection and operant reinforcement. *Eros* is usually taken to mean sexual love, in part no doubt because the word erotic is derived from it. It is that part of making love that is due to natural selection; we share it with other species. (Many forms of parental love are also due to natural selection and are also examples of *eros*. To call mother love erotic is not to call it sexual.) Erotic lovemaking may also be modified by operant conditioning, but a genetic connection survives, because the susceptibility to reinforcement by sexual contact is an evolved trait. (Variations which have made individuals more susceptible have increased their sexual activity and hence their contribution to the future of the species.) In most other species the genetic tendency is the stronger. Courtship rituals and modes of copulation vary little from individual to individual and are usually related to optimal times of conception and seasons for the bearing of offspring. In *homo sapiens* sexual reinforcement predominates and yields a much greater frequency and variety of lovemaking.

Philia refers to a different kind of reinforcing consequences and, hence, a different state to be felt and called love. The root *phil* appears in words like philosophy (love of wisdom) and philately (love of postage stamps), but other things are loved in that way when the root word is not used. People say they "love Brahms" when they are inclined to listen to his works—perform them, perhaps, or go to concerts where they are performed, or play recordings. People who "love Renoir" tend to go to exhibitions of his paintings or buy them (alas, usually copies of them) to be looked at. People who "love Dickens" tend to acquire and read his books. We say the same things about places ("I love Vienna"), subject-matters ("I love astronomy"), characters in fiction ("I love Daisy Miller"), kinds of people ("I love children"), and, of course, friends in whom we have no erotic interest. (It is sometimes hard to distinguish between *eros* and *philia*. Those who "love Brahms" may report that they play or listen to his works almost erotically, and courtship and lovemaking are sometimes practiced as forms of art.)

If we can say that *eros* is primarily a matter of natural selection and *philia* of operant conditioning, then *agape* represents a third process of selection—cultural evolution. Agape comes from a word meaning to welcome or, as a dictionary puts it, "to receive gladly." By showing that we are pleased when another person joins us, we reinforce joining. The direction of reinforcement is reversed. It is not our behaviour, but the behaviour of those we love that is reinforced. The principal effect is on the group. By showing that we are pleased by what other people do, we reinforce the doing and thus strengthen the group.

The direction of reinforcement is also reversed in *eros* if the manner in which we make love is affected by signs that our lover is pleased. It is also reversed in *philia* when our love for Brahms, for example, takes the form of founding or joining a society for the promotion of his works, or when we show our love for Venice by contributing to a fund to preserve the city. We also show a kind of *agape* when we honour heroes, leaders, scientists, and others from whose achievement we have profited. We are said to "worship" them in the etymological sense of proclaiming their worth. (When we say that we venerate them the *ven* is from the Latin *venus*, which meant any kind of pleasing thing.) Worship is the commoner word when speaking of the love of god, for which the New Testament used *agape*.

A reversed direction of reinforcement must be explained, especially when it calls for sacrifice. We may act to please a lover because our own pleasure is then increased, but why should we do so when it is not? We may promote the works of Brahms or help save Venice because we then have more opportunities to enjoy them, but why should we do so when that is not the case? The primary reinforcing consequences of *agape* are, in fact, artificial. They are contrived by our culture and contrived, moreover, just because the kind of thing we then do has helped the culture solve its problems and survive.

ANXIETY. Very different states of the body are generated by aversive stimuli, and they are felt in different ways. Many years ago W. K. Estes and I were rash enough to report an experiment in the *Journal of Experimental Psychology* (1941, 29, pp. 390–400) under the title, "Some quantitative properties of anxiety," although we were writing about rats. A hungry rat pressed a lever at a low, steady rate, under intermittent reinforcement with bits of food. Once or twice during an hour-long session, we sounded a tone for three minutes and then lightly shocked the rat through its feet. At first neither the tone nor the shock had any marked effect on the rate of responding, but the rat soon began to respond more slowly while the tone was sounding and eventually stopped altogether. Under rather similar circumstances a person might say, "I stopped what I was doing because I felt anxious."

In that experiment, the disrupted behaviour was produced by intermittent operant reinforcement, but the disruption would usually be attributed to respondent (classical or Pavlovian) conditioning. There is a problem, however. A change in probability of responding or rate of responding is not properly called a response. Moreover, since the shock itself did not suppress responding, there was no substitution of the stimuli. The reduced rate seems, paradoxically, to be the innate effect of a necessarily conditioned response.

A paraphrased comment of Freud's begins as follows: "A person experiences anxiety in a situation of danger and helplessness." A "situation of danger" is a situation that resembles one in which painful things have happened. Our rat was in a situation of danger while the tone was sounding. It was "helpless" in the sense that it could do nothing to stop the tone or escape. The state of its body was presumably similar to the state a person would feel as anxiety, although the verbal contingencies needed for a response comparable to "I feel anxious" were lacking.

The paraphrase of Freud continues: "If the situation threatens to recur in later life, the person experiences anxiety as a signal of impending danger." (It would be better to say "impending harm," because what threatens to recur is the aversive event—the shock for the rat and perhaps something like an automobile accident for the person, but what actually recurs is the condition that preceded the event—the tone, or say, riding with a reckless driver.) The quotation makes the point that the condition felt as anxiety begins to act as a second conditioned aversive stimulus. As soon as the tone began to generate a particular state of the rat's body, the state itself stood in the same relation to the shock as the tone, and it should have begun to have the same effect. Anxiety thus becomes self-perpetuating and even self-intensifying. A person might say, "I feel anxious, and something terrible always happens when I feel that way," but the contingencies yield a better analysis than any report of how self-perpetuated anxiety feels.

FEAR. A different result would have followed in our experiment if the shock had been contingent upon a response—in other words, if pressing had been punished. The rat would also have stopped pressing, but the bodily state would have been different. It would probably have been called fear. Anxiety is perhaps a kind of fear (we could say that the rat was "afraid another shock would follow"), but that is different from being "afraid to press the lever" because a shock will follow. A difference in the contingencies is unmistakable.

Young behaviorists sometimes contribute to an example of fear, relevant here, when they find themselves saying that something pleases them or makes them angry and are embarrassed for having said it. The etymology of embarrassment as a kind of fear is significant. The root is *bar*, and young behaviourists find themselves barred from speaking freely about their feelings because those who have misunderstood behaviourism have ridiculed them when they have done so. An analysis of how embarrassment feels, made without alluding to antecedents or consequences, would be difficult if not impossible, but the contingencies are clear enough. In general, the more subtle the state felt, the greater the advantage in turning to the contingencies.

Such an analysis has an important bearing on two practical questions: how much can we ever know about what another person is feeling, and how can what is felt be changed? It is not enough to ask other people how or what they feel, because the words they will use in telling us were acquired as we have seen, from people who did not quite know what they were talking about. Something of the sort seems to have been true of the first words to describe private states. The first person who said, "I'm worried" borrowed a word meaning "choke" or "strangle." ("Anger," "anguish" and "anxiety" also come from another word that meant "choke.") But how much like the effect of choking was the bodily state the word was used to describe? All words for feelings seem to have begun as metaphors, and it is significant that the transfer has always been from public to private. No word seems to have originated as the name of a feeling.

We do not need to use the names of feelings if we can go directly to the public events. Instead of saying, "I was angry," we can say, "I should have struck him." What was felt was an inclination to strike rather than striking, but the private stimuli must have been much the same. Another way to report what we feel is to describe a setting that is likely to generate the condition felt. After reading Chapman's translation of Homer for the first time, Keats reported that he felt "like some watcher of the skies/When a new planet swims into his kin." It was easier for his readers to feel what an astronomer would feel upon discovering a new planet than what Keats felt upon reading the book.

It is sometimes said that we can make direct contact with what other people feel through sympathy or empathy. Sympathy seems to be reserved for painful feelings; we sympathise with a person who has lost a fortune but not with one who has made one. When we empathize, we are said to project our feelings into another person, but we cannot actually be moving feelings about, because we also project them into things—when, for example, we commit the pathetic fallacy. What we feel of Lear's rage is not quite what we feel in a raging storm. Sympathy and empathy seem to be effects of imitation. For genetic or personal reasons we tend to do what other people are doing and we may then have similar bodily states to feel. When we do what other *things* are doing, it is not likely that we are sharing feelings.

Sympathy and empathy cannot tell us exactly what a person feels, because part of what is felt depends upon the setting in which the behaviour occurs, and that is usually missing in imitation. When lysergic acid diethylamide first attracted attention, psychiatrists were urged to take it in order to see what it felt like to be psychotic, but acting like a psychotic because one has taken a drug may not create the condition felt by those who are psychotic for other reasons.

That we know what other people feel only when we behave as they behave is clear when we speak of knowing what members of other species feel. Presumably we are more likely to avoid hurting animals if what they would do resembles what we should do when hurt in the same way. That is why we are more likely to hurt the kinds of animals—fish, snakes, and insects, for example—which do not behave very much as we do. It is a rare person, indeed, who would not hurt a fly.

To emphasize what is felt rather than the feeling is important when we want to change feelings. Drugs, of course, are used for that purpose. Some of them (aspirin, for example) break the connection with what is felt. Others create states that appear to compete with or mask troublesome states. According to American television commercials, alcohol yields the good fellowship of *agape* and banishes care. But these are temporary measures, and their effects are necessarily imperfect simulations of what is naturally felt in daily life because the natural settings are lacking.

Feelings are most easily changed by changing the settings responsible for what is felt. We could have relieved the anxiety of our rat by turning off the tone. When a setting cannot be changed, a new history of reinforcement may change its effect. In his remarkable book *Émile*, Rousseau described what is now called desensitization. If a baby is frightened when plunged into cold water (presumably an innate response), begin with warm water and reduce the temperature a degree a day. The baby will not be frightened when the water is finally cold. Something of the sort could also be done, said Rousseau, with social reactions. If a child is frightened by a person wearing a threatening mask, begin with a friendly one and change it slightly day by day until it becomes threatening, when it will not be frightening.

Psychoanalysis is largely concerned with discovering and changing feelings. An analysis sometimes seems to work by extinguishing the effects of old punishments. When the patient discovers that obscene, blasphemous, or aggressive behavior is tolerated, the therapist emerges as a non-punitive audience. Behaviour "repressed" by former punishments then begins to appear. It "becomes conscious" simply in the sense that it begins to be felt. The once offending behaviour is not punished, but it is also not reinforced, and it eventually undergoes extinction, a less troublesome method of eradication than punishment.

Cognitive psychologists are among those who most often criticize behaviourism for neglecting feelings, but they themselves have done very little in the field. The computer is not a helpful model. Cognitive psychologists specialize in the behaviour of speakers and listeners. Instead of arranging contingencies of reinforcement, they often simply describe them. Instead of observing what their subjects do, they often simply ask them what they would probably do. But the kinds of behaviour most often associated with feelings are not easily brought under verbal control. "Cheer up" or "Have a good time" seldom works. Only operant behaviour can be executed in response to advice, but if it occurs only for that reason, it has the same shortcomings as imitative behaviour. Advice must be taken and reinforcing consequences must follow the bodily condition that is the intended effect of the advice will be felt. If consequences do not immediately follow, the advice ceases to be taken or the behaviour remains nothing more than taking advice.

Fortunately, not everything we feel is troublesome. We enjoy many states of our bodies, and because they are positively reinforcing, do what is needed to produce them. We read books and watch television and, to the extent that we then tend to behave as the characters behave, we feel and possibly enjoy relevant bodily states. Drugs are taken for positively reinforcing effects (but the reinforcement is negative when they are taken primarily to relieve withdrawal symptoms). Religious mystics cultivate special bodily states—by fasting, remaining still or silent, reciting mantras, and so on. Dedicated joggers often report a jogging high.

To confine an analysis of feelings to what is felt may seem to neglect an essential question: what is *feeling*, simply as such? We can ask a similar question about sensory process—for example, what is *seeing*? Philosophers and cognitive psychologists avoid that question by contending that to see something is to make some kind of copy—a "representation," to use the current word. But making a copy cannot be seeing, because the copy must in turn be seen. Nor is it enough, of course, to say simply that seeing is behaving; it is only part of behaving. It is "behaving up to the point of acting." Unfortunately, what happens up to that point is out of reach of the instruments and methods of the behaviour analyst and must be left to the physiologist. What remains for the analyst are the contingencies of reinforcement under which things come to be seen and the verbal contingencies under which they come to be described. In the case of feeling, both the conditions felt and what is done in feeling them must be left to the physiologist. What remain for the behaviour analyst are the genetic and personal histories responsible for the bodily conditions the physiologist will find.

There are many good reasons why people talk about their feelings. What they say is often a useful indication of what has happened to them or of what they may do. On the point of offering a friend a glass of water, we do not ask, "How long has it been since you last drank any water?" or "If I offer you a glass of water, what are the chances you will accept it?" We ask "Are you thirsty?" The answer tells us all we need to know. In an experimental analysis, however, we must have a better account of the conditions that affect hydration and a better measure of the probability that a subject will drink. A report of how thirsty the subject feels will not suffice.

For at least 3,000 years, however, philosophers, joined recently by psychologists, have looked within themselves for the causes of their behaviour. For reasons which are becoming clear, they have never agreed upon what they have found. Physiologists, and especially neurologists, look at the same body in a different and potentially successful way, but even when they have seen it more clearly, they will not have seen initiating causes of behaviour. What they will see must in turn be explained by ethologists, who look for explanations in the evolution of the species, or by behaviour analysts, who look at the histories of individuals. The inspection or introspection of one's own body is a kind of behaviour that needs to be analysed, but as the source of data for a science it is largely of historical interest only.

After reading: CONSOLIDATE INFORMATION

1. Reread Skinner's analysis of love as a behaviour and apply what he says to another emotion such as anger, hatred, or jealousy.
2. Skinner suggests that an analysis of the nature of human emotions leads us inevitably to the question "How can we know what another person feels?" Write a freewrite response to the question and share it with another student in your class.
3. Skinner implies that there is an outline or pattern to be discerned in the ways in which human beings feel. How would you explain that pattern?

Emotions: A Trinity
Elaine Hatfield and Richard Rapson

Professors of Psychology Elaine Hatfield and Richard Rapson collaborated on the article from which the following excerpt is taken. Collaboration—in research and in writing—is a common practice in the social sciences. In their article, Hatfield and Rapson respond to what they view as Skinner's overly simple explanation of the nature of emotions. The article first appeared in Emotions and the Family: For Better or Worse *(1990), a textbook of essays in psychology addressed to an audience of researchers, teachers, and students of psychology.*

Before reading: FIRST THOUGHTS
LOOK AHEAD

1. Read the title and the short anecdote quoted at the beginning of the article. What do you think you will learn about the emotions from this article?
2. Read the subheadings of each section:
    Defining Emotion
    The Nature of Emotion
    Cognitive Aspects of Emotion
    Biological Aspects of Emotion
    Behavioral Aspects of Emotion
What can you predict about this article from these subheadings?
3. Write short, freewritten definitions of the following words: cognitive, psychological, and behavioral.

During reading: REACT
          QUESTION
          SUMMARIZE

1. Summarize the main objection Hatfield and Rapson have to Skinner's outline of the emotions.
2. Hatfield and Rapson write that they view human emotions as a system. What do you think they mean by that?

Recently, at the University of Iowa's summer program on social psychophysiology, I watched a demonstration. An undergraduate who worked in John Cacioppo's laboratory was wired up with electrodes designed to measure facial EMG, heart rate, breathing rate, and skin conductance. He was instructed to think about anything he wished. Some trainees watched the student on a television monitor. All they saw was a blank, relaxed, impassive face. Others of us watched the pens on a 10-channel Grass ployograph recorder. Now and then we would spot dramatic changes on the printout. For example, at one point, the electrodes connected to the corrugator supercilli muscle showed a sudden jump. "What are you thinking about?" we asked. "An argument with my roommate." Later there was a powerful movement around the orbicular oris. It was so powerful that it was interfering with all the other readings. We looked at the television monitor to see what the student was doing, but we could detect no sign of movement. "What is going on?", we asked. "I've just thought of a great argument," he answered. "Well, quit," we said. "Just imagine you are listening to what he has to say." He did, and the pens immediately quieted down. (Carlson & Hatfield, in press)

    IN CHAPTER 1 OF THIS BOOK, B. F. Skinner argued that intimate conversations will go best if people speak the same emotional language—the language of behavior. We disagree. We believe that, in the light of abundant and remarkable new research, Skinner's concept of the nature of emotion is too simple. In this chapter, we review what scientists now know about emotion. In the process, it becomes clear that emotional experiences leave complex cognitive and physiological, as well as behavioral tracings. To understand emotion, one must be prepared to speak many languages. Let us begin our discussion by defining what we mean by emotion.

DEFINING EMOTION

    We, like many other theorists, view emotions as a *system* that activates cognitive, physiological, and behavioral components. For example, consider Izard and Buechler's (1986) definition:

> A fundamental emotion is defined as a complex motivational phenomenon, with characteristic neurophysiological, expressive, and experiential components. No

single component of the three suffices as a description of an emotion; all three are essential to the concept. At the neurophysiological level, a fundamental emotion is defined as a particular, innately programmed pattern of electrochemical activity in the nervous system. The expressive component consists mainly of a characteristic pattern of facial activity, but may also include bodily responses (postural-gestural, visceral-glandular) and vocal expressions. At the experiential level, each fundamental emotion is a unique quality of consciousness. (p. 167.)

In the last 2 decades, scientists have learned a great deal about the nature of emotion. In this paper we are only able to present a scattering of this voluminous research. For a more complete review, see Carlson and Hatfield (in press). Scientific discoveries make it clear that: (a) people do, in part, speak a universal language of emotion. Many aspects of emotional experience and expression are genetically "hard-wired" into humans. (b) However, peoples' emotional socialization and emotional experiences are very different. The historical era in which people live, the cultural and social groups to which they belong, and the type of family in which they are raised, insure that, in part, the language of emotion that they speak must be their own.

The Nature of Emotion

Darwin (1872/1965) proposed an evolutionary model for understanding emotional expression. In prehistory, animals (including man) were confronted again and again with certain problems of survival. Those animals that best fitted their environments survived. In *The Expression of the Emotions in Man and Animals*, Darwin proposed that, as a consequence of their shared evolutionary history, animals and man came to experience and express emotions in much the same way. The facial, postural, physiological, and behavioral reactions associated with emotion evolved because they "worked", that is, they increased the species' chances of survival. In recent years, scientists have begun to make some impressive strides in detailing just how these basic inherited emotional systems operate.

Cognitive Aspects of Emotion

A variety of cognitive psychologists have attempted to spell out how cognitive factors shape intimates' emotional experiences. For example, Lazarus (Lazarus, Kanner, & Folkman, 1980) argued that the first step in an emotional sequence is a "cognitive appraisal." In the process of "primary appraisal," people try to decide what consequences impending events are likely to have for their well-being. Once they have assessed the situation they must proceed to a "secondary appraisal." What *should* they do about the situation? What *can* they do? Finally, "reappraisal" highlights the interactive nature of peoples' encounters with other persons and with the world. Individuals perceive and react; the environment counterreacts. Individuals, in turn, must appraise these reactions. People never stop making evaluative judgments about themselves and the world around them.

Cognitive theorists such as Lazarus attempt to provide a sort of universal framework, which outlines how all people at all times will analyze challenging situations. Theorists from a variety of related disciplines add complexity and variability to this picture.

For example, anthropologists (see Lutz & White, 1986), sociologists (see Kemper, 1986), and historians (see Degler, 1980; Gay, 1984; Stearns & Stearns, 1985; or Stone, 1979) have begun to document the profound impact of culture in shaping peoples' perceptions of how they are supposed to feel about various events and how they can legitimately express those feelings. This work makes it clear that the historical and cultural contexts play a mighty role in determining how emotions ultimately take shape and gain expression in real life.

Social psychologists have also documented the impact that families have on family members' emotional experiences, and on: (a) their ability to express their emotions with clarity; (b) the intensity with which they express their emotions; and (c) their ability to read others' most subtle emotional expressions, (see, for example, Buck, 1979; Ekman & Friesen, 1969; Izard, 1971; or Jones, 1960). Obviously, people possess very different interests and skills in dealing with emotion. For example, someone with a literary, theatrical, artistic, or psychological bent may well find it rewarding to spend a great deal of time in analyzing the minute details of their *own feelings*, and may also enjoy looking at portraits, watching Masterpiece Theater (where the dramatists are often deeply concerned with the subtleties and contradictions of character), and talking with friends and acquaintances about their personal problems. Such people are likely to know exactly what they feel in a given situation. Others, "macho men" for example, convinced that masculinity equals *lack* of emotional responsiveness, might find their rewards in insisting, in even the most trying of situations, that for them it is "no sweat." They may indeed turn things off to such an extent that they are totally unaware of their feelings. The same holds true with regard to emotional *expression*. Some of my colleagues try very hard to convey, in measured, precise, verbal expression, the nuances of their inner lives. Others think that to express emotions means to shout, cry, pound pillows, and hit one another over the head with batakas (or worse). Finally, people have learned to be differentially attentive to others' emotional displays. Some people are sharply attuned to the tiniest movement of another's eyebrow. The most minute change in facial expression throws them into a panic. "Is he angry?" "Have they hurt her feelings; is she going to cry?" Social psychologists have begun to explore the ways in which families socialize children in these areas. For example, some social psychologists find a strong correlation between parental expressiveness and the expressiveness of infants as young as 3 months old. (Malatesta & Haviland, 1982). Lanzetta and Kleck, 1970, proposed that individuals who have been punished by socializing agents for engaging in overt displays of emotionality learn to inhibit their own emotional expression. At the same time, however, they become unusually sensitive to the displays of others. Halberstadt (1986) observed: "When the family environment is low in expressiveness, individuals must become sensitive to the most subtle displays of emotion in order to relate effectively with other family members." (p. 827).

Interestingly, then, some researchers have proposed that often there is a negative relationship between peoples' sending and receiving skills: The people who send the clearest, most intense emotional messages themselves are often the poorest at recognizing other, more subtle, forms of expression. Those whose own emotional responses are muted and difficult to fathom are often expert readers of the emotions of others (Buck, 1979; Halberstadt, 1986; Izard, 1971; Morency & Krauss, 1982; Zuckerman, Hall, DeFrank, & Rosenthal, 1976). Obviously, there is no reason a person would have to be either a poor sender or receiver. It would seem that people who are taught to be comfortable with a variety of forms of emotional expression—to carefully analyze emotion-laden situations, sometimes; to be spontaneous, sometimes; to express emotions softly when that is appropriate and more fiercely when that is necessary; and to be capable of reading subtle and powerful expressions of emotion—would do best in close relationships.

The research of historians, anthropologists, sociologists, social psychologists, and developmentalists, then makes it clear that there would be both universality and idiosyncrasy in emotional expression.

Biological Aspects of Emotion

From evolutionary biology, we are learning *when* the various layers of the brain evolved. From neuroanatomy, we are discovering how the brain is structured. From neurophysiology, we are beginning to understand how the brain functions chemically.

THE ANATOMY OF EMOTION

MacLean (1986) argued that, in the course of evolution, humans have ended up with a brain that has a triune structure. In a sense, the brain consists of three different types of brains, with different anatomical structures and chemical processes layered one upon the other. The oldest type of brain is basically reptilian. The second is inherited from the early mammals. The third is from the late mammals/primates. MacLean pointed out that the reptilian brain was primarily concerned with preservation of self and species. Its primitive structures were designed to guide the reptile in the processes required for obtaining food (search, angry attacks, self-defense, feeding, and mates).

In the neo-mammalian brain three new patterns of behavior, which were primarily designed to facilitate mother–child relationships, emerged through evolution. These included nursing of the young, "audiovocal communication" for facilitating mother–child contact and play behavior. MacLean contended that such affects as desire, fear, anger, dejection and depression, ecstasy and affection, all derive from activities in the limbic system.

It was not until the neo-cortex evolved in the late mammalian primate period that symbolic or verbal information became important in shaping primate emotional experience and expression. MacLean (1986) reviewed over 40 years of clinical and experimental findings in support of his contention that it is not cognition alone, but emotions that guide the behavior required for self-preservation and preservation of the species.

The Physiology of Emotion

Psychologists are beginning to learn more about the chemistry of emotions and the way various emotions interact. Liebowitz (1983), for example, offered some speculations about the chemistry of the "highs" and the "lows" that crisscross people's consciousness. These include the highs of euphoria, excitement, relaxation, spiritual feelings, and relief, as well as the lows of anxiety, terrifying panic attacks, the pain of separation, and the fear of punishment.

Liebowitz proposed that naturally occurring brain chemicals produce emotions. *Joy and excitement:* (Chemicals resembling stimulants (such as amphetamine and cocaine) produce the "rush" felt by joyous people, lovers, and those engaging in exciting activities. *Relaxation:* Chemicals related to the narcotics (such as heroin, opium, and morphine), tranquilizers (such as Librium and Valium), sedatives (such as barbiturates, Quaaludes, and other "downers"), alcohol, and marijuana all produce a mellow state and wipe out loneliness, panic attacks, and depression. *Spiritual peak experiences:* Chemicals similar to the psychedelics (such as LSD, mescaline, and psilocybin) produce a sense of beauty, meaningfulness, and timelessness.

Physiologists do not usually try to produce painful experiences in the laboratory. Thus, we know a bit less about the chemistry of pain. Such painful feelings may, however, arise from two sources: (a) withdrawal from the chemicals that produce the highs; (b) the infusion of chemicals which, in and of themselves, produce anxiety, pain, or depression. (A great deal is known about the physiology and chemistry of emotion. For a review of relevant sources see Carlson and Hatfield, in press.)

The basic emotions, then, are associated with chemical neurotransmitters or with chemicals that increase/decrease the receptors' sensitivity. The basic emotions may well be, in part, chemically distinct. Yet, at the same time, emotions have more similarities than differences. Chemically, joy, love, sexual desire, and excitement, as well as anger, hate, fear, jealousy, and anxiety have much in common: for example, they are all intensely arousing. They all produce a sympathetic response in the automatic nervous system (ANS). This is evidenced by the symptoms associated with all of these emotions—a flushed face, sweaty palms, weak knees, butterflies in the stomach, dizziness, a pounding heart, trembling hands, and accelerated breathing. Lacey (1967) made a surprising discovery. In emotional situations people seemed to react in stereotyped, *but very different*, ways. For example, Person A's heart might start to beat wildly in response to feeling frightened *or* excited *or* joyous—and that would be the only ANS reaction manifested. Person B might start to breathe heavily and perspire whenever becoming emotional, and those would be the only reactions visible. Lacey pointed out that it was therefore misleading to speak of ANS "arousal," as if all people at all times showed a uniform ANS reaction, one in which the various indicants of ANS arousal were perfectly correlated. Different people experience different patterns of ANS arousal.

The reactions shown by one person will not be strongly correlated with those shown by others in the same emotional situation, and the various indicants of ANS arousal themselves will not be correlated. Once again we see that people seem to share *some* emotional experiences (most show some type of ANS arousal), but that some aspects of their experiences are unique.

There are other factors that contribute to the difficulty people have both in articulating their own emotional experiences with precision much less making assumptions about what other people might be experiencing. Recent neuroanatomical/neurophysiological research suggests that the various emotions probably are more tightly interrelated than psychologists once thought. Hatfield (1970) and Hatfield and Walster (1978) pointed out that when people are caught up in an intensely emotional situation, "chemical spill-over" is likely to occur— that is, peoples' feelings get all mixed up. Everything gets intensified. People can move from elation through terror into the depths of despair and back again in a matter of seconds. They know that they are feeling intensely but it is difficult to disentangle their complicated interlocking feelings. They literally do not know whether to laugh or to cry.

Skeletomotor Reactions

A variety of researchers have studied the impact of emotional experiences on facial reactions (For recent reviews, see Cacioppo, Petty, & Tassinary, in press).

The facial response system. When we think about things (as evidenced in the anecdote that began this chapter) our bodies play out our thoughts. As we think about what we will say next, the *orbicularis oris* (the muscle around the mouth) invisibly sounds out the words. When we think about writing, small muscle movements occur in our fingers and arms. Although these movements are invisible to the naked eye, scientists can easily detect them via EMG (electromyographic) recordings. Scientists have demonstrated that facial EMG activity is capable of distinguishing positive from negative emotional states, even when there are no changes in overt facial action or autonomic activity (Cacioppo et al., in press, or Fridlund & Izard, 1983). Since this research is just in its infancy, researchers are optimistic that they may be able to distinguish the basic emotions via their EMG signatures.

Perhaps the most powerful way we communicate with one another is via visible facial expressions. Ekman (1972) and Izard (1971) have argued that the face speaks a universally understood language. Recently, psychologists have uncovered some compelling evidence that the basic emotions *are* expressed in much the same way in all cultures. (Of course, every culture also possesses its own display rules). Recent research illustrates how both these processes operate. Scientists studying infants, children, and adults from a variety of cultures have linked happiness, sadness, fear, anger, disgust, and surprise to a series of distinctive facial displays (Ekman, 1972; Izard, 1977; Scherer & Ekman, 1982; Steiner, 1979).

These same studies, however, show that peoples' emotional reactions are most similar when observed in private. In public, powerful "display rules" partially shape our responses. (For example, we try to look happy at weddings and sad at funerals, regardless of how we might really feel.)

Behavioral Aspects of Emotion

Many eminent learning theorists have explored the link between emotion and motivation, and the link between both those factors and behavior. For example, Skinner (1953) argued that emotional patterns of responding may arise from two very different sources. First, the evolutionary history of the species may favor certain unlearned or unconditioned responses. "For example, in some species biting, striking and clawing appear to be strengthened during anger before conditioning (that is, learning) can have taken place" (Skinner, 1953, p. 164). In short, we may strike out in anger simply because we are "wired" that way. Second, some emotional behaviors are learned. For example, an angry child may have been conditioned to "teasing the other child, taking toys away from him, destroying his work, or calling him names" (Skinner, 1953, p. 164). Such children have learned that such irritating behavior causes their enemies to suffer.

In the case of innate behaviors, such as instinctive anger, the history of the species may have insured that certain behavioral consequences are rewarding or punishing. That is, those patterns of angry behavior that fostered survival (such as biting or clawing one's enemies) came to be wired in. Reactions that were ineffective dropped out. Learned emotional behavior continues because it is reinforcing. People soon learn that an angry outburst "works." They cause the timid to give them what they want (a positive reinforcer) or at least to quit causing trouble (a negative reinforcer).

More recently, theorists such as Baron and Byrne (1981) and Berscheid and Hatfield (1969) attempted to explain why people are attracted to some people and repelled by others by citing the principle of reinforcement. They contend that people come to like and love those who reward them and dislike and hate those who punish them. Baron and Byrne's (1981) argument goes as follows:

1. Most stimuli can be identified as either rewarding or punishing.

2. Rewarding stimuli arouse positive feelings; punishing stimuli arouse negative feelings. These feelings, or affective responses, fall along a continuum from extremely positive to extremely negative.

3. The evaluation of any given stimulus as good or bad, enjoyable or unenjoyable, depends on whether it arouses positive or negative feelings. How positively or negatively a person evaluates another depends on the strength of the aroused effect. They illustrate their theory with this example:

> To take an obvious example, if a stranger were to walk up to you on the street and give you a swift kick in the shins, negative feelings would be aroused. If asked to evaluate the experience, you would no doubt say you also learned to associate negative feelings with the person, you would also indicate dislike for him in the future, but that is not all you learned in the situation. It may be less obvious, but your negative feelings aroused by a kick would also be likely to extend to any

innocent bystander who happened to be there, ... to the street where the kicking took place, and to anything else that was associated with the unpleasant interaction. In an analogous way, if on the following day, another passing stranger gave you a year's supply of free movie passes, your feelings would be positive and you would probably express liking toward your surroundings. (p. 212)

In this view, the human mind functions like a giant computer. The mind tallies up how emotionally pleasurable versus painful a lifetime of intimate encounters with Person X have proved to be, sums, and "spits out" an emotional reaction. A very handy tally indeed. Byrne (1971) even proposed a simple formula, a "law of attraction" to predict how people will evaluate others (See Fig. A).

$$Y = \left[\frac{\Sigma PR}{(\Sigma PR + \Sigma NR)} \right] + k$$

FIGURE A Byrne's "Law of Attraction."

The Y in Byrne's formula stands for attraction. On the other side of the equation the only symbols that really matter are PR (which stands for positive reinforcement—i.e., reward) and NR (which stands for negative reinforcement—which Byrne equates with punishment). Y (attraction) is greatest when there is a great deal of PR and very little NR. In *The Attraction Paradigm*, Byrne (1971) provided an encyclopedic review of evidence in support of these propositions.

Learning theorists make it clear that people may learn very different things about what is appropriate to feel, express, and observe in social situations.

What rewards seem most critical in love relationships? Hatfield and her colleagues (1984) interviewed over 1,000 dating couples, 100 newlywed men and women, and 400 elderly women as to the rewards (or lack thereof) the interviewees found to be most critical in their love relationships (Hatfield, Traupmann, Sprecher, Utne, & Hay, 1984). Their answers were surprisingly similar. The following rewards were critically important to almost everyone:

Personal Rewards

1. *Social grace.*
   Having a partner who is sociable, friendly, and relaxed in social settings.
2. *Intellect.*
   Having a partner who is intelligent and informed.
3. *Appearance.*
   Having a physically attractive partner.
   Having a partner who takes care of his or her appearance and conditioning; who attends to such things as personal cleanliness, dress, exercise, and good eating habits.

Emotional Rewards

1. *Liking and loving.*
   Being liked by your partner.
   Being loved by your partner.

2. *Understanding and concern.*
   Having your personal concerns and emotional needs understood and responded to.
3. *Acceptance.*
   Because of your partner's acceptance and encouragement, being free to try out different roles occasionally—for example, being a baby sometimes, a mother, a colleague or a friend, an aggressive as well as a passive lover, and so on.
4. *Appreciation.*
   Being appreciated for contributions to the relationship; not being taken for granted by your partner.
5. *Physical affection.*
   Receiving open affection—touching, hugging, kissing.
6. *Sex.*
   Experiencing a sexually fulfilling and pleasurable relationship with your partner.
   Sexual fidelity; having a partner who is faithful to your agreements about extramarital relations.
7. *Security.*
   Being secure in your partner's commitment to you and to the future of your relationship together.
8. *Plans and goals for the future.*
   Planning for and dreaming about your future together.

Day-to-Day Rewards

1. *Day-to-day operations.*
   Having a smoothly operating household, because of the way you two have organized your household responsibilities.
2. *Finances.*
   The amount of income and other financial resources that you may gain through your "joint account."
3. *Sociability.*
   Having a pleasant living together situation, because your partner is easy to live with on a day-do-day basis.
   Having a good companion, who suggests enjoyable things to do and who also goes along with your ideas for what you might do together.
   Knowing your partner is interested in hearing about your day and what is on your mind, and in turn will share concerns and events with you.
   Having a partner who is compatible with your friends and relatives; who is able to fit in.
4. *Decision making.*
   Having a partner who takes a fair share of the responsibility for making and carrying out decisions that affect both of you.

5. *Remembering special occasions.*
   Having a partner who is thoughtful about sentimental things; who remembers, for example, birthdays and other special occasions.

Opportunities Gained and Lost

1. *Opportunities gained.*
   Having the opportunity to partake of the many life experiences that depend on being married—for example, the chance to become a parent and even grandparent, the chance to be included in "married couple" social events, and, finally, having someone to count on in old age.

2. *Opportunities foregone.*
   Necessarily giving up certain opportunities in order to be in this relationship. The opportunities could have been other possible mates, a career, travel, etc.

SUMMARY

To understand emotion, scientists have found it necessary to acknowledge that emotions are a complex system, with multiple components. In part, the three components of the emotional trinity interact with one another. Candland (1977) proposed that emotional stimuli quickly elicit a response in the cognitive and physiological systems. The two elements combine to produce an emotional experience and then to generate appropriate emotional behavior. Each of the three elements is an indispensable part of a continuous emotional feedback loop. Each element modifies and is modified by the others. Each is both a stimulus and a response. Cognitive appraisals shape and are shaped by physiological reactions. The experience feeds back and shapes the perception of the eliciting stimuli. The various aspects of emotion continually feed back on one another, affecting the course of an emotional experience (see Figure B).

Nonetheless, each component of the emotional trinity provides unique information. This information is not redundant. For example, Lazarus (1977) pointed out that the various aspects of emotion are not always in sync:

> "... the three components correlate very poorly with each other. An individual might report no distress yet exhibit strong physiological reactions, or the behavioral responses signifying anger or fear might be inhibited as a result of social or internal pressures.... In short, the somatic changes connected with an emotion usually appear in a complex pattern of end-organ responses rather than in a simple, highly correlated one." (pp. 69–70)

To truly understand an intimate's inner life, one ideally would have some glimmering of how they *thought* about emotional events, and *felt* (physiologically) in addition to how they *behaved*. In the next section, we argue that intimates would do well to broaden their skills at speaking their mates' and families' emotional languages. We think Skinners' advice (chapter 1) is misleading because he suggests that intimates narrow the way they speak about their feelings and that they rule out entire forms of discourse. We think people will do better if they expand their skills at emotional communication, adding those of Skinner and others to their existing repertoire, rather than trying to force themselves and those they love into a narrow, artificial form of expression. This richer repertoire fits with the more complex view of emotions derived from recent research.

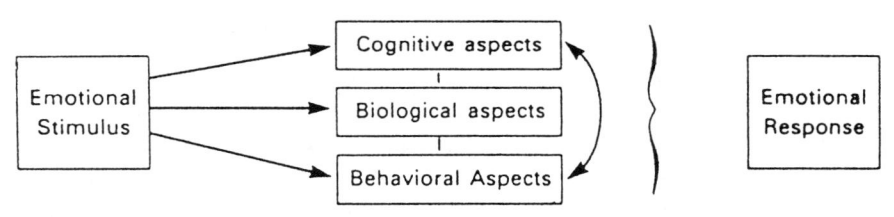

FIGURE B An emotional sequence.

References

ARGYLE, M. (1967). *The psychology of interpersonal behavior*. Baltimore, MD: Penguin Books.

BARON, R. A., & BYRNE, D. (1981). *Social psychology: Understanding human interaction*. (3rd ed.). Boston: Allyn and Bacon.

BERSCHEID, E. (1983). Emotion. In H. H. Kelley, E. Berscheid, A. Christensen, J. H. Harvey, T. L. Huston, G. Levinger, E. McClintock, L. A. Peplau, & D. R. Peterson (Eds.), *Close relationships*. (pp. 110–168). New York: Freeman.

BERSCHEID, E., & HATFIELD, E. (1969). *Interpersonal attraction*. Reading, MA: Addison-Wesley.

BUCK, R. (1979). Individual differences in nonverbal sending accuracy and electrodermal responding: The externalizing—internalizing dimension. In R. Rosenthal (Ed.), *Skill in nonverbal communication: Individual differences*. (pp. 140–170). Cambridge, MA: Oelgeschlager, Gunn, & Hain.

BYRNE, D. (1971). *The attraction paradigm*. New York: Academic Press.

CACIOPPO, J. T., PETTY, R. E., & TASSINARY, L. G. (in press). Social psychophysiology: A new look. To appear in L. Berkowitz (Ed.) *Advances in experimental social psychology*.

CANDLAND, D. K. (1977). The persistent problems of emotion. In D. K. Candland, J. P. Fell, E. Keen, A. I. Leshner, R. Plutchik, & R. M. Tarpy (Eds.), *Emotion*. (pp. 1–84). Monterey, CA: Brooks-Cole.

CARLSON, J., & HATFIELD, E. (in press). *The psychology of emotions*. Lanham, MD: University Press of America.

DARWIN, C. (1965). *The expression of the emotion in man and animals*. Chicago, IL: University of Chicago Press. (Original work published 1872).

DEGLER, C. N. (1980). *At odds: Women and the family in America from the revolution to the present*. New York: Oxford University Press.

EKMAN, P. (1972). Universals and cultural differences in facial expressions of emotion. In J. Cole (Ed.), *Nebraska Symposium on Motivation, 19,* (pp. 207–282) Lincoln: University of Nebraska Press.

EKMAN, P. (1985). *Telling lies*. New York: Berkley Books.

EKMAN, P., & FRIESEN, W. V. (1969). Nonverbal leakage and clues to deception. *Psychiatry, 32,* 88–106.

FRIDLUND, A. J., & IZARD, C. E. (1983). Electromyographic studies of facial expressions of emotion and patterns of emotions. In J. T. Cacioppo & R. E. Petty (Eds.), *Social psychophysiology: A sourcebook.* (pp. 243–286). New York: Guilford Press.

GAY, P. (1984). *The bourgeois experience: Victoria to Freud. Vol. 1: Education of the senses.* New York: Oxford University Press.

HALBERSTADT, A. G. (1986). Family socialization of emotional expression and nonverbal communication styles and skills. *Journal of Personality and Social Psychology, 51,* 827–836.

HATFIELD, E. (1970). Studies testing a theory of positive affect. National Science Foundation Grant GS 30822X, Washington, DC.

HATFIELD, E., TRAUPMANN, J., SPRECHER, S., UTNE, M., & HAY, J. (1984). Equity and intimate relations: recent research. In W. Ickes (Ed.), *Compatible and incompatible relationships.* (pp. 1–27). New York: Springer-Verlag.

HATFIELD, E., & WALSTER, G. W. (1978). *A new look at love.* Lanham, MD: University Press of America.

IZARD, C. E. (1971). *The face of emotion.* New York: Appleton-Century-Crofts.

IZARD, C. E. (1977). *Human emotions.* New York: Plenum Press.

IZARD, C. E., & BUECHLER, S. (1986). Aspects of consciousness and personality in terms of differential emotions theory. In R. Plutchik & H. Kellerman (Eds.), *Emotion: Theory, research and experience. Vol. 1* (pp 165–188). New York: Academic Press.

LANZETTA, J. T., & KLECK, R. E. (1970). Encoding and decoding of nonverbal affect in humans. *Journal of Personality and Social Psychology, 16,* 12–19.

LAZARUS, R. S. (1977). A cognitive analysis of biofeedback control. In G. E. Schwartz & G. Beatty (Eds.), *Biofeedback: Theory and Research* (pp. 69–71). New York: Academic Press.

LAZARUS, R. S., KANNER, A. D., & FOLKMAN, S. (1980). Emotions: A cognitive phenomenological analysis: In R. Plutchik & H. Kellerman (Eds.), *Emotion: Theory, research and experience. Vol. 1.* (pp. 189–218). New York: Academic Press.

LIEBOWITZ, M. R. (1983). *The chemistry of love.* Boston, Little, Brown, and Co.

LUTZ, C., & WHITE, G. M. (1986). The anthropology of emotions. *Annual Review of Anthropology, 15,* 405–436.

MACLEAN, P. D. 1986). Ictal symptoms relating to the nature of affects and their cerebral substrate. In R. Plutchik & H. Kellerman (Eds.), *Emotion: theory, research, and experience. Vol. 3. Biological foundations of emotion.* (pp. 61–90) New York: Academic Press.

MALATESTA, C. A., & HAVILAND, J. M. (1982). Learning display rules: The socialization of emotion expression in infancy. *Child Development, 53,* 991–1003.

MORENCY, N. L., & KRAUSS, R. M. (1982). Children's nonverbal encoding and decoding of affect. In R. Feldman (Ed.), *Development of non-verbal behavior in children.* (pp. 181–199). New York: Springer-Verlag.

SCHERER, K. R., & EKMAN, P. (1982). *Handbook of methods in nonverbal behavior research.* Cambridge: Cambridge University Press.

SKINNER, B. (1953). *Science and human behavior.* New York: The Macmillan Co.

STEARNS, P. N., & STEARNS, C. Z. (1985). Emotionology: Clarifying the history of emotions and emotional standards: *American Historical Review, 90:* 4, 813–836.

STEINER, J. E. (1979). Human facial expression in response to taste and smell stimulation. *Advances in Child Development and Behavior, 13,* 257–295.

STERNBERG, R. J. (1988). Triangulating love. In R. J. Sternberg & M. L. Barnes (Eds.), *The psychology of love.* (pp. 119–138). New Haven: Yale University Press.

STONE, L. (1979). *The family, sex, and marriage: In England 1500–1800.* New York: Harper Torchbooks.

ZUCKERMAN, M., HALL, J. A., DEFRANK, R. S., & ROSENTHAL, R. (1976). Encoding and decoding of spontaneous and posed facial expressions. *Journal of Personality and Social Psychology, 34,* 966–977.

After reading: CONSOLIDATE INFORMATION

1. Summarize how Hatfield and Rapson see the relationship of behavior to the emotions.
2. According to Hatfield and Rapson, how do family and cultures affect the ways in which people express emotion?
3. From Hatfield and Rapson's summary, can you make some inferences about how a person can understand another person's inner feelings?

Family Life and the Politics of Talk

Mary Field Belenky, Blythe McVicker Clinchy, Nancy Rule Goldberger, Jill Mattuck Tarule

The following excerpt is taken from a collaboratively written study, Women's Ways of Knowing: The Development of Self, Voice, and Mind *(1986). Basing their study on interviews with 135 female students, the four co-authors isolate and analyze patterns of the ways in which women work out meaning, interpret their understandings of the world, and use language either to remain silent or to make their voices heard. The following section is taken from Chapter 8, "Family Life and the Politics* of Talk," in which the young women discuss the ways family talk and language influenced their own development and attitudes.

Note: The authors use two terms which they define within the context of their study: procedural knowing and constructivist knowing. By procedural knowing they mean the procedures or strategies a person develops to interpret what happens to her. Constructivist knowing refers to a person's ability to understand how she constructs meaning from the knowledge she has of the world.

Before reading: FIRST THOUGHTS
LOOK AHEAD

1. How can family life be linked to the politics of talk? How, in your own experience, does talk and language function in your family life?
2. Do you think that there is a difference in the way male and female children communicate with their parents?
3. Respond to the two metaphors the authors use to characterize family emotional structures:
    net/web
    mountain/pyramid

During reading: REACT
QUESTION
SUMMARIZE

1. Why do you think that the women described in this chapter thought it noteworthy and admirable that their fathers had become good listeners and that their mothers had developed strong voices?
2. React to the subheading "Healing the Split between Intellect and Emotion." What is the split? Why does it have to be healed?

THE WOMEN WHO QUESTIONED the infallibility of the gut and who were consciously cultivating and integrating the voices of reason and emotion wove still another pattern in the family story. While not all these women came from happy homes, they were much more likely than the women who held other perspectives to describe family relationships characterized by images of connection, care, mutuality, and reciprocity. Because the themes in the family histories told by the procedural and the constructivist knowers were so similar, we combined their stories, noting the exceptions when they occur.

MOTHERS AND DIALOGUE

Daughters who integrated the voices of reason and feelings were likely to be interested in the quality of the voices of their mothers. Many noted with admiration that their mothers developed strong, clear voices of their own. As one young woman said, "My mother is only five feet tall, but if you heard her over the phone, why you would think that she is at least five feet and seven inches."

Again we see that it is important to daughters that parents have a voice. Those who receive knowledge from others look to their parents for truth and direction and often feel helped when their voices are loud and clear. At this new juncture daughters wish their parents to have voices of their own so that they might be full participants in an ongoing conversation. A twenty-three-year-old college alumna described such talk. "I was her confidante. She would tell me things about herself. It was sort of a relationship of equals." It was only in this last collection of stories that family conversations routinely involved two-way talk. In these stories both parents and daughters were given a voice, each spoke and listened, each had an equal say.

These daughters were disappointed if their mothers did not have the courage to speak their minds straight out, or if their mothers only provided others "with a forum for discussion, but is never a participant in that discussion herself."

Some noticed their fathers listening with care. When that occurred it was highly valued. However, none of these daughters particularly admired their fathers for speaking out. For fathers to have a voice was a given—not an achievement. For fathers to develop a listening ear and for mothers to "gain a voice" were the feats that those who were integrating the voices of reason and feeling noted and appreciated.

CONNECTEDNESS BETWEEN MOTHERS AND DAUGHTERS

Although the basic themes of attachment and autonomy were interwoven, a greater sense of connection and of commonalities pervaded the daughters' portraits of mothers, while the sense of distance and difference continued to predominate in the descriptions of life with father. This pattern was also observed by James Youniss and Jacqueline Smoller (1985) in their extensive study of adolescents' perceptions of mothers and fathers. This pattern was also reflected in the descriptions of family life Lillian Rubin heard in the interviews she conducted with husbands and wives in her study of lower-class family life, *Worlds of Pain* (1976). Chodorow (1978) argued that the basic sense of living connected or separated from others—different conceptions of self and of the self-world relationship—is deeply rooted in the experience of the infant's earliest relationships with his or her caregiver. Universally, mothers and/or other women attend to the care of the young, with fathers and other men remaining on the periphery. Chodorow maintains that when caregivers ordinarily from only one sex nurture infants, the stage is set for two distinctive developmental consequences, depending on the match or mismatch of the caregiver's and the infant's gender. The female infant nurtured by her mother has only to affirm her connectedness and sense of sameness as she begins to develop an understanding of gender and of her own identity as a person in the world. The male baby, on the other hand, has to declare his separateness from his mother, his primary caregiver and first source of identification, in order to build a conception of his gender and identity.

Chodorow's argument is compelling and helps explain the differing sense of connectedness and separateness that can readily be observed in well-developing boys and girls from the earliest ages on. However, as we reexamined these stories of family life, two considerations emerged that threw Chodorow's argument into a different light. With an increasing awareness of how much the sense of connectedness to others deepens with maturity, we believe that important causal factors that occur later in the life cycle must also be considered. For many women being a mother as well as having a woman as a mother provides a profound experience of human connection. That adult experiences as well as childhood experiences contribute to the evolution of a sense of connection is consistent with our observations that connectedness with others is one of the most complicated human achievements, requiring a high level of development. As Jerome Kagan (1984) suggests, there is a general tendency to attribute characteristics to the infant that are opposite to those that are prized in adults in the culture. Thus, he argues, Americans valuing independence and individuality in adults tend to see the baby as being dependent and undifferentiated from others. In contrast, the Japanese, valuing a close interdependence between people, see the infant as too autonomous and needing to be coaxed into a dependent role in order to encourage the mutual bonding necessary for adult life. The more we come to understand and value attachment and connectedness in adults, the more likely we will conceptualize autonomy and independence as part of the infant's nature and act to encourage the development of the capacity for connection with others.

Guiding Metaphors

Whatever the roots of connectedness, communal and family life is threatened whenever members fail to see the interdependence of all. As Gilligan and her colleagues suggest, the individual who conceptualizes the self as basically connected to others sees the bonds that knit human relationships together as bonds of attachment. They spin visions of the ties between persons, which can best be suggested by the metaphor of webs and nets. Webs and nets imply opposing capacities for snaring or entrapment and for rescuing or safety. They also suggest a complexity of relationships and the delicate interrelatedness of all so that tension and movement in one part of the system will grow to be felt in all parts of the whole. In the complexity of a web, no one position dominates over the rest. Each person—no matter how small—has some potential for power; each is always subject to the actions of others. It is hard to imagine other ways of visioning the world that offer as much potential for protection to the immature and the infirm.

In contrast, the self premised in autonomy sees individuals relating through bonds of agreements, such as contracts, laws, and the like. Their metaphors for suggesting the world are more often images of pyramids and mountains. On the metaphorical mountain the few at the top dominate the many on the bottom. Those near the base must move the whole mountain to affect those near the apex; in the image of the net, even the least can affect all others by the slightest pull on the gossamer thread.

Those on a mountain find it easier to maintain the view that some must lead and others must follow, that some will win while the rest will lose. In the hierarchical world that the players with these limited epistemologies construct, the game is rigged. Typically, it is the men who dominate the women and the parents who hold sway over the children. Mothers taking this either/or stance believe that they must choose to lose in order for their children to succeed. Thus mothers try to remain voiceless, powerless, and selfless so that their children will prosper (Miller 1976).

Carole Klein (1984), in *Mothers and Sons*, tells us that the mothers of sons feel more guilt and receive more condemnation from others when they pursue their own interests than do the mothers of daughters. Because women are expected to subordinate themselves to males, it may take longer for mothers and sons to realize that the win/lose model is not the best model for most human relationships than it takes mother and daughters. It is the relationship between mothers and daughters in which the possibility of common interests and a win/win game is most likely to become apparent. Because mothers and daughters can affirm and enjoy their commonalities more readily, they are more likely to see how they might advance their individual interests in tandem, without one having to be sacrificed for the other—an understanding that most of the constructivist women and their mothers have achieved.

Healing the Split between Intellect and Emotion

When the procedural knowers first began to cultivate the voice of reason, they were more likely to see intrapsychic powers being allocated to their parents according to the conventional pattern. They saw their fathers as imbued with intelligence, while they portrayed their mothers as warm and sensitive. While they saw each of their parents as having developed one aspect of their powers rather fully, they portrayed them as denying other aspects of their selfhood.

Occasionally when this bifurcation was sharply drawn, the volcanic eruptions that were so typical of the earlier stories remained a theme, albeit the theme was now largely muted and the level of violence greatly diminished. While these mothers were depicted as hot-tempered and hysterical, it was the cold, unemotional fathers who erupted with volcanic force. The fathers relied on their wives to mediate and interpret their feelings to others. Such fathers were unemotional only in the sense that they did not articulate feelings. Indeed, it often appeared that it was the mother who was actually the thinker and the father who was the feeler—at least in terms of dealing with the personal and the interpersonal. A smooth relationship between such fathers and their daughters was often dependent on the mediation services provided by sensitive, feeling mothers. Such mothers tried to imagine, understand, and articulate each person's feelings. The conversations of these fathers and daughters could enter into the personal only when the mother became an interpreter and supplied them with the language of emotions.

It may be that the father's unmet need for the absent mother to intercede as an intermediary and translator explains why marital separation is so often followed by the abandonment of children by fathers. When a separation or divorce occurs, a father has to face his children directly, without the services of a mediator. Some fathers may feel so uncomfortable without an intermediary that they withdraw altogether. Teaching children and fathers to talk with each other directly might go a long way toward reducing the amount and intensity of such estrangements.

The descriptions of volcanic activity, alcoholism, violence, and abandonment were markedly diminished in the stories of family life told by procedural and constructivist knowers—in terms of both prevalence and virulence—when compared with the stories told by women who held the earlier perspectives. While fully 75 percent of the silent and the received knowers depicted one or both of their parents as alcoholic, only two (6 percent) of the reflective and constructivist knowers combined gave a parent this label. A third woman had a mother she proudly called a "sober alcoholic." "I really respect her for her progress in stopping drinking and being successful at it. That's one of the great accomplishments of her life. Being able to accept that she had a problem and that she could be doing something about it and being successful in it."

While a few of these women had parents who were separated or divorced, none of the fathers abandoned the father-daughter relationship altogether—an event that occurred with remarkable frequency in the previous collection of stories. When all family members were encouraged to draw on their whole range of capacities to deal with both the personal and the impersonal, they no longer needed to rely on the use of either power or abandonment for the resolution of conflicts. Instead, talking things through—however heatedly—became the preferred alternative. As Patti, the adolescent mother who helped us understand procedural knowing, said, "My mother and I can fight, argue, and scream about different points of things and yet end up saying, 'Well, thank you!' You know, appreciating each other no matter how much we disagree."

Mothers and Developing the Voice of Reason

The tendency to allocate intellectual capacities to fathers and emotional ones to mothers was largely overcome in the stories told by women who were integrating the voices of reason and emotions themselves. These women were much more likely to see mothers and fathers as endowed with both intellectual and emotional capacities. Almost all of them portrayed their mothers as having good minds and many of their fathers as having some capacity to acknowledge and articulate their feelings.

While subjectivists' mothers had the ability to speak from the gut and say what they felt, it was only in this last group of stories that the daughters consistently depicted their mothers as also having the ability to speak from the mind and to say what they thought. As Patti said,

> My mother is a wonderful person to talk to. I can talk to her about anything now. She is the type that can draw stuff out of a person. *She stands up for what she thinks* (emphasis added).

Another elaborated,

> My mother is very independent, very strong—a very verbal kind of person. She has got her opinions and she is not the least bit afraid to express them. When she gets into arguments there is a lot of love—but there is that independence of thought.

Mildred illustrates the pleasure that constructivist women and their mothers often take in each other's intellectual powers.

> My mother is a liberated woman who has a wonderful mind. After getting a Ph.D. in philosophy, she produced nine children and became the perfect housewife. About the age of forty she realized that she spent her whole life making other people happy and there are a lot of other things for women out there. She has gotten a second degree and now she teaches. She is very successful. Her students adore her and her children adore her.

Another college student saw her mother in similar terms.

> My mother is a wonderful person! She is really a miracle. Very creative, very political, very involved with life. She is complicated. I was always her friend. She included me in her life. She always comes to something with understanding.

These women portrayed their intelligent mothers as being very active learners.

> My mother always wants to be on top of the news. She is always questioning, investigating, and looking for something else, making challenges and demands on herself, in her job and with her children.

Like their daughters, these mothers had two inner voices at their command: a voice for expressing emotions and a voice for sharing reasons. Both could be heard. The use of one did not drown out the other.

Fathers and Developing the Voice of Emotions

As these women came to value their mothers for their good minds, many also began to find in their fathers emotional capacities that they never knew existed. As Patti said, "My father is trying to be more understanding, which makes it easier for me to express myself. He realizes now that emotions play a much larger part than logical thinking. While Patti saw her father changing, others saw that it was their own view of their fathers that was undergoing change. As one college student said, "My father is an emotional man who doesn't let you know that he is emotional. He is very intelligent, very logical, and very accepting. I can see now that he really has a depth of emotions that I've never really seen before."

The shift that these women noticed—their fathers became more tolerant of their nurturant and affiliative responses and mothers became more active and agentic—has been documented in many studies of adult men and women approaching midlife (Cumming and Henry 1961; Gurin, Veroff, and Feld 1960; Gutmann 1964, 1975; Lowenthal, Thurnher, and Chiriboga 1975; Neugarten 1969;

Rossi 1980). Again, it appears that when all goes well parents and children develop in tandem, that in the natural course of things the different generations can provide each other with the mutual supports that each requires for continued growth and development.

The Mother-Daughter Relationship and the Development of Connected Knowing

However much the parents of these women moved toward developing and integrating their intellectual and emotional capacities, distinctive differences remained between the ways the women depicted their mothers and fathers and related to them as knowers. While fathers served as models of knowing, it was in the relationships with mothers that these daughters found the most developed models of and opportunities for connected knowing. Connected knowing rises out of the experience of relationships; it requires intimacy and equality between self and object, not distance and impersonality; its goal is understanding, not proof.

Most of the procedural knowers reported that they talked with their mothers about personal things and they talked to their fathers—if they talked at all—about relatively impersonal topics. (In no case did this pattern reverse.) For example, a woman in her mid-twenties said,

> My mother is the one that I have more intimate discussions with. I can talk with her about stuff that I don't discuss with my father.... My mother deals more with that part of me which is able to deal with people, and sympathize with people, and communicate with people. My father has more to do with my intellectual development and my appreciation of literature.

And Faith said, "My dad has this dislike of what he calls 'idle chitchat,' but that's sort of necessary for a person. Faith's father liked to talk about "world affairs and crossword puzzles."

When fathers do talk to their daughters about matters of personal importance to the daughters, they tell them what they ought to do. One senior told us that her father was "still in the advice-giving mode." The father offered his advice out of loving concern. He wanted his daughter to major in economics in order to get a good job in business and become financially secure. But to the daughter, who was interested in painting and taking care of animals, the father's advice felt cold and controlling. When she failed to pursue her father's goals, she was aware that she had disappointed him. "My father categorizes me, and he always finds me wanting."

The intelligent mothers these women depicted were more like students, trying to understand; and they spoke of their intelligent fathers as being more like conventional teachers, bent on passing out truths. Linda's description of her parents provided an outstanding example. Both of her parents were psychiatrists involved as researchers and practitioners with adolescents and young adults (Linda's age group). Linda's mother looked to Linda as an expert she could consult. "She asks me—We talk a lot about her cases and her work. I kind of help her see the point of view of my generation—or whatever." Linda's mother asked, she did not tell. To her father, Linda was not an expert but a case that proved his points. She believed that her father was not interested in her as a unique person but as a general case for fitting into his "little classifications." She believed that he had little interest in the classifications that she might offer. "He makes me a case study. I'm just a little piece of evidence.... He is not interested in what goes on in my head." As Linda saw it, her father did not look to her for help to expand his understanding of her age group. Instead of asking her about her experience, he told her what she was experiencing. "Since I'm in this position, I must feel this way, this way, or this way. He has all of these little classifications which he fits everything into." She also believed that he was only interested in proving his old theories, not in generating new ones. She tested out this hunch: "I said, 'Dad, are you still learning new things?' And he goes, 'Well, not particularly.'" To her mother, Linda was a colleague or a teacher; to her father, Linda was a research subject, a student, or a child.

That such differences between mothers and fathers are so common may be accounted for by the fact that many men are used to being the expert, while many women are used to consulting others; many men are interested in how experience is generalized and universalized, while many women are interested in what can be learned from the particular; and the work of men frequently involves maintaining or increasing the status differences between persons, while the life work of many women focuses on maternal practice, where the main goal is to bring the smallest, least members up into relations of equality. While mothers and daughters slip into chairs around the kitchen table with ease, only occasionally do fathers abdicate their platforms without pressure from below.

To see themselves as equals, daughters often had to cut their fathers down to size. As one college alumni recounted,

> I am awed by my father. He is very smart, very intelligent, and very articulate. He can really pop the bubble. I can pop his bubble now and then! (Both laugh.) I never knew it before, but I can throw it right back to him—and he can be devastating!

By being devastating herself, she could meet him on equal ground. She continued,

> Eventually I began to realize that my father wasn't perfect. That he was a human being—with frailties and problems of his own. If my father said something, that was that. You never argued with him. I began to realize that he could be wrong about stuff and that he did have deficiencies as a person. I think that helped our relationship in the sense that I could be a little more equal to him and able to communicate with him more. I think that's when we really started being very good friends.

Another woman definitely had seen her father, the professor, as God. She had once called him "Zeus" and said he was "a magnificent sight to look at." She agreed with one of his students that if her father "was running for God," she, too, would have voted for him. This father seemed to have campaigned for such a role. "He tends to have the approach that he is better than anyone else. He really has an overinflated ego. I think that any person will admit that early on in life parents are God—the authority. Later on they don't know a damn thing. And then after a while, you realize that they are reasonable people after all." In saying this, she paraphrased the words that Mark Twain put in the mouth of a young man: "My parents were so dumb when I was seventeen and so much smarter when I was twenty-one; I can't believe how much they learned in just four years."

While fathers of the constructivists occasionally still required dethroning, such images were largely absent from their stories of mothers. Indeed, the women in this group characterized the relationship between mothers and daughters as one of great intimacy, equality, and collegiality. While one might worry that such close, personal ties might hamper the individuation and development of these women, it was rare for women in this group to express such concerns. Indeed, Bertram Cohler and Henry Grunebaum (1981), in their study of daughters, mothers, and grandmothers, were also surprised at the intimate relationships they observed between different generations of women and revised their opinions about the difficulties such closeness might necessarily entail.

Not only did these women tend to cultivate relationships with their mothers that were very close and collegial, such relationships served as models for guiding and assessing many other relationships. As such, most of the constructivists were able to turn at least one of their professors into a colleague/friend of the highest order. Whenever such relationships took place, the sense of pleasure and accomplishment was unmistakable. Bridget shared her delight in the changes that even she and her father were able to bring about. "I tease him about the fact that I am finally getting myself established in life and that now he can start learning things from me."

> (Laughs) I am going to love it! (Laughs.) It makes me feel great! He agrees!" These women, along with many of their mothers, some of their professors and a few of their fathers, became perpetual students *and* perpetual teachers. In trading these roles back and forth, they made colleagues of one another.

References

CHODOROW, N. (1978). *The reproduction of mothering*. Berkeley: University of California Press.

COHLER, B., & GRUNEBAUM, H. (1981). *Mothers, grandmothers, and daughters*. New York: Wiley & Sons.

CUMING, E. & HENRY, W. H. (1968). *Growing old: The process of disengagement*. New York: Basic Books.

GILLIGAN, C. (1982). *In a different voice: Psychological theory and women's development*. Cambridge: Harvard University Press.

GURIN, G., VEROFF, J. & FELD, S. (1960). *Americans view their mental health*. New York: Basic Books.

GUTMANN, D. (1964). An exploration of ego configurations in middle and later life. In B.L. Neugarten (Ed.), *Personality in middle and later life* (pp. 114–148). New York: Atherton.

Gutmann, D. (1975). Parenthood: A key to the comparative study of the life cycle. In N. Datan & L. Ginsberg (Eds.), *Life-span developmental psychology: Normative crisis* (pp. 167–184). New York: Academic Press.

Kagan, J. (1984). *The nature of the child.* New York: Basic Books.

Klein, C. (1984). *Mothers and sons.* Boston: Houghton Mifflin.

Miller, J.B. (1976). *Towards a new psychology of women.* Boston: Beacon Press.

Neugarten, B.L. (1969). Continuities and discontinuities of psychological issues into adult life. *Human Development, 12,* 121–130.

Rossi, A. (1980). Aging and parenting in the middle years. In P. Baltes & O. G. Brim (Eds.), *Life-span development and behavior* (Vol. 3). New York: Academic Press.

Rubin, L. (1976). *Worlds of pain: Life in the working-class family.* New York: Basic Books.

Youniss, J. and Smoller, J. (1985). *Adolescent relations with mothers, fathers and friends.* Chicago: University of Chicago Press.

After reading: CONSOLIDATE INFORMATION

1. After reading this section, what can you infer about the authors' belief about what shapes a woman's way of perceiving and understanding what goes on around her?
2. How do you think the women described here will act in their own marriages and families?
3. What can you infer from this chapter about what the authors evaluate as positive in family talk?

Effects of Physical Attractiveness, Intelligence, Age at Marriage, and Cohabitation on the Perception of Marital Satisfaction

Michael W. Tucker and Kevin E. O'Grady

Michael Tucker and Kevin O'Grady report the results of their research in a familiar form for social scientists, that of the experimental research report. This article, which was written for a scholarly audience, appeared in The Journal of Social Psychology. *Portions of this research report were part of Michael Tucker's senior honors thesis, which he wrote under the direction Kevin O'Grady at the University of Maryland.*

Before reading: FIRST THOUGHTS
                    LOOK AHEAD

1. What kinds of characteristics do you think affect a person's happiness in marriage?
2. Much is written about the high rate of divorce in the United States. Before reading this article, freewrite a quick list of causes you think may account for that rate.
3. Read the title; then read the abstract. What can you predict about the researchers' findings?

During reading: REACT
                   QUESTION
                 SUMMARIZE

1. Read the survey of research or literature review which begins the article. Do the research findings summarized agree or disagree with your own perceptions about marriage?
2. Do you think that the composition of the researchers' study group, which was composed of college students, affected their findings? How?

ABSTRACT. Factors used in predicting the likelihood of marital satisfaction were investigated. Sixty-four male and 64 female American undergraduates evaluated eight bogus marriages in which male and female physical attractiveness, age at marriage, and intelligence and cohabitation were systematically varied, using a partially balanced incomplete blocks design. Evaluation was based on a 15-item, Likert-type questionnaire specifically developed for use in this study. Results of a multivariate analysis of variance revealed seven significant main effects and three significant interaction effects. Significant main effects were found for the gender of subject and all within-subject factors except cohabitation. In addition, two hypothesized first-order interactions, Male Attractiveness × Female Attractiveness and Male Intelligence × Female Intelligence, were significant. However, the hypothesized Male Age at Marriage × Female Age at Marriage interaction did not emerge. Results are interpreted in the context of prior research on physical attractiveness, the matching hypothesis, and perceived similarity of needs.

IN THE LAST 20 YEARS there has been an alarming increase in the incidence of separation and divorce in the United States. Brehm (1985) reported that the divorce rate had more than doubled since the mid 1960s. Because most people will continue to marry and many of these marriages may end in divorce, research into what factors influence the stability of marriage is becoming increasingly important.

One factor of interest to any discussion of marital satisfaction is similarity of any of a variety of demographic and background characteristics. Most studies conclude that people tend to marry people similar to themselves, and further, that couples appear to be more satisfied when they are similar (Blazer, 1963; Murstein, 1976; Murstein & Beck, 1972; Schellenberg & Bee, 1960; White & Hatcher, 1984).

Another factor that may affect marital satisfaction is physical attractiveness. Research has consistently shown that good things are attributed most often to the physically attractive (e.g., Dion, Berscheid, & Walster, 1972; Miller, 1970; Sigall & Landy, 1973; Walster, Aronson, Abrahams, & Rottman, 1966), though there are clear exceptions to this general rule (e.g., Dermer & Theil, 1975; Sigall & Ostrove, 1975). It appears that attractive people are perceived as possessing desirable characteristics merely on the basis of their attractiveness, even if the characteristics are unrelated. According to the matching hypothesis, people usually end up dating and subsequently marrying people of about the same level of attractiveness as themselves (Berscheid, Dion, Walster, & Walster, 1971; Murstein, 1976).

Intelligence also may well influence marital satisfaction. Research directly assessing the effects of intelligence on subsequent marital satisfaction is largely lacking; however, some studies suggest an inverse relationship between educational attainment level and marital separation rates (Bumpass & Sweet, 1972; Glick, 1957; Udry, 1966). Nonetheless, Bumpass and Sweet suggested that age-at-marriage differences may explain this relationship better than intellectual differences. Little research clearly demonstrates the effects of intelligence on marital satisfaction, but it is reasonable to assume that satisfaction would be highest when partners are of similar intellectual abilities (Murstein, 1976).

Age at first marriage is another factor that may well influence subsequent marital satisfaction. Demographic research indicates a clear relationship between age and marriage failure rates. Marriages in which the partners are younger than 20 years are much more likely to fail than those of older partners (Booth & White, 1980; Bumpass & Sweet, 1972; Carter & Glick, 1970). The effects of age discrepancy could also be important. Cowan (1984) found that subjects felt the likelihood of having a successful marriage decreased as age discrepancy between partners increased.

A final factor is cohabitation. Research in the 1970s theorized that cohabitation would serve as a form of compatibility test for marriage (Lewis, Spanier, Storm-Atkinson, & LeHeckla, 1977; Macklin, 1972; Trost, 1975). However, more recent research in the United States on cohabitation suggests that it has little or no effect on subsequent marital satisfaction (Bentler & Newcomb, 1978; Jacques & Chason, 1979; Newcomb & Bentler, 1980; Watson, 1983).

The present study was concerned with whether people perceive this relationship to be true or believe that cohabitation increases a couple's chances of having a successful marriage. It investigated what individuals perceive as the factors that affect marital satisfaction and focused on the effects similarity of a married couple in terms of attractiveness, intelligence, and age at marriage might have on the perception of the satisfaction of the partners. The purpose was twofold. First, little research has addressed the implicit norms and stereotypes that might be used in evaluating marital partners; hence, it seems important to evaluate popular beliefs about marital satisfaction. Second, it was also possible to compare what factors individuals *perceived* to be important with what factors prior research has shown to be *actually* critical determinants of a satisfying marriage. The determination of significant discrepancies would serve to shed additional light on the role these various factors might play in marital discord, under the assumption that discrepancies between one's expectations about marriage in general and one's actual experience may produce significant discord in the marriage.

To assess the effects of similarity, the three previously discussed factors—attractiveness, intelligence, and age at marriage—were systematically manipulated for each of the partners. Premarital cohabitation was also included as a factor in the design in order to study its effects alone and in conjunction with the other independent variables.

Thus, there were eight main effects in the study. The first two main effects were male and female physical attractiveness. It was hypothesized that attractive people would be perceived more favorably than unattractive people (Dion et al., 1972; Miller, 1970; Sigall & Landy, 1973). The third and fourth main effects were male and female age at marriage. It was hypothesized that older individuals would be perceived more favorably than the younger (Booth & White, 1980; Bumpass & Sweet, 1972; Carter & Glick, 1970). The fifth and sixth main effects were male and female intelligence. It was thought that the more intelligent would be perceived more favorably than the less intelligent (Bumpass & Sweet; Glick, 1957; Udry, 1966). The seventh main effect was cohabitation. It was hypothesized that a significant difference would be found, despite the fact that more recent research (Macklin, 1980; Newcomb, 1979) failed to support unambiguously the existence of this effect. The eighth main effect was subject gender. Abramowitz (1985), in a similar experiment involving physical attractiveness, found neither a subject gender main effect nor any significant interaction effects involving subject gender; therefore, no significant differences involving subject gender were hypothesized.

There were also several important interaction effects for which specific hypotheses were formulated. For the Male Attractiveness × Female Attractiveness interaction it was expected that high-attractiveness couples would be perceived most positively and low-attractiveness couples most negatively (Dion et al., 1972; Miller, 1970). Thus, the notion here is that the attractiveness of one member of the couple must be considered in the context of the other member's attractiveness, which may serve to enhance the perception (i.e., when both are attractive), to moderate the perception (when members of the couple are disparate on attractiveness), or to degrade the perception (when both members are unattractive). It is of interest that this hypothesis partially contradicts the results of Bar-Tal and Saxe (1976), who reported that their subjects evaluated wives independently of their husbands' attractiveness, whereas evaluations of husbands were dependent on their wives' attractiveness.

The Male Age at Marriage × Female Age at Marriage interaction was also of interest. It was hypothesized that older would be perceived more favorably than younger couples (Booth & White, 1980; Bumpass & Sweet, 1972; Carter & Glick, 1970). It was further hypothesized that for age-discrepant couples, the female-older couples would be perceived most negatively (Cowan, 1984).

For the Male Intelligence × Female Intelligence interaction, it was hypothesized that couples of similar intelligence would be perceived more favorably than disparate couples (Murstein, 1976) and also that high-intelligence couples would be seen more positively than low-intelligence couples (Glick, 1957; Solomon & Saxe, 1977; Udry, 1966). Solomon and Saxe found that higher intelligence resulted in a more positive evaluation of a female stimulus person; we were interested in whether intelligence of a spouse within the context of the partner's intelligence would moderate this effect.

METHOD

Subjects

Sixty-four male and 64 female undergraduate psychology students in the United States participated in this experiment and received extra course credit for participation.

Materials

Materials were a set of 16 photographs and a series of bogus data sheets. The photographs had previously been used successfully in an experiment involving physical attractiveness (Abramowitz, 1985). Abramowitz obtained, from three independent samples of 98 undergraduates in total, ratings of physical attractiveness (using a 9-point Likert-type scale) of 48 black-and-white photographs of White seniors drawn from a high school yearbook. Each individual picture was carefully chosen so that the initial pool of 48 individuals showed considerable variability in terms of attractiveness, each individual appeared appropriately dressed for a responsible young adult, and each individual would be seen as between the ages of 18 and 22 years. (Subsequent research suggested that college students guessed the ages of the individuals in the final 16 photographs to be between 17 and 25 years.) The yearbook picture of each of the 48 individuals was then photographed and enlarged professionally.

A final set of 16 photographs was selected for further use based on the ratings. In this set, half of the individuals of each sex had been rated approximately one standard deviation above average attractiveness and the other half were rated approximately one standard deviation below average attractiveness. Within each of the four groups of photos, none of the photos differed significantly (all $ps > .05$) from one another in terms of their rated physical attractiveness. Moreover, the male high-attractiveness photos ($M = 5.87$; range, 5.78–5.99) did not differ significantly from the female ($M = 5.66$; range, 5.60–5.80); this was also true for the male low-attractiveness ($M = 3.46$; range, 3.42–3.50) and female low-attractiveness photos ($M = 3.56$; range, 3.48–3.66), both $ps > .05$. However, both male and female high- and low-attractiveness photos were rated significantly different from each other, both $ps < .05$. Furthermore, selecting photos that were only one standard deviation from the mean ensured that the attractiveness manipulation was not overwhelming. Nonetheless, Abramowitz (1985) found that his subjects did discriminate along the lines of attractiveness.

Other materials were a folder and a series of data sheets. Each folder contained two sheets, one for the male and one for the female member of each bogus couple, with information on all independent variables except attractiveness. Data sheets were intended to provide each subject with a consistent but limited amount of information about each couple, and they allowed for systematic manipulation of the independent variables. In addition, some filler questions (e.g., health status, criminal record, history of drug, alcohol, or mental health problems) were included to disguise the true nature of the experiment. No problems were indicated in any of these areas for any member of any couple.

Intelligence was varied by use of SAT scores; the manipulation was approximately one standard deviation above and below the mean: 32 high-intelligence SAT total scores ($M = 1200$; range, 1171–1228); 32 low-intelligence SAT total scores ($M = 800$; range, 772–827); 32 high-intelligence verbal scores ($M = 603$); 32 low-intelligence verbal scores ($M = 400$); 32 high-intelligence quantitative scores ($M = 597$); 32 low-intelligence quantitative scores ($M = 399$). Grade point averages (GPAs) were also included and closely corresponded with the SAT scores. The high-intelligence GPAs had a range of 3.12 to 3.28 ($M = 3.20$); low-intelligence GPAs had a range of 2.12 to 2.28 ($M = 2.20$).

Age at marriage was varied by using the ages of 18 and 22 years. According to the U.S. Department of Health, Education, and Welfare (1976), the median age at first marriage was 21 years for women and 22.9 for men and the modal ages were 19 for women and 21 for men. These statistics suggest that manipulating age at marriage around a mean of 20 was reasonable.

Cohabitation was varied by supposedly having asked the couple whether they had lived together prior to their marriage, and their response was indicated on the data sheet.

Dependent Variables

This experiment contained 15 questions on a 7-point Likert-type scale with endpoints labeled *not at all* and *very much*. The first 4 questions were based largely on the first 2 questions from the Kansas Marital Satisfaction Scale (Schumm et al.,

1986). The remaining 11 questions were intended to further assess the extent to which the subjects thought the couple was likely to have a satisfying marriage.

Items 1 and 2 asked the subject to estimate the likelihood that each member was satisfied with the marriage; Items 3 and 4, the likelihood that one member was satisfied with the other as a spouse; Items 5 and 6, the likelihood of either member seeking an extramarital affair; Items 7 and 8, the likelihood of each member of the couple to influence decisions to any great extent; Items 9 and 10, the likelihood that one member of the couple was in love with the other; Items 11 and 12, the likelihood that the couple was satisfied sexually with each other; Items 13 and 14, the likelihood that each member was seriously committed to the relationship; and Item 15, the likelihood that the couple communicated well.

Procedure

Subjects signed up for an experiment on marital relations. They were tested in mixed-sex groups of fewer than 10 by a male experimenter, who explained that they would be asked to evaluate eight recently married couples. The rationale offered was that the research was part of a larger, longitudinal study examining various aspects of marital relationships. They were then given the eight folders and asked to complete the attached questionnaire for each couple. They were later debriefed and given an opportunity to ask questions when all subjects had completed all questionnaires.

Design and Analysis

The design was 2 (Gender of Subject) × 2 (Male Attractiveness) × 2 (Female Attractiveness) × 2 (Male Intelligence) × 2 (Female Intelligence) × 2 (Male Age) × 2 (Female Age) × 2 (Cohabitation). All effects except subject gender were within-subject factors. This design allowed for 128 possible combinations of within-subject factors. Each subject was asked to read 8 of the 128 possible conditions. Of these 8, complete combinations of male attractiveness, female attractiveness, and cohabitation were presented. They were paired with 8 of the remaining 16 possible conditions; moreover, these pairings were balanced across subjects. Thus, the basic experimental design was a partially balanced incomplete blocks design. One result of the partial balancing was that some effects, which generally involved higher order interactions, were confounded. All effects, both unconfounded and confounded, were included in the statistical model and tested for significance. It should be clearly noted that the male age at marriage was the only hypothesized effect that was confounded. Moreover, due to the incomplete nature of the design, some effects in the model could not be estimated; again, they generally involved higher order interactions. Of the 255 possible effects in the model, 84 were unconfounded, 140 were confounded, and 31 were inestimable.

The design was translated into an analysis of variance model, which allowed for both estimation and tests of significance for all estimable effects in the model, both confounded and unconfounded. Moreover, because there were multiple dependent measures, the effect of each term in the model was assessed for all dependent variables simultaneously. Hence, the statistical model was a partially balanced incomplete blocks multivariate analysis of variance.

To control the cumulative error rate due to the large number of tests of significance, a two-part familywise error rate was used. Nominal α was .05. Two families were then defined: those effects for which hypotheses were stated and the remaining estimable effects. Nominal α was then divided equally among each of these two families, that is, α was .025 for each. A Bonferroni adjustment, based on the number of estimable effects within each family, was made to create a per effect error rate. Because there were 10 hypothesized effects, the per effect error rate for the first family was .0025 (i.e., .025/10) and that for the second family was .0001 (i.e., .025/214).

All tests of significance were based on Roy's greatest characteristic root test θ (Harris, 1985). Theta represents the proportion of variance explained in the linear combination of the dependent variables by the independent variable. All post-hoc tests used a common critical value based on Gabriel's (1968) simultaneous test procedure, which simply requires that any subeffect examined, for any subset of the dependent variables, produce a value for θ equal to or greater than the critical value for the effect from which the subeffect was taken. This procedure is analogous to Scheffé's multiple comparison procedure in univariate analysis of variance and holds the error rate to at most the per effect error rate.

The general strategy followed in conducting post-hoc tests for main effects was straightforward. First, the discriminant function coefficients were examined to determine a best linear composite of the 15 dependent variables. Then, various likely subsets of the dependent variables were tested for significance. Finally, a subset of the dependent variables was selected, based on these tests, that explained the largest proportion of variance with the smallest number of variables. This strategy simply isolates those dependent variables that were primarily responsible for determining the group differences.

In the case of interaction effects, a two-stage strategy was employed. First, tests of simple effects were conducted using all dependent variables. Then, for the significant simple effects, simple effects tests were again conducted for those subsets of dependent variables considered to form the best linear composite based on an examination of the discriminant function coefficients. Again, the purpose of this procedure was to help isolate those group differences that were significant for identified subsets of the 15 dependent variables.

Following isolation of a specific subset of the dependent variables for a given effect, interpretation focused on the relevant combined cell means for those specific variables in the subset.

Results

For the main effects, significant results were obtained for subject gender [θ (1, 6.5, 328.5) = .207, $p < .0001$], male attractiveness [θ (1, 6.5, 328.5) = .153, $p < .0001$], female attractiveness [θ (1, 6.5, 328.5) = .342, $p < .0001$], male age at marriage [θ (1, 6.5, 328.5) = .103, $p < .0001$], female age at marriage [θ (1, 6.5, 328.5) = .126, $p < .0001$], male intelligence [θ (1, 6.5, 328.5) = .473, $p < .0001$], and female intelligence

[θ(1, 6.5, 328.5) = .394, p < .0001]. Cohabitation failed to reach significance [θ(1, 6.5, 328.5) .023, p > .4].

Two unconfounded first-order interactions were significant: Male Attractiveness × Female Attractiveness [θ(1, 6.5, 328.5) = .079, p < .0001] and Male Intelligence × Female Intelligence [θ(1, 6.5, 328.5) = .154, p < .0001]. The Male Age at Marriage × Female Age at Marriage interaction was not significant [θ(1, 6.5, 328.5) = .037, p > .06].

One unconfounded second-order interaction reached significance: Female Age at Marriage × Cohabitation × Male Intelligence [θ(1, 6.5, 328.5) = .074, p < .0001]. No other interaction effects reached statistical significance (all θ's < .095). Concerning the main effect for subject gender, the best linear composite appeared primarily to involve five dependent variables that yielded θ = .1720, a reduction of .0346 from the θ involving all dependent variables. Subsequent examination of the combined means relevant to this effect for these five dependent variables revealed that female subjects, in comparison with male subjects, perceived the men to be more satisfied with the women as spouses (M = 5.43 vs. 4.99), the women to be more satisfied with the men as spouses (M = 5.36 vs. 5.00), the women to be more likely to influence decisions (M = 4.86 vs. 4.60), the men to be more likely to be sexually satisfied (M = 5.37 vs. 4.98), and the couples to be likely to have good communication (M = 4.86 vs. 4.80).

Regarding the main effect of male attractiveness, the best linear composite appeared primarily to involve four dependent variables that yielded θ = .1280, a reduction of .0283 from the θ involving all dependent variables. Subsequent examination of the combined means relevant to this effect for these four dependent variables indicated that high-attractiveness men, in comparison with low-attractiveness men, were seen as more likely to have satisfied spouses (M = 5.29 vs. 5.07), as more likely to seek extramarital affairs (M = 3.81 vs. 3.41), as less likely to have spouses who would seek extramarital affairs (M = 3.13 vs. 3.35), and as more likely to have spouses who were sexually satisfied (M = 5.25 vs. 4.95).

For the female attractiveness main effect, the best linear composite primarily involved six dependent variables that yielded θ = .3116, a reduction of .0308 from the θ involving all dependent variables. Examination of the combined means for these six dependent variables indicated that high-attractiveness women, compared with low-attractiveness women, were seen as more likely to have husbands who were satisfied with the marriage (M = 5.28 vs. 4.92), as more likely to have husbands who were satisfied with their spouses (M = 5.41 vs. 5.00), as less likely to have husbands who would seek extramarital affairs (M = 3.90 vs. 3.31), as more likely to have sexually satisfied husbands (M = 5.49 vs. 4.85), as less likely to be satisfied with their marriage (M = 5.16 vs. 5.11), and as less committed to the relationship (M = 5.40 vs. 5.22).

For the male age at marriage main effect, the best linear composite appeared primarily to involve four dependent variables that yielded θ = .0730, a reduction of .0299 from the θ including all variables. Subsequent examination of the combined means indicated that older men were seen as more likely to be satisfied with their marriages (M = 5.24 vs. 4.96) and with their spouses (M = 5.27 vs. 5.15), as more likely to have spouses who were satisfied with them (M = 5.27 vs. 5.15), and as more likely to influence decisions (M = 5.23 vs. 4.85) than were the younger men.

Regarding the female age at marriage main effect, the best linear composite appeared primarily to involve three dependent variables that yielded $\theta = .1183$, a reduction of .0080 from the θ involving all dependent variables. Examination of the combined means for these three dependent variables revealed that older women were seen as more likely to be satisfied with their marriages ($M = 5.21$ vs. 5.06), as more likely to influence important decisions ($M = 4.91$ vs. 4.55), and as less likely to have spouses who influenced important decisions ($M = 5.24$ vs. 4.84) than were younger women.

Concerning the female intelligence main effect, the best linear composite appeared primarily to involve six dependent variables that produced $\theta = .3649$, a reduction of .0291 from the θ including all dependent variables. Examination of the combined means for these six dependent variables revealed that high-intelligence women, in comparison with low-intelligence women, were seen as more likely to have husbands who were satisfied with them ($M = 5.34$ vs. 5.07), as less likely to be satisfied with their husbands ($M = 5.12$ vs. 5.24), as more likely to influence important decisions ($M = 5.11$ vs. 4.36), as less likely to have husbands who influenced decisions ($M = 5.34$ vs. 4.74), as less likely to have sexually satisfied husbands ($M = 5.19$ vs. 5.15), and as more likely to communicate well ($M = 4.96$ vs. 4.71).

For the male intelligence main effect, the best linear composite appeared to involve primarily six dependent variables that yielded $\theta = .4268$, a reduction of .0464 from the θ involving all dependent variables. Examination of the combined means for these six dependent variables indicated that high-intelligence men were seen as more likely to have spouses who were satisfied with their marriages ($M = 5.38$ vs. 4.89), as more likely to be satisfied with their spouses ($M = 5.24$ vs. 5.18), as more likely to have spouses who were satisfied with them ($M = 5.44$ vs. 4.92), as more likely to influence decisions ($M = 5.47$ vs. 4.61), as more likely to have sexually satisfied wives ($M = 5.21$ vs. 4.99), and as more likely to communicate well ($M = 5.09$ vs. 4.57) than were low-intelligence men.

Tests of simple main effects for the Male Attractiveness × Female Attractiveness interaction revealed that three such tests were significant (all θ's > .0860), the single exception being the male attractiveness within high female attractiveness condition ($\theta = .0364$).

For the male attractiveness within low female attractiveness effect, the best linear composite appeared primarily to involve six dependent variables that yielded $\theta = .1831$, a reduction of .0127 from the θ involving all dependent variables. Inspection of the relevant cell means indicated that attractive men were seen as more likely than unattractive men to have wives who were satisfied with them as husbands ($M = 5.36$ vs. 5.02). Further, the attractive men were seen as more likely to seek extramarital affairs ($M = 4.21$ vs. 3.61), as less likely to have wives who would seek extramarital affairs ($M = 2.95$ vs. 3.38), as less likely to be in love with their wives ($M = 5.35$ vs. 5.07), as less likely to be sexually satisfied ($M = 5.04$ vs. 4.66), and as more likely to have sexually satisfied wives ($M = 5.28$ vs. 4.89) than were the unattractive men.

For the female attractiveness within low male attractiveness effect, the best linear composite appeared to involve four dependent variables that yielded $\theta = .0861$, a reduction of .0277 from the θ involving all dependent measures. Examination of the relevant means for these four dependent variables indicated that high-attractiveness women were seen as more likely to have spouses who were satisfied with them ($M = 5.45$ vs. 5.04), as more likely to have spouses who were in love with them ($M = 5.41$ vs. 5.35), as being less in love with their spouses ($M = 5.37$ vs. 5.46), and as more likely to have sexually satisfied husbands ($M = 5.47$ vs. 5.04) than were low-attractiveness women.

For the female attractiveness within high male attractiveness effect, the best linear composite appeared to involve four dependent variables that produced $\theta = .2628$, a reduction of .0451 from the θ involving all dependent variables. Inspection of the relevant means showed that attractive women were seen as less likely to be satisfied with their partner as a spouse ($M = 5.31$ vs. 5.12), as less likely to have husbands who would seek extramarital affairs ($M = 3.41$ vs. 4.21), as more likely to have sexually satisfied husbands ($M = 5.52$ vs. 4.66), and as less likely to be committed to the relationship ($M = 5.50$ vs. 5.22) than were low-attractiveness women.

Tests of simple main effects for the significant Male Intelligence × Female Intelligence interaction revealed that all such tests were significant (all θs > .1726).

For the female intelligence within low male intelligence effect, the best linear composite appeared predominantly to involve six dependent variables that yielded $\theta = .2062$, a reduction of .0293 from the θ involving all dependent variables. Inspection of the relevant cell means indicated that high-intelligence women were seen as more likely to have husbands who were satisfied with them as spouses ($M = 5.25$ vs. 5.10), as less likely to be satisfied with their husbands as spouses ($M = 4.75$ vs. 5.09), as less likely to have husbands who would seek extramarital affairs ($M = 3.88$ vs. 3.56), as less likely to have husbands who influenced decisions ($M = 4.28$ vs. 4.94) and as more likely to influence decisions themselves ($M = 5.27$ vs. 4.58) than low-intelligence women. Further, intelligent women were seen as less likely to have a marriage in which there was good communication ($M = 4.41$ vs. 4.74) than were less intelligent women.

For the female intelligence within high male intelligence effect, the best linear composite appeared to involve primarily five dependent variables that produced $\theta = .2777$, a reduction of .0353 from the θ involving all dependent variables. Examination of the cell means relevant to this effect indicated that more intelligent women, in comparison with less intelligent women, were perceived as more likely to have husbands who were satisfied with them as spouses ($M = 5.43$ vs. 5.04), as more likely to be satisfied with their husbands as spouses ($M = 5.49$ vs. 5.39), as less likely to have husbands who influenced decisions ($M = 5.20$ vs. 5.73), and as more likely to influence decisions themselves ($M = 4.94$ vs. 4.14). Finally, intelligent women were seen as more likely than less intelligent women to have a marriage in which there was good communication ($M = 5.48$ vs. 4.69).

For the male intelligence within low female intelligence effect, the best linear composite appeared to involve six dependent measures that yielded $\theta = .1728$, a reduction of .0496 from the θ involving all dependent variables. Examination of the cell means revealed that more intelligent men were perceived as less likely to be satisfied with their spouses ($M = 5.10$ vs. 5.04), as more likely to have wives who were satisfied with them as spouses ($M = 5.39$ vs. 5.09), as more likely to influence decisions ($M = 5.73$ vs. 4.94), as less likely to have wives who influenced decisions

(M = 4.14 vs. 4.58), as more likely to have wives who were committed to the relationship (M = 5.51 vs. 5.18), and as less likely to communicate well (M = 4.69 vs. 4.73) than were less intelligent men.

For the male intelligence within high female intelligence effect, the best linear composite involved primarily five dependent variables that yielded θ = .3870, a reduction of .0283 from the θ involving all dependent variables. Inspection of the relevant cell means for these five dependent variables indicated that the more intelligent men were seen as more likely to have wives who were satisfied with the marriage (M = 5.46 vs. 4.78), as more likely to be satisfied with their wives as spouses (M = 5.43 vs. 5.25), as more likely to have wives who were satisfied with them as spouses (M = 5.49 vs. 4.75), as more likely to influence decisions (M = 5.20 vs. 4.28), and as more likely to communicate well (M = 5.48 vs. 4.41) than were less intelligent men.

Tests of simple interaction effects for the significant Female Age at Marriage × Cohabitation × Male Intelligence interaction revealed that one of four such estimable tests was significant; Female Age at Marriage × Cohabitation within low male intelligence yielded θ = .0570. Of the 12 possible simple main effects, only 4 were estimable (due to the inestimability of the Cohabitation × Male Intelligence interaction), and of the 4, only female age at marriage within cohabitation within low male intelligence was significant (θ = .1260). The best linear combination involved four dependent variables that yielded θ = .1049. Inspection of the relevant cell means for these four dependent variables indicated that the older women were seen as more likely to be satisfied with their marriage (M = 5.12 vs. 4.87), as less likely to have husbands who influence decisions (M = 4.32 vs. 5.02), as more likely to influence decisions themselves (M = 5.16 vs. 4.40), and as more likely to have husbands who were in love with them (M = 5.31 vs. 5.29) than were younger women.

Discussion

Results for the main effects were largely unsurprising. Attractive, intelligent, and older people were all perceived more favorably than were their counterparts. The male and female intelligence main effects explained the largest proportions of the variance, and there was clearly a halo effect around the attractive men and women. One interesting point concerning attractiveness was that the attractive men were seen as more likely to seek extramarital affairs. This coincides with Dermer and Theil's (1975) finding that attractive American people are, in certain instances, seen as more divorce prone than less attractive people. It appears that the halo effect does not extend to the realm of sexual fidelity.

Two interesting results were obtained for the main effects. Contrary to hypothesis, cohabitation was not significant and subject gender was. Concerning the significant subject gender effect, results indicated that female subjects seemed to hold more optimistic or romantic notions about what marriage is likely to involve, which is not to say that their ratings were necessarily any more or less realistic than male ratings. Rather, there is the possibility that women hold slightly higher expectations for happiness in marriage than men do. This incongruity suggests that a husband and wife may enter marriage with different beliefs about happiness in a marriage, and thus may well have different expectations regarding happiness in their own marriage.

Concerning the nonsignificant cohabitation main effect, it appears that subjects did not put as much emphasis on this variable as was hypothesized. This finding is congruent with the more recent research that suggests that cohabitation has little effect on subsequent marital satisfaction (Macklin, 1980; Newcomb, 1979).

Of the three hypothesized first-order interactions, only two were significant. Contrary to our hypotheses, the Male Age at Marriage × Female Age at Marriage interaction was not significant. This finding is noteworthy in light of research that clearly indicates that age of Americans at first marriage is a critical factor in subsequent marital satisfaction (Booth & White, 1980; Bumpass & Sweet, 1972; Carter & Glick, 1970). The fact that the age at marriage main effects were significant suggests that the manipulation was sufficiently salient. Evidently, subjects did not feel that partners' relative age differences would have any substantial effect on marital satisfaction. Moreover, this result is contrary to Cowan's (1984) finding in which subjects reacted negatively toward age-discrepant couples; however, age differences in the current study were not pronounced, and this relatively small age difference could explain both the inability to find the hypothesized interaction effect as well as the inconsistency with Cowan.

The most noteworthy findings of this study involve the Male Attractiveness × Female Attractiveness and the Male Intelligence × Female Intelligence interactions. Results from the former interaction are complex; however, our hypotheses concerning the interaction were generally supported: The attractive were seen more favorably than the unattractive couples. Interestingly, it appears that although subjects perceived being attractive as improving one's chances of having a satisfied partner, it lessened the chances of the attractive member being happy. Subjects felt that an attractive woman, for instance, was more likely to have a spouse who was satisfied with the arrangement but was less likely to be happy about it herself.

Whereas the students attributed all sorts of good things to attractive people on the basis of their attractiveness, they also perceived these attractive people to be less satisfied, ironically, on the basis of their own attractiveness. In a certain sense this finding is contrary to what research has shown to be typically attributed to attractive people (Dion, Berscheid, & Walster, 1972; Miller, 1970; Sigall & Landy, 1973; Walster et al., 1966). Furthermore, this is one noteworthy instance in which results were contrary to our hypothesis that attractive people would be seen more favorably.

The interaction of greatest strength, between male and female intelligence, explained more of the variance than any other interaction term in the model. It appears that subjects felt this to be an important determinant in whether the couple was likely to have a satisfying marriage. Moreover, results of this interaction clearly revealed that these undergraduates perceived intellectually similar more favorably than intellectually disparate couples. This finding supports our hypothesis concerning the interaction and also coincides with previous similarity research (Murstein, 1976). Our hypothesis that couples of higher intelligence would be perceived more favorably (Glick, 1957; Udry, 1966) was unsupported. Subjects perceived similarity of intellectual abilities as being most important and being more intelligent as an asset only if the spouse was similarly intelligent. This observation is made particularly clear by the fact that disparate couples were seen as less likely to communicate well.

Although these results support our hypotheses concerning how subjects would perceive the interactive effects of intelligence, a similar phenomenon was not seen in the attractiveness interaction. There was no evidence that subjects attempted to do any matching up within this interaction, as the matching hypothesis and similarity research might suggest (Berscheid, Dion, Walster, & Walster, 1971; Murstein, 1976). Moreover, the pattern of results associated with this interaction was not consistent with the results of Bar-Tal and Saxe (1976), who reported that the ratings of husbands were dependent on the attractiveness of the wife, whereas the ratings of wives were independent of the attractiveness of the husband. They found that unattractive husbands married to attractive wives received the most positive evaluations and that unattractive women married to attractive men received the least positive ratings. However, the lack of a significant simple main effect for male attractiveness within the high female attractiveness condition, as well as the overall pattern of the relevant cell means in the current study, clearly contradicts Bar-Tal and Saxe's findings.

A possible explanation for this latter finding is that, when considering attractiveness, subjects looked upon the couple as two separate individuals, but when considering intelligence, subjects approached the couples as a whole, and further, were considering the dynamics that were likely to occur within that whole. The implications, when considering intelligence, are encouraging, because some research suggests that similarity of intellectual abilities might be most conducive to marital satisfaction (Murstein, 1976).

An obvious caution in interpreting all the results is the fact that subjects were asked to provide their perceptions of each individual within the couple, rather than a rating of the couple itself. This procedure was consistent with our interest regarding the perception of marital satisfaction and the possibility that subjects might tend to rate one of the two spouses in a given marital pair more positively and the other more negatively as a function of one or more of the factors under examination. Indeed, this is exactly what happened in many instances. Asking subjects to provide ratings of the couples themselves would be quite interesting, particularly so in regard to how they might attempt or not attempt to rectify any seeming conflict between the ratings of the couple and the individuals in the couple.

Although the present results indicate that subjects perceived intelligence as being an important criterion in their perceptions of these marriages, it is the variable on which there is the least amount of research. Two important issues with research in this area are whether noncollege populations also perceive intelligence as being a crucial factor in marital satisfaction and the effects of the wife's intelligence on the marriage dyad. Results indicated that more intelligent women were seen as less likely to be satisfied with their marriages. This is a particularly relevant finding, given the fact that more and more women are pursuing higher education.

References

Abramowitz, I. A. (1985). *The effect of physical attractiveness and intelligence on same-sex and opposite-sex evaluations of job applicants.* Unpublished master's thesis, University of Maryland, College Park.

Bar-Tal, D., & Saxe, L. (1976). Perceptions of similarly and dissimilarly attractive couples and individuals. *Journal of Personality and Social Psychology, 33,* 772–781.

Bentler, P. M., & Newcomb, M. D. (1978). Longitudinal study of marital success and failure. *Journal of Consulting and Clinical Psychology, 46,* 1053–1070.

Berscheid, E., Dion, K., Walster, E., & Walster, G. W. (1971). Physical attractiveness and dating choice: A test of the matching hypothesis. *Journal of Experimental Social Psychology, 7,* 173–189.

Blazer, J. A. (1963). Complementary needs and marital happiness. *Marriage and Family Living, 25,* 89–95.

Booth, A., & White, L. (1980). Thinking about divorce. *Journal of Marriage and the Family, 42,* 605–616.

Brehm, S. S. (1985). *Intimate relationships.* New York: Random.

Bumpass, L. L., & Sweet, J. A. (1972). Differentials in marital instability: 1970. *American Sociological Review, 37,* 754–766.

Carter, H., & Glick, P. C. (1970). *Marriage and divorce: A social and economic study.* Cambridge, MA: Harvard University Press.

Cowan, G. (1984). The double standard in age-discrepant relationships. *Sex Roles, 11,* 17–23.

Dermer, M., & Theil, D. L. (1975). When beauty may fail. *Journal of Personality and Social Psychology, 31,* 1168–1176.

Dion, K., Berscheid, E., & Walster, E. (1972). What is beautiful is good. *Journal of Personality and Social Psychology, 24,* 285–290.

Gabriel, K. R. (1968). Simultaneous test procedures in multivariate analysis of variance. *Biometrika, 55,* 489–504.

Glick, P. C. (1957). *American families.* New York: Wiley.

Harris, R. J. (1985). *A primer of multivariate statistics* (2nd. ed.). New York: Academic.

Jacques, M. M., & Chason, K. J. (1979). Cohabitation: Its impact on marital success. *Family Coordinator, 28,* 35–39.

Lewis, R. A., Spanier, G. B., Storm-Atkinson, V. L., & LeHeckla, C. F. (1977). Commitment in married and unmarried cohabitation. *Sociological Focus, 10,* 367–374.

Macklin, E. D. (1972). Heterosexual cohabitation among unmarried college students. *Family Coordinator, 21,* 463–472.

Macklin, E. D. (1980). Nontraditional family norms: A decade of research. *Journal of Marriage and the Family, 42,* 905–922.

Miller, A. G. (1970). Role of physical attractiveness in impression formation. *Psychonomic Science, 19,* 241–243.

Murstein, B. I. (1976). *Who will marry whom?* New York: Springer.

Murstein, B. I., & Beck, G. D. (1972). Person perception, marriage adjustment, and social desirability. *Journal of Consulting and Clinical Psychology, 39*, 396–403.

Newcomb, M. D., & Bentler, P. M. (1980). Assessment of personality and demographic aspects of cohabitation and marital success. *Journal of Personality Assessment, 44*, 11–24.

Newcomb, P. R. (1979). Cohabitation in America: An assessment of consequences. *Journal of Marriage and the Family, 41*, 597–603.

Schellenberg, J. A., & Bee, L. S. (1960). A re-examination of the theory of complementary needs in mate selection. *Marriage and Family Living, 22*, 227–232.

Schumm, W. R., Paff-Bergen, L. A., Hatch, R. C., Obiorah, F. C., Copeland, J. M., Meens, L. D., & Bugaighis, M. A. (1986). Concurrent and discriminant validity of the Kansas Marital Satisfaction Scale. *Journal of Marriage and the Family, 48*, 381–387.

Sigall, H., & Landy, D. (1973). Radiating beauty: The effects of having a physically attractive partner on person perception. *Journal of Personality and Social Psychology, 28*, 218–224.

Sigall, H., & Ostrove, N. (1975). Beautiful but dangerous: Effects of offender attractiveness and nature of the crime on juridic judgment. *Journal of Personality and Social Psychology, 31*, 410–414.

Solomon, S., & Saxe, L. (1977). What is intelligent, as well as attractive, is good. *Personality and Social Psychology Bulletin, 3*, 670–673.

Trost, J. (1975). Married and unmarried cohabitation: The case of Sweden with some comparisons. *Journal of Marriage and the Family, 37*, 905–922.

Udry, J. R. (1966). Marital instability by race, sex, education, and occupation using 1960 census data. *American Journal of Sociology, 31*, 203–209.

United States Department of Health, Education, and Welfare (1976). *Vital and health statistics: First marriages, United States: 1968–1976, Series 21*. Washington, DC: U.S. Government Printing Office.

Walster, E., Aronson, V., Abrahams, D., & Rottmann, L. (1966). Importance of physical attractiveness in dating behavior. *Journal of Personality and Social Psychology, 4*, 508–516.

Watson, R. E. (1983). Premarital cohabitation vs. traditional courtship: Their effects on subsequent marital adjustment. *Family Relations, 32*, 139–147.

White, S. G., & Hatcher, C. (1984). Couple complementarity and similarity: A review of the literature. *American Journal of Family Therapy, 12*, 15–25.

After reading: CONSOLIDATE INFORMATION

1. Summarize what Tucker and O'Grady found to be significant factors in the perception of marital satisfaction.
2. Go back to your list of factors contributing to the high divorce rate. How do Tucker and O'Grady's findings confirm or modify your perceptions about marital happiness?
3. Given Tucker and O'Grady's findings and their interpretation of their findings, what advice would you give to a college freshman who was trying to decide whether or not to get married?

Learning to Romance: Cultural Acquisition in College

Margaret A. Eisenhart

In this scholarly article, Professor Margaret Eisenhart applies research methodology to the question of how college students become participants in the culture of college life. In her research, Professor Eisenhart has developed an ethnography, a study which combines interviews or informant reports, case studies, and detailed observations to reach some conclusions about human behavior.

Before reading: FIRST THOUGHTS
           LOOK AHEAD

1. Respond to the title; how do you think learning to romance is connected to the process of understanding and participating in the culture of college life?
2. Read the abstract; in your own words, how would you explain the idea of cultural acquisition?
3. Write a short freewrite reacting to the quotation from the student, Sandy, at the beginning of the article.

During reading: REACT
           QUESTION
           SUMMARIZE

1. What is your reaction to the story of Linda's relationship with Donny?
2. Why do you think Eisenhart describes Sandy's route to the cultural system as "blocked"?

This article addresses the topic of cultural acquisition in terms of the question: What is the process by which individuals "take meaning" (Heath) from culture and make it a part of who they are? Relying on the work of Dreyfus, Holland, and materials from an ethnographic and interview study of a small group of college women, cultural acquisition is described as stages of increasing individual expertise and identification with a given cultural system—stages in which access to the more advanced levels is limited by an individual's social relationships, a process with both positive and negative implications for individuals, and with a developmental trajectory that can be discontinuous. The social parameters of the cultural acquisition process are stressed. CULTURAL ACQUISITION, INDIVIDUAL LEARNING, UNIVERSITY WOMEN

> SANDY: I don't know exactly how it happened. It bothers me a lot because when I came to college I was very content with myself as I was.... And I kind of, all of a sudden started [hearing]: "You are going to have all the right clothes ... do the right things." And, "you don't talk right." I started being very insecure—which really pissed me off. Because I am a very strong person. Strong-willed and have a very strong sense of what I like and what I don't like, what is acceptable, what isn't acceptable and here was something, being, I felt, being thrown at me that I had to accept. I didn't have a choice because it was all around me. And I thought, oh, my god, how did you get yourself into this situation?

THE WOMAN IN THE PASSAGE ABOVE, newly arrived from the North at a southern university, seems to be acquiring culture; that is, she seems to be in the process of learning about a somewhat new set of behaviors, new ways of thinking, and new views of herself in her encounters on campus. What was "being thrown on" Sandy[1] was a peer culture—promoted within the campus peer group—that was unfamiliar to her. Her response was to reconsider old knowledge, question her self-identity, and wonder what she would be like, in this context, in the future.

Although evidence of this process—in which individuals work to "take meaning" (Heath 1982) from their environment and make it a part of themselves—appears in the field notes and transcripts gathered during our ethnographic study of women in college (Holland and Eisenhart 1988a, 1988b, 1989, 1990), educational anthropologists' frameworks for understanding it are limited. It seems that the *process or steps* by which individuals take or internalize meaning from culture[2] have only occasionally been studied in any detail within anthropology and education. For example, although Heath (1982) and Hymes (quoted in Heath 1982) have encouraged us to conceive of learning culture as ways of taking meaning from environment, their attention has been focused on the different ways that groups, not individuals, take meaning. Fred Erickson (1982) got close when he discussed Helen Keller's learning of early language, but his attention was drawn to the immediate scenes of social life that the individual learner encounters, not the process of internalizing culture. And Ochs and Schieffelin's work (1984), while demonstrating the value of investigating children's accumulating linguistic and social knowledge as a means of studying cultural acquisition, emphasized the ways that novices' speech and actions in learning environments link them to cultural patterns extending beyond specific interactions.

In commenting on Ochs and Schieffelin's work, LeVine (1984) writes,

> One lesson emerging from this work is that research into how children acquire adult patterns can only be as strong as the analysis of the adult patterns being acquired. [p. 84]

This statement echoes an earlier and more general one by Harrington who wrote (1982:330) that before anthropologists could turn their attention to learning processes, they had to lay out the sociocultural frames within which learning occurs. But, as LeVine continues, this is a complicated move.

> The multiplexity of culture [by which LeVine means both the accumulating layers of an individual's experience as she grows up and the "enormous disparity in equally valid types of knowing permitted by ... cultures" (p. 86)] and particularly the property of multiple meanings in cultural symbols, presents a difficult question for research into the acquisition of culture: How shall we conceptualize the means by which a child acquires the combination of meanings for a cultural symbol that anthropologists have claimed gives that symbol its ... power? [1984:85]

Our recent study of university women, which followed Sandy and her cohort from 1979 to 1987, brought these questions and the limitations of previous work to the fore. For one thing, because the women were not acquiring culture for the first time—thus, not like the young children who have been the subjects of most work on cultural acquisition, the learning process they were engaged in was not as obvious. Second, the women were not acquiring a totally new culture—the usual assumption in acquisition studies. However, because we studied women who were freshmen and then sophomores at residential universities away from their homes, they were all facing the prospect of finding themselves in, forming, or joining new social groups with the possibility that these groups would use or produce cultural forms that differed in some respects from what the women had known before. For some like Linda, who will be introduced below, her new peer group and the cultural system she encountered in it were familiar extensions of what she had known in high school. For her, acquiring the peer group culture meant drawing more direction from a cultural system she already knew something about, accepting portions of it as descriptive of her own situation, and condensing its meanings for her own use. Although Linda expressed some discontent with the way her participation according to the system affected her, by the end of her sophomore year she had ceased to pay attention to her own or others' misgivings about it. In other words, she seemed to have fully internalized a major part of the cultural system. For Sandy, too, some aspects of the peer culture on campus were already familiar, but as the opening quote hints, Sandy found her route to increased internalization of this cultural system blocked. In contrast to Linda, Sandy's discontents grew, and her previously internalized view of herself came more and more into question in the face of her peers' misgivings about her. These were two of many individual variations in the process by which the 23 women in our study learned to take meaning from the peer culture that surrounded them on campus. The variations we discovered were not very well accounted for by the symbolic interactionist theory of Fred Gearing and associates (Gearing et al. 1979) that guided the original design of our study (Holland and Eisenhart 1979) or by the neo-Marxist theory that inspired our final interpretation of what was most significant about the full study (Holland and Eisenhart 1990). To explain these variations, another kind of theory was needed; a theory that would focus attention on the process by which the women's experiences on campus were differentially internalized.

Given this framing of the problem to be explained, the work of activity theorists seemed promising. Relying on Vygotsky's theory of development in which the social enactment of knowledge precedes and constitutes its internalization, activity theorists would seem to be interested in the process by which socially encoded meanings come to be internalized by individuals. However, educational anthropologists inspired by Vygotsky have focused primarily on the practical activities in which people engage as they acquire proficiency in a skill, rather than on changes in ideas or representations of self that follow from these activities (Kozulin 1986). Lave (1988), for example, has studied the contexts of activities for arithmetic problem solving; Gallimore and Goldenberg (1989), the components of family activities in which beginning literacy emerges; Weisner, Gallimore, and Jordan (1988), the home-based activities of sibling caretaking and peer assistance; and Wertsch, Minick, and Arns (1984), adult-child interaction in the completion of a specified task. Although the process of internalization, what Dorothy Holland (1986) has called "the winnowing of possible interpretations" to make some of them one's own, is certainly implied in these works, it has not been examined directly.

Some of Holland's writing suggests a somewhat different direction for pursuing this topic. Holland (1986) proposed that internalization be defined as an individual's increasing grasp of, and motivation to act in response to (for or against) cultural systems in a given social context. Based on ideas from her own work in cognitive anthropology, as well as the work of Dreyfus, Spiro, and Vygotsky, and from data from Sandy and her cohort, Holland broadly characterized the internalization process as codevelopment of individual expertise, cognitive salience, and (personal) identification with a cultural system.

In what follows and consistent with points made earlier about the need to specify first the cultural system available to be acquired, I will briefly describe the cultural system of romance that pervaded the campus peer groups of our study (see also Holland and Eisenhart 1988a, 1990; Holland and Skinner 1987). Next, I review some of our data to illustrate how the idea of codevelopment can be used to categorize steps in the process of cultural acquisition we observed, and I discuss Holland's argument that "identification," or "developing a concept of one's self as an agent in a cultural system" is the key point in the process. Finally, I take Holland's ideas a step further by illustrating—through a detailed examination of two cases, Linda's and Sandy's—some additional aspects of the process.

The Cultural System of Romance at SU

In the study of the university, SU,[3] where Linda and Sandy were students, we relied on ideas and techniques from cognitive anthropology to represent culture—those collective interpretations of social and material experience that are more or less shared by members of a group and available to be acquired by individuals who interact in the group. Using the concept of "cultural model" (Quinn and Holland 1987)—a set of coherent, taken-for-granted ideas about the world—and the findings from two cognitive elicitation studies at SU (Holland and Skinner 1987), we posited a "cultural model of romance" that underlay and gave significance to much of campus social life.[4]

According to the cultural model of romance, a woman's attractiveness and prestige on campus are validated by the men who find her attractive, who want to go out with her, and who treat her well. For women and men, attractiveness to the opposite sex is a very desirable quality to have and attractiveness is validated—prestige is gained—by having romantic partners. This ranking system is related to what seemed to be a shared notion of intimate cross-gender relationships. In the taken-for-granted relationship, an attractive man and an attractive woman are drawn to one another. The man learns about the woman and appreciates her qualities and uniqueness as a person. Sensitive to her desires, he shows his affection by treating her well. For example, he buys things for her, takes her places she likes, and shows that he appreciates her. She in turn acts on her affection and interest in the man and allows the relationship to become more intimate (Holland and Eisenhart 1988a:121).

The model directs attention to what women should expect and what they should be upset about in their relationships with men. When a man is drawn to an attractive woman, he is supposed to treat her well, appreciate her special qualities as a woman and a person, be responsive to her concerns, and give her gifts. Bad treatment is being handled as if one were an object or without individual characteristics. If the woman is not judged attractive—relative to the man's prestige and attractiveness—then she cannot expect much good treatment. She is expected to reveal her good feelings about the man and allow the relationship to become more intimate without concomitant attention and special treatment from the man. Likewise, if a man is not considered attractive, then a woman need not put up with a lot of demands from him (Holland and Eisenhart 1988a:121–122).

In the peer culture at SU in the early 1980s, a romantic relationship develops in stages. The first stage begins with a search for an attractive partner. A woman's activities during this stage are focused on making herself physically appealing to men and getting herself into settings where she can be seen by and meet men. Some SU women spend, in the words of women in the study, "every minute not in class" beside the pool, "working on their tans." Women diet, exercise, go shopping, and trade clothes with an eye toward making themselves "look good" to men. They "dress up" to go almost everywhere, including the lounges of their dorms, because "there might be some guys in there." In addition, women who are searching for men organize groups of women to go together to mixers, clubs, bars, restaurants, and sports events ostensibly, at least, to meet attractive men. As a result of such efforts, a woman hopes to find an attractive man who is interested in her.

The second stage involves increasingly regular, frequent, and close contact between a man and a woman who are attracted to each other, often culminating in "going steady." The relationship becomes a more exclusive one in which the partners are not "seriously" dating anyone else. As this stage develops, partners are expected to want to spend more and more time together. Women speak of couples who want to be together 24 hours a day, of those who exchange extravagant gifts, and of those who write to, call, and see each other every day.

As this stage continues, especially if it develops into an exclusive relationship, the women begin to arrange their lives to be available to their boyfriends. They do things to help and support their boyfriends, and participate in social activities chosen by their boyfriends.

The time frame associated with the sequence calls for women to be involved in one or both of these two stages while they are in college. There is also a third, more "serious" stage in which a romantic relationship leads to marriage and a family. This stage gives some form to the women's thinking about their futures. When a woman has had a steady relationship for some time, she begins to consider this third stage. One said, "[My boyfriend] and I have been together so long, it's inconceivable that we wouldn't have talked about marriage." Another said, "We're getting engaged [soon].... I'm sure I'm gonna marry him ... probably in the next one to two years" (Holland and Eisenhart 1990:134–136).

With the cultural system of romance outlined in this way, we can turn to the individual women who participated in our study on the same campus. We discovered that individual women participated differently in the cultural system defined by romance, but that their participation showed a pattern of covariance and codevelopment (Holland 1986).

The Individual Level

At the individual level, we found that the women varied in their use of language to communicate about romance and romantic relationships. Some used the words associated with romance tentatively and euphemistically. One used the word "it" to refer to sex; others could produce elaborate verbal analyses of romantic relationships; and still others used a few well-chosen words to convey a complex image or idea, for example, the label, "add-a-bead," a kind of necklace, was used to refer to the sorority girl type—a type likely to wear certain clothes, behave in certain ways, and form a romantic relationship with a "frattybagger."

A second way in which the women varied was in their active participation in the social system dominated by romance. Some were mainly bystanders to the main action: They did not have boyfriends or regular dates and so could only vicariously or infrequently engage in or practice the activities associated with the romantic world. Others participated very actively, either because they already had boyfriends on campus or they had no lack of requests to date.

A third way the women differed was in their effectiveness at handling the social pressures to participate in the romantic world. Some found it difficult to establish or maintain desired friendships with women without a boyfriend to provide a focal point for discussion. Others seemed socially trapped (more than they wanted to be) by being part of an established relationship with a boyfriend and, with him, part of a group that did many things together. Still others finessed their way into favorable status positions among their peers without devoting much time or energy to romantic relationships. One found an attractive boyfriend who was almost always busy with his own work.

A fourth difference appeared in the women's ways of handling the emotions associated with romantic relationships. Some did not seem to be very emotionally involved at all. Others sounded truly upset and hurt when their attempts at romantic relationships were rebuffed. Others seemed paralyzed into inaction by a fear of what would happen if they gave up the intimacy associated with a romantic relationship—even a bad one. And others took pride in being able to manipulate men to advantage.

The final way the women varied was in their pattern of response to the social identities they believed were available to them. Some debated—at great length—the pros and cons of the various identities that comprised the romantic prestige system. Some seemed to accept a position in the system, sometimes gladly, sometimes not. Still others rejected—at least temporarily—the identities associated with the romantic world; and a few were able to creatively circumvent them. In a summary of these differences, Holland wrote:

> If the woman had not developed a clear identification of herself in the world of romance—an image of herself that mattered to her—then romance was not likely to be very salient for her and she was not likely to be very expert in conducting romantic relationships. Similarly, if, for some reason, she had not been able to develop expertise then she was unlikely to have formed much of a romantic identification. Salience, identification, and expertise appear to develop together as an interrelated process—a process that was continually supported and shaped in the context of social interaction. [1986:27]

Holland connects these phases of codevelopment with Dreyfus's levels of developing expertise and Spiro's levels of increasing cognitive salience. Building on their work, she proposes that identification is the pivotal point of internalization.

> Identification ... seems to describe ... the point or phase in internalization where the system that one has been socially interacting—according to the instructions and directions of others—becomes a system that one uses to understand and organize one's self and at least some of one's own feelings and thoughts. [1986:33]

The model of cultural acquisition proposed by Holland fits well the case of Linda, who will be discussed next. It does not fit Sandy's case as well. By comparing Linda with Sandy, some additional features of the acquisition process are highlighted.

Linda

For some of the SU women in the study (5 of 11), the acquisition of the campus peer culture seemed to unfold as an extension or elaboration of what they had learned about the cultural system of romance before coming to college. These women were fairly comfortable with romantic relationships as interpreted in the culture of romance. And, they became more comfortable during college. Linda was one of these women.

When Linda went to college, she already had a boyfriend, Donny, whom she had met and begun to date three years earlier. Because of Donny, Linda started her college career with a fairly high ranking in the prestige hierarchy. That is, her social position as quite an attractive woman was validated by her having a steady boyfriend at the beginning of her college career.

At the beginning of her second semester, Linda and Donny decided to end their steady relationship. She did not see him for weeks, although they did talk on the phone. She started dating other men, and he, other women. About this, she said,

> We both have just come to the decision that we've got so many things we want to do ... and we both want to date other people.... We were dating more or less steady ... but I want to go out with other people now, whereas then I didn't.

Soon thereafter, Linda planned to spend a weekend with one of her new dates and told Donny about it. Based on the cultural system of romance, it can be inferred that she might have told him in order to raise her attractiveness rating. Her description of her expectations for his response confirm that she intended to make such a "statement" with her announcement and that she expected him to award her the point. But she was not successful.

> I just figured he'd get mad and say "you can't go." He's a very jealous person, and he tends to be a little bit possessive, so I figured he'd get upset about it. But he didn't.

At this point and again consistent with the cultural system of romance, Linda interpreted Donny's response as an indicator that she was not as attractive as she had thought she was. Although she did not lack for dates, she seemed to lose status in her own eyes in the face of Donny's disinterest in her new date. Donny's rejection hurt her feelings. She moved to reestablish their relationship, and by April they were back together.

But then Donny proceeded to make her life miserable in a different way. He claimed to disbelieve her statement that she had stopped dating others and so telephoned her or her friends persistently, at odd hours of the day and night, to check on her whereabouts. If he could not find her, he accused her of being with other men. In other words, he seemed to be trying to establish his attractiveness as the greater of the two.

Linda's response was to try harder to please him, thereby conceding the point to him in the game of romance. And Donny's demands presented special difficulties for Linda because he attended college miles away. It soon became clear that Donny expected Linda to travel to visit him at his campus (although she did not have a car) and to attend numerous social events sponsored there by his fraternity. Linda found these demands a "strain," but she accepted them.

> I don't need to be part of a big group.... I have to find a ride all the time.... I don't need that much social life. But Donny wants me to be a little sister—you know, a hostess—to his fraternity. He wants me to be a part of it because it's so important to him. [It's] such a strain [for me]. You just don't need that when you're going to college, but I know how important the fraternity is to him.

Linda became a little sister and began to do other things for Donny too. Sometimes at his request and sometimes on her own, she began to cook for him, wash his clothes, and help him out when he got behind in his studying. He also continued to subject her to his unexpected phone calls to "test" her explanations of how she spent her time on her own campus. At one point, Linda's dormmates overheard her telephone conversation with Donny. When the call ended, they accused him of upsetting her, and they called him a "jerk." Linda seemed to acknowledge that Donny was not always the perfect boyfriend, but she was convinced that he was "Mr. Right" for her. When asked to account for her continued interest in him, she acknowledged that Donny could be difficult to put up with but said she knew she would continue to do so. When asked why, Linda responded with a sigh, "It must be love." She went on to say:

> I depend on Donny for attention. . . . he makes me feel good, he compliments me, he's attentive to me. . . . I know that I will be happy with him.

Soon after graduating from college, Linda married Donny.

While she was attending college, Linda found herself in a social arena that permitted and encouraged her to further develop her expertise in the world defined by the culture of romance. For Linda and the others like her who had steady boyfriends, social life in college could be a time to learn how to refine and elaborate information, ways of talking, social skills, and emotional commitments consistent with the cultural system of romance. Although resentful at times, Linda seemed to come to accept her discontents and her subordinate status (to Donny's) as part of being in a romantic relationship. Her sighful statement, "It must be love," seems to encapsulate both her commitment and her willingness to accept the situation entailed in becoming a steady girlfriend and ultimately, a wife. As we have noted elsewhere (Holland and Eisenhart 1988a), at least for women like Linda, this acquisition process begins early in young adulthood. Linda had dated Donny for three years before coming to SU. Thus, at the time of her marriage to him, she had been developing the pattern of her relationship with him for seven years.

Linda's experiences acquiring the cultural system of romance while in college can be described as falling within the highest three stages of developing expertise that Holland presented, borrowing from Dreyfus (1984). Altogether, Dreyfus proposed five stages—novice, advanced beginner, competent, proficient, and expert—distinguishable by the way rules (information and knowledge) are used in a given social situation and by the amount of personal investment in a successful outcome. In the novice and beginner stages that we must presume Linda has already passed through before coming to college, the learner is presented with a simplified task environment in the form of a set of rules for determining actions. Novices' and beginners' actions are hesitant, often not-quite-right, and relatively unconcerned, as they try to learn all the rules and come to recognize some of their situational limitations.

In the third or competent stage, learners choose a plan or perspective from which to view a situation and then implement rules in order to pursue the plan. In other words, some rules are highlighted while others are ignored in order to follow the plan. This phase seems to characterize Linda's move to increase her prestige in Donny's eyes. She does not seem to consider other rules that might apply or be used; nor does she seem to anticipate what will occur if her plan fails. It also seems to characterize her reaction when the plan does fail. Dreyfus writes,

> the competent performer... after wrestling with the question of a choice of perspective or goal, feels responsible for, and thus emotionally involved in, the result of this choice.... Successful plans induce euphoria, and mistakes are felt in the pit of the stomach. [Dreyfus 1984:30–31]

Holland restates the crucial change entailed in developing beyond beginner as: the individual coming to identify herself as an agent in the world described by the cultural system (1986:30–31). She also points out that emotional involvement and salience are implicated in Dreyfus's words, though they do not receive his special attention. Linda's identification with the system defined by the campus culture of romance never seemed to be in doubt. When we first encountered her, she was making moves as an active participant in the system. The system was salient to her, and she was emotionally involved.

Dreyfus's proficient learner is no longer involved in conscious planning and becomes dispassionate. Based on the accumulation of information about successful plans in similar situations, the learner spontaneously (intuitively) adopts an appropriate plan and then considers rules as tools to use to manipulate the environment to advantage. When Linda begins to arrange her life to meet Donny's demands, she can be viewed as entering this stage. She is no longer taking risks with her prestige as defined by the culture of romance, and she seems to be unreflexively subsuming her feelings under her actions to please Donny. In other words, she seems to have accepted as her own one set of rules for acting, in steady romantic relationships—the rules that apply when the woman is less attractive than the man.

Finally, according to Dreyfus, the expert understands, acts, and learns from results without any conscious awareness of the process. A situation,

> seen as similar to [previous ones in which the same perspective and subsequent actions (manipulations) were taken] is not only thereby understood but simultaneously the associated decision, action, or tactic presents itself.... These reference situations... bear no names and, in fact, defy complete verbal description.... The expert... experiences a compelling sense of the issue and the best move. [He acts quickly,] depending almost entirely on intuition and hardly at all on analysis and comparison of alternatives. [p. 33]

When Linda condenses her situation in "it must be love," she seems to have, in this sense at least, become an expert in the cultural system of romance. She is no longer considering alternatives or taking her misgivings seriously. The relationship she and Donny have is defined and organized for her, and it is guiding some of the actions she takes in her life. She expects her peers to understand this when she calls her circumstances "love," and they seem to.

Sandy

Sandy's situation was quite different from Linda's and not as well accounted for by the Dreyfus-Holland model of developing expertise. When Sandy began her college career, her acquisition of the culture of romance was more problematic (as was true, in some form, for five other women in our SU sample). Sandy explained that in high school she did not date much, but she hoped to enter the romantic world while in college. During the first observation of Sandy (January of her freshman year), one of her suitemates, Debby, had just returned to the dorm room from "checking out" a party downstairs.

> SANDY: Who's there?
> DEBBY: All girls.
> SANDY: All girls . . . ? [as in: why bother?]

The conversation drifted to upcoming parties and possible dates for them.

> DEBBY asks SANDY: How 'bout that cute guy in your Spanish class?
> SANDY: There's another cute guy in class, too.
> DEBBY: Keep your hands off!
> SANDY: You can have the blonds, I get the dark-haired, cute ones.
> DEBBY: Why the blond ones [for me]?
> SANDY: Because I don't want them.

Although Sandy could talk a good line in the romantic domain (she had the knowledge to banter about attractiveness and men in order to fit in socially with her girlfriends in the dorm), she did not seem to plan her activities or work on her appearance in an attempt to make herself available or attractive to men. She also did not feel like she was a full participant. She expressed this feeling in the excerpt that opened this article. Shortly after that, she blew up in an encounter with a male acquaintance.

> One of my friends, Debby, knew this guy [Ron] from high school, they were acquaintances. . . . I'd met him, you know, no big thing. We were in my suitemate's room. It was Debby and I and Ron, and I don't know what was said but something made me mad, and I turned around and let out a slew of words that aren't fitting to hear, and out of the clear blue sky, he said, "You know, I don't know why you take such perverse pleasure in swearing like that. You know, first of all, it's unladylike, and girls in the south just don't do that." I stood there for the longest time thinking, "Where did this come from?" And he went on to tell me that only people who lack intelligence swear, and you won't find girls in the south swearing because they knew their manners, and they'd say "yes ma'am, no ma'am, yes sir, no sir," all this type stuff. And they do this and they do that. . . . And here I was. It hit me right in the face. Here was someone saying this to me. And I stood there, and then he went on to tell me that my parents did not raise me properly. Then it wasn't me anymore, he wasn't attacking me. He was attacking my parents. They didn't know how to raise a child. Which is when I totally flew off, and went into fifty million more words I know he didn't want to hear to prove to him that I could swear and hold my own. And then I told him to get out of my room. He called my friend the next day, and she said he acted like nothing happened. . . .

In no uncertain terms, Sandy got the message that her way of doing things—of dressing, of talking, of expressing her feelings—was not acceptable in the campus culture she found around her. By her account, no one stood up for her actions, either during the exchange or afterwards, and no one seemed to realize how much the encounter had upset her. For her, this encounter and others like it began to erode her sense of involvement with the campus peer culture and her identity.

> Where I was brought up and raised ... I felt that no matter where I went or what I did I would be comfortable.... Anyone would talk to me ... not because I wore the right things or said the right things or had the right last name. And when I came down here, that's what hit me in the face because all of a sudden everyone was talking about their prep schools and you have to wear ... your penny loafers and your hose ... and your Izod and have long hair and put it in a ponytail.... I got the impression that here I was a sloppy little girl and I didn't have any class or I didn't have any style.... I have some preppie clothes, and sometimes I wear them but I don't feel that what you wear puts you in a certain circle. But, all of a sudden I felt that I was put either to one side or to the other side ... and I didn't have a choice because it was all around me ... and I didn't like that.... And it really bothered me.

As her freshmen year progressed, Sandy still occasionally acted like she was interested in the romantic world. When her dormmates teased her about being short, she replied, "Well, I haven't had any six-foot men in my life lately, so I guess it doesn't matter." Or, when talking about seeing some old friends during a trip home, Sandy reported on a conversation with an old girlfriend: "We all talked about where all these cute guys are because we can't find them...."

But, as much as Sandy talked as if she wanted a romantic relationship, she did not get into one. She could never "see herself" with the men she dated. She also did not change her way of dressing or talking. In fact, she seemed to be retreating into a world dominated by her friendship with an older woman, Leslie.

Soon some of Sandy's other friends began to object to the amount of time she and Leslie spent together, but Sandy felt that her friendship with Leslie was too precious to jeopardize. Sandy said that she wanted to spend as much time as possible with Leslie:

> Our relationship is terrific ... I just would like to spend more time ... [so far] it's all been crammed into one semester ... probably not gonna be another time in my life when I can just sit down and just be friends. [Holland and Eisenhart 1988a:129]

By the end of Sandy's freshman year, she and Leslie became virtually inseparable and rarely interacted with others.

But Sandy's campus acquaintances would not let her retreat from the romantic scene unnoticed. During her sophomore year, they charged that she and Leslie were "queers."

> I came back one day and there were a whole bunch of obscene things written all over my door: no whites, no dykes, you know. It was an elementary school scene. It was ... it was, it was so unrealistic to me I was, I thought, damn this is college, this isn't what you're supposed to be! And um ... then she [one of Sandy's

MARGARET A. EISENHART / *Learning to Romance: Cultural Acquisition in College* 183

dormmates] decided to generate a rumor about me. OK, that, my relationship with Leslie is off color, and it's a queer relationship. OK, and she based this on the night that Leslie slept over.... And I just I don't believe this, because in the dormitory situation... you know, this whole damn university is gonna be gay!

OK, it doesn't matter whether I am or not, even though I am *not*..... I don't like anything like that to be said, I mean it's off color and... to me it's just an atrocity all the way around. I don't see how anyone could draw that conclusion between Leslie and I.

At first Sandy totally rejected the gay label and tried to "clear" her name by appealing to the resident adviser to judge her story in light of the allegation. After she failed to get an unequivocal answer from the dorm adviser and some others, she began to really wonder about herself.

For awhile I went through a stage where I thought well maybe this girl is telling the truth, maybe, maybe I'm doing something wrong. And I went through a very guilty stage when, well to me it was unfounded, but I'm a sensitive person and I thought, well geez, someone's upset you know, I've gotta be doing something.... But, I couldn't think of anything! I really couldn't think of anything!

I just, I got so paranoid because it just seemed so unbelievable to me that... I got to the point where I thought, maybe this is true, maybe people do think this of me. And... I had to ask 'em, I said, "I know you haven't known me very long but do you think that I'm queer?!" [laughs] Helluva question to ask someone! Because you just... you shouldn't let what other people say about you, because you should know what you are yourself, but you get to a point that you keep hearing it and you keep hearing it and you think, well is this the way it really looks to other people?

Sandy's route to expertise in the cultural system of romance was blocked because she never started dating in earnest. She turned to another kind of relationship. Unfortunately for Sandy, the cultural system of romance that dominated the peer groups at SU seemed to admit only one kind of appropriate relationship characterized by intimacy and spending long periods of time together: heterosexual romantic relationships. Thus, Sandy's relationship with Leslie could be and was interpreted by others (at least by some) as an aberration. It was a familiar style of relationship but with one major defect—her partner was homosexual, rather than heterosexual. In the game defined by the cultural model of romance, Sandy made a bad and unacceptable move, and some of her peers attacked her. The attack left her unsure how to handle herself on campus and how to identify herself. By the end of her sophomore year, she had found that she couldn't play the romance game, she had lost sight of who she was at SU, and (not surprisingly) she had dropped out of school.

Sandy's college experiences call for some additional thinking about the Dreyfus-Holland model. How are we to understand the obstacles that prevented Sandy's development of expertise? How should we interpret, in acquisition terms, what she learned about the cultural system of romance while in college? And, when she switched her attention to her relationship with Leslie, was she beginning to learn another cultural system or only reacting against the system of heterosexual romance?

Discussion

The process of taking meaning from the cultural system of romance is occurring differently for these two women. Linda, with a relatively high position in the campus status hierarchy by virtue of having a boyfriend, with the disagreeable experience of trying to increase her prestige behind her, and with her knowledge that the social trajectory for wife and motherhood, which she desired, proceeds from a steady relationship such as the one she has with Donny, is becoming an expert with the cultural system of romance. Following Dreyfus's scheme and Holland's additions to it, Linda must have already (before college) had opportunities to learn *about* the rules or norms of this cultural system; when we encountered her, she was already taking responsibility as an actor in the system and feeling the distressing results of making a mistake. With her comment, "It must be love," she seems to have reached Dreyfus's highest level of expertise, where she no longer takes seriously her own misgivings about, or any alternatives for, what the culture of romance means to her.

Sandy, with a neutral position (not actively engaged yet but trying; not rejected) in the status hierarchy at the beginning of college, who has the experience of not being able to find a boyfriend and finds no peer group or family support for an alternative close relationship with a woman, does not develop expertise in the cultural system of college romance. Sandy found her efforts to acquire that system blocked in the early stages of development. Without a boyfriend, or at least some men to date, it seemed that Sandy could become no more than Dreyfus's advanced beginner with the cultural system of romance. She knew how to talk romance with her girlfriends and she knew *about* some of the rules of the romance game. But without a man in her life, she could not play any more advanced form of the game; thus she could not move on to learn the cultural system as Linda did.

Sandy's situation, compared to Linda's, suggests how crucial to advanced cultural learning is the ability to establish the "right" social relationships. Holland suggests that pressures to individual commitment or resistance arise in social interaction, thereby connecting identification (specifically) and internalization (more generally) to the social distribution of knowledge and the social reproduction of power relations, but she is not explicit about how these social forces work.

Comparison of the two cases reveals that what Linda and Sandy learned about the cultural system of romance in college was initially set up by the social experiences they had previously had and found themselves in when they entered college. Their entering social characteristics placed them at different starting points in the acquisition process that would take place in college. Linda had a boyfriend and thus a higher standing than Sandy. From there, the levels of expertise to which they had access differed. Linda could continue to identify herself as an agent in a long-term romantic relationship with a man; she could come to expect her relationship and her prestige to develop and be judged in certain ways, and she could come to condense the meanings of her romantic relationship and a significant portion of her future life to a few ideas that she no longer thought about consciously. As this process unfolded for Linda, it appeared that once her prestige relative to Donny's had been established, she encountered no more challenges to her identification with and actions in the context of the cultural system of romance. This is not surprising; she was, of course, by accepting a portion of the cultural system of romance as her own, on track to reproduce a traditional role and status for an American woman and her man. Sandy had no opportunity to acquire this part of the cultural system of romance because she had no boyfriend. Without one, she had to rely on her skills at talking a good romantic line in the dorm and hope that a boyfriend would eventually come along. When one did not, Sandy could not increase her expertise with or her commitment to the cultural system of romance.

The two cases also reveal how important to learning is the group's interpretation of an individual's actions and the availability of alternative cultural systems. Linda's behaviors and statement that "it must be love" were accepted as appropriate, given her relationship with Donny, according to the cultural model of romance. In other words, her peer group exerted no pressure on Linda to change her developmental course; the group's response propelled her toward greater expertise with the cultural system of romance. When Sandy started to withdraw from the romantic scene and devoted more and more of her time to Leslie, the campus peer group, again apparently applying the cultural system of romance, cast her in a very unfavorable light. Sandy, having taken the socially salient but disapproved step of establishing a close relationship with a woman, found herself set on a course she had never anticipated or learned anything about. As a consequence, she seemed to lose all indicators of expertise in the campus peer group: she lost her sense of identity, she came to question how she should act, and she found she could not effectively use the cultural system of romance with the campus peer group. The peer group had propelled Sandy out of a context for acquiring expertise in its cultural system.

Sadly for Sandy, she seemed unable to find a viable cultural alternative for someone of her gender, class, and age. She seemed to be in the position of having to abandon one cultural system without an alternate from which she could start to take meaning. For Sandy, unlike Linda, her life during college seemed to be on hold. Without a cultural system to guide her, she had no clear direction, no purpose, no goal. Sandy was certainly experiencing something, but whether she was acquiring a cultural system at this point is questionable. With no group context in which to articulate her alternative views, develop expertise, or practice alternative identities, she would seem to have no organized way to take meaning from her campus peer group environment, except to view herself as a failure in the cultural system they promoted. She handled this void by withdrawing from the social environment that pressured her to romance: she dropped out of school, became estranged from her parents and friends, and lived with Leslie who remained at least a friend. Perhaps the two of them constructed an alternative system for themselves. We have no evidence that they ever affiliated with any groups associated with alternative cultural systems.

In light of the importance Holland gives to "identification," it is also interesting to consider Sandy's level of identification with the cultural system of romance. Following Dreyfus's and Holland's stages, Sandy seems to have proceeded no higher than advanced beginner. However, she must have had some sense of herself as an actor in the cultural system; otherwise, why would her words (see, for example, the opening quote) convey the emotional pain and confusion about self that they do? And later after she has chosen to spend time with Leslie, why does she care so deeply about her dormmate's attack?[5] It seems that Sandy did identify somewhat with the cultural system of romance although the Dreyfus-Holland model would not recognize her as "competent."

These findings point to two additional areas of the Dreyfus-Holland model that need revision. First, identification, or at least emotional investment, with a cultural system may emerge before the competent stage. Sandy, although she was not in a social position to execute the plans associated with full participation in the cultural system of romance, seemed somewhat committed to herself as an actor in the system. Perhaps it would be more useful to consider identification as a dialectic (rather than a point) that emerges as one's view of self comes in contact with socially defined categories of identity. Such a view is consistent with a Vygotskian approach to ontogenetic development (Wertsch et al. 1984).

Second, socially defined categories of developing expertise cannot be omitted from a model of cultural acquisition. In Vygotskian terms, these social forms can be viewed as mediators that facilitate and constitute individual development. They are the social expectations about the public accomplishments necessary to move from stage to stage. Surely the chess player who never wins a game will not be judged competent at it, regardless of her knowledge of the rules. The same was true for Sandy: without dating regularly or coming up with an appropriate alternative, she would not be judged competent (at romance) by the campus peer group. Correspondingly, the range of experiences necessary to intuit an appropriate course of action, to manipulate one's environment, and to condense one's ideas would likely not be available for social reasons, as they were not for Sandy.

In addition, the comparison of Linda and Sandy alerts us that we must come to terms with the idea that the process of cultural acquisition has both positive and negative results for individuals. Although it is certainly possible to consider people like Linda who become expert as "successful," it is also the case that part of learning a cultural system well is learning to disregard personal experiences (frustrations, discontents, misgivings) that are not noticed or labeled in the system. After her attempts to impress Donny with her attractiveness failed, Linda seemed to give in to the cultural system, that is, she learned to accept some bad treatment in the name of love. In doing so, she seemed to be consigning herself to a subordinate (but appropriate for the status quo) position in the relationship and for her future.

For individuals like Sandy, who for whatever reason cannot make the social arrangements necessary to obtain access to higher levels of expertise, the negative personal consequences are more apparent. When Sandy found herself unable to succeed in romance, she tried to retreat from the cultural system of romance, and she found herself charged with one of the most negatively viewed labels of the system. Although at first she adamantly denied the accusation that she was gay, she eventually bowed to the pressure and began to wonder if, in fact, she really was. Her frustration and pain were almost tangible.

On the other hand, with her heightened awareness of her actions and feelings as well as the potential for others' negative interpretations of them, Sandy was not (while she was in college) in danger of giving herself over to the cultural system as Linda had done. In sum, developing cultural expertise means burying one's frustrations with the cultural system as well as experiencing the advantages of expert moves. Failure to develop expertise has the opposite drawbacks and advantages.

At this point it is interesting to note that, in neither case, did the women remain long in the positions described above. Although our more recent information about Linda and Sandy is limited, we know that by 1987 Linda and Donny were divorced, and Linda was preparing to marry someone else. We also know that in 1987 Sandy had a boyfriend. About him she said: "My personal feelings are that I would like that person to be in my life permanently." One wonders what happened to Linda during her divorce: did she bring up to a conscious level the misgivings she suppressed as an expert; that is, did she fall back to a lower level of expertise? Similarly, what will happen to Linda when she outlives the socially defined stage of her life in which the cultural system of romance dominates her peer groups? Will she abandon her expertise, that is, stop viewing herself as an actor in this cultural system? Or, will she cling to her expertise in the face of numerous challenges to it?

We are also left wondering what happened to reattach Sandy to the cultural system of romance and whether she later developed expertise with the same cultural system she had to abandon in college. These examples suggest that developing expertise is not a one-way street. Rather, individuals may move up and down levels, depending on their personal circumstances and their social positions.

Conclusion

The cases of Linda and Sandy support, up to a point, the usefulness of conceiving cultural acquisition in terms of the process of developing expertise in a given cultural system. The Dreyfus-Holland model permits us to view individual differences as well as individual development or change in conjunction with a given cultural system.

What is not explicit in their model is how inevitably social is the cultural acquisition process. The data on Linda and Sandy suggest that the process is both constrained and motivated by (1) the cultural forms available to individuals within the groups where they interact; (2) the individual's previous experiences with similar cultural forms; (3) the individual's success at meeting the social requirements of the social category she is in or wishes to be in; and (4) the individual's progress through socially defined developmental stages. The codeveloping stages of expertise, salience, and identification provide a framework for understanding steps by which individuals take more and more (or fail to take) meaning from their cultural environment, but it seems that these steps can be interpreted only in conjunction with social group membership, with the use or application of cultural systems promoted by social groups, and in light of group definitions of growth and development. These social processes seem to be the medium in which individuals are propelled into, stalled at, or diverted from acquiring expertise with a cultural system. Some individuals, because of their social circumstances, are able to acquire high levels of cultural expertise, others cannot because they lack certain social characteristics. When they are able, they pass through stages in which they increasingly take for granted and accept about themselves the constraining definitions and the organizational formulae provided by the cultural system. They also appear to take more direction and feel more compulsion from the cultural system. When individuals do not exhibit or cannot arrange the necessary social characteristics, they cannot gain access to higher stages of expertise. In some situations, people like Sandy may reject or abandon the cultural system that denies them access, rather easily find others like themselves, and together form social groups in which alternative cultural forms are produced, for example, the "lads" in Willis's (1977) study. Individuals like those who become lads may then take more and more meaning from the alternative cultural form produced within the group. Of course, we would expect, as was true among members of the campus peer groups at SU, that internal social divisions, within a group like the lads, may limit access to higher levels of expertise in the alternative cultural system, such that only a few members are "expert" at any given time.

Unlike the lads, Sandy found no such group to join or alternative cultural system from which she could make sense of her world or herself while she was at SU. Unfortunately we know little about her experiences after she dropped out, or about how she eventually came, once again, to take meaning from the cultural system of romance. Future studies that follow closely the lives of individuals like Sandy can shed more light on this, yet another aspect of cultural acquisition.

Notes

Acknowledgements. Portions of this article were originally presented at the meeting of the American Anthropological Association, November 1988, Phoenix, Arizona. I am grateful to Katharine Cutts, Paul Deering, M. Elizabeth Graue, Evelyn Jacob, Ofelia Miramontes, and the *AEQ* reviewers for their comments on the original paper. The research on which this article was based was supported by the National Institute of Education, the University of North Carolina–Chapel Hill, Virginia Polytechnic Institute and State University, and the University of Colorado at Boulder. To them, to the women who participated in the research, and to my co-principal investigator—Dorothy Holland—I am especially grateful.

1. All proper names used for study participants or settings are pseudonyms.
2. Wolcott (1988) has argued for a return to the concept of "propriospect" (Goodenough 1971) in order to capture *what* individuals learn from culture. My interest is in trying to understand the process, as well as the content, of cultural acquisition.
3. The study from which these data are taken was conducted on two campuses—one predominantly black, one predominantly white. At the black school we followed the lives of 12 women; at the white school, we followed the lives of 11 women. In this article, I discuss data from the white school only. For information about other aspects of the complete study, see Holland and Eisenhart (1988a, 1988b, 1989, 1990).
4. The definition of culture is hotly debated within cultural anthropology and the definition I use, based on work in cognitive anthropology, is only one of many possible alternatives. The reader should be aware that noncognitive anthropologists may dispute this definition and thus question whether "romance" is properly labeled a cultural system.

Also, I will refer, throughout the article, to *a* cultural system (of romance). I do so because this system was so pervasive for peer groups at SU (Holland and Eisenhart 1990) and for simplicity's sake. I recognize, however, that individuals are exposed to and may be in the process of simultaneously acquiring more than one cultural system.

5. I am grateful to Katharine Cutts for clarification of this question.

References Cited

DREYFUS, HUBERT L.
 1984 What Expert Systems Can't Do. Raritan 3(4):22–36.

ERICKSON, FREDERICK
 1982 Taught Cognitive Learning in Its Immediate Environments: A Neglected Topic in the Anthropology of Education. Anthropology and Education Quarterly 13(2):149–180.

GALLIMORE, RONALD and CLAUDE GOLDENBERG
 1989 The School's Effects on Home Contexts for Literacy Acquisition. Paper presented at the meeting of the American Educational Research Association, San Francisco.

GEARING, FREDERICK, THOMAS CARROLL, LETTA RICHTER, PATRICIA GROGAN-HURLICK, ALLEN SMITH, WAYNE HUGHES, ALLAN B. TINDALL, WALTER PRECOURT, and SIGRID TOPFER
 1979 Working Paper 6. *In* Toward a Cultural Theory of Education. F. O. Gearing and L. Sangree, eds. Pp. 9–38. The Hague: Mouton.

GOODENOUGH, WARD
 1971 Culture, Language, and Society. McCaleb Module in Anthropology. Reading, Mass.: Addison-Wesley.

HARRINGTON, CHARLES
 1982 Anthropology and Education: Issues from the Issues. Anthropology and Education Quarterly 13(4):323–335.

HEATH, SHIRLEY BRICE
 1982 What No Bedtime Story Means: Narrative Skills at Home and School. Language in Society 11:49–76.

HOLLAND, DOROTHY C.
 1986 How Cultural Systems Become Desire: A Case Study of American Romance. Paper presented at the meeting of the American Anthropological Association, Philadelphia, Pennsylvania.

HOLLAND, DOROTHY C. and MARGARET A. EISENHART
 1979 Women's Peer Groups and Choice of Career. Project Proposal. Washington, D.C.: National Institute of Education.
  1988a Moments of Discontent: University Women and the Gender Status Quo. Anthropology and Education Quarterly 19(2):115–139.
  1988b Women's Way of Going to School: Cultural Reproduction of Women's Identities as Workers. *In* Class, Race, and Gender in American Education. L. Weis, ed. Pp. 266–301. Albany: SUNY Press.
  1989 On the Absence of Women's Gangs in Two Southern Universities. *In* Women in the South: An Anthropological Perspective. H. Mathews, ed. Pp. 27–46. Athens: University of Georgia Press.

1990 The Culture of Romance: Women, Resistance, and Gender Relations on Campus. Chicago: University of Chicago Press (in press).

HOLLAND, DOROTHY C. and DEBRA SKINNER
1987 Prestige and Intimacy: The Cultural Models Behind Americans' Talk about Gender Types. *In* Cultural Models in Language and Thought. D. Holland and N. Quinn, eds. Pp. 78–111. Cambridge: Cambridge University Press.

KOZULIN, ALEX
1986 The Concept of Activity in Soviet Psychology: Vygotsky, His Disciples and Critics. American Psychologist 41(3):264–274.

LAVE, JEAN
1988 Cognition in Practice: Mind, Mathematics and Culture in Everyday Life. Cambridge: Cambridge University Press.

LEVINE, ROBERT
1984 Properties of Culture: An Ethnographic View. *In* Culture Theory: Essays on Mind, Self, and Emotion. R. Shweder and R. LeVine, eds. Pp. 67–87. Cambridge: Cambridge University Press.

OCHS, ELINOR and BAMBI SCHIEFFELIN
1984 Language Acquisition and Socialization: Three Developmental Stories and Their Implications. *In* Culture Theory: Essays on Mind, Self, and Emotion. R. Shweder and R. LeVine, eds. Pp. 276–320. Cambridge: Cambridge University Press.

QUINN, NAOMI and DOROTHY C. HOLLAND
1987 Culture and Cognition. *In* Cultural Models in Language and Thought. D. Holland and N. Quinn, eds. Pp. 3–40. Cambridge: Cambridge University Press.

WEISNER, THOMAS, RONALD GALLIMORE, and CATHIE JORDAN
1988 Unpackaging Cultural Effects on Classroom Learning: Native Hawaiian Peer Assistance and Child-Generated Activity. Anthropology and Education Quarterly 19(4):327–353.

WERTSCH, JAMES V., NORRIS MINICK, and FLAVIO J. ARNS
1984 The Creation of Context in Joint Problem-Solving. *In* Everyday Cognition: Its Development in Social Context. B. Rogoff and J. Lave, eds. Pp. 151–171. Cambridge: Harvard University Press.

WILLIS, PAUL
1977 Learning to Labor: How Working Class Kids Get Working Class Jobs. New York: Columbia University Press.

WOLCOTT, HARRY
1988 Propriospect. Paper presented at the meeting of the American Anthropological Association, Phoenix, Arizona.

After reading: CONSOLIDATE INFORMATION

1. Write a brief summary of how cultural acquisition works (or does not work) in the case study of Linda or Sandy.

2. How would you desribe the cultural system at SU? How does that cultural system compare with what you perceive to be the cultural system at your university or college?
3. Analyze Eisenhart's interpretation of her findings about Linda and Sandy.

Sport in the Black Urban Community
Steven A. Reiss

In a comprehensive, scholarly study of the evolution of American urban society and the rise of sports entitled City Games, *Steven A. Reiss examines sports as a sociological phenomenon. The following excerpt is taken from a chapter entitled "Sport, Race, and Ethnicity."*

Before reading: FIRST THOUGHTS
                     LOOK AHEAD

1. What do you think is the connection between sports and the Black community in America?
2. If segregation was a fact of American life until World War II and even after, what effect do you think it (in schools, public facilities, and neighborhoods) would have had on the participation of Blacks or African-Americans in organized sports?
3. With what sport do you associate Black players?

During reading: REACT
                    QUESTION
                    SUMMARIZE

1. What professional sports were the first to be truly integrated in the United States?
2. What did Joe Louis and Jackie Robinson mean to Black Americans?

THE SPORTING OPTIONS of black urban residents were influenced not only by such factors as class, culture, and space but also by their race. At the turn of the century most urban blacks lived in southern cities. They comprised the majority in Charleston and Savannah, nearly half of Memphis, and two-fifths of Atlanta, Birmingham, Charlotte, Nashville, and Richmond. Unlike the European immigrants, blacks were completely familiar with and actively involved in the American sporting culture. However, in the post-Reconstruction South their athletic experiences were totally segregated, by either law or custom. Black athletes could not compete with whites, and seating at commercialized spectator sports like horse racing and baseball was segregated. The black sporting life was, by necessity, centered within their own neighborhoods. Black communities in larger cities supported at least two black baseball clubs while fraternal organizations, churches, and politicians organized picnic games at black-owned fairgrounds or in black sections of municipal parks. By 1876 there were black YMCAs in Richmond and Nashville, described by historian Howard Rabinowitz as middle-class social centers which "gave [blacks] a chance to seek the reformation of their erring brethren" who enjoyed billiards and other pleasures of "the sporting life."[1]

The one exception to the pervasive segregation of southern urban sports facilities was in New Orleans, with its peculiar racial traditions. Dale Somers, in his extensive study of Delta City sports, found that although most sports were segregated, there was considerable interracial competition and that "until the mid-eighties, participants in racially mixed contests encountered little hostility." Until 1871 local racetracks had always permitted blacks into the general admission section, but that year the Metairie Course erected a separate stand for blacks. Black economic pressure promptly reversed that policy. But even in New Orleans, segregation existed at the various lakefront athletic facilities, and since white clubs would not admit them, blacks had to form their own athletic clubs. In the 1880s the color line was drawn tighter: game laws were passed to protect wildlife—aimed at curtailing black hunters who were blamed for depleting the woods (probably for food)—and also white baseball teams that played blacks were threatened with a boycott. Finally, in the 1890s local cyclists withdrew from the LAW because northern units had black members.[2]

The last sport in New Orleans to draw the color line was boxing. Since fighters were seen as merely entertainers rather than as the social equals of spectators, mixed bouts were traditionally accepted. However, blacks were not allowed to attend these fights until 6 September 1892, when black featherweight champion George Dixon defended his crown against Jack Skelly at the Olympic Arena; then, of course, they sat in a segregated section. Dixon won the fight with a brutal eighth-round knockout which citizens saw as a shocking blow to the prestige of the white race, and as a result, no more mixed matches were allowed in New Orleans.[3]

At the turn of the century black populations in northern cities were rather small—15,000 in Chicago, for example—but beginning in 1915 large numbers of blacks migrated north to escape racial violence, get better jobs, secure civil rights, and enjoy a more sophisticated life-style. Black populations in industrial cities like Chicago more than tripled in a decade, and by 1920 New York had over 150,000 black residents. Consequently, black ghettoes fostered an enormous development and expansion of black social and cultural institutions in segregated settings.

Although black amateurs were usually able to compete against whites, black athletes in northern cities encountered considerable discrimination. Like the Irish and the new immigrants, black athletes had to form many of their own sports clubs, which ranged from track and field and baseball to cycling, because white status and ethnic clubs would not admit them. Black athletic associations themselves sorted out individuals by class or origin, just as white clubs did. In Boston, for instance, Stephen Hardy found that long-time and upwardly mobile residents formed tennis clubs just like the white elite, while new arrivals from the South "found a common bond in social networks at neighborhood gymnasiums where the latest boxing news might be discussed." West Indian newcomers formed cricket clubs to facilitate competition and sustain their Caribbean heritage.[4]

Black access to semipublic and public sports facilities was limited by expense, discretionary time, accessibility, and discrimination. In the late nineteenth century separate black YMCAs were established in Boston, Brooklyn, New York, and Philadelphia; in Detroit, only the black elite could use the white Y. As early as 1889, black community leaders in Chicago considered establishing a separate black branch, but integrationist sentiment at the time defeated the proposal. After the turn of the century, white hostility to blacks in the Y movement became so sharp that they were virtually shut out. As a result, prominent black Chicagoans in 1910 initiated a campaign for a Y in their own neighborhood. The building was completed three years later at a cost of $190,000, with generous contributions from philanthropist Julius Rosenwald and various local meatpackers and industrialists who further demonstrated their concern by purchasing memberships for their black employees.[5]

Black or integrated teams that traveled outside the growing black neighborhoods to play white teams in white neighborhoods often encountered rough treatment on the playing field and even tougher situations off the field. In the 1910s, when an integrated Chicago basketball team went to play in a white section, trouble often followed: "On the way over here fellows on the outside bailed them out, but our fellows sure got them on the way home. There were three black fellows on the team and those three got just about laid out. Our team wouldn't play them, so there was a great old row. Then, when they went home some of our boys were waiting for them to come out of the building to give them a chase. The coons were afraid to come out, so policemen had to be called to take them to the car line. The white fellows weren't hurt any, but the coons got some bricks."[6]

Boxing

The most popular spectator sports in the black community were prize fighting and baseball. Although black fighters encountered less discrimination than other black athletes—which reflected the low status of the sport—they were subject to terribly abusive language from white fans. At a time when black professional athletes were being forced out of thoroughbred racing, cycling, and organized baseball, blacks were achieving considerable renown in the prize ring. Between 1890 and 1908 there were five black world champions, though many prominent contenders never even got title matches because champions like John L. Sullivan drew the color line.[7]

Top black fighters usually lived in northern black communities, where they would be treated with respect, could get more fights, found opportunities for investment in businesses like Jack Johnson's Café de Champion (a cabaret in Chicago's black belt), and enjoyed the pleasures of the demi-monde. In working-class black communities black pugilists were heroes and had such a wide following that an historian of black Boston discovered that "black attendance at boxing matches outdrew the Sunday sermon." Black fans preferred to see mixed bouts in which their idols could win symbolic racial victories, but local customs or city and state laws often restricted inter-racial contests for fear of fomenting racial antagonisms. Immediately after Jack Johnson successfully defended his heavyweight crown on 4 July 1910 against former champion Jim Jeffries, "The Great White Hope," there were racial conflicts in cities across the country. Many communities subsequently barred exhibitors from showing the film of the fight for fear of generating more incidents.[8]

Over the next several decades boxing continued to attract black interest because it was the only democratic professional sport. One expert estimated there were as many as 1,800 black pros during the 1930s. Like their white peers, they were attracted by the opportunity to make a name for themselves, earn a living, escape the ghetto, and maybe get rich. At a time when no other major professional sport was open to blacks, Afro-American pugilists were achieving great success. The 1930s produced five black champions, including Henry Armstrong, who won three different titles, and Joe Louis, the first black to fight for the heavyweight championship since Jack Johnson. Champion from 1937 to 1949, Louis represented to white America what the ideal negro should be, but for his own community, Louis symbolized black power, racial pride, and an insistence that blacks be accepted in American society. He was a role model for ghetto youth like Malcolm Little (Malcolm X), who became an amateur fighter. His victories were received with great glee in northern black communities, where thousands took to the streets to celebrate, deriving, as Lena Horne remembered, "all the joy possible from this collective victory of the race."[9]

Blacks quickly achieved dominance in the ring. By 1948, nearly half of all contenders were black—a reflection of widespread black poverty and the success of role models like Joe Louis. Italians were second in the number of contenders and Mexican-Americans, a new group to achieve prominence in boxing, third.[10] The ethnic succession in the ring reflected the changing racial and ethnic complexion of the inner city as older ethnic groups who were doing better economically moved out and were replaced by the new urban poor. This dynamic was epitomized by the absence of Jewish fighters from the lists of contenders. Jews had formerly dominated the sport, but as they became better educated or succeeded as entrepreneurs, they moved to the urban periphery or the suburbs. Jews no longer needed to get their brains knocked out to make a living.

Basketball: The Ghetto Game

Class and environment—the main reasons that blacks achieved ethnic succession in boxing—are also the primary factors behind current black dominance in professional basketball (75 percent of the NBA in 1980). Professional ballplayers had always been disproportionately urban, particularly from major cities, and that pattern still holds. In the 1960s and 1970s nearly all NBA players (91.3 percent) were urban; and nearly half, from large cities (49.5 percent)—usually from the inner city, where boys did not have much money or many constructive alternatives for their free time other than sports.[11] As Bob Gibson, a Hall of Famer and one-time Harlem Globetrotter, remembered from his youth in Omaha during the early 1950s: "It always seemed to me that the Negro kids in the project spent more time in sports and participating in things like this than the average white kid. The white kid had more things to do. He could go to the movies, but we could not. We never had the money. So we ran footraces and played ball because there was nothing else to do, unless you wanted to go out and get in trouble."[12] Over the past thirty years basketball has been the major athletic passion of black ghetto youth, as it had once been for Jewish, German, and Irish youth. As Pete Axthelm pointed out a few years ago, "Other young athletes may learn basketball, but (inner) city kids live it." The playground is their heaven, wrote journalist Rick Telander, where city youths study the moves of their heroes, develop their own, and try to make a reputation for themselves. They practice diligently for hours a day, all year long, motivated by the immediate gratification of prestige at neighborhood courts and the longer-term goals of starring in high school, getting a college scholarship, and ending up in the NBA. This of course is a pipe dream, since only 4 percent of high school players are good enough to play in college, much less the NBA. Unlike earlier cohorts of inner-city basketball players, the latest generation devoted *all* their attention to their game and little to their brain, with the result that even if they excelled in basketball and achieved a degree of fame, there was a strong chance they would end up right back in the ghetto where they had started.[13]

Baseball In the Urban Black Community

Baseball was the most important sport in the black communities. Unlike the immigrants from overseas, rural black migrants were very familiar with the national pastime. Until 1898, when blacks were barred from organized baseball by a common understanding among racist owners, there had been around fifty professional black ballplayers, including two in the majors in 1884. Blacks responded to being shunned by forming their own professional teams. By 1900 there were five salaried black teams, including two in Chicago despite the small size of its black community. Chicago teams played on Sundays, when black fans were off work; during the week they toured the Midwest playing local town teams. The preeminent black team then was Chicago's Leland Giants, owned by local black politicians. The club played at their own park four miles south of the Black Belt, next door to their proprietors' amusement park. The Leland Giants played from 1907 to 1909 in the otherwise all-white City League, the finest semiprofessional league in the United States. The club was so good that in 1909 they played a postseason series with the Chicago Cubs. The Giants, a great draw at the box office, brought out to 15,000 fans of both races. Management problems led to the team's demise in 1910; a year later the club was succeeded by the American Giants, jointly owned by white tavern keeper John M. Schorling and former star pitcher Rube Foster. They played on the site of the old White Sox Park across the street from the growing Black Belt. The team became a symbol of pride in the community, and one black editor urged "all race loving and race building men and women" to support it. The American Giants were so popular that on one Sunday, when the local major league clubs were at home, the Giants outdrew both of them with a crowd of 11,000 black and white fans.[14]

The success of black baseball was strongly influenced by the great migration north that began in the mid-1910s and continued in subsequent decades. Between 1920 and 1950 the black populations of Chicago, Cleveland, Detroit, and New York all quadrupled, and other northern cities also had substantial increases. These newcomers could secure only low paying jobs and, because of their income and discrimination, had little choice over where to live. The resulting northern black ghettos—with inadequate housing, high rates of crime, and poor municipal services—created new opportunities for businesses that catered to a predominantly black clientele—particularly businesses in the entertainment field, like baseball.

Before 1920 most black teams had been owned by white entrepreneurs, who scheduled games and rented ballparks. Black journalists deplored these conditions, urging that profits "should be received by the Race to whom the patrons of the game belong." After World War I Rube Foster, sole owner of the Chicago American Giants since 1916, initiated a movement to wrest control of black baseball from white promoters and put it into the hands of black entrepreneurs. Foster believed that the growing black urban communities provided a potential market for a top-flight negro league, and he also argued that since all players and two-thirds of the spectators were black the profits should remain with the race.[15]

In 1920 Foster organized the Negro National League (NNL), with eight mainly midwestern franchises, all but one of which were owned and operated by black businessmen. NNL teams played from forty to eighty league contests and a total of about 200 games a year, including exhibitions. Tickets cost twenty-five cents. The leading expert on the negro leagues estimated weekend crowds exceeded 5,000, but the average attendance was only about one-third of that. Although the league was highly regarded by the black press and urban fans, it struggled financially, lasting through twelve shaky seasons. Of the original eight teams, only the American Giants lasted from start to finish. A crucial problem was lack of control over their playing area: only the American Giants had their own field; the others leased local parks, where they were usually secondary tenants and could not schedule choice dates. In 1926 Foster suffered a mental breakdown, and the subsequent absence of sustained leadership plus the impact of the Depression led to the death of the NNL in 1931.[16]

In 1933 a new NNL was organized by numbers bankers, one of the few lucrative, if illegal, occupations in the black neighborhoods during the Depression. The most prominent owner was Gus Greenlee, king of the Pittsburgh numbers racket, owner of the city's leading "black and tan" resort, and manager in the mid-1930s of light-heavyweight boxing champion John Henry Lewis. Greenlee first got involved in baseball in 1930, when he sponsored the Crawfords, a well-known independent black nine, and two years later he spent $100,000 for the first black-built ballpark. Greenlee and his fellow owners were well regarded by the black press, which saw them as strong race men who provided hundreds of jobs through their business ventures and supplied badly needed cheap entertainment.[17]

The NNL started out inauspiciously, playing its games at old minor league fields, former federal league parks, or second-rate semiprofessional fields. In the inaugural season Greenlee lost $50,000, but he justified it as an investment in the future. But within a few years business perked up, and the NNL and its rival—the Negro American League, founded in 1937—were on a "reasonably sound financial ground." Most teams at least broke even except for the star-laden, high-salaried Crawfords. As the NNL became more successful, its teams began to rent major-league parks, where there was a better ambiance and more space for the large crowds coming out to see exciting and high-quality play. White landlords profited handsomely from fees that ranged from 10 to 20 percent of the gate. In the 1940s the Yankees were earning about $100,000 a year from their black tenants. The negro leagues reached their zenith during World War II, when urban black populations grew dramatically because of the opportunities for jobs in war-related industries.[18]

In the interwar era the negro league teams were prominent community institutions, and cities without NNL franchises were regarded as second rate. Opening-day games became important public rituals, embellished with such ceremonies as pregame parades or the throwing out of the first ball by celebrities like Lena Horne or politicians like Congressman William Dawson of Chicago. Fans dressed up for opening day, and according to historian William Rogosin, "society pages of the black newspapers gushed with baseball stories that suggested opening day's importance for a culture with limited opportunities to partake in American tradition." Games during the season were employed for community activities ranging from beauty contests to "Stop Lynching" campaigns.[19]

The biggest event in black baseball—and the single most important sporting event in the black community, outside of Joe Louis's fights—was the annual East-West All-Star Game. In 1933 Gus Greenlee initiated the All-Star Game, which became so popular that by 1943 it was attracting 50,000 spectators. Most contests were held at Comiskey Park, located across the street from one of the most important black communities in the United States. Fans from all social backgrounds, including out-of-town tourists, flocked to the stadium. The game became one of the highlights in the social calendar of the black elite, who sat in expensive $1.50 seats where everybody could see them.[20]

Ironically, at the same time the negro leagues reached their height, a major movement developed to integrate organized baseball, which eventually meant the end of the negro leagues. Black sportswriters, civil-rights organizations, and left-wing political groups made the integration of baseball a political issue. In 1945 a Boston councilman threatened the city's teams with the loss of their Sunday permits unless they gave blacks tryouts, and New York's Fiorello LaGuardia formed the Mayor's Committee on Baseball to encourage local teams to sign black ballplayers. A Communist councilman running for reelection in New York distributed flyers captioned "Good enough to die for his country, but not good enough for organized baseball."[21]

The integration of baseball by Jackie Robinson, and his courage, perseverance, outstanding play, and "class," made him a great hero in black communities and his exploits front-page news in the black press. As Branch Rickey had hoped, Robinson's presence in the Brooklyn Dodgers lineup had a positive impact on black attendance, which had previously been limited. During his rookie season in 1947, black Kansas Citians took a five-hour-long train ride to St. Louis, traveling under Jim Crow conditions, to see Jackie play in segregated Sportsman's Park. When Robinson made his first appearance at Wrigley Field, he drew a record crowd of 46,000. Thousands of blacks attended, wearing their best Sunday clothes. At the time blacks were almost never seen on the North Side, and as journalist Mike Royko remembered, "It was probably the first time ... (blacks and whites) had been so close to each other in such large numbers."[22]

The integration of baseball, a slow and torturous process, was not completed on the major-league level until 1959, when the Boston Red Sox signed their first black player. The process had a significant impact on black urban life, promoting racial pride, securing begrudging respect from white fans, and demonstrating a potential for future gains in race relations. However, during the 1950s, southern training camps remained segregated, and several teams moved to Arizona to escape Jim Crow. Modest advances did occur in the South; for example, the Dodgers scheduled integrated exhibition games in cities like Atlanta, Macon, and Miami, where inter-racial sport was previously forbidden. In addition, by 1953, every professional league except the Southern Association was integrated; blacks played in such Deep South cities as Jacksonville, Montgomery, New Orleans, and Savannah, albeit in front of segregated crowds.[23]

The worst abuses of black athletes and spectators did not end until the civil-rights demonstrations and economic boycotts of the 1960s and the implementation of federal civil-rights legislation that forbade discrimination in such public facilities as municipal parks, swimming pools, and golf courses, as well as restaurants, hotels, and common carriers. Organized baseball did not do everything in its power to eliminate Jim Crow, though Casy Stengel did insist that hotels in Chicago and Kansas City cease discriminating against his black players. Historian Jules Tygiel argues that professional baseball was one of the first American institutions to accept blacks on virtually equal terms, and because baseball is the national pastime, that was an important symbolic achievement.[24]

Conclusion: Sport, Race and Ethnicity in the American City

The sporting culture of urban ethnic groups was a product of their cultural heritage, social class, and discrimination. Yet while these variables affected all groups, some were more important for different categories of ethnic cohorts than others—the old-world heritage for the European immigrant, economics for second-generation white ethnics, and racism for blacks.

European immigrants who settled in cities alleviated their alienation and facilitated their adjustment to strange and hostile environments by developing ethnic subcommunities as much like the Old World as possible. In zones of emergence and slums the newcomers established ethnic villages to sustain their language, customs, and religion and a sense of peoplehood. These communities nurtured such old institutions as the Church and such new ones as mutual aid societies and foreign-language newspapers, which helped the newcomer cope with urban America. The old immigrants brought over a sporting heritage which remained a vital part of their cultural life in their new land. The turnverein's gymnasiums and community centers played a central role in German neighborhoods. Irish sports clubs promoted nationalism, and their traditional love of sport enabled them to readily fit into a male bachelor subculture, in which they could find friends and possible routes of social mobility. However, sporting traditions were far weaker among the new immigrants, and with the exception of slavic groups, who were beginning to develop an oppositional and revolutionary sporting subculture in eastern Europe, sport had no appeal to these newcomers.

Sport did play a prominent role among all second-generation immigrants. Success in sports was a step towards assimilation—a means of disproving negative ethnic stereotypes, gaining respect from the outside community, and cementing social relationships among street corner youth; a source of ethnic pride and feelings of community; and a possible vehicle for vertical mobility. The sons of the old immigrants had distinct advantages over the new immigrants; they had parental approval and often lived in the zone of emergence, where they had opportunities to participate in a wide variety of sports. But Italian, Jewish, and Polish youths faced parental opposition, needed to work, and lived in crowded slums that placed severe limitations on their athletic options. Since it was difficult to become proficient in baseball because of the lack of space for playing fields, inner-city youth mainly participated in sports within their own communities. Because of accessibility, cost, and fear for their security in strange neighborhoods, inner-city youth favored sports like basketball, boxing, billiards, and bowling, which did not require much space, could be played indoors at night, and provided status to good players. Boxing was especially appropriate for young men living in tough neighborhoods, where fighting was part of daily life. Park districts, social agencies fighting against juvenile delinquency, and ethnic voluntary organizations trying to maintain a sense of peoplehood among the American-born youth provided facilities for basketball and boxing. Once the white ethnics moved into better neighborhoods, the second and third generation had the time and the necessary space to enjoy whichever sports they preferred.

Black urbanites, completely familiar with the American sporting culture, still faced severe limitations because of class and racism. Black use of sports facilities was restricted in the South by social custom and laws and in the North by discrimination and ghettoization. Their neighborhoods, always underfunded, were the last to get public parks and other facilities. Nonetheless, sport was very important in black localities for recreational and other purposes. Urban blacks, less successful at building their own community institutions than the European immigrants, used sport, along with the church, press, and politics, to develop a sense of community in their neighborhoods. Blacks established their own voluntary sports associations, their own teams, and even their own heroes. Success in sports raised black pride, provided fans with a sense of self-worth by vicarious identification with athletic heroes, and gained some begrudging respect from the broader community. Sport also provided hopes of social mobility—less from college scholarships, which were very rare for blacks, than through professional sports, either segregated baseball or integrated boxing, a meritocratic sport that was a natural outlet for impoverished, tough ghetto youth. As white ethnics moved out of the inner city, they were replaced by blacks, who also succeeded in boxing and basketball, the two major sports most congruent with the physical and cultural character of inner-city life. But unlike the white groups, blacks have not been able to escape urban poverty and the ghetto, and one result has been the unfortunate over-reliance on athletics as a means of getting ahead.

Notes

1. David Goldfield and Blaine Brownell, *Urban America: From Downtown to No Town* (Boston, 1979), 260; Howard Rabinowitz, *Race Relations in the Urban South, 1865–1890* (Urbana, Ill., 1980), 185, 187, 189–90, 389n30, 228–30.

2. Dale A. Somers, *The Rise of Sports in New Orleans, 1850–1900* (Baton Rouge, 1972), 11–12, 29, 87, 96–97, 120–21, 142–44, 199–200, 209, 222–24, 241–42, 286 (quote), 286–90.

3. Ibid., 181.

4. Hardy, *How Boston Played*, 138 (quote), 153; *Brooklyn Eagle*, 5 May 1894; *NYT*, 18 Oct. 1914, 14 Aug. 1917. For a detailed study of sport in one black community, see Rob Ruck, *Sandlot Seasons: Sport in Black Pittsburgh* (Urbana, Ill., 1987).

5. C. Howard Hopkins, *The History of the Y.M.C.A. in North America* (New York, 1951), 213, 472; David M. Katzman, *Before the Ghetto: Black Detroit in the Nineteenth Century* (Urbana, Ill., 1973), 79, 161; W. E. B. Du Bois, *The Philadelphia Negro: A Social Study* (1899; rep. New York, 1967), 232; Kenneth L. Kusmer, *A Ghetto Takes Shape: Black Cleveland, 1870–1930* (Urbana, Ill., 1976), 50–58; Spear, *Black Chicago*, 46–47, 52, 100–101, 162, 174, 227.

6. Chicago Commission on Race Relations, *Negro in Chicago*, 253.

7. See, e.g., Riess, *Touching Base*, 194–96, 217n124; Robert Peterson, *Only the Ball Was White* (Englewood Cliffs, N.J., 1970), chaps. 1, 2; Marshall W. Taylor, *The Fastest Bicycle Rider in the World* (Worcester, Mass., 1928); David K. Wiggins, "Isaac Murphy: Black Hero in Nineteenth-Century American Sport, 1861–1896," *Canadian Journal of History of Sport and Physical Education* 10 (May 1979): 15–32; idem, "Peter Jackson and the Elusive Heavyweight Championship: A Black Athlete's Struggle against the Late-Nineteenth-Century Color-Line," *JSpH* 12 (Summer 1985): 143–68; Randy Roberts, *Papa Jack: Jack Johnson and the Era of White Hopes* (New York, 1983); Al-Tony Gilmore, *Bad Nigger! The National Impact of Jack Johnson* (Port Washington, N. Y., 1975).

8. Elizabeth Pleck, "Black Migration to Boston in the Late Nineteen Century" (Ph.D. diss., Brandeis University, 1974), 188 (quote). (My thanks to Stephen Hardy for bringing this to my attention.) Roberts, *Papa Jack*, chaps. 5, 7–9; Gilmore, *Bad Nigger!* chaps. 5–6; *NYT*, 6, 9, 10–12, 14, 17 July 19 10; "The Prize Fight Moving Pictures," *Outlook* 95 (16 July 1910): 541–42. Mixed bouts were barred in New York from 1912 to 1916. See, e.g., *NYT* 29 Dec. 1911, 7 Jan. 1912, 6 June 1915, 17 Jan., 18 Feb. 1916; *NPG* 103 (6 Sept. 1913): 10, 107 (12 Feb. 1916): 10, 108 (1 Apr. 1916): 10; "Smith-Langford Cancelled," *Boxing and Sporting World* 1 (4 Oct. 1913): 4; *New York World*, 17 Jan., 29 June, 7, 8, 11, 12 July, 8 Aug. 1916.

9. On white attitudes toward Louis, see Anthony Edmonds, *Joe Louis* (Grand Rapids, 1972), chaps. 4–6; and Frederick C. Jaher, "White America Views Jack Johnson, Joe Louis and Muhammed Ali," in *Sport in America: New Historical Perspectives*, ed. Donald Spivey (Westport, Conn., 1985), 158–73, 177–82. For black attitudes, see Lawrence W. Levine, *Black Culture and Black Consciousness: Afro-American Folk Thought from Slavery to Freedom* (New York, 1977), 433–38. Quote is from Lena Horne and Richard Schickel, *Lena* (Garden City, L.I., 1965), 75, in ibid., 434.

11. In the late 1940s boxers were typically ex-street fighters, often from broken homes, with unemployed fathers. Weinberg and Arond, "Occupational Culture," 460.

12. Computed from Ronald L. Mendell, *Who's Who in Basketball* (New Rochelle, 1973). See also John F. Rooney, Jr., *A Geography of American Sports: From Cabin Creek to Anaheim* (Reading, Mass., 1974), 154–74. Between 1946 and 1983, two-thirds of all College All-Ameri-

cans (Division 1) came from metropolitan areas with over 500,000 residents at a time when those cities comprised just half (49.5 percent) of the national population. New York produced the most (13.5 percent), followed by Chicago (6.3 percent), Philadelphia, and Los Angeles (3.8 percent each). In 1970 they were the leading procurers of Division I players with ratios approximately equal to their share of the national population. *Chicago Sun-Times*, 13 Dec. 1983.

13. Bob Gibson with Phil Pepe, *From Ghetto to Glory: The Story of Bob Gibson* (Englewood Cliffs, N.J., 1968), 6.

14. Pete Axthelm, *The City Game* (New York, 1970), ix-x, book iii; Rick Telander, *Heaven Is a Playground* (New York, 1976).

15. The standard history of black baseball is Peterson, *Only the Ball Was White*, esp. chaps. 2-3. On black baseball in Chicago, see ibid., 62-66; Spear, *Black Chicago*, 117-18; *Spalding's Official Baseball Guide of Chicago, 1906 ... 1910* (New York, 1906-10); *Chicago Defender*, 12 Dec. 1908, 23 Apr. 1910, 20 Feb. 1915; *CDN*, 10 Jan. 1910; *New York Age*, 14 Apr., 5 May, 21 July 1910, 5 Jan. 1911. Quote is in Peterson, *Only the Ball Was White*, 66.

16. Riess, *Touching Base*, 38, 196-97; Peterson, *Only the Ball Was White*, 257.

17. Foster's team averaged $85,000 in each of its first six years in the NNL, but other clubs took in as little as $10,000 at the gate. Peterson, *Only the Ball Was White*, 86, 86, 89, 90, 114-15.

18. Donn Rogosin, *Invisible Men: Life in Baseball's Negro Leagues* (New York, 1983), 14-17, 103-8, 213. On the early Crawfords, see Ruck, *Sandlot Seasons*, 46-62.

19. Rogosin, *Invisible Men*, 18-19, 23-24, 105, 107, 110, 209; Peterson, *Only the Ball Was White*, 93, 94, 135-36.

20. Rogosin, *Invisible Men*, 22-23, 93-94.

21. Ibid., 25-26.

22. Jules Tygiel, *Baseball's Great Experiment: Jackie Robinson and His Legacy* (New York, 1983), 40-41, 69 (quote).

23. Rogosin, *Invisible Men*, 218. Quote is from *CDN*, 26 Oct. 1972, cited in Tygiel, *Baseball's Great Experiment*, 196.

24. Tygiel, *Baseball's Great Experiment*, 265-84.

After reading: CONSOLIDATE INFORMATION

1. Summarize the significance of basketball for urban Blacks.
2. What is the connection between sports and the integration and assimilation of Blacks into mainstream society?
3. Does Reiss think that sports have been a positive influence on Black life in America?

The Attitude Towards Personality
Margaret Mead

Margaret Mead (1901–1978) became famous for her landmark study of adolescence on the remote South Sea Island of Samoa, Coming of Age in Samoa *(1934). In recent years, Mead's work has become the subject of controversy and criticism for what some anthropologists view as a romanticization of the people she studied. The following is an excerpt from* Coming of Age in Samoa. *Although she undertook her study as a scholarly research project, Mead intended her work to be read by a wide audience.*

Before reading: FIRST THOUGHTS
            LOOK AHEAD

1. What kind of traits do you think make up a person's personality?
2. How does where you live, who you are, and the social group to which you belong [in short, your culture] affect what personality traits you value?
3. Mead describes the Samoans' attitude toward personality as being a mixture of caution and fatalism. What do you think she means by this?

During reading: REACT
            QUESTION
            SUMMARIZE

1. Do the Samoans seem to recognize personality traits? Which traits do they seem most concerned with?
2. How much do Samoans emphasize motivation? How do they describe emotional causes?

THE EASE with which personality differences can be adjusted by a change of residence prevents the Samoans from pressing one another too hard. Their evaluations of personality are a curious mixture of caution and fatalism. There is one word *musu* which expresses unwillingness and intractability, whether in the mistress who refuses to welcome a hitherto welcome lover, the chief who refuses to lend his kava bowl, the baby who won't go to bed, or the talking chief who won't go on a *malaga*. The appearance of a *musu* attitude is treated with almost superstitious respect. Lovers will prescribe formulæ for the treatment of a mistress, "lest she become *musu*," and the behaviour of the suppliant is carefully orientated in respect to this mysterious undesirability. The feeling seems to be not that one is dealing with an individual in terms of his peculiar preoccupations in order to assure a successful outcome of a personal relationship, appealing now to vanity, now to fear, now to a desire for power, but rather that one is using one or another of a series of potent practices to prevent a mysterious and widespread psychological phenomenon from arising. Once this attitude has appeared, a Samoan habitually gives up the struggle without more detailed inquiry and with a minimum of complaint. This fatalistic acceptance of an inexplicable attitude makes for an odd incuriousness about motives. The Samoans are not in the least insensitive to differences between people. But their full appreciation of these differences is blurred by their conception of an obstinate disposition, a tendency to take umbrage, irascibility, contra-suggestibility, and particular biases as just so many roads to one attitude—*musu*.

This lack of curiosity about motivation is furthered by the conventional acceptance of a completely ambiguous answer to any personal question. The most characteristic reply to any question about one's motivation is *Ta ilo*, "search me," sometimes made more specific by the addition of "I don't know." This is considered to be an adequate and acceptable answer in ordinary conversation although its slight curtness bars it out from ceremonious occasions. So deep seated is the habit of using this disclaimer that I had to put a taboo upon its use by the children in order to get the simplest question answered directly. When this ambiguous rejoinder is combined with a statement that one is *musu*, the result is the final unrevealing statement, "Search me, why, I don't want to, that's all." Plans will be abandoned, children refuse to live at home, marriages broken off. Village gossip is interested in the fact but shrugs its shoulders before the motives.

There is one curious exception to this attitude. If an individual falls ill, the explanation is sought first in the attitudes of his relatives. Anger in the heart of a relative, especially in that of a sister, is most potent in producing evil and so the whole household is convened, a kava ceremony held and each relative solemnly enjoined to confess what anger there is in his heart against the sick person. Such injunctions are met either by solemn disclaimers or by detailed confessions: "Last week my brother came into the house and ate all the food, and I was angry all day"; or "My brother and I had a quarrel and my father took my brother's side and I was angry at my father for his favouritism towards my brother." But this special ceremony only serves to throw into strong relief the prevalent unspeculative attitude towards motivation. I once saw a girl leave a week-end fishing party immediately upon arrival at our destination and insist upon returning in the heat of the day the six miles to the village. But her companions ventured no hypothesis; she was simply *musu* to the party.

How great a protection for the individual such an attitude is will readily be seen when it is remembered how little privacy any one has. Chief or child, he dwells habitually in a house with at least half a dozen other people. His possessions are simply rolled in a mat, placed on the rafters or piled carelessly into a basket or a chest. A chief's personal property is likely to be respected, at least by the women of the household, but no one else can be sure from hour to hour of his nominal possessions. The tapa which a woman spent three weeks in making will be given away to a visitor during her temporary absence. The rings may be begged off her fingers at any moment. Privacy of possessions is virtually impossible. In the same way, all of an individual's acts are public property. An occasional love affair may slip through the fingers of gossip, and an occasional *moetotolo* go uncaught, but there is a very general cognisance on the part of the whole village of the activity of every single inhabitant. I shall never forget the outraged expression with which an informant told me that nobody, actually nobody at all, knew who was the father of Fa'amoana's baby. The oppressive atmosphere of the small town is all about them; in an hour children will have made a dancing song of their most secret acts. This glaring publicity is compensated for by a violent gloomy secretiveness. Where a Westerner would say, "Yes, I love him but you'll never know how far it went," a Samoan would say, "Yes, of course I lived with him, but you'll never know whether I love him or hate him."

The Samoan language has no regular comparative. There are several clumsy ways of expressing comparison by using contrast, "This is good and that is bad"; or by the locution, "And next to him there comes, etc." Comparisons are not habitual although in the rigid social structure of the community, relative rank is very keenly recognised. But relative goodness, relative beauty, relative wisdom are unfamiliar formalisations to them. I tried over and over again to get judgments as to who was the wisest or the best man of the community. An informant's first impulse was always to answer: "Oh, they are all good" or, "There are so many wise ones." Curiously enough, there seemed to be less difficulty in distinguishing the vicious than the virtuous. This is probably due to the Missionary influence which if it has failed to give the native a conviction of Sin, has at least provided him with a list of sins. Although I often met with a preliminary response, "There are so many bad boys"; it was usually qualified spontaneously by "But so-and-so is the worst because he . . ." Ugliness and viciousness were more vivid and unusual attributes of personality; beauty, wisdom, and kindness were taken for granted.

In an account given of another person the sequence of traits mentioned followed a set and objective pattern: sex, age, rank, relationship, defects, activities. Spontaneous comment upon character or personality were unusual. So a girl describes her grandmother: "Lauuli? Oh, she is an old woman, very old, she's my father's mother. She's a widow with one eye. She is too old to go inland but sits in the house all day. She makes tapa."* This completely unanalytical account is only modified in the case of exceptionally intelligent adults who are asked to make judgments.

In the native classification attitudes are qualified by four terms, good and bad, easy and difficult, paired. A good child will be said to listen easily or to act well, a bad child to listen with difficulty or act badly. "Easy" and "with difficulty" are judgments of character; "good" and "bad" of behaviour. So that good or bad behaviour have become, explained in terms of ease or difficulty, to be regarded as an inherent capability of the individual. As we would say a person sang easily or swam without effort, the Samoan will say one obeys easily, acts respectfully, "easily," reserving the terms "good" or "well" for objective approbation. So a chief who was commenting on the bad behaviour of his brother's daughter remarked,

"But Tui's children always did listen with difficulty," with as casual an acceptance of an irradicable defect as if he had said, "But John always did have poor eye sight."

Such an attitude towards conduct is paralleled by an equally unusual attitude towards the expression of emotion. The expressions of emotions are classified as "caused" and "uncaused." The emotional, easily upset moody person is described as laughing without cause, crying without cause, showing anger or pugnaciousness without cause. The expression "to be very angry without cause" does not carry the implication of quick temper, which is expressed by the word "to anger easily," nor the connotation of a disproportionate response to a legitimate stimulus, but means literally to be angry without cause, or freely, an emotional state without any apparent stimulus whatsoever. Such judgments are the nearest that the Samoan approaches to evaluation of temperament as opposed to character. The well-integrated individual who approximates closely to the attitudes of his age and sex group is not accused of laughing, crying, or showing anger without cause. Without inquiry it is assumed that he has good typical reasons for a behaviour which would be scrutinised and scorned in the case of the temperamental deviant. And always excessive emotion, violent preferences, strong allegiances are disallowed. The Samoan preference is for a middle course, a moderate amount of feeling, a discreet expression of a reasonable and balanced attitude. Those who care greatly are always said to care without cause.

The one most disliked trait in a contemporary is expressed by the term *fiasili*, literally "desiring to be highest," more idiomatically, "stuck up." This is the comment of the age mate where an older person would use the disapproving *tautala laititi*, "presuming above one's age." It is essentially the resentful comment of those who are ignored, neglected, left behind upon those who excel them, scorn them, pass them by. As a term of reproach it is neither as dreaded nor as resented as the *tautala laititi* because envy is felt to play a part in the taunt.

In the casual conversations, the place of idle speculation about motivation is taken by explanations in terms of physical defect or objective misfortune, thus "Sila is crying over in that house. Well, Sila is deaf." "Tulipa is angry at her brother. Tulipa's mother went to Tutuila last week." Although these statements have the earmarks of attempted explanations they are really only conversational habits. The physical defect or recent incident, is not specifically invoked but merely mentioned with slightly greater and more deprecatory emphasis. The whole preoccupation is with the individual as an actor, and the motivations peculiar to his psychology are left an unplumbed mystery.

Judgments are always made in terms of age groups, from the standpoints of the group of the speaker and the age of the person judged. A young boy will not be regarded as an intelligent or stupid, attractive or unattractive, clumsy or skilful person. He is a bright little boy of nine who runs errands efficiently and is wise enough to hold his tongue when his elders are present or a promising youth of eighteen who can make excellent speeches in the *Aumaga*, lead a fishing expedition with discretion and treat the chiefs with the respect which is due to them, or a wise *matai*, whose words are few and well chosen and who is good at weaving eel traps. The virtues of the child are not the virtues of the adult. And the judgment of the speaker is similarly influenced by age, so that the relative estimation of character varies also. Pre-adolescent boys and girls will vote that boy and girl worst who are most pugnacious, irascible, contentious, rowdy. Young people from sixteen to twenty shift their censure from the rowdy and bully to the licentious, the *moetotolo* among the boys, the notoriously promiscuous among the girls; while adults pay very little attention to sex offenders and stress instead the inept, the impudent and the disobedient among the young, and the lazy, the stupid, the quarrelsome and the unreliable as the least desirable characters among the adults. When an adult is speaking the standards of conduct are graded in this fashion: small children should keep quiet, wake up early, obey, work hard and cheerfully, play with children of their own sex; young people should work industriously and skilfully, not be presuming, marry discreetly, be loyal to their relatives, not carry tales, nor be trouble makers; while adults should be wise, peaceable, serene, generous, anxious for the good prestige of their village and conduct their lives with all good form and decorum. No prominence is given to the subtler facts of intelligence and temperament. Preference between the sexes is given not to the arrogant, the flippant, the courageous, but to the quiet, the demure boy or girl who "speaks softly and treads lightly."

After reading: CONSOLIDATE INFORMATION

1. What can you infer about the Samoans' attitude toward personality from Mead's observations?
2. Explain what is fatalistic about the Samoans' evaluation of personality.
3. Why do you think the Samoans seek explanations for physical illness but not for emotional or psychological states?

Margaret Mead and Samoa: *Coming of Age* in Fact and Fiction
Richard Feinberg

Professor Richard Feinberg's "re-analysis" of Mead's work appeared in a scholarly journal, American Anthropologist. *Feinberg re-evaluates Mead's work in the light of contemporary criticisms as well as the actual evidence of a close reading of Mead's work.*

Before reading: FIRST THOUGHTS
                     LOOK AHEAD

1. React to professor Feinberg's title. Why does he use the words "fact and fiction"?
2. What do you know about the concepts of cultural determinism and biological determinism?
3. What can you predict about Feinberg's article after reading the abstract?

During reading: REACT
                    QUESTION
                    SUMMARIZE

1. What does the word *dysphoric* mean? Try to make a reasonable guess from its context here, and then look it up in the dictionary. What elements in Mead's work does Feinberg see as dysphoric?
2. From Feinberg's summary, what do you think are the major criticisms of Mead's work?

Derek Freeman's 1983 critique of Margaret Mead's *Coming of Age in Samoa* has prompted one of the most heated debates in recent anthropological memory. Yet even Mead's defenders have generally accepted the view that she saw Samoa as a romantic paradise. Here I argue that a careful reading of *Coming of Age* shows quite a different picture. In my reanalysis, Mead's work emerges as complex and somewhat enigmatic, with facile conclusions standing in contrast to much rich and sensitive ethnography. My goal in this article is to highlight what Mead actually said, pointing up the notable discrepancy between the popular perception and her actual account.

DEREK FREEMAN'S RINGING CRITIQUE of *Coming of Age in Samoa* by Margaret Mead has, since 1983, been reverberating through professional anthropology as well as the educated lay public. In the informed opinion of Freeman, a recognized expert on Samoa, not only was a landmark work of our discipline mistaken in its findings, but it was almost a direct inversion of the truth. Not only was one of our most illustrious ancestresses in error, but those errors had resulted from her violation of our discipline's most sacred canons of field research.

Not surprisingly, the anthropological community's initial tendency was to choose sides and join in the debate. From almost every quarter, we have heard opinions as to which of the "combatants" was correct. What is Samoa really like? Did Mead go to the field determined to prove Boas right about the paramountcy of culture over biology? And if Freeman is correct about Samoan ethnography, what are the implications for the "nature/nurture debate"? Often, as might be expected, the result was generation of more heat than light. Yet even Mead's defenders have accepted, for the most part, Freeman's version of her picture of Samoa.[1]

Now, despite such periodic aftershocks as Freeman's recent vehement attack (Freeman 1987) on Lowell Holmes's book, *Quest for the Real Samoa* (1987), the passage of almost five years has calmed the sensibilities of most commentators. Thus, this may be a good time to reexamine Mead's initial work and attempt a balanced appraisal of her contribution.

In this essay I will argue that, contrary to popular opinion, *Coming of Age* is a complex and somewhat enigmatic book in which facile conclusions stand in contrast to much rich and sensitive ethnography. I will not address the issue of just what Samoan life is really like or which of the protagonists was closer to "the truth." Rather, I will try to highlight what Mead actually said, pointing up the notable discrepancy between the popular perception and her actual account.

Freeman's View of Mead's Samoa

According to both Freeman and popular imagination, "Mead depicted the Samoans as a people without jealousy, for whom free lovemaking was the pastime *par excellence*, and who, having developed their emotional lives free from any warping factors, were so amiable as to never hate enough to want to kill anybody" (Freeman 1983:95). She is said to have characterized Samoan life as "easy and casual," and adolescence as "the easiest and most pleasant time of life" (Freeman 1983:xi). She is said to portray "a family system without bonding or guilt," and to use this depiction "to explain the remarkable case that, so she claims, characterizes life in Samoa, especially during adolescence" (1983:87).

Freeman's book is filled with quotes appearing to give substance to the common view of Mead's Samoa. Nor did he invent the quotes. *Coming of Age* contains dozens of passages presenting an idyllic image to rival any Hollywood set. This nowhere more apparent than in the second chapter, entitled "A Day in Samoa." Here we read:

> As the dawn begins to fall among the soft brown roofs and the slender palm trees stand out against a colourless, gleaming sea, lovers slip home from trysts beneath the palm trees or in the shadow of beached canoes, that the light may find each sleeper in his appointed place. [Mead 1970(1928):26]

Then, as the day ends at the chapter's culmination,

> A white-clad, ghostly throng will gather in a circle about the gaily lit house, a circle from which every now and then a few will detach themselves and wander away among the trees. Sometimes sleep will not descend upon the village until long past midnight; then at last there is only the mellow thunder of the reef and the whisper of lovers, as the village rests until dawn. [p. 29]

She describes clandestine love affairs as "usually of short duration and both boy and girl may be carrying on several at once" (p. 77). In one of her more sweeping passages, she asserts that there are no neurotic pictures, no frigidity, no impotence, except as the temporary result of severe illness, and the capacity for intercourse only once in a night is counted as senility. [p. 116]

In considering the rare cases in which genuine adjustment problems arose, she asks:

Were there no conflicts, no temperaments which deviated so markedly from the normal that clash was inevitable? Was the diffused affection and the diffused authority of the large families, the ease of moving from one family to another, the knowledge of sex and freedom to experiment a sufficient guarantee to all Samoan girls of a perfect adjustment? *In almost all cases, yes.* [p. 121, emphasis added]

In other places, she notes the supposed ease of adolescence; the general casualness of Samoan society; the tendency to coddle the slow and discourage the precocious; and the importance of tradition, which results in a narrow range of choices and eliminates what is a major source of stress in Western society; and she asserts that no one feels deeply and therefore no one becomes too upset when things fail to work out.

Trouble In Paradise: Dysphoric Elements in Mead's Samoa

The view of Samoa that Freeman attacks, then, can unquestionably be found in Mead's work. She often exaggerates for impact. And her tendency to exaggerate and oversimplify is particularly apparent in her general summaries and programmatic statements. In short, to the extent that Mead may have been widely misinterpreted, she must bear the brunt of responsibility for such misinterpretation. Still, when one carefully examines her substantive ethnographic descriptions, one finds another side of her account—a side that presents a remarkable balance, subtlety of insight, and awareness of conflicting cultural demands and consequent psychological stress.

Mead's awareness of the conflict running through Samoan life emerges on the first page of her acknowledgements, where she explains her decision to live in the dispensary rather than the village. There she notes that she "could study all the individuals in the village and yet remain aloof from *native feuds and lines of demarcation*" (p. 7, emphasis added). Boas, in his foreword, makes reference to Mead's "lucid and clear picture of the joys *and difficulties*" encountered by Samoan adolescents (1970[1928]:10, emphasis added). And even Mead's idyllic portrait of Samoan life in chapter II depicts a boy "who is taunted by another, who has succeeded him in his sweetheart's favor, [and] grapples with his rival!" (p. 26).

Obviously, then, Mead was aware that Samoan life was not all harmony and bliss. Perhaps still more important, she recognized that disputes and difficulties were not a matter of accident or personal idiosyncrasy, but rather are produced by pressures and contradictions in the very fabric of Samoan culture.

In chapter III and elsewhere, she describes the irritation and frustration faced by children assigned (as they invariably are) to care for younger siblings (see particularly pages 32–33). Then, as youngsters approach adolescence, they are increasingly spared the burdensome responsibility for caring for small children, and it is largely in this sense that Mead sees adolescence as a period of freedom. Still, adolescence brings its own share of difficulties.

At 17 or 18 years of age, a boy becomes a member of the *'aumaga*, the society of untitled men. Of this group, Mead says that it

> is called, not in euphuism but in sober fact, "The strength of the village." *Here he is badgered into efficiency by rivalry, percept and example.* The older chiefs who supervise the activities of the *Aumaga* gaze equally sternly upon any backslidings and upon any undue precocity. The prestige of his group is ever being called into account by the *Aumaga* of the neighbouring villages. *His fellows ridicule and persecute the boy who fails to appear when any group activity is on foot.* . . . [p. 38, emphasis added]

As the boy makes the transition to adulthood, he is caught in a dilemma. His reputation and self-esteem are bound to his success at acquiring a title—the more prestigious the title, the better. Titles are bestowed by kin groups in recognition of outstanding ability and community service. The aspirant "has many rivals," against whom he "must always pit himself . . . in group activities" (p. 39). Yet, among a person's most admired characteristics are humility and the ability to cooperate with others. To embarrass others by comparing them unfavorably to oneself, through either word or deed, is bad manners in the extreme. Thus, to achieve his much-desired social recognition, a young man must compete without appearing to compete. He must constantly impress his fellow villagers and kin with his skills as a fisherman, a carpenter, an orator. He must demonstrate his leadership abilities. Yet,

> with this goes the continual demand that he should not be too efficient, too outstanding, too precocious. He must never excel his fellows by more than a little. [p. 39]

Rivalry for succession to titles involves not only individuals, but may cause strains in the entire descent group as factions develop around each of the candidates. On pages 51–53, Mead discusses in some depth the complexity of rival claims to a title and the strategies for succession.

When at last the young man gains his hard-earned prize, the unenviable burdens of rank immediately descend upon him. As a *matai* or titled man, he must speak and walk slowly and with dignity. He gives up the companionship of his youthful friends and may no longer participate in their activities—their games and dances. He is under constant scrutiny, lest he make a mistake. He must take responsibility for the economic well-being of his extended family, settle their disputes, and approve—perhaps even arrange—their marriages. And easy familiarity in most of his relationships gives way to extreme formality. Mead summarizes the youth's dilemma in the following terms:

He dislikes responsibility, but he wishes to excel in his group; skill will hasten the day when he is made a chief, yet he receives censure and ridicule if he slackens his efforts; but he will be scolded if he proceeds too rapidly; yet if he would win a sweetheart, he must have prestige among his fellows. [pp. 40–41]

Is it any wonder then, that Samoans often develop the kind of tense, insecure personality that Freeman so compellingly describes?

A girl is spared the trial of having to compete for titles. This is not to say, however, that stress and strain have been eliminated. If she wishes to marry well, she must demonstrate proficiency at her feminine tasks, particularly those involved in plaiting mats and cultivation. Furthermore, there is a female analogue to the *matai*: the *taupou* or ceremonial maiden. Such a girl "is snatched [at adolescence] from her age group and sometimes from her immediate family also and surrounded by a glare of prestige" (p. 44). Nor is the "glare of prestige" an unequivocal blessing.

The *taupou*, like the *matai*, becomes a center of attention. She must take care always to conduct herself with special grace and decorum. She has grave responsibilities in entertaining dignitaries from neighboring villages. She must learn special courtesies, perform special dances, and assume a role of special honor at the sacred kava ceremonies. She is expected to be sexually alluring and yet, upon pain of death, retain her virginity until after marriage. It goes almost without saying that the burdens, responsibilities, and public attention associated with being a *taupou* are not universally attractive to Samoan girls, and Mead describes in some detail the tribulations of a prospective *taupou* who finds the role for which she is being groomed decidedly uncongenial (pp. 49–51).

Freeman portrays Mead's view of Samoan life as one of easy emotional adjustment, with few demands upon the individual and only the mildest of sanctions when those few demands are not met. Again, in her interpretive passages, Mead indeed makes statements to this effect. Yet, when she describes specifics of the enculturation process, she characterizes young girls as "possessed by a fear of the chiefs, a fear of small boys, a fear of their relatives, and by a fear of ghosts" (p. 57). This considerable array of fears, then, enforces a substantial degree of discipline, and it is for this reason that small children rarely go about at night in groups of fewer than four or five.

For a writer supposedly preoccupied with the ease of social life, Mead devotes a surprising amount of space to what she calls "the phenomenon of the isolated child in a village full of children of her own age" (p. 57). This phenomenon, she suggests, may occur among children from small households or children whose houses are inauspiciously located. Then she goes on to discuss the isolation felt by adolescent girls as they are separated from their childhood playmates, given adult tasks and responsibilities, and limited in their social circle to members of their own kin groups.

Perhaps the most controversial and dramatic aspect of Mead's book is that which deals with premarital sexual experimentation. Most of her readers have come away with the impression that Samoan adolescents routinely practice "free love," and that such behavior is readily accepted by public opinion. Many Samoans have taken umbrage at the picture of their archipelago as a land of reckless promiscuity, and it may be on this point more than any other that Freeman has taken Mead's ethnography to task. Yet, Mead's own descriptions indicate that sexual relations out of wedlock meet with less than general approval.

In describing the perceptions of the adolescent girl engaged in a romantic adventure, Mead notes:

> All of the adult and near-adult world is hostile, spying upon her love affairs in its more circumspect sophistication, supremely not to be trusted. No one is to be trusted who is not immediately engaged in similarly hazardous adventures. [60–61]

But why would the adult world wish to spy on the girl's sexual activity, and why would the girl care who knew of her activities unless there were some feeling that they were more than a little bit improper? Nor, if premarital sex were not something to hide, would children find the sport of hunting for young couples in the bush so entertaining as apparently they do (p. 107).

The cooperative relationships enforced upon the boys and young men through the 'aumaga organization are absent among young women. From the breakup of play groups and the onset of adolescence, female life is far more atomistic than male life. Nor is this relative social isolation nullified by the girl's new-found interest in romantic intrigue. The boy-girl antagonism developed in the early children's play groups makes the development of comfortable emotional attachments between males and females later in life most difficult to achieve.

> The lack of precocious sex experimentation is probably due less to the parental ban on such precocity than to the strong institutionalised antagonism between younger boys and younger girls and the taboo against amiable intercourse between them. This rigid sex dichotomy may also be operative in determining the lack of specialisation of sex feeling in adults. Since there is a heavily charged avoidance feeling towards brothers and cousins, a tendency to lump all other males together as the enemy who will some day be one's lovers, there are no males in a girl's age group whom she ever regards simply as individuals without relation to sex. [pp. 108–109]

Music and dance are of central importance in Polynesian life, and Samoa is no exception. In *Coming of Age*, Mead devotes an entire chapter to "The Role of the Dance" (pp. 90–97). The dance, in Mead's view, is the one place in Samoan life where unrestrained precocity, creativity, and even a degree of open exhibitionism is accepted and, indeed, encouraged. From Mead's discussion, it is clear that she perceives considerable psychic stress and deprivation to result from the overwhelmingly communal emphasis in Samoan culture. It is to compensate for this decided deprivation that the opportunity for individual achievement and recognition through dance is so important.

Mead repeatedly asserts that Samoans typically abstain from strong emotional commitments, and that the absence of such feelings precludes development of either strong personal loyalties or jealousy. It helps to keep Samoan life on an even keel and to prevent outbreaks of physical violence. Freeman takes exception to this characterization and demonstrates that Samoans are quite capable of strong feelings and close personal attachments, that they have a markedly competitive side to their personalities, and that they sometimes come to blows over sexual jealousy.

However, despite passages supporting Freeman's interpretation of Mead's position, other sections make it clear that she did recognize a passionate, competitive, possessive side to the Samoan personality. She describes a well-respected woman who was "married at fifteen, while still a virgin" and "adored her husband" (pp. 110–111). She recognizes that "cases of passionate jealousy do occur" (p. 122). And she describes the "rage" of a girl whose erstwhile lover had turned his attentions to a rival, as "unbounded" (p. 133).

Allusions to such cases are dispersed throughout the book, and Mead devotes a lengthy chapter (pp. 121–137) to examination of such situations, carefully dissecting, in each instance, the underlying contradictions. Thus we see repeatedly the stresses placed upon a child who grows up in a nuclear family household in a society organized on the assumption that people will live in extended family groups, and the dilemma suffered by an individual cursed with a volatile temperament in a society that values calmness, dignity, and grace. True, she views these cases as anomalous. Yet she cites enough of such "anomalies" that the critical reader has reason to ask just how atypical they really are.

Conclusions

Illustrations of the discrepancies between Mead's ethnographic descriptions and the popular perception of her book could be multiplied indefinitely. And in the end, one almost must conclude that *Coming of Age* is two books in one. The first of these must be understood in terms of the purpose for which the book was written. As explained in the preface to the 1961 edition, her intention was to champion "the future of young people who in the United States were becoming less than they might be because we understood so little about what a difference culture can make" (1961:12). In order to accomplish this, she felt it necessary to reach an audience not of professional scholars but of "teachers and of the world for their children" (1961:12). And to reach the widest possible audience, she recognized the value of a dramatic writing style combined with a clear and simply stated message.[2]

Nonetheless, she was a serious ethnographer, and in her actual descriptions, the complexity, contradictions, trials, and tribulations that permeate Samoan culture were clearly apparent. Nor, in her concluding chapters, in which she attempted to derive lessons from Samoa that might be applied to ourselves, did she present the South Sea archipelago as an earthly paradise. She did suggest that we face certain problems that are muted in Samoan culture. This is not to say, however, that Samoa is without its own problems. In particular, she argued that among Samoans stress is mitigated at the expense of individuality, while emotional equilibrium and sexual adjustment are maintained at the expense of creativity and romantic love. And this, contrary to the popular image, she viewed as far too high a price to pay. Still, she maintained that lessons may be gleaned from the Samoan case and that with innovative social engineering it might well be possible to obtain some of the best of both worlds.

One may disagree with Mead's conclusions. And undoubtedly Samoa scholars—Freeman included—will find much to criticize in the details of Mead's substantive ethnography. Yet, she was neither blind nor stupid. She was well aware of the "darker side" of Samoan life that Freeman has so studiously recorded. Indeed, a careful reading of *Coming of Age* gives one a picture of Samoa that is far less at variance with Freeman's than has generally been recognized.

If Mead's ethnography is not so simple (or so simple-minded) as is commonly imagined, however, was she not dishonest in her sweeping generalizations? If she was not more than a little disingenuous, how can one account for the discrepancy between her complex ethnographic observations and her simplistic interpretations? And is she not herself—because of the manner in which she chose to present her material—to blame for popular misapprehension of her work?

Many Samoans and some anthropologists argue that Mead "lied" in order to promote her social program.[3] Accusations that she engaged in purposeful deception, however, find little support among her more responsible critics. Even Freeman is inclined to understand Mead's errors as resulting from inadequate training, her informants' duplicity, and the theoretical blinders with which she had been fitted by her mentor, Boas.

I join with Freeman in rejecting the perception of Mead as a charlatan but attribute *Coming of Age*'s inconsistencies to somewhat different causes. In fact, to a greater or lesser degree, I see the same duality as almost intrinsic to anthropological writing, particularly when it involves the attempt to present the results of social scientific research to a popular audience. Programmatic passages always involve simplification of a complex reality by attempting to distill major themes. Even in a work presenting the most sensitive analyses, summary statements, by their nature, are bound to exclude much that is significant in favor of what the author takes to be most important. In the case at hand, Mead was aware of tension in Samoan culture and society; but in her considered judgment, emphasis on smooth relations was preeminent.

Second, I submit that anthropology has something of a built-in bias toward reporting what is startling and different at the expense of the expected and mundane. After all, one does not build a reputation by reporting what is "common knowledge." This bias makes it easy to tune into that which is unusual, while phenomena that are familiar from the viewpoint of our own cultural experience we tend to take for granted and not notice. Further, we are often unaware of our cultural biases, and to the extent that this is true, we cannot compensate for them through self-conscious reflection.

The latter point becomes especially problematic when one approaches one's work with a sense of "mission," as Mead manifestly did. Clearly, she hoped that her findings would force us to rethink our cultural assumptions, thereby helping make this world a better place. Such an approach tends to reinforce the other biases inherent in ethnographic writing and influences one's decision as to which aspects of a sociocultural system deserve emphasis. This point, of course, comes very close to certain aspects of Freeman's critique. But again, to some degree, it is a defect in all ethnographic writing. At least Mead was open about her political agenda. Thus forewarned, readers should have taken her pronouncements with a healthy dose of skepticism.

Finally, was Mead not herself to blame for the misreading of her data? To a degree she was. Bald assertions are easier to remember than finely honed analyses—and make better review and advertising copy. And by making programmatic passages as sweeping and dramatic as she did, she helped create an atmosphere in which many details were likely to get lost. Still, should we fault an author for crediting her readers with some critical faculties? Shouldn't readers—particularly in academic circles, where Mead's most vocal critics have resided—be expected to read a book carefully and in its entirety before they criticize it? In short, should responsibility for sloppy scholarship be placed on an author who presents a complex mass of data but fails to take full cognizance of the complexity in her interpretations, or the reader who sees only the interpretations without noticing the data? From that perspective, I suggest that *Coming of Age* contains much sensitive ethnography, and the failure of an academic audience to notice what is plainly there is unprofessional at best.

In sum, then, Freeman has performed a worthwhile service in helping to make the educated public aware of the inaccuracies in Mead's glib generalizations about Samoan culture and society. Human cultures always are complex and richly textured, and simple descriptions are inevitably distortions of the truth. Still, one may glean much insight from a careful reading of Mead's work, and it is to her credit that the rich descriptions in the ethnographic portions provide sufficient information for the critical reader to arrive at conclusions substantially different from those for which her book has become famous.

In this essay, I have not attempted to evaluate the Samoan data or determine which of the competing ethnographies is closer to the truth. Rather, I have tried to show that *Coming of Age* is quite a different book from what is commonly imagined. On matters of sex, Mead tended to focus on social behavior, while her passages on violence and emotional control depicted cultural values. In Freeman's case this bias was reversed. And both writers have a tendency to shift their levels of analysis without clearly acknowledging that they are doing so. Despite the major differences in theoretical emphasis and interpretation, however, data presented in the two accounts are largely compatible. Finally, if this suggestion is correct, perhaps a reevaluation of Mead's book may help provide us with a truer picture of Samoa after all.

Notes

1. Thus even such a sympathetic, and generally insightful, author as Mageo can write, "Mead's work is marred by her unwillingness to acknowledge the presence and importance of Samoan aggression" (Mageo 1988:28).

2. In this respect, it also should be noted that the final chapters of *Coming of Age*, in which Mead drew her most explicit comparisons between life in Samoa and the West, were added to the original manuscript at her publisher's suggestion (see Mead 1972: 163–164, 165).

3. Shore's report (1981:213) of Samoan suspicions in this regard is confirmed by Freeman (1983:288). In personal conversations, I have heard similar assertions from a number of anthropologists; to my knowledge, however, no professional anthropologist has committed such accusations to the printed page.

References Cited

BOAS, FRANZ
    1970[1928] Foreword. *In* Coming of Age in Samoa. Margaret Mead, auth. New York: Dell.

FREEMAN, DEREK
    1983 Margaret Mead and Samoa: The Making and Unmaking of an Anthropological Myth. Cambridge, MA: Harvard University Press.
    1987 Comment on Holmes's *Quest for the Real Samoa*. American Anthropologist 89(4):930–935.

HOLMES, LOWELL D.
    1987 Quest for the Real Samoa: The Mead/Freeman Controversy and Beyond. South Hadley, MA: Bergin and Garvey.

MAGEO, JEANETTE MARIE
    1988 Malosi: A Psychological Exploration of Mead's and Freeman's Work and of Samoan Aggression. Pacific Studies 11(2):25–65.

MEAD, MARGARET
    1970[1928] Coming of Age in Samoa: A Psychological Study of Primitive Youth for Western Civilization. New York: Dell.
    1972 Blackberry Winter. New York: William Morrow.

SHORE, BRADD
    1981 Sexuality and Gender in Samoa: Conceptions and Missed Conceptions. *In* Sexual Meanings: The Cultural Construction of Gender and Sexuality. Sherry B. Ortner and Harriet Whitehead, eds. Pp. 192–215. Cambridge: Cambridge University Press.

After reading: CONSOLIDATE INFORMATION

1. Summarize, in your own words, Feinberg's evaluation of Mead's depiction of Samoan culture.
2. How does Feinberg explain the inconsistencies in Mead's analysis in *Coming of Age in Samoa*? How does Feinberg analyze the notion of audience in evaluating Mead's work?
3. What purpose do you think underlies Feinberg's writing? Do you think that he successfully achieves that purpose?

A Republic of Couch Potatoes: The Media Shrivel the Electorate
Wilson Carey McWilliams

Wilson Carey McWilliams is a Professor of Political Science at Rutgers University. He excerpted the following essay from a forthcoming book, The Election of 1988, *for the lay or non-scholarly readers of* Commonweal. *Note that he deals with a question similar to the one which prompted Professor Christine Ridout (in the next article) to undertake a statistical study of the media coverage of primary elections in 1988.*

Before reading: FIRST THOUGHTS
                     LOOK AHEAD

1. After reading the title and subtitle, what can you predict about McWilliams's article?
2. What effect do you think television has had on political campaigns, particularly the presidential campaigns?
3. Do you think the term *couch potato* carries a positive or negative connotation? Do you think McWilliams uses the term negatively or positively?

During reading: REACT
                     QUESTION
                     SUMMARIZE

1. In comparing the nastiness of the 1888 and the 1988 presidential campaigns, why does McWilliams seem to imply that the 1988 campaign was the nastier of the two?
2. What does McWilliams mean when he refers to the "demobilization" of the electorate?

THE ELECTION OF 1988 sent an urgent signal that something is wrong with the political soul of American democracy. The campaign was more than negative. It was a year when civility "took it on the chin," one in which, on talk shows as in politics, nastiness "became a commodity" (Lena Williams, *New York Times*, December 18, 1988). Even so, it had precedents.

In 1888, President Grover Cleveland, who had survived considerable tarring four years earlier, faced smears and distortions at least the equal of 1988. His former opponent, James G. Blaine, charged that Cleveland had appointed to office 137 convicted criminals, including two murderers, seven forgers, and several brothel keepers. Mrs. Cleveland was forced to deny the rumor that the president beat and abused her. It was said that Cleveland was a dogmatic liberal (of the nineteenth-century variety) and the equivalent of a "secular humanist" because he was reported to have said, "I believe in free trade as I believe in the Protestant religion."

Most notoriously, Matt Quay, the Republican boss of Pennsylvania, engineered a scheme by which a Republican supporter, posing as a former British subject, wrote to the British ambassador asking which candidate would best advance Britain's interest. The ambassador, Mr. Sackville-West, injudiciously replied that Cleveland's free trade sympathies made him preferable, and Republicans exultantly portrayed Cleveland as unpatriotic and, especially in Irish wards, as the tool of British imperialism.

Nevertheless, there is something new and alarming about the incivilities of the presidential campaign in 1988. In the first place, the electronic media give greater force and currency to scurrilities, just as television makes innuendo visible: Blaine's attack on Cleveland's appointments had nothing like the impact of a glowering Willie Horton, illustrating Republican claims that Dukakis had been "soft on crime," or of pictures of garbage afloat in Boston harbor. Moreover, contemporary voters are more exposed to and dependent on mass media.

In Cleveland's day, the press could still be described, in the terms Tocqueville used earlier, as a form of political association. There was a mass press, but the great majority of newspapers were local, the voices and guardians of community. Information from national campaigns and leaders reached most voters only through local editors, leaders, and opinion makers who interpreted it and passed on its propriety and authenticity. In 1988, the media spoke to more and more citizens directly, without intermediaries; gatekeepers could not protect us when the fences had been trampled or pulled down.

At the most fundamental level, politics is about invisible things. A political society can be symbolized—for example, by the flag, George Bush's talisman in 1988—but it cannot be seen. Especially in a polity as diverse as the United States, political community is not a matter of outward semblance but of inward likeness, common ideas and ideals. In this sense, television almost necessarily distorts politics, since it is forced to visualize and personalize things that are impalpable or objective. When events suit the medium, as in television's coverage of the southern civil rights movement, it speaks with unique power, but more often it is apt to be misleading, silly (Dukakis's tank ride), or mischievous.

To classical political theory, speech, not sight, is the most political of the faculties because it is in and through speech that we discover the boundaries and terms of political community. But political speech—and, especially, *listening* to political speech—is a skill and pleasure that must be learned. It demands an extended span of attention, the capacity for critical reflection, and that art of hearing that lets us separate meaning from its disguises. Always difficult, that command of rhetoric is harder to cultivate in a society as supersonic as ours, and the electronic media actually undermine the arts of speech and hearing.

Preoccupied with holding their audience, television programmers shun anything that might bore us (the Republican argument, this year, against more than two presidential debates), a logic that tends toward the lowest common public denominator. The 1988 debates were question-and-answer sessions in which no comment could run longer than two minutes; in 1960, Kennedy and Nixon began their debates with eight-minute opening statements. In the 1970s, the average "sound bite" allowed a public figure was fifteen to twenty seconds, and the president was given as much as a minute. Pretty thin at best. But in the 1980s, the figure has declined to ten seconds for all public figures. It symbolizes the decline of speech that George Bush, admiring the refrain, made "Don't Worry, Be Happy" into a campaign song, either ignoring the words or trusting that American voters would not notice their very contrary lesson.

Even at its best, however, television reporting (and increasingly, all reporting) shies away from evaluating the substance, or even the accuracy, of what is said in campaigns preferring to discuss the strategy and process of campaigning. Nominally neutral, this emphasis on stratagems effectively tells citizens that the public side of politics—and, especially, those questions being argued—is of secondary importance. Even pure quantities, like results of polls and elections, need to be interpreted in the light of momentum and expectations. In this implicit teaching, "real politics" is covert, a business for professionals that can be approached only through inside information supplied by the media.

Parties and candidates, of course, struggle to control the process of interpretation, bypassing the press whenever possible and controlling photo opportunities through carefully contrived events. In 1988, for example, the Dukakis campaign, after beginning with relatively frequent press conferences, followed the Republicans' example in shielding the candidate from the press. Similarly, both national conventions were transparently staged to avoid any appearance of conflict and to project optimism, harmony, and concern for "family values." Ironically, the 1988 conference of the Communist party of the Soviet Union featured heated debate, resembling an old-style American party convention as much as the 1988 American conventions called to mind the traditional, totalitarian gatherings of the Communist party.

"Packaging," however, only redefines the role of the media; by pushing debate and decision offstage, it makes citizens even more dependent on the media to search what is said in public for clues to the real deliberations behind the scenes. Public life, increasingly, is mirroring the media's art. Portrayed as trivial or superficial, political events become lifeless and shallow, arguments for cynicism and indifference.

Inherently, the electronic media emphasize the private, self-protective, and individualistic side of American culture at the expense of citizenship and public life. Traditional politics, like older forms of entertainment, drew citizens into public places; the media bring politics to individuals in private retreats. In those settings, private concerns are naturally uppermost, making it harder than usual—and it is always difficult—to appeal to public goods and goals. Politics is dramaturgical: It asks us to step beyond the day-to-day, to see the present in the light of the possible, judging practice by theory. Great politics, like great theater, requires a special space, a precinct for its particular sort of fantasy, from which we reemerge into everyday life. Such distinctions hone and heighten experience; by blurring fantasy and reality so pervasively, television weakens reality's force and fantasy's charm.

Above all else, television is a visual medium, confined to what can be seen and hence to externalities. Sight is our quickest sense, but it is also superficial, and the media's discontinuity of image and affect encourages emotional detachment, adaption rather than commitment. A politics of the visible comes naturally to, and teaches us to be, a world of strangers.

Be that as it may, citizens *are* dependent on mass media for news and for the interpretation needed to make sense out of the bewildering ravelments of contemporary life. At the same time, the media are great concentrations of power, remote and distant "private governments" that decide who will speak to us and on what terms. In the media's version of deliberation, citizens have no voices; one cannot "talk back" to a television set, and citizens can assert their dignity only by refusing to listen. Of course, a displeased viewer can also change channels, but this "receiver control" is almost entirely negative, given the media's tendency toward a homogenized message.

Yet media decision makers know that, while the power of the media as a whole is overawing, any *single* medium is vulnerable, its position still more precarious because media domination invites resentment. Changing channels is as easy as it is because national television has no organic relation to our lives; a local newspaper or radio station is part of, and often indispensable to, the day-to-day life of a community, but there is no reason why I should prefer ABC to NBC or CBS. The older media, especially the local press, had a position that permitted them to offer "cue giving"—guidance as well as protection—and evaluation was an integral part of their reporting. The electronic media are more anxious to "resonate"; more fearful of giving offense, they cultivate nonpartisanship and a professional neutrality.

Better than the Democrats, the Republicans have understood that this desperate neutrality makes it easy to neutralize the media. Fairly consistently, Republican candidates criticize the media, appealing to the public's fear of hidden persuaders and joining its resentment of media power. George Bush virtually began his campaign with a contrived face-off with Dan Rather, and he continued to fault the media's coverage of the election. This media bashing takes the form of asking for fair play or balanced treatment, but its real aim is to insulate a candidate—or a president—from criticism, Teflon-coating its beneficiaries.

The success of this strategy was evident in the media response to this year's presidential and vice-presidential debates. After the first debate, the media pronounced the exchange a draw, a defensible stance even if a plurality of viewers thought Dukakis had edged Bush. Even John Chancellor's astonishing claim that Dan Quayle had done well, despite Lloyd Bentsen's one-sided victory, might be explained as a too-rigid refusal to take sides. But television newsmen showed no reluctance to declare that Bush had won the second presidential debate. Taken as a whole, these comments suggest that if the media did not approach Republican candidates "on bended knee"—Mark Hertsgaard's description of the Reagan years—they did bend over backward.

In 1888, American politics was still dense with associations, and for both parties, the presidential candidate was only the chief figure in a campaign made up of a myriad of local campaigns in states and wards. Cleveland, in fact, did not campaign at all, considering huckstering beneath the dignity of his office, and Benjamin Harrison's more active office-seeking was very limited by our standards.

Law and technology have combined to create a centralized presidential politics dominated by national media and party committees. In campaigns, as in voting, congressional and local elections are sharply distinct from the presidential contest, so much so that it seemed anomalous, on election night, when candidates for governor and U.S. senator in Montana received about the same percentage of the vote as their party's nominee for president.

The "nationalization of the electorate" has been a major political theme of the century, the result of an effort to open politics to individual citizens, freeing them from the control of local elites. Progressive reformers, advocates of the primary system, were also inclined to celebrate the mass media, just as their successors urged a more responsible two-party system. In one respect, the breaking down of racial barriers to political participation, the process has been pure gain. It has become increasingly clear, however, that the grand design of the reform tradition has failed.

Despite prolonged campaigning, despite vast expenditure of money (in which, in 1988, the two parties were virtually equal), despite the advice of experts and the easing of rules for voter registration, turnout fell—as it has, with the exception of the New Deal years, throughout this century. This "demobilization" of the electorate is too profound and too persistent to be explained by the requirement of registration or other barriers to voting. In 1988, the fraction of adult Americans who went to the polls was almost 20 percent lower than it was in 1960, when racial discrimination still kept masses of black Americans off the electoral rolls. In Todd Gitlin's axiom, "As politics grows more professional, voting declines."

The affective distance between citizens and public life is great and growing. When they vote for president, voters must evaluate candidates, whose characters they know only superficially, for an office in which character is crucial. We lack the peer review that, in earlier years, was provided by party leaders and opinion makers who controlled nominations and guided campaigns. In 1884, the discovery that Grover Cleveland apparently had fathered an illegitimate child provoked the response that such private failings, then as now the focus of media attention, are not the most important indices of political character, and Cleveland won the election. In 1988, by contrast, while Gary Hart's derelictions shattered his candidacy, voters did not appear to notice that, after all his years in the Senate, Hart was endorsed by only one incumbent Democratic senator. Judgment by peers is yielding to an audition by the media, and private proprieties may now outweigh public virtues.

"Almost the only pleasure of which an American has any idea," Alexis de Tocqueville wrote, "is to take part in government and to discuss the part he has taken," and even women "listen to political harangues after their household labors." More recently, Frank Skeffington, Edwin O'Connor's fictional mayor, spoke of politics as America's "greatest spectator sport," in which performers could, at least, rely on a critical mass of knowledgeable fans, but Skeffington was already sounding "the last hurrah." In 1988, public speech seemed to be degenerating into shouted incivility, the tough talk of playground squabbles, at best a preface to politics.

America cannot be an ancient Greek *polis* or a homogeneous community; political life must find room for our diversities and our privacies, just as prudence must acknowledge the impact of technology and economic change. American democracy needs, and can stand, only so many stanzas of epic poetry. Contemporary politics calls for the more prosaic effort to protect and rebuild locality, association, and party, the links between private individuals and public goods. Even such limited goals, however, presume policy guided by a ruling principle, that middle term between repression and relativism whose better name is citizenship. For both Republicans and Democrats, the election of 1988 indicates the need for a new civility, and for the kinds of word and deed necessary to affirm the dignity of self-government.

After reading: CONSOLIDATE INFORMATION

1. What are the major elements of McWilliams's critique of political coverage by electronic media?
2. How does McWilliams analyze the role of media bashing in political campaigns?
3. What are the implications for political journalism of McWilliams's analysis of television as a visual medium?

The Role of Media Coverage of Iowa and New Hampshire in the 1988 Democratic Nomination

Christine F. Ridout

Professor Christine Ridout applied statistical or quantitative analysis to the media coverage of the 1988 Iowa and New Hampshire presidential primaries. This report on her research appeared in a scholarly publication, American Politics Quarterly.

Before reading: FIRST THOUGHTS
LOOK AHEAD

1. Read the title and the abstract; what predictions can you make about Professor Ridout's findings?
2. What do you think the phrase "Media momentum cycle" means as it refers to the media coverage of the presidential primary campaigns and elections?
3. Do you think that the presidential electoral process, beginning with the state primaries and ending with the November election, works as a process of democratic choice?

During reading: REACT
QUESTION
SUMMARIZE

1. As you read Professor Ridout's description of the media influence on the primary election process, how does her account compare with your own observations of presidential campaigns?
2. To what is Ridout referring when she uses the term *horse race*?

Media coverage of Iowa and New Hampshire has traditionally played a significant role in presidential nominations. The 1988 Democratic race is no exception. However, the media's effect was not particularly dramatic, and no candidate ever acquired media-driven momentum. The absence of momentum should not, however, obscure the fact that early coverage was essential to Dukakis's victory. This finding points to three relatively stable aspects of presidential nominations that help explain early media effects. These are the sequential nature of the nominating process, the low information levels and unstable opinions typical of the electorate early in the process, and the media's emphasis on the early contests and on the horse race. These characteristics interact to produce significant early media effects on presidential nominations.

IN FEBRUARY 1984, the Iowa caucuses and the New Hampshire primary transformed Gary Hart from an unknown candidate into the alternative to Walter Mondale for the Democratic presidential nomination. Much of the responsibility for Hart's sudden viability lay with the media, which paid enormous amounts of attention to his candidacy after Iowa and New Hampshire. Hart's media coverage, most of which was positive in the early stages, increased dramatically after Iowa and New Hampshire, and his standing in the polls rose significantly. He thus rode a crest of media and momentum that nearly swept him to the Democratic nomination. Hart's rapid rise confirmed the importance of Iowa and New Hampshire in the nominating process because of the media-momentum cycle that they frequently generate. This cycle can have a profound impact on the final outcome of the race by eliminating some candidates and elevating others.

In February 1988, Richard Gephardt, the winner of the Iowa caucuses, did not fare so well. He based his strategy on a win in Iowa that he believed would generate sufficient momentum to enable him to challenge Michael Dukakis in New Hampshire. He hoped that a strong New Hampshire showing would generate additional momentum and would eventually lead to the nomination. But post-Iowa momentum never materialized for Gephardt and his candidacy died rather quickly. What happened to Gephardt, and what does his candidacy tell us about the role of early media coverage in presidential nominations?

In contrast, Michael Dukakis finished third in Iowa, first in New Hampshire and subsequently won the Democratic nomination. How did a candidate who was at 6% in the polls in mid-January win the nomination? What role, if any, did early media coverage play in his eventual victory?

And what of Albert Gore's strategy of skipping Iowa and New Hampshire? How did this decision affect his candidacy and what does it illustrate about the impact of early media coverage?

Finally, what can be learned from the 1988 Democratic race about the effects of early media coverage on presidential nominations? Why does early coverage frequently exert such an influence on the final outcome? Are there characteristics of early coverage and of the nominating process that make a strong media effect likely?

In the 1988 Democratic race, media effects were the result of the unknown nature of the candidates and of media decisions on how to cover them. Early coverage shaped voter perceptions of the candidates and was particularly influential in 1988 because of Super Tuesday. Curiously however, early media influence occurred without the drama of momentum and of an early frontrunner. How this occurred explains the influence of early coverage in 1988. More generally, it illustrates why early coverage can have such an effect on presidential nominations.

News Decisions and Political Effects

The 1988 Democratic nomination illustrates the political effects of news decisions. Election coverage is the product of media choices that reflect the interests of journalists and news organizations. Because television is governed primarily by entertainment and profit values, election coverage is geared to entertaining and attracting audiences. To this end, the media emphasize the strategic nature of elections; coverage consists of polls, the candidates' strategies, and their electoral prospects. However, this approach is not politically neutral and "candidates are helped or hurt depending on how news values interact with campaign developments" (Patterson 1989, 108). This is evident in the phenomenon of media and momentum.

The concept of media and momentum grows out of the disproportionate attention the media pay to Iowa and New Hampshire. The media's fascination with the first results of the primary season leads them to overemphasize Iowa and New Hampshire (Bartels 1988; Orren and Polsby 1987). In 1984, for example, Iowa and New Hampshire accounted for 32% of coverage of the entire nominating season (Adams 1987, 45). In 1988, they accounted for 34% of primary coverage

(Lichter, Amundsen, and Noyes 1988, 12). After Iowa and New Hampshire, candidate coverage is allocated on the basis of these two races, with a strong showing usually resulting in a major increase in media attention. This is particularly true if the winner was not expected to win. Increased media attention is also given to the "perceived winner." This occurred in 1984 when Hart's unexpected second place in Iowa resulted in a major increase in media exposure. After Iowa, Hart's share of exposure on NBC rose from approximately 3% to almost 30%; on CBS, Hart's airtime rose five-fold (Adams 1985, 12). Also important is that the tone of coverage is usually positive. In 1984, Hart's early "coverage was virtually free of any harsh criticism, unflattering issues, or cynical commentary" (Adams 1985, 12). An increase in positive media attention enables a candidate to increase name recognition and frequently results in a rise in the opinion polls. From this comes a cycle of more media attention and additional momentum (Mayer 1987, 13–20).

Effect on Public Opinion

Although it is difficult to assert a causal relationship between candidate coverage and changes in the opinion polls, the well-documented and repetitive pattern of change suggests that a relationship does exist. From 1936 to 1972 the New Hampshire winner gained an average of 8% in the opinion polls (Beniger 1976). This pattern continued from 1976 to 1984, with Iowa and New Hampshire winners registering significant gains in the polls (Mayer 1987, 14–16).

Gary Hart offers the most dramatic example: after Iowa and New Hampshire, his standing in the polls increased from 3% to 30% (Mayer 1987, 15).

Further substantiating this relationship is what we know about media influence during the early primary season. During this phase, there are frequently many unknown candidates in the field and voters typically have either no opinions or very unstable opinions of the candidates. Compounding voter confusion is the fact that party identification is not a useful guide during primary elections. In this situation, media influence is significant because voters are dependent on the media to form opinions and because there are no preexisting opinions to mediate new information. As Patterson (1980) noted: "When voters' attitudes are weak, their perceptual defenses also are weak. When this occurs . . . voters are likely to accept incoming information in a rather direct way, thus developing a conception of the situation consistent with this information. Their perspective becomes that of the communicator" (p. 126). This is particularly true of information about the horse race. Several studies have found that voters retain information about winners and losers at a significantly higher rate than they do other campaign information (Bartels 1988, 41–44). In addition, voters tend to have more favorable views of candidates who they think have a good chance of winning. In 1976 for example, "Democrats' opinions about a candidate tended to align with their perceptions of his chances. If they regarded a candidate as having a good chance, they usually had acquired more favorable feelings toward him. . . . On the other hand, less favorable thoughts usually followed the perception that a candidate did not have much of a chance" (Patterson 1980, 128). Formed early in the race when voter opinion is highly malleable, perceptions of candidate viability are hard to change later on (Traugott 1985, 108).

The 1988 Democratic Nomination: The "Seven Dwarfs" Seek News Coverage

Unlike most nominating contests, the 1988 Democratic race consisted entirely of unknown candidates with no significant early front-runner. Coverage of Iowa and New Hampshire therefore provided the voters' first glimpse of the candidates and was important in determining public opinion. Because no candidate had a broad base of public support, each candidate's primary goal was to increase his name recognition and expand his political base (Pomper 1989, 38–39). The essential ingredient in this expansion was an adequate amount of positive coverage coming out of Iowa and New Hampshire.

The other unique aspect of 1988 was Super Tuesday. The large number of delegates chosen on Super Tuesday meant that any candidate who did not do well would not survive. Given the unknown character of the Democratic field, each candidate had to emerge from Iowa and New Hampshire with enough positive name recognition to get "*to* Super Tuesday as a viable candidate." Whatever Super Tuesday voters learned about the candidates from early coverage would have a major impact on Super Tuesday's outcome. Thus, "for the unknown candidates of 1988, [Iowa and New Hampshire] would be even more important preliminaries to the main bout of Super Tuesday" (Pomper 1989, 39).

Ironically, given the significance of early coverage, the media's effect was not particularly dramatic or short term. No Democratic candidate acquired media-driven momentum, and the race remained multicandidate for an unusually long time. This was largely the result of the unknown character of the candidates, which made it difficult for one of them to move quickly to the front of the pack. This was reflected in the Iowa results. The media were therefore confronted with a politically inconclusive outcome that offered no opportunity for dramatic coverage. Instead, the media focused on the candidates' viability in light of Iowa. In this process, doubt was cast on Gephardt's candidacy. In contrast, Dukakis was declared viable and was predicted to do well in New Hampshire. However, his prospects for Super Tuesday were questioned, and this mitigated the possibility of momentum. The absence of momentum should not, however, obscure the fact that the positive tone of Dukakis's early coverage was essential to his eventual victory. Dukakis enjoyed "smooth sailing" and "his horse-race evaluations remained highly positive throughout the early primaries" (Lichter, Amundson, and Noyes 1988, 66). In addition, the amount of his coverage increased. Thus began the slow development of a favorable image for Dukakis. This got him to Super Tuesday and made it possible for him to expand his political base. As Pomper (1989) noted: "Dukakis started with limited recognition. Over time, he gained more attention, and almost all of it was positive" (p. 49).

The Iowa Outcome: Or, Why the Winner Was a Loser

In the immediate post-Iowa period, Richard Gephardt's media attention declined. In the weeks before Iowa, Gephardt moved to a leading position in the polls and was designated the front-runner by the media. Coverage was allocated accordingly, and in the week before Iowa, Gephardt received more media attention than his Democratic rivals (see Table 1). However, in the week after Iowa, Gephardt's network coverage dropped from 6:10 minutes (40% of Democratic coverage) to 4:55 minutes (20%), while Dukakis's coverage increased from 2:15 minutes (13%) to 8:10 minutes (32%). Even more damaging was that Gephardt's share of *total* campaign coverage slipped from 15.5% to 5.3%. Why did this happen? What were the circumstances surrounding Gephardt's win and Dukakis's third-place position that led the media to downplay Gephardt and focus on Dukakis?

The first point is that Gephardt was a victim of expectations. Because he was leading in the polls, he was expected to win. Thus his actual win was not a surprise and was not worthy of additional media attention. Also important was the small margin of victory. Because he invested large amounts of time and money on Iowa, and because he was from neighboring Missouri, the small margin of victory minimized the significance of his win. These points are illustrated in NBC's election-night coverage (February 8). Tom Brokaw described the Democratic race as "very close," with "three men bunched at the top," and he described Gephardt as the candidate "who spent more days in this state than any of the candidates." Later in the broadcast, in an interview with Gephardt, Brokaw noted: "A good showing for you, but if those other two stay as close to you as they are, it looks like it will be pretty much a dead heat going into New Hampshire." Brokaw further stated: "You spent a lot of time in this state, almost a half a year, you spent a lot on money, you're from nearby Missouri, now you go into a New England state, then you move rapidly down south where you weren't able to spend that kind of time. Do you think what you were able to do here will translate as effectively there?" According to this interpretation, Gephardt did not really win; it was a "dead heat." And, considering all the time and money spent in Iowa and the fact that Missouri is a neighboring state, it was really a pretty poor showing! This interpretation not only downplayed his Iowa win, but also raised serious questions about his future prospects. In this light, the decline in Gephardt's media attention is not surprising. Contrast this with the interpretation of Dukakis's third place by John Chancellor, also of NBC (February 8): "Dukakis, third place, far from home, is no disgrace for him. I think he's in rather good shape. He has a huge lead in New Hampshire going up there a week from today. He ought to do very well." Similarly, Brokaw stated about Dukakis: "He's holding third. He'd hoped for second, but the guess probably will be tomorrow that he did well enough in Iowa to move on to New Hampshire, which is after all *his* neighboring state. He had a run against two regional candidates. But what it indicates is that he's in a real dead heat now as you go into New Hampshire." Thus, Dukakis did not come in third; it was a "dead heat." Actually, it was better than that because he was far from home and ran strongly against two regional candidates, both of whom invested significant resources in Iowa. Thus "the interpretation was up for grabs, but in the end Dukakis won the spin control."[1] He therefore emerged from Iowa as a viable candidate, a fact that was carried on national news at a time when voters were beginning to form opinions of the candidates.

The media's interpretation of the candidates' electoral viability illustrates how news values influence candidate coverage. Gephardt suffered because his win was expected and because of the perception that it was a weak showing. His first place therefore lacked the drama and excitement that would elicit a positive tone and an increased amount of coverage. In contrast, Dukakis was judged to have done reasonably well. Coupled with his commanding lead in New Hampshire, he was seen as viable; the amount and tone of his coverage followed accordingly. Emphasis on the candidates' prospects also illustrates the impact of horse race coverage. The media choice to focus on the horse race influenced the Democratic race by shaping voter perceptions of the candidates' prospects. This focus hurt Gephardt.

The media's interpretation of Iowa is particularly striking in light of the fact that the Dukakis camp had feared the opposite: that "a third or fourth place finish ... would be judged 'worse than expected' by the press, cast doubts about his national stature, and allow the Iowa victor to arrive in New Hampshire on a wave of hype."[2] This is exactly what Gephardt had hoped for. As one Dukakis adviser said: "You gotta love it, huh? The winnowing process has begun, and we've been winnowed in."[3] The role of early media coverage in making or breaking candidate is illustrated by these points.

The second and perhaps more damaging aspect of Gephardt's coverage after Iowa had to do with the allegation that he was a "flip-flopper." The questioning of his record began immediately and it projected a highly negative view of Gephardt. In an election-night interview with Gephardt (February 8), Tom Brokaw stated: "But now they're going to concentrate on your record. You've been in Washington, you've been a man of the Establishment. You're campaigning as an outsider. You've changed your mind on abortion, on ERA. . . . You're going to be accused [as] the 'candidate of the flip-flop.' You know what's coming. That's part of the price of popularity coming out of Iowa." Brokaw later stated that "Gephardt is going to have to answer a lot of questions." And indeed, accusations that he was a "flip-flopper" dominated his post-Iowa coverage. The result was that Gephardt spent most of his time defending himself.

Also important was that pre-New Hampshire coverage emphasized the increasingly nasty fight between Gephardt and Simon and it characterized the bitter battle for second place as a "struggle for survival" (CBS February 15). CBS also reported "big 'M and M' trouble for Gephardt [and Simon]—money and momentum" (February 10). The negative tone of this coverage did little to enhance Gephardt's image either nationally or in New Hampshire. In contrast, Dukakis's coverage was highly favorable. He was portrayed as "above the fray" (WCVB [Boston's ABC affiliate] February 13), the "man to beat" (NBC February 11), "sailing along in relatively calm waters," and the candidate with "lots of money and heavy favorite status in New Hampshire" (CBS February 10).

Another important facet of media coverage in the week after Iowa was the role of Boston-based television. According to Arbitron, 86% of New Hampshire voters watch Boston television.[4] In this setting, the years of positive coverage accorded to Dukakis by Boston television and the particularly favorable coverage of his presidential campaign made it difficult for Gephardt to challenge Dukakis in New Hampshire (Knopf 1970). Coverage of Iowa was no exception. On the night of the caucuses (February 8) the Boston NBC affiliate, WBZ, devoted four minutes to Dukakis's "bronze medal" speech but did not carry Gephardt's speech or do an interview with him. In addition, WBZ interpreted Dukakis's third place in a very favorable light. WBZ characterized Iowa as "such a close bronze ... Dukakis [is] a *credible national presidential candidate* [emphasis added] on the basis of these results."[5] Based on this interpretation, Dukakis's huge lead in the polls held, and Gephardt's ability to generate Iowa "bounce" fizzled. Perhaps even more important was that favorable Boston coverage put Dukakis in an unusually strong position to capitalize on the pivotal role of New Hampshire and to translate that into favorable *national* coverage.

Another dimension of Gephardt's post-Iowa flop lies in the Robertson-Bush story on the Republican side. Robertson's surprise second and Bush's subsequent struggle for survival so dominated the news that Gephardt's Iowa win was eclipsed. On the night of the Iowa caucuses, NBC devoted 10 minutes to the Republicans before discussing the Democrats, a clear disadvantage for Gephardt. In addition, in the week after Iowa, Bush was the top story on both national and local news, and his post-Iowa network coverage skyrocketed to 24:30 minutes (33% of *total* campaign coverage) from 10:00 minutes in the week before Iowa (Table 1). Similarly, Robertson's coverage increased from 5:20 to 14:10 (18.6% of total coverage). Compare this to Gephardt's 5.3% of total coverage and it is clear why he was unable to generate momentum out of Iowa.

The emphasis on the Bush-Robertson story illustrates how the interaction of news values and campaign developments can help some candidates and hurt others. Bush's struggle to survive represented the type of continuing nightly drama that tends to receive large amounts of coverage. This emphasis damaged Gephardt because it denied him the coverage he needed.

It can be argued that the negative interpretation of Gephardt's Iowa win, coupled with the positive interpretation of Dukakis's third place, had a long-term affect on the race by shaping voter perceptions during the critical early phase of the campaign. During this phase, both Gephardt's credibility and viability were questioned, seriously damaging his candidacy. In contrast, Dukakis's image as electorally viable increased his chances of doing well, and national coverage gave him name recognition outside New England. This helped later on in what proved to be a long and bumpy ride to the nomination.

These conclusions are supported by polling data from before Iowa and after New Hampshire. According to a January poll (Table 2), Dukakis was favored by a meager 6% of the national electorate. Immediately after New Hampshire, his national favorability rating rose to 21%, an increase of 15% in one month (Table 3). Excluding southern and border states, Dukakis was favored by 26% of the electorate. In contrast, Gephardt's national favorability rating increased from 4% in January to 12% in February, an increase of only 8% (Tables 2 and 3). Again excluding southern and border states, Gephardt was favored by only 13% of the electorate, a 13% difference with Dukakis. These data support the hypothesis that early coverage played a role in altering public opinion. Importantly, the 1988 data are consistent with pre-1988 relationships between the tone and quantity of early coverage and shifts in public opinion. This pattern indicates that the candidate with the most favorable media exposure after Iowa and New Hampshire registers the greatest gains in the opinion polls. The year 1988 was no exception.

TABLE 1 Network Coverage Before and After Iowa (By Number of Minutes on Evening Network News, Monday Through Friday)

	WEEK BEFORE CAUCUSES	WEEK AFTER CAUCUSES	OWN PARTY COVERAGE BEFORE (%)	OWN PARTY COVERAGE AFTER (%)	TOTAL COVERAGE BEFORE (%)	TOTAL COVERAGE AFTER (%)
George Bush	10:00	24:30	40.6	48.4	25.0	32.4
Robert Dole	8:50	9:15	35.7	18.3	22.0	12.2
Pat Robertson	5:20	14:10	21.5	28.1	13.3	18.8
Jack Kemp	:20	2:20	1.2	4.5	0.8	3.1
Pete du Pont	:15	:25	1.0	0.8	0.6	0.5
Michael Dukakis	2:15	8:10	14.9	32.0	5.6	10.6
Richard Gephardt	6:10	4:55	41.0	20.0	15.5	5.3
Paul Simon	2:45	5:55	17.4	24.0	6.5	7.9
Gary Hart	2:50	:45	18.6	2.6	7.0	0.9
Albert Gore, Jr.	—	3:15	—	13.0	—	4.3
Bruce Babbitt	:35	:55	3.3	4.0	1.2	1.3
Jesse Jackson	:15	:40	1.7	2.4	0.6	0.9
Democratic Total	15:10	25:00	—	—	37.5	33.1
Republican Total	24:45	50:40	—	—	62.5	66.9
Total Coverage	39:55	75:40				

NOTE: Percentages are approximate.
SOURCE: DWJ Associates, Inc, a New York-based firm that maintains a computer data base of network news. Data courtesy of DWJ Associates, Inc. All totals and percentages calculated by the author.

TABLE 2 Candidate Support Before the Iowa Caucuses (In Percentages)

SUPPORT FOR DEMOCRATIC CANDIDATES AMONG DEMOCRATIC PRIMARY VOTERS:	
Hart	23
Jackson	17
Simon	9
Dukakis	6
Gephardt	4
Gore	4
Babbitt	2
Undecided	35[a]

a. Percentage in this category was calculated by the author.
SOURCE: *New York Times*/CBS News Poll. Based on telephone interviews with 1,663 adults nationwide from January 17–21, 1988. *New York Times*, January 26, 1988. Copyright © 1988 by The New York Times Company. Reprinted by permission.

The January poll is also important for the 35% of voters who were undecided. Because the Democratic candidates were unknown, many voters had no opinion of them. Significantly, the 35% dropped to 23% in February, indicating that voters were beginning to make up their minds. Also important was that much of Hart's early support (23%) was based on name recognition and was extremely unstable.[6] Hart supporters were therefore vulnerable to new information and opinion change during the early primaries. In this volatile electoral environment, the quantity and tone of each candidate's early coverage had a long-term effect on voter perceptions.

TABLE 3 Candidate Support After the New Hampshire Primary (In Percentages)

WHO DO YOU WANT THE DEMOCRATS TO NOMINATE FOR PRESIDENT IN 1988?			
	Total U.S.	Southern Border States[a]	Rest of U.S.
Dukakis	21	13	26
Gephardt	12	11	13
Gore	8	16	1
Hart	10	10	11
Jackson	13	19	9
Simon	6	4	7
Other	3	2	4
No one	4	3	5
No opinion	23	23	23

a. Alabama, Arkansas, Florida, Georgia, Kentucky, Louisiana, Maryland, Mississippi, Missouri, North Carolina, Oklahoma, South Carolina, Tennessee, Texas, Virginia
SOURCE: *New York Times*/CBS News Poll. Based on telephone interviews conducted with 2,734 people nationwide from February 17–21, 1988. *New York Times*, February 23, 1988. Copyright © 1988 by The New York Times Company. Reprinted by permission.

Albert Gore Skips Iowa and New Hampshire

Albert Gore chose to skip Iowa and New Hampshire because they have an insignificant number of delegates. His strategy was to focus on Super Tuesday, where he had a natural base, and where lots of delegates would be chosen. What Gore overlooked however, was that Iowa and New Hampshire have something more important than delegates; they have media coverage. This was particularly true in 1988 when early coverage comprised 34% of total network coverage and 2,000 reporters covered the Iowa caucuses, twice as many as in 1984. CNN and C-Span also played an important role and most local television stations were, in Iowa, an important factor in introducing the candidates to the national electorate ("Adventures in Campaignland" 1988, 18).

By skipping Iowa and New Hampshire, Gore skipped the media coverage associated with them. While the other candidates were being introduced to the nation, Gore was locked out of coverage, and he remained unknown outside the South. No unknown candidate can afford to skip such a large portion of primary coverage, particularly since it occurs early in the process. Gore also suffered from the negative cast put on his strategy by the media. Gore was referred to as the candidate who "chose not to campaign in Iowa . . . who quit campaigning here" because he "wasn't doing well and said it's not a representative state" (Tom Brokaw NBC Iowa Election Night coverage). Gore also became too closely identified as a regional candidate, a fact that contrasted with Dukakis's emphasis on running a national campaign. Lesley Stahl of CBS referred to Gore as the "candidate the southern power brokers are pinning their hopes on" and as "the one with the southern accent and southern roots" (February 11). Gore's predicament was apparent in the polls taken after New Hampshire, which showed him as favored by 8% of the national electorate. Even more damaging was that, outside the South, Gore was favored by a meagre 1% of the electorate (Table 3). Most likely, voters did not know who he was and the few who did may have thought of him as the southern candidate who skipped Iowa and New Hampshire. Thus as Gore tried to move north, his showing was dismal and his candidacy died.

Conclusion

The 1988 Democratic nomination is an important confirmation of the influence of early media coverage on presidential nominations. The importance of the 1988 nomination stems from the fact that coverage of Iowa and New Hampshire exercised an influence in a manner that was not typical of previous years. The nomination also indicates that the influence of early coverage can occur under a variety of circumstances. More importantly, the 1988 nomination indicates that much of the influence of early coverage is the result of characteristics of voters and of the nominating process itself that are independent of the media. In this sense, 1988 requires us to look beyond the specifics of each contest to identify relatively stable and ongoing characteristics of the nominating process that create an early media effect from year to year. Three characteristics in this respect are the sequential nature of primaries, the low levels of information and unstable opinions typical of the electorate early in the process, and the media's emphasis on the early contests and on the horse race. These dimensions of the nominating process interact to produce early media effects regardless of the idiosyncrasies of each contest or of the specific content of early coverage.

The sequential nature of primaries and the low levels of information and unstable opinions of voters during the early primaries are important. These two characteristics render the nominating process uniquely vulnerable to early media influence. As these two characteristics interact, they produce an effect that magnifies the influence of early coverage. Because their opinions are so unstable and their information levels so low, voters are unusually susceptible to learning and opinion change from early coverage. That learning then becomes a major determinant of electoral choice in future primaries. The sequential nature of primaries is therefore a major component of the influence of early learning from the media.

Another aspect of early voter learning is the media's emphasis on Iowa and New Hampshire and on the horse race. These two emphases represent the third ongoing characteristic of the nominating process. At a time when voters' opinions are most unstable and most vulnerable to incoming information, voters are deluged with horse race information. Significantly, voters retain horse race information at a high rate and it has a major affect on their perceptions of the candidates. This represents a second interactive effect, this one between voter vulnerability to information and media choices about the amount and content of coverage: the media deliver large amounts of the kind of information readily retained by voters at a time when they are most susceptible. The result is learning and the formation of opinions that are resistant to change from new information later in the process. The significance of this is again magnified by the sequential nature of primaries.

These characteristics were important in 1988. The unknown character of the candidates meant that early coverage would have a powerful impact on voters' long-term perceptions of the candidates. Combined with Super Tuesday and with the media's usual emphasis on the horse race, coverage of Iowa and New Hampshire assumed dramatic importance. That it did so without the drama of momentum and of an early frontrunner points to the significance of the underlying variables discussed above. We can assume that if these three general characteristics of the nominating process continue, and there is no reason to think they will not, then the influence of early coverage of Iowa and New Hampshire will remain a permanent part of presidential nominations.

Notes

1. J. A. Farrell, "For Dukakis, Victory Forged by Familiarity," *Boston Globe*, 17 February 1988, p. 1. (Reprinted courtesy of the *Boston Globe*)
2. J. A. Farrell and J. Vennochi, "Iowa a Boost for Dukakis Camp," *Boston Globe*, 10 February 1988, p. 16. (Reprinted courtesy of the *Boston Globe*)
3. Ibid.
4. C. Black, "Candidates Tailor Message to N. H. in Media Warfare," *Boston Globe*, 11 February 1988.
5. WBZ (Boston NBC affiliate), televised commentary on 8 February 1988 of Michael Dukakis's "Bronze Medal" speech. Reprinted with permission.
6. E. J. Dionne, "Reagan Influence Wanes, Poll Finds," *New York Times*, 26 January 1988, p. 1. Copyright © 1988 by the New York Times Company. Reprinted by permission.

References

ADAMS, WILLIAM C. 1985. Media coverage of campaign '84: A preliminary report. In *The mass media in campaign '84*, edited by Michael J. Robinson and Austin Ranney. Washington, DC: American Enterprise Institute.

———. 1987. As New Hampshire goes.... In *Media and momentum: The New Hampshire primary and nomination politics*, edited by Gary R. Orren and Nelson W. Polsby. Chatham, NY: Chatham House.

Adventures in campaignland. 1988. *Newsweek*, 1 February, 18–23.

BARTELS, LARRY M. 1988. *Presidential primaries and the dynamics of public choice*. Princeton, NJ: Princeton University Press.

BENIGER, JAMES R. 1976. Winning the presidential nomination: National polls and state primary elections, 1936–1972. *Public Opinion Quarterly* 40.

COLUMBIA BROADCASTING SYSTEM (CBS). 1988. Television coverage of the 1988 democratic nomination for president of the United States.

KNOPF, TERRY ANN. 1987. Duke fever: The boosterism and bias in local TV coverage of the Dukakis candidacy becomes a national issue. *Boston Magazine*, November, 148–60.

LICHTER, S. ROBERT, DANIEL AMUNDSON, and RICHARD NOYES. 1988. *The video campaign: Network coverage of the 1988 primaries*. Washington, DC: American Enterprise Institute.

MAYER, WILLIAM G. 1987. The New Hampshire primary: A historical overview. In *Media and momentum: The New Hampshire primary and nomination politics*, edited by Gary R. Orren and Nelson W. Polsby. Chatham, NJ: Chatham House.

NATIONAL BROADCASTING COMPANY (NBC). 1988. Television coverage of the 1988 democratic nomination for president of the United States.

ORREN, GARY R., and NELSON W. POLSBY, eds. 1987. *Media and momentum: The New Hampshire primary and nomination politics*. Chatham, NJ: Chatham House.

PATTERSON, THOMAS E. 1980. *The mass media election: How Americans choose their president*. New York: Praeger.

———. 1989. The press and its missed assignment. In *The elections of 1988*, edited by Michael Nelson. Washington, DC: Congressional Quarterly Press.

POMPER, GERALD M. 1989. The presidential nominations. In *The election of 1988: Reports and interpretations*, edited by Gerald M. Pomper. Chatham, NJ: Chatham House.

TRAUGOTT, MICHAEL W. 1985. The media and the nominating process. In *Before nomination: Our primary problems*, edited by George Grassmuck. Washington, DC: American Enterprise Institute.

After reading: CONSOLIDATE INFORMATION

1. Explain why early media coverage was so influential in the 1988 Democratic Race.
2. Study Table 1, which summarizes the amount of network news coverage of the candidates. What inferences can you draw about the amount of coverage received

by the incumbent, George Bush? Compare the amount of coverage Bush received with that of the other candidates.
3. What do Ridout's findings and analysis imply about the American voter?

Nonverbal Communication
Lori A. Rose

Lori Rose, a Behavioral Sciences major at the University of Indianapolis, wrote the following essay for a Social Psychology class. Note that Rose uses the format and documentation specified by the American Psychological Association (APA).

Before reading: FIRST THOUGHTS
    LOOK AHEAD

1. What do you think of when you hear the term *nonverbal communication*?
2. How does Rose set up the context for her paper in the first paragraph?
3. What do you know about the field of proxemics?

During reading: REACT
    QUESTION
    SUMMARIZE

1. How do you think the proximity of a speaker to you affects the way you react to that speaker?
2. Do the results of the three studies Rose analyzes surprise you? Why or why not?

NONVERBAL COMMUNICATION IS A CHANNEL through which we communicate a great deal of information in addition to our verbal messages. The way we say things, the positions we assume as we talk, and the movements our body makes, all communicate to the listener about our liking or disliking, our dominance or submissiveness, and our responsiveness to them. Proxemics, the examination of human territories, is one aspect of nonverbal communication. This paper will examine Hall's theory of nonverbal communication, and examine research in the area of proxemics. Next, proxemic behavior in American ethnic groups will be examined. Finally, Hall's theory will be evaluated in light of the research presented.

In his book, *The Hidden Dimension*, Dr. Edward Hall outlines his theory of nonverbal communication. Dr. Hall studied personal space and territoriality. He developed a proxemic classification system. His hypothesis behind the classification system is as follows:

> It is the nature of animals, including man, to exhibit behavior which we call territoriality. In doing so, they use the senses to distinguish between one space or distance and another. The specific distance chosen depends on the transaction; the relationship of the interacting individuals, how they feel, and what they are doing (128).

Hall noted that much of our perception of distance occurs unconsciously. Hall's perception of space was dynamic, he saw actions that could occur in a space as important, rather than what is seen through passive viewing (Hall 115).

The classification system that Hall devised was based on middle-class, healthy adults from the northeastern seaboard of the United States. Hall does not intend for this classification system to be generalized to all humans or even all Americans. They are only accurate for the group in the sample. Hall contends that Afro-Americans and Hispanic Americans will have very different proxemic patterns. There are four basic distances, each of which has a near and a far phase.

The closest distance that Hall identified is the intimate distance. At this distance, the presence of another is unmistakable and produces sometimes overwhelming sensory inputs. The sensory perceptions of this distance include distorted sight, heat from the other person's body, sound, smell, and feel of breath. All of these indicate intimate involvement with another person (Hall 116).

The close phase of the intimate distance is the distance for love-making, comforting, and protecting. The communication process at this distance consists of contact, especially via muscles and skin, close-ranged, detailed vision when possible, and increased olfaction and radiant heat sensation. Vocalization plays a very small part in the communication process at this phase (Hall 117).

The far phase of the intimate distance is six to eighteen inches. Contact at this phase involves mainly extremities. At this stage visual focus is much easier, which facilitates eye contact. However, visual distortions do occur at this distance, which Americans find uncomfortable. The voice is used for communication, but usually at a low level or a whisper. Heat and odor of breath are sometimes noticed. Hall notes that middle-class adults in America do not consider it polite or correct to use the intimate distance in public, but it is common for young people to do so (Hall 118).

Personal distance is a term that was first used by Hediger to indicate the distance that non-contact species consistently kept between themselves. It is the protective bubble that we keep between ourselves and others. This space is reserved for those we are friendly with.

The close phase of the personal distance is one and a half to two and a half feet. At this distance, there is no visual distortion, and the face is seen with clarity. Small details of the face are perceived here that are not perceived at any other distance. This distance signals a close relationship or a particular liking for the other person (Hall 119).

The far phase of the personal distance is between two and a half and four feet. This is the traditional arm's length away. This is the distance at which items of personal interest and involvement can be discussed. Most details of the other person's features can be seen, and movements of the hands are perceived. Voice level is moderate. No body heat is perceptible and neither are most normal scents (Hall 120).

The third distance is called social distance. At this distance, visual detail of the face is not seen and touch is not expected. The amplitude of voice is normal for Americans. Conversations at this distance can be overheard at up to twenty feet (Hall 121).

In the close phase, which is four to seven feet, details of skin and hair are perceptible, but not facial details. Impersonal business occurs at this phase. To look down at a person at this phase has a domineering quality (Hall 121).

Seven to twelve feet mark the far phase of the social distance. At this phase very formal business and social functions are conducted. Fine details of the face are further obscured at this phase. The whole face can be seen at once during conversations at this distance. It is extremely important to maintain eye contact during transactions at this distance. The voice level is much louder at this phase than at the close phase, and conversations are easily overheard outside of the room where the conversation occurs. At distances over ten feet, conversation is not necessary (in order to be polite), if it is not desired (Hall 123).

Public distance, the fourth and final distance, is a great deal different than social distance. It involves numerous sensory shifts. This distance is well outside the area of involvement (Hall 123).

The close phase of the public distance is twelve to twenty-five feet. At this phase the voice is loud, but not at full volume. Several types of grammatical, syntactic, and stylization shifts occur at this distance; speech becomes quite formal. Fine details of the body are no longer noticeable (Hall 123-124).

The far phase of the public distance is twenty-five feet or more. This space is usually the amount of space that is automatically reserved for very important public figures. It can also be used by anyone an a public occasion. At this distance, the voice and nonverbal cues must be amplified and exaggerated. Speech slows and words are enunciated more clearly (Hall 124-125).

Much research has been conducted testing Hall's hypothesis and classification system. I analyzed three such studies in detail. The first examined the effects of interpersonal distance between a police officer and a citizen. The second examined reactions to nonverbal expectancy violations. The final study involved initial interaction distance between individuals of unequal and equal military rank.

The first piece of research, by Baxter and Rozelle (1982), studied the effects of interpersonal space during interviews between a policeman and a citizen. The subjects were twenty-nine white, undergraduate male student-subjects who were randomly assigned to the control or experimental group. An interviewer, playing a policeman, was also used. The interview consisted of four phases during which the distance between the policeman and citizen was varied. For both the experimental and control groups, the interview began at a four-foot distance. This phase lasted for two minutes. Then the interviewer moved to within two feet for the next two minutes for both groups. This distance was maintained for the rest of the eight minute interview for the control group, while the experimental group was varied. During the third phase the interviewer moved to an eight inch distance in the experimental group. For the final phase in the experimental group the policeman regained his two-foot distance. The police interviewer maintained eye contact for the entire interview.

Baxter and Rozelle's results were consistent with Hall's findings. The students were fairly comfortable at the four-foot distance. The policeman remained at their social distance. When the policeman came within two feet, or within their personal space, the students began to exhibit nonverbal behaviors that indicated discomfort. For the experimental group, when the officer was eight inches away, or in the intimate space, nonverbal behaviors of extreme discomfort were exhibited. Speech was disrupted and disorganized, eye movements increased, gaze aversion occurred, and subjects placed their arms and hands between themselves and the officer (96–98).

The second study that I examined was conducted by Burgoon and Hale (1988). This study examined negative and positive violations of nonverbal expectancy. Participants were pairs of undergraduate students, one of which was enrolled in a communications class; the other was a friend chosen by the first member of the pair. Participation was voluntary. The communications student was enlisted as a confederate to manipulate the immediacy variable. The other member of the pair was simply instructed to engage in two ten-minute conversations, one with a stranger and the other with a friend. During these conversations the students were to discuss two social-moral problems on their choice of specified topics. Confederates who were in the nonimmediacy situation were instructed to begin the violation after one minute of conversation by doubling the space between them, taking an indirect body position, leaning backwards, crossing their arms, and decreasing eye contact. Those in the high immediacy condition conversely, halved the distance between them, maintained direct body orientation, leaned forward, assumed open posture, and increased eye contact. Each confederate exhibited the same violation for both interviews.

The results of the research conducted by Burgoon and Hale showed that nonimmediacy produced more negative ratings than normal or high immediacy. Nonimmediate confederates were judged to be less competent by the other pair member. Both violations communicated dominance, with high immediacy being significantly more dominant. Friends were more sensitive to the violations than were strangers. Overall, nonimmediacy communicated detachment, nonintimacy, dissimilarity, and dominance. Increases in immediacy communicated more involvement, intimacy, similarity, and dominance (75–78).

The third proxemic study that I examined involved initial interaction distances for members of the military with unequal rank. Subjects were 562 uniformed active duty members of the Navy. Interactions were observed during duty hours in nonworking settings. All the interactions involved one stationary member being approached by another (Dean 295).

The results of this study indicate that interaction directed toward superiors is characterized by larger interpersonal distance than interaction directed toward peers. It also indicates that the distance increases as the rank gradient increases. Superiors seemed to have the option of formal or intimate interactions, while subordinates were required to initiate formal interactions. This study also supported Hall's classification system because most of the interactions occurred in the far phase of the personal distance, which would be appropriate for these ordinary interactions between acquaintances (Dean 298–299).

Hall specifically states that his theory only applies to the specific class of people that he studied. Following Hall's study, many other studies were done to compare the proxemic behavior of other groups. I will discuss two other studies that deal with the proxemic behavior of Afro-Americans as compared to white Americans.

The first comparative study (Aiello and Jones, 1973) dealt with the proxemic behavior of black and white children in first, third, and fifth grades. The children who were studied were from two New York City elementary schools. One school served primarily white, middle-class children, while the other served lower-class blacks. 192 children served as subjects, and were randomly drawn in equal numbers from the three classes. The children were placed in dyads with same sex partners. Two pairs of children were taken at a time, and were introduced to one of two judges, who appeared similar to many of the young white teachers in both schools. Each judge invited her pair to discuss their favorite commercial and prepare to act it out. The judge than acted as though she had work to do, looking up only occasionally, as a teacher would. Every twenty seconds, the judge recorded the distance and axis orientation of the dyad. Six or seven judgements were collected for each pair (Aiello and Jones 21–23).

The hypothesis for this study was that black children would stand closer and adopt a less direct axis orientation than white children, as black adults do. However, this was not the case. Black children did stand closer in first grade, but this difference disappeared in older children and overall. Black children did, however, stand in a less direct axis than white children. This study supports Hall's theory that patterns are learned early in life, but only partially supports his idea that such behaviors are basic to subcultures and unlikely to change (Aiello and Jones 23–27).

The other comparative study that I analyzed dealt with race differences in female black-black and white-white dyads. The dyads were randomly selected from a particular fast food restaurant in several locations in a large eastern city. The subjects were observed and the distance between them was observed at several intervals. After they left the restaurant, they completed a four item questionnaire about their relationship. The results of this study showed that black females stood more closely and leaned toward each other more than white females, in agreement with previous research (Smith 61–63).

In conclusion, Hall's theory and classification system seem to be very effective in explaining proxemic behaviors. His theory predicts that Americans are uncomfortable when acquaintances come into their close personal or intimate space, as exhibited by the policeman and student interviews. His theory also explains the negative reactions to violations of nonverbal expectancies and explains negative evaluations of violatees. His theory also includes explanations of the issues of dominance and rank as illustrated in the military study. Hall also contends that there will be differences in proxemic behaviors in different groups. This is affirmed by the studies that contrast the proxemic behaviors of white and black children and adults.

References

Aiello, J. & Jones, S. (1973). Proxemic behavior of black and white first-, third-, and fifth-grade children. *Journal of Personality and Social Psychology*, 25, 21–27.

Baxter, J., Druckman, D., & Rozelle, R. (1982). *Nonverbal communication: Survey, theory, and research*. Newbury Park CA: Sage Publishing.

Burgoon, J. & Hale, J. (1988). Nonverbal expectancy violations: Model elaboration and application to immediacy behaviors. *Communications Monographs*, 55, 75–78.

Dean, L., Willis, F., & Hewitt, J. (1975). Initial interaction distance among individuals of equal and unequal military rank. *Journal of Personality and Social Psychology*, 32, 294–299.

Hall, E. *The hidden dimension*. (1966). New York: Doubleday.

Smith, A. (1983). Nonverbal communication among black female dyads: An assessment of intimacy, gender, and race. *Journal of Social Issues*, 39, 55–67.

After reading:

1. How is nonverbal communication related to the study of proxemics?
2. Why do you think that different racial or ethnic groups have different proxemic patterns?
3. Summarize Rose's evaluation of Hall's theory.

A Survey of Dating Violence on a University Campus

Richard Shea and Daniel Zona

Richard Shea and Daniel Zona based the research in this paper on a survey they developed collaboratively to study the prevalence of dating violence on their own campus, the University of Rhode Island. The paper was written for a 200 level Sociology course.

Before reading: FIRST THOUGHTS
LOOK AHEAD

1. What do you think of when you read the words *dating violence*?
2. How prevalent do you think violence among dating couples is on your college campus?
3. Shea and Zona surveyed students concerning the prevalence of dating violence on their university campus; freewrite a short list of what you think they might have found out about dating violence.

During reading: REACT
QUESTION
SUMMARIZE

1. Why do you think Shea and Zona define violent acts in the broad way that they do?
2. Do you think the categories in the co-authors' questionnaire were complete? Would you add or change any of the categories? Why or why not?

Abstract: Courtship and dating violence at the University of Rhode Island is examined by means of a survey of students in two introductory sociology classes. Incidence figures are given for the various violent means of resolving conflict. The relationship between violence and other variables is also discussed. The findings resemble those of previous researchers and confirm the prevalence of dating violence among college students. It is suggested that further research is needed to understand the causes of dating violence.

IN THE PAST TWENTY YEARS a social phenomenon has surfaced concerning the family. Family violence has received widespread attention from a variety of sources. The research conducted on family violence, particularly spouse abuse, has stimulated further research on dating and courtship violence. Dating violence, according to Makepiece (1981, 1983) is a major key to understanding family violence. The patterns of interpersonal relationships of those dating and courting form the foundation for future family dynamics. By examining dating violence and the maladaptive patterns that may form in courtship, family violence can be better understood.

The research of Straus, Gelles, and Steinmetz (1980) into family violence provided many insights into the world of family violence. Straus, Gelles, and Steinmetz provide a working definition of what violent acts fall within the parameters of family violence. They define violent acts as those "carried out with the intention, or perceived intention, of causing physical pain or injury to another person" (Straus, Gelles, & Steinmetz, p. 20).

Their research explored different variables such as children, sex, money, and social activities that influence violence in the family. Another variable they detected was stress as an indicator of violence. This is a variable that should be examined closely since the average person in American society experiences high levels of stress for a variety of reasons. Straus and his colleagues (1980) also found that couples experiencing sexual problems increase the rate of household violence as compared to couples not experiencing sexual problems.

Building on the work of Straus, Gelles, and Steinmetz, Makepiece (1981; 1983) surveyed large numbers of dating couples and found that 21.2% of the subjects had experienced violence in the form of actual or threatened violence. Makepiece also found that alcohol served a critical role in violent relationships. The percentage of respondents who said they had been drinking when the violence occurred was 31.6%.

More recent studies (Cate et al, 1982; Henton et al., 1983; Muehlenhard & Linton, 1987) demonstrate that violence is a fact of the American dating scene. And Gelles and Cornell (1985) point out that violence in dating and courtship are learned behavior patterns which prefigure marital violence (p. 66).

The present study seeks to demonstrate incidence rates for violence, and to examine how stress and conflict relate to these incident rates for dating couples at the University of Rhode Island. For the purpose of the study, violent behavior as defined by Straus, Gelles, and Steinmetz (1980) is broadened to include threatening to hit or to throw something, throwing, smashing, hitting or kicking an object, or hitting or kicking the other person. The data collected from the respondents is analyzed for the respondents' violent behavior, not their partners'. Data was collected on how often the subjects experienced stress in their relationships, and also on the amount of stress they experienced in their lives. The couples' sexual relationship was assessed for conflict as well as the presence of alcohol.

It was hypothesized that higher levels of stress and conflict would be related to higher rates of violence. Alcohol was also thought to be a factor in violent behavior, as was the presence of problems in a couple's sexual relationship. Finally, data on the amount of time couples had been dating, and their future plans were collected in order to test the theory of the "marriage license as a hitting license" (Straus, Gelles and Steinmetz, 1980, p. 31). That is, it was thought that those couples who had made some plans of engagement or marriage would be more prone to use violence because it would be more socially sanctioned, as it is within the marriage context.

Method

Subjects

A survey was administered at the University of Rhode Island to 200 undergraduate students enrolled in two introductory sociology courses. Of the 200 students surveyed, 123 students were currently dating. These 123 students constituted the sample for the study. There were 38 males and 85 females. The mean age for all subjects was 19.345. Respondents were predominantly Catholic and Protestant (82.9%), and the vast majority were white (98%).

Procedure

A questionnaire was designed which assessed the demographic characteristics of sex, age, religion, and race for all respondents. All subjects were asked if they were currently dating someone. Subjects who were not dating were told that they had completed the survey. Those who were currently dating were asked to proceed with the survey. Subjects were then asked how long they had been dating their partner, what plans had been made as a couple, and it they were currently living with their dating partner.

This information was followed by two 5-point scales asking the subjects how often the stress and/or frustration they experienced in selected areas of school, work, family, career plans, and health affect their dating relationship, and their overall life. Responses could range from 1 (Always) to 5 (Never). Subjects were then asked one question to determine the degree to which they agree with their partner on managing money, social activities and entertainment, affection and sexual relations, future plans, and birth control. These scales were also scored from 1 (Always) to 5 (Never). A value of 9 was assigned if subjects responded "doesn't apply" to any of the above questions.

The above indexes were variations of the ones used by Straus, Gelles, and Steinmetz to measure conflict and stress in their study of family violence. Some of the items were modified in order to make them more salient for college students.

The "Conflict Tactics Seals" (see Straus, Gelles, and Steinmetz, 1980, for the actual scale and reliability and validity data) was then used to assess the subjects' means of resolving conflict with their partners. The "Conflict Tactics Scale" was exactly like the one used by Straus, Gelles, and Steinmetz to measure inter-spousal conflict, except that "choking" was added following "beat up the other one." Subjects were also asked if they, their partners, or both of them were under the influence of alcohol when any of the violent means of resolving conflict were used.

The final section of the survey was concerned with the sexual activity and relationship of the couple. Subjects were asked if they had ever engaged in any sexual activity with their current partner, and if yes, who initiated it most often. Also, they were asked if they had ever felt pressured to engage in sex with their partner. Finally, they were asked if, in general, they were satisfied with their sexual relationship, and with the level of love and intimacy in their relationship.

The questionnaire was administered in two different sociology classes during regular class time. Subjects were told that the researchers were exploring the personal dynamics of relationships, and that all responses would be kept strictly confidential. The questionnaire took approximately 30 minutes to complete. Upon completion, all subjects were thanked for their participation.

Results

Frequency data was collected for all variables on the questionnaire. A crosstabs procedure was run on several of the scale items to see how they related to the violent or potentially violent means of resolving conflict yielded by the "Conflict Tactics Scale." Violent and potentially violent acts were defined differ-

TABLE 1 Respondents' Use of Violence in Their Relationships

Type of Violence	Incidence	
	n	%
Threatened to hit	24	20
Threw, smashed, or hit something	45	37.5
Pushed, grabbed, shoved	14	11.6
Slapped	17	14
Kicked, bit, hit	10	8.3
Hit with something	6	5
Beat up	2	1.7
Choked	1	.8
Threatened with gun or knife	0	0
Used a gun or knife	0	0

ently; they began with the item "threatened to hit or throw something at your partner," and continued through "Used a knife or gun."

The incidence of both actual and threatened physical violence in dating relationships was examined. The results of this analysis are displayed in Table 1.

As expected, the more extreme forms of violence were far less common than the milder forms like "pushing" or "slapping."

The involvement of alcohol in dating violence was also examined. The percentage of subjects who reported that both they and their partners were under the influence of alcohol at the time of the violent incidents was 38.6%.

In order to assess the effect stress may have on respondents' relationships and on their overall lives, data was analyzed for those subjects who said that they were "almost always" experiencing stress in the areas of school, work, family and career plans. Tables 2 and 3 show the percentage of individuals who responded in this way, broken down by the violent means they used to resolve conflicts.

It appears that stress caused by work is the best predictor of the use of violence by the respondent, followed by the stress caused by family. Further analysis of the remaining scale responses is beyond the scope of this paper, and

TABLE 2 Stress in the Relationship*

	Threatened To Hit[+]	Threw/ Smashed Something[+]	Pushed, Grabbed, Shoved[+]	Slap[+]	Hit, Bit, Shoved[+]	Hit with[+] Something
School	11	33.3	4	11	4	0
Work	12.5	50	0	12.5	12.5	12.5
Family	12.5	37.5	12.5	12.5	0	0
Career	11	33.3	11	11	0	0

* in percent
+ at least once

TABLE 3 Stress in Life*

	Threatened To Hit[+]	Threw/ Smashed Something[+]	Pushed, Grabbed, Shoved[+]	Slap[+]	Hit, Bit, Shoved[+]	Hit with[+] Something
School	17	41	10	12	5	2
Work	18	75	25	12.5	0	0
Family	17	33.3	11	11	0	0
Career	12.5	33.3	0	8	0	0

* in percent
+ at least once

therefore, no conclusive statements can be drawn about the relationship between stress and violence.

To get some idea of the relationship between conflict and violence, data was examined for subjects who said that they agreed "sometimes" with their partners on the issues of managing money, social activities, sexual relations, future plans, and birth control.

It appears that conflict about no specific issue can be used as an indicator of violence in the relationship when couples "sometimes" agree. Conflict caused by sometimes disagreeing about sexual relations appears to be most related to violence, but no conclusive statements can be made about this variable.

A crosstabs procedure was also run on the variable of couples' future plans by the violent items on the "Conflict Tactics Scale."

This analysis indicated that subjects who are planning marriage used the highest percentage of violent acts against their partners. For example, 28% of those respondents who are planning to marry their dating partners have slapped them at least once, compared to 4.8% of those who are merely planning to continue dating.

TABLE 4 Agreement*

	Threatened To Hit[+]	Threw/ Smashed Something[+]	Pushed, Grabbed, Shoved[+]	Slap[+]	Hit, Bit[+]	Hit with+ Something
Money	25	50	15	18	6	3
Social Activities	17	45	13	22	17	14
Sex	22	59	11	22	17	17
Future Plans	26	32	13	13	10	6
Birth Control	8	25	0	0	0	0

* in percent
+ at least once

TABLE 5 Future Plans*

	Threatened To Hit[+]	Threw/ Smashed Something[+]	Pushed, Grabbed, Shoved[+]	Slap[+]	Hit, Bit[+]	Hit with+ Something
Dating Indefinitely	9.5	38	9.5	4.8	4.8	0
Engagement	33.3	33.3	8.3	25	8.3	8.3
Living Together	20	30	20	10	10	10
Marriage	24	41	21	28	17	10
Relationship Termination	0	0	0	0	0	0

* in percent
+ at least once

A similar analysis run on the length of respondents' dating relationship indicated that, generally, those subjects who have been dating longest committed the highest percentage of violent acts.

The percentage of those subjects who have been dating for 2 years to 35 months, and have slapped their partner is 31%, as opposed to 7% of the subjects who have been dating from 1 year to 23 months.

Table 7 shows the breakdown of respondents' sex by the violent items on the "Conflict Tactics Scale."

The data indicates that, in general, the females in this sample were more likely to threaten to hit, slap, and hit, bite or kick their partners. Males, however, were more likely to throw things, push, grab, or shove, or hit their partners with some object.

The quality of the respondents' sexual relationships was examined by collecting data on 2 questions. Firstly, subjects were asked if they had ever felt

TABLE 6 Length of Relationship*

	Threatened To Hit[+]	Threw/ Smashed Something[+]	Pushed, Grabbed, Shoved[+]	Slap[+]	Hit, Bit[+]	Hit with+ Something
0–6 Mo.	14.3	29	14.3	0	0	0
6–11 Mo.	29	24	9.5	24	9.5	9.5
1 Yr.–23 Mo.	21.4	36	21.4	7	21.4	7.8
2 Yrs.–35 Mo.	15	54	23	31	23	15.4
More than 3 Yrs.	16.67	44	11	16.67	0	0

* in percent
+ at least once

TABLE 7 Sex*

	Threatened To Hit+	Threw/ Smashed Something+	Pushed, Grabbed, Shoved+	Slap+	Hit, Bit+	Hit with+ Something
Males	16	53	13	5.3	5.3	5.3
Females	22	30	11	18	9.6	4.9

* in percent
+ at least once

pressured to engage in sex with their partners, then, they were asked if they were satisfied, in general, with their sexual relationship.

Those respondents who report having felt pressured to engage in sex with their partners use a higher percentage of violence than those subjects who have never felt pressured. Finally, subjects who say that they are satisfied with their sexual relationship appear to be less likely, on the whole, to use violent acts against their partners.

DISCUSSION

The results of the study lend support to the findings of dating violence. The study does in fact remain consistent with previous research done by Makepiece, and Straus, Gelles, and Steinmetz. Unfortunately, the variables of stress and conflict were not fully explored, however, there were relationships that did tend to be an indicator of violent and potentially violent behaviors. The relationship between the length of time the couple were involved, and the couple's future plans did interact with one another to have the respondent report of exercising violent behavior. Another aspect of the study which supported other research conducted by Makepiece was the presence of alcohol. The findings show that alcohol was involved in a large number of violent incidents. Again, the findings support other research concerning the link between a couple's sexual problems and violent behavior. The presence of sexual problems did seem to lead to a higher percentage of violence among couples.

The overall incidence rates for the different violent and potentially violent behaviors closely resemble the findings of Cate et al. (1982), Henton et al.(1983)

TABLE 8 Pressure*

	Threatened To Hit+	Threw/ Smashed Something+	Pushed, Grabbed, Shoved+	Slap+	Hit, Bit+	Hit with+ Something
Yes	24	45	12	21	9	6
No	18	32	10	9	7.5	4

* in percent
+ at least once

TABLE 9 Satisfaction*

	Threatened To Hit[+]	Threw/ Smashed Something[+]	Pushed, Grabbed, Shoved[+]	Slap[+]	Hit, Bit[+]	Hit with[+] Something
Yes	24	40	12	15	7.8	4.5
No	18	50	18	12	12	12

* in percent
+ at least once

and Makepiece (1981; 1983) and therefore reinforce Makepiece's assertion (1981) that dating violence is a prevalent problem and does not consist of a few isolated incidents.

Straus, Gelles, and Steinmetz (1980) and Gelles and Cornell (1985) report that sexual difficulties in relationships greatly increase the potentiality of violent behavior. These data do lend support to their findings. The evidence suggests that the violent acts were used to resolve conflict. The data collected on these couples' future plans show that couples who have planned a marriage show a higher percentage of violence and thus supports the theory that the marriage license is a "hitting license" (Gelles & Cornell, 1985, p. 66). Obviously there are many possible variables as to why this theory holds true, but nonetheless, it does raise the issue that the specific form of commitment needs to be closely examined. It is clearly evident that dating couples who are planning marriage but not married during the survey do use a greater degree of violence than couples who do not have marriage plans. Further research may provide explanations which will lead to therapy or treatment strategies which could permeate the population and reduce violent behavior. To understand fully the phenomena of violent behaviors during courtship and dating, further research is needed. Through further research, social policies and programs can be developed to aid individuals who find themselves locked in a violent situation. Through further research, an understanding of why college students remain in abusive or violent relationships may be gained.

Many questions are unanswered and will remain unanswered unless researchers and practitioners from all fields of social study work together to terminate old myths and stereotypes, and replace them with constructive, healthy, loving relationships in which men and women can live without the threat of violence.

References

CATE, R.M., J.M. HENTON, F.S. CHRISTOPHER, & S. LLOYD. (1982). "Premarital abuse: A social psychological perspective." *Journal of Family Issues*, 3 (March):79–90.

GELLES, R.J. & C. CORNELL. (1985). *Intimate Violence in Families*. Beverly Hills CA: Sage Publications.

HENTON, J.M., R.M. CATE, J. LOVAL, S. LLOYD, & S. CHRISTOPHER. (1983). "Romance and violence in dating relationships." *Journal of Family Issues* 4 (September):467–470.

MAKEPIECE, J. (1981). "Courtship violence among college students." *Family Relations* 30 (January):97–102.

———. (1983). "Life-events stress and courtship violence." *Family Relations* 32 (1):101–109.

MUEHLENHARD, C.L. & M.A. LINTON. (1987). "Date rape and sexual aggression in dating situations: Incidence and risk factors." *Journal of Counseling Psychology*, 34 (2), 186–96.

STRAUS, M.A., R.J. GELLES, & S.K. STEINMETZ. (1980). *Behind Closed Doors: Violence in the American Family.* New York: Anchor/Doubleday.

After reading: CONSOLIDATE INFORMATION

1. Shea and Zona surveyed their fellow students and wrote their report in 1988; since that time there has been a noticeable increase in the attention paid to dating violence, date rape, and other forms of social abuse on college campuses. How do you think their study, even their results, would be changed if it were done today?
2. Why do you think Shea and Zona conclude that a reliable study of the relationship between stress and dating violence is outside the scope of their paper?
3. What do you think are the advantages of collaborative research and writing projects among students? Do you think there are any disadvantages?

The Diagnosis and Treatment of *Bulimia Nervosa*
Tamara S. Peters

Tamara Peters is a Biology major at the University of Indianapolis. She wrote the following paper synthesizing research on the eating disorder, bulimia nervosa, *for an introductory Abnormal Psychology class.*

Before reading: FIRST THOUGHTS
LOOK AHEAD

1. What do you know about bulimia and anorexia?
2. Read the introduction; what predictions can you make about Peters's paper from what she writes in the introduction?
3. Why do you think eating disorders occur in young American women?

During reading: REACT
	QUESTION
	SUMMARIZE

1. Do you think that eating disorders such as bulimia and anorexia are connected to Americans' attitude toward food?
2. Why do you suppose that most people who suffer bulimia are from the middle class?

Introduction

Bulimia nervosa IS AN EATING DISORDER that consists of reoccurring binge eating followed by self-induced purging. Binge eating is defined as the consumption of thousands of calories at one sitting of short duration. Bulimic individuals are more concerned with the amount of food they intake than their caloric intake or the consumption of one particular food group. Binge eating usually occurs after a period of fasting or starvation. At times, the vomiting portion of the cycle is followed by an additional fasting period that is sometimes enhanced by diuretics, laxatives, or a combination of both. Individuals suffering from bulimia nervosa follow this eating pattern, generally, in order to lose weight.

Diagnosis

Individuals who follow a binging and purging pattern of eating frequently followed by a period of fasting, are classified as suffering from *bulimia nervosa*. Bulimics show signs of depression and anger or frustration before and after their binging and purging episodes. They often complain of irritation and deterioration of their gums and inner cheeks of their mouths. Temper tantrums may also follow these situations, often because they become disgusted and overwhelmed by their actions and behavior. Because of their body's need to compensate for the damage it receives, these individuals complain often of being exhausted and sleep frequently as their bodies attempt to compensate for their lack of food consumption.

Bulimics tend to have their binging and purging sessions while they are alone. At one sitting, it is not uncommon for a bulimic individual to consume up to twenty thousand calories within a two hour period. Most bulimics deny to other people that they suffer from any type of eating disorder. Most research indicates that bulimics are usually aware of their actions; sometimes, however, they are unaware of their binging and purging cycle until they have finished it and are exhausted. It takes most of these individuals four to five years before they admit that they have a problem and seek professional counseling. They are usually too embarrassed, disgusted, and ashamed to admit their problem. They hate to feel inferior.

As with many people who suffer from eating disorders, bulimic individuals tend to have a distorted or incorrect image of their bodies. One study (Fairburn and Beglin, 1990) has shown through random surveys that the average bulimic female desires to lose 16.2 pounds. This average desired weight loss is twice the amount that individuals who do not suffer from eating disorders wish to lose on a diet.

Bulimics are usually within fifteen percent of their normal body weight. Their weight tends to fluctuate constantly up and down with about ten to thirty pounds either way because of their altering between the binging and purging half and the starvation half of the cycle.

Statistics

The average person who suffers from bulimia nervosa is a female in her early twenties. The majority of the bulimics detected through surveys or through those who have sought professional help are female college students. Bulimia nervosa seems primarily to affect women: 80–90 percent of those afflicted are female, whereas, 10–20 percent are male. Generally, these young adults come from middle class families and are usually college girls who strive toward high academic achievement and extreme perfection.

After viewing many surveys, a majority of which were compiled on various college campuses, the results of these surveys show that only one percent of all women and two tenths of a percent of men suffer from bulimia. However, one survey detected up to nineteen percent of females and up to five percent of males battle this eating disorder day after day. All of the data collected from these surveys was correlated against the symptoms of bulimia listed in the Diagnostic and Statistical Manual, 3rd ed. (DSM-III R).

Treatment

Many types of treatment are used to treat individuals who suffer from bulimia nervosa. All of these treatments are similar in their structure. Some of the most widely used forms of treatment for bulimia nervosa are group therapy, cognitive-behavioral treatment, response prevention treatment, and nutritional intervention.

Nutritional intervention can be used to eventually teach the bulimic to possess normal eating habits. Through analyzing their current eating habits and gradually controlling their urges to where they are consuming reasonable amounts of food, their binging and purging cycle will be eventually limited. A majority of bulimics never fully recover, but the cycle can be limited and under near full control. Nutritional intervention tries to get the bulimic individual to follow, maintain, and understand a nutritional diet, to maintain an appropriate body weight, to achieve a correct perception of her body appearance, and to form a normal eating pattern.

Cognitive-behavioral treatment is used to make the bulimic aware of her eating pattern: how many times she eats, how much food she consumes, and what types of food are consumed each day. This form of therapy is also involved with correcting the bulimic's perception of her body, since bulimics overestimate their body weight and have an abnormal view of their body structure.

Another form of treatment for bulimia nervosa is response prevention. Response prevention forces the bulimic to face her binging and purging cycle with a therapist. During a treatment session, the bulimic has food placed in front of her that she might normally include in one of her binging sessions, she eats, and then she is kept in the therapy session through her average time lapse between the binging and purging. This prevents the bulimic from vomiting her food and also usually limits her food consumption because she is in the presence of others. Bulimic individuals use their binging and purging, followed by starvation cycle as a way of solving their problems. The purging part of the cycle is thought to be an anxiety releaser. Through this form of therapy, the bulimic is taught that she can overcome her problems without using her bulimic tendencies as an outlet for her problems.

Group therapy is one of the most widely used forms of treatment for bulimia nervosa. Group therapy usually contains up to ten bulimics per group who meet to resolve physical, physiological, and social aspects of bulimia nervosa. Depending on the group size and severity of the individual cases, the number of times the group meets, how often they meet and the duration of their sessions are determined. The longer term therapy sessions have been most effective.

Summary

Bulimia nervosa is a cyclic eating disorder which consists of a binging and purging period followed by a fasting or starvation period. Bulimics generally complain of dental problems, physical and mental exhaustion. Of all the individuals who suffer from eating disorders, college women in their early twenties comprise the largest population who suffer from bulimia nervosa. Treatments such as nutritional intervention, cognitive-behavioral treatment, response prevention treatment, and group therapy have been most effective.

Bulimia nervosa is an eating disorder that can be overcome. It takes a strong individual to admit she has the disorder, reorganize her lifestyle, and battle the behavior she has learned to live her life by.

References

American Psychiatric Association (1987). *Diagnostic and statistical manual of mental disorders* (3rd ed.). Washington DC: Author.

Agras, W. S., Schneider, J. A., Arnow, B., Raeburn, S. D. & Telch, C. F. (1989). Cognitive behavior and response-prevention treatments for bulimia nervosa. *Journal of Consulting and Clinical Psychology*, 2, 215–221.

Clark, K., Parr, R., & Castelli, W. (Eds.) (1988 October). The prevalence of bulimia nervosa in the U.S. college student population. *American Journal of Public Health*, 78, 1322–1325.

Fairburn, C. G. & Beglin, S. (1990 April). Studies of the epidemiology of bulimia nervosa. *American Journal of Psychiatry*, 147, 401–408.

GIANNINI, A. J., NEUMANN, M. & GOLD, M. (1990 April). Anorexia and bulimia. *American Family Physician*, 41, 1169–1176.

GRAY, J. J. & HOAGE, C. M. (1990 April). Bulimia nervosa: Group behavior therapy with exposure plus response prevention. *Psychological Reports*, 66, 667–674.

SLAGERMAN, M. & YAGER, J. (1989). Multiple family group treatment for eating disorders: A short term program. *Psychiatric Medicine*, 7, 269–283.

WHITE, M. B. & WHITE, W. C. JR. (1983). *Bulimarexia: The binge/purge cycle.* New York: WW Norton.

After reading: CONSOLIDATE INFORMATION

1. Peters's paper is a synthesis of research on bulimia. What are her conclusions?
2. Evaluate the sources Peters uses for her paper.
3. Reread Peters's summary of the treatment of bulimia. What is the prognosis for someone who suffers from this disorder?

Further Explorations for Readings in the Social Sciences

1. Elaine Hatfield and Richard Rapson's article "Emotions: A Trinity" responds directly to B.F. Skinner's article "Outlining a Science of Feeling." Evaluate each article and decide which one seems to give the most credible account of human emotions.
2. The articles by Margaret Eisenhart, Belenky, Clinchy, Goldberger and Tarule and Margaret Mead use ethnography rather than quantitative or statistical methods to describe and define their subjects. Review these essays and develop your own definition of ethnography based on what you read.
3. Review Lori Rose's paper on nonverbal communication and read Belenky, Clinchy, Goldberger and Tarule on the ways women perceive and develop ways of knowing and talking. How do you think family backgrounds influence the ways people develop modes of nonverbal communication?
4. Social scientists frequently collaborate in their research and in the writing of their research reports. In this section four articles are collaboratively written by two, and in one case four, authors. Review these articles and evaluate how effectively the co-authors create one voice.
5. Steven Reiss and Margaret Eisenhart study the social identity of two groups who have held minority status in the United States, African-Americans (Reiss) and women (Eisenhart). What conclusions can you infer from their essays about the ways members of these two groups form a social identity and a self-concept?
6. The two pairs of articles by Skinner (1986) and Hatfield and Rapson (1990), and Mead (1933) and Feinberg (1990), represent the kind of dialogue that goes on within a discipline or field. Review and examine these two pairs of articles and write a

short evaluation in which you demonstrate how the later writers build on, modify, or contradict ideas in the earlier essays.
7. Christine F. Ridout and Wilson Carey McWilliams both write about the effect of news media on presidential elections and American voters, although they do so for different kinds of readers. What specific examples of documentation and evidence, style, language, and tone demonstrate the differences in the two audiences?

3

Readings in the Sciences

Occupational and Environmental Cancer: Radical Chic and Mau-Mauing the Carcinogens
Howard Frumkin

This article appeared in Science for the People *(SftP), a magazine which focuses on public policy and environmental health issues for a non-specialist audience. Howard Frumkin is a professor and researcher at the University of Pennsylvania Medical School. Frumkin seems well aware that some of his readers are the very people (progressive scientists and activists) he is arguing against, so he carefully documents his argument with references to medical research.*

Before reading: FIRST THOUGHTS
                LOOK AHEAD

1. What do you think the phrase "occupational cancer" means?
2. What occupations do you think may have high cancer rates?
3. Do you think that cancer rates have increased in the past twenty years?

During reading: REACT
                QUESTION
                SUMMARIZE

1. How do you react to Frumkin's contention and subsequent analysis that cancer rates have, for the most part, decreased?
2. Why does Frumkin make it a point to question animal studies of various cancers?

Is Cancer On the Rise or not? What proportion of cancers is due to occupational and environmental causes? What is the role of tobacco smoking? When identifying carcinogens, how should in vitro and animal evidence be utilized? When regulating carcinogen exposures, how should low levels of exposure be approached? And finally, what is the significance of quantitative risk assessment? These six separate questions have each been central to the debate over the threat posed by occupational and environmental cancers.

As progressive scientists, environmentalists, community groups, and labor unions have rallied around the issue of environmental and occupational cancers for the last three decades, a paradigm has developed which can be seen in the popular press, in the pages of journals like *SftP* and *Health/PAC Bulletin*, and in books like Samuel Epstein's *The Politics of Cancer*. Industry, the paradigm posits, releases thousands of toxic substances into workplaces, communities, and the general environment; these substances are potent carcinogens; an epidemic of cancer is resulting. This paper, like this issue of *SftP*, will attempt to examine some of the issues raised by that paradigm. Specifically, I want to raise a caution: that despite a coherent political framework, some progressive scientists have made arguments not adequately grounded in facts, and that we need to remedy that problem.

Cancer Rates: Up or Down?

The first question, regarding cancer rates, should be the simplest. Larry Agran, in *The Cancer Connection*, provided one answer: "In truth, what we are witnessing is the unmistakable emergence of a national cancer epidemic. An epidemic of frightful proportions. A cancer pox. The numbers and the trends point clearly to the calamity that is already upon us."[1] Samuel Epstein, in *The Politics of Cancer*, expressed a similar view. He wrote that "there has been a real and absolute increase in cancer incidence and mortality during this century." He called cancer a "killing and disabling disease of epidemic proportions," and dubbed it "the plague of the twentieth century."[2]

The answer that emerges from reviewing data is considerably less dramatic. According to the most recent American Cancer Society report, mortality is increasing for some cancers, decreasing for others, and stable for still others.[3] Among women, lung cancer mortality is rising, colorectal, uterine, and gastric cancer mortality are declining, and breast cancer mortality is stable. Mortality from leukemia and ovarian and pancreatic cancer rose until about 1960 and then stabilized. Among men, lung cancer mortality increased rapidly during the last five decades, although that increase has recently begun to slow. Prostatic cancer mortality is increasing slightly and gastric cancer mortality is falling, but no other sites show major changes. Combining men and women, and excluding lung cancer, overall cancer mortality since 1950 has shown a 13 per cent decline.[4] (All these figures are age-adjusted.) Brain cancer and multiple myeloma mortality show increases among those aged over 75[5] (although accurate data may be elusive in this age category[6]). Of course, mortality data must be viewed circumspectly. They are based on death certificates, which are often inaccurate, and changes over time may reflect changes in diagnosis, treatment and other factors.

Incidence data show prominent increases in lung cancer among both men and women. In addition, there are slight increases in breast cancer among women and in prostatic cancer among men.[7] Bladder cancer, a type related to chemical exposures, has increased in incidence; leukemia incidence increased until the last decade, when it began to decline. In sum, certain site-specific cancers do appear to be increasing, particularly in selected age groups, as shown in disaggregated incidence and mortality data. This is certainly a serious concern. However, if there is an "epidemic" of cancer, it probably involves only lung cancer.

Cancer from Occupational and Environmental Exposures

What proportion of cancers can be attributed to occupational and environmental causes? During the 1960's, Higginson estimated that up to 90% of cancer is environmentally induced, based principally on geographic comparisons.[8] Of course, "environmental" in this context includes all extrinsic factors, such as diet, tobacco, and sunlight. Much of the debate has focused specifically on occupational causes of cancer, and we can review that narrower debate here.

In the context of political and scientific struggle during the 1970's, both high and low estimates of the workplace contribution to cancer emerged. An important document was prepared and circulated by the National Cancer Institute and other agencies in 1978, but never published.[9] In this report, a group of prominent federal agency scientists noted the cancer risk ratios that had been observed in occupational cohorts heavily exposed to any of six substances. They applied these risk ratios to all workers currently exposed to the substances, and they projected numbers of cancers that would result. From these calculations, they estimated that 20–40% of all U.S. cancers were (or would soon be) attributable to occupational factors. This argument was widely criticized after its release.[10] It ignored differences in dose between the study cohorts and the currently exposed workers, and it generated numerical predictions that diverged dramatically from observed rates. Despite these problems, many of us at the time accepted the high estimates and cited them uncritically. Three years later, Doll and Peto published *The Causes Cancer*, in which they estimated that about four percent of cancers are attributable to occupational exposures.[11] Their analysis considered specific cancers with known occupational etiologies, estimated the proportion of each ascribable to workplace exposures, and summed these. These authors, too, have been criticized, along several lines.[12] They excluded data for nonwhites and for people over 65 years of age, they accounted only for known carcinogens and excluded potential (and animal) carcinogens, and they did little to approach the issue of possible synergistic effects from exposure to multiple carcinogens. However, it is unlikely that these problems caused more than a twofold error in their estimates, and the four percent estimate accords well with prior work.[13] In summary, the weight of current evidence suggests that something under 10% of cancer is occupational in origin, despite higher claims by some progressive scientists.

Of course, that amounts to a lot of avoidable deaths, concentrated for the most part among unwitting victims from the working class. We are right to be profoundly concerned. We should be alert to revelations of new occupational and environmental carcinogens that may alter our quantitative estimates. But in the meantime, we only weaken our case when we stretch the numbers!

The Smoking Cigarette

A third question, regarding the role of tobacco smoking, poses a different sort of problem. Progressives are justifiably concerned that undue focus on lifestyle factors, including smoking, may divert attention from such involuntary exposures as occupational carcinogens. (This is a strategy amply exploited by corporate interests in workplace health promotions programs, "prostituted" epidemiological studies, and similar efforts.) It may seem more congruous to our political views to target environmental toxins rather than smoking as our major environmental health concern. And at the level of practice, many of us have undoubtedly squirmed uncomfortably at union or community meetings while people raged against relatively low-level chemical exposures while filling the meeting room with cigarette smoke.

The facts are fairly clear. Tobacco is by far the major single environmental cause of cancer, not only in the general population, but in most working populations as well. Accordingly, we have good progressive analyses of the social causes of smoking and of the political economy of tobacco. The "question," then, is one of emphasis. There has been a tendency among some researchers and activists in occupational and environmental health to minimize the role of smoking in causing cancer, to overstate the relative role of chemical toxins, and to justify this all more in political terms than in scientific terms. Certainly, there are compelling reasons to struggle against toxic exposures in the workplace and community. But there are equally compelling reasons to acknowledge honestly that smoking causes a lot of cancer.[14]

Animal Studies

The fourth question concerns the role of in vitro and animal evidence in establishing carcinogenicity. These methods have been controversial for at least two reasons. First, we attempt to extrapolate human cancers from nonhuman data. Second, we attempt to extrapolate low-dose outcomes from high-dose data. In both efforts, we need to make assumptions that are difficult to verify.

The standard progressive position has been to argue that animal carcinogens "may be" human carcinogens, and that public health prudence requires that we regulate based on this "conservative" assumption. That is a sensible approach, and it has been adopted by most regulatory agencies worldwide. The corporate response has been one of cynicism. Bacteria and animals, it is argued, are metabolically distinct from humans (so extrapolation is unjustified). In some cases, test animals are so resistant to cancer that many species must be tested before just one demonstrates a response (so the stuff probably isn't carcinogenic in humans). And animals typically are tested with extremely high doses, far higher than typical human exposures.

In fact, it *is* difficult to extrapolate from animals to humans, because species *do* differ considerably in their biology. But we are on firm intellectual ground here, it seems to me, precisely because we don't need to pretend that our position is rooted in data. This is an issue that clearly centers on political assumptions rather than on data interpretation.

The Dose-Response Curve

The high-dose to low-dose issue is more controversial; like the issue of animal evidence, it embraces both conflicting political interests and profound scientific ignorance, but the political assumptions tend to be buried more deeply in scientific debate.

Briefly, we do not know the molecular mechanisms of carcinogenesis, and we do not know the shape of the dose-response curve that relates carcinogenic exposures and resulting disease. Therefore, using data based on high-dose exposures (whether from animal studies or epidemiology), we cannot predict with any certainty how much cancer will be caused by low-dose exposures. There are many mathematical models in currency, so you can pick a curve that bends at low doses according to your political preferences. The curves of progressive scientists have tended to predict more cancers at low doses, while corporate curves have tended to minimize the effect of low-dose exposures.

An extreme form of this argument concerns the existence of threshold levels of carcinogenic exposure. These are exposures below which no cancers will be induced, presumably because our bodies have repair mechanisms that can protect us at low levels of exposure. Progressives have argued that thresholds cannot be demonstrated noting correctly that both animal studies and epidemiology are insensitive to subtle effects occurring at low dose levels. In any case, the argument goes, it theoretically takes just one molecule to induce a malignancy. Opponents have argued that thresholds do exist, based on several considerations: there are recognized cellular repair mechanisms; some carcinogens function at late stages of carcinogenesis (promoters) and may have reversible effects; in some cases carcinogenic exposures seem to induce cancers only when abnormalities like tissue scarring are present.

Here again, scientific theories and data provide precious few certain answers. It surely makes sense, as with animal data, to err on the side of safety, and to proceed as if there were no thresholds. But we need to admit that some of the arguments in favor of thresholds are plausible, and we need to be open-minded on this issue: we may well learn someday that certain carcinogens have thresholds.

The Role of Risk Assessment

This leads to the final question I want to discuss, the role of quantitative risk assessment. This practice is an attempt to characterize dose-response relationships quantitatively, based either on animal data or on epidemiology. The goal is to predict the incremental public health gain achieved by particular regulatory strategies.

Needless to say, the development of risk assessment was driven more by regulatory mandate than by adequate data. In occupational health, for example, the need for risk assessment grew out of the stringent benzene standard proposed by the Occupational Safety and Health Administration (OSHA) in 1977. Industry challenged the standard, claiming that OSHA had failed to demonstrate a "reasonable relationship" between the benefits of the standard and the costs of implementing it. The appeal went to the the Supreme Court, which vacated OSHA's proposed standard.[16] This was interpreted by OSHA and other regulatory agencies as requiring quantitative risk assessment and cost-benefit analysis in subsequent standard-setting.

Accurate quantification of risk requires extensive, precise exposure and outcome data that are almost never available.[17] On this basis alone, there is plenty of reason to doubt the conclusions of quantitative risk assessment. But progressive scientists have pointed to other problems. First, attempts to quantitate effects of low-level exposures may harbor the assumption that some low level is safe, violating the no-threshold argument. Second, certain quantitative risk assessments have purported to demonstrate that politically charged exposures are safe, and even that natural exposures and common foods are more carcinogenic than many industrial contaminants.[18] For example, current evidence indicates that household radon exposure is a far more important cause of cancer in the U.S. than air pollution and contaminated drinking water combined.[19] We may take issue with particular risk assessments, citing inadequate data or arbitrary assumptions, and we will usually be correct. But the very existence of risk assessment suggests a nagging possibility: that exposures with considerable political significance may have a trivial effect on health. Obviously, this would undermine political efforts that depend on the perception of hazard.

There is a larger political challenge in quantitative risk assessment. Implicit in the practice is the assumption that tradeoffs are inevitable and that some cancer risk may be justified by economic or other benefits. Progressive critics have pointed out that those who bear the risks, such as workers, are usually not those who reap the benefits, such as capitalists. Moreover, the assumption of risk in these circumstances is rarely voluntary or informed. Equity considerations therefore compel the argument that workers and communities should not "buy into" risk calculations.

But that position begs the question. In a perfectly egalitarian socialist society, there would in fact be tradeoffs between safety and productivity, and among various social spending options. It is quite conceivable that people in that society would voluntarily assume some cancer risk in return for some other benefits. This tradeoff would be unpleasant and unfortunate, but it is not inherently evil or exploitative. It might even be the case that some workers and community groups would make such a choice today. Progressive scientists, environmentalists, and occupational health workers have been conspicuously reticent to take up these calculations.

Responsibility of Progressive Scientists

In summary, I have suggested that progressive positions on occupational and environmental carcinogenesis have from time to time contained certain problems: arguments that cannot be supported by existing data, a failure to acknowledge the limitations of existing data, and a failure to address some difficult but important dilemmas raised by these matters.

If my observations are correct, at least in part, then they raise the questions of why the problems exist, and how they might be corrected. The cynic might answer this way: progressive scientists are distracted from the dispassionate search for truth by the exigencies of political struggle. Our political views subvert our scientific judgment.

That analysis is both simple and complex. It implies a duality between scientific "truth" and sociopolitical "opinion" that is certainly false.[20] It implies that there is a single correct truth, rather than a multiplicity of viable interpretations. It suggests a range of intriguing insights about the sociology of both science and political activism beyond the scope of this article.

It must also be said, in our defense, that the excesses of progressive scientists pale in comparison to those of corporate interests. Suppression of data, gagging of scientists, and outright prevarication are all well documented.[21] In fact, the debates rarely take place on a level stage; the customs of scientific discourse, in which a hypothesis is assumed false until proven true and a statistically nonsignificant study is equated with a negative study, stacks the odds against a progressive viewpoint.

For all of this, it still seems true that we are sometimes given to excess. There is no virtue to being dispassionate in the face of exploitation, injustice, and preventable suffering. Political activism is not only acceptable; it is necessary. And we should take care never to be paralyzed by excessive caution masquerading as good science. But as we undertake to be activists, we need to be faithful to the facts, and frank about what we don't know. Exaggeration and distortion are unacceptable and in the long run counterproductive. These are the challenges, and the potential, of progressive science.

Notes

1. Agran, L. *The Cancer Connection, And What We Can Do About It* (New York: St. Martin's Press, 1979), p. xvi.

2. Epstein, S. *The Politics of Cancer* (San Francisco: Sierra Club Books, 1978). pp. 21, 15, 8.

3. Silverberg, E. and Lubera, JA. Cancer statistics, 1988. *Ca-A Cancer Journal for Clinicians 1988*; 38:5–22.

4. Bailar, JC and Smith, EM. "Progress against cancer?" *New England Journal of Medicine*, 1986; 314:1226–32.

5. Davis, DL and Schwartz, J. "Trends in cancer mortality: U.S. white males and females, 1986–83." *Lancet* 1988; 1:633–36.

6. Doll, R and Peto, R. *The Causes of Cancer* (New York: Oxford University Press, 1981).
7. Bailar and Smith, op. cit.
8. Higginson, J. "Present trends in cancer epidemiology." *Proceedings of the Canadian Cancer Conference 1969*; 8:40–75
9. Bridbord, K., Decoufle, P., Fraumeni, J.F., Hoel, D.G., Hoover, R.N., Rall, D.P., et al. "Estimates of the fraction of cancer in the United States related to occupational factors." Prepared by NCI, NIEHS, NIOSH. September 15, 1978. Unpublished.
10. See for example, Peto, R. "Distorting the epidemiology of cancer: the need for a more balanced overview." *Nature* 1980; 284:297–300.
11. Doll and Peto, op. cit.
12. See for example Davis, D.L., Bridbord, K. and Schneiderman, M. "Cancer Prevention: assessing causes, exposures, and recent trends in mortality for U.S. males, 1968–78." *Teratogen Carcinogen Mutagen* 1982; 2:105–35.; Davis, D.L., Lilienfeld, A.M., Gittelsohn, A.M. and Scheckenback, M.E. "Increasing trends in some cancers in older Americans: fact or artifact?" *International Journal of Health Serv.* 1988; 18:35–68.; Infante, P.F. and Pohl, G.K. "Living in a chemical world: actions and reactions to industrial carcinogens." *Teratogen Carcinogen Mutagen* 1988; 8:225–49.
13. Wynder, E.L. and Gori, G.B. "Contribution of the environment to cancer incidence: an epidemiological exercise." *Journal of the National Cancer Institute* 1977; 58:825–32.
14. See, for example Tye, J.B., Warner, K.E. and Glantz, S.A. "Tobacco advertising and consumption: evidence of a causal relationship." *Journal of Public Health Policy* 1987; 8:492–508; Whelan, E.M., Sheridan, M.J., Meister, K.A. and Mosher, B.A. "Analysis of coverage of tobacco hazards in women's magazines" *Journal of Public Health Policy 1981*, 2:28–35; Sterling, T.D. "Does smoking kill workers or working kill smokers? or the mutual relationship between smoking, occupation, and respiratory disease." *International Journal of Health Serv 1978*; 8:4347–52. But thumb through the pages of *International Journal of Health Services, Health/PAC Bulletin*, or *Science for the People*; you'll find surprisingly little on tobacco.
15. See, for example, two recent papers on asbestos, both by Kevin Browne: "Is asbestos or asbestosis the cause of the increased risk of lung cancer in asbestos workers?" *British Journal of Ind. Medicine* 1986; 43:145–49, and "A threshold for asbestos related lung cancer," *Brit J Ind Med* 1986; 43:556–58.
16. Industrial Union Department v. American Petroleum Institute, 448 U.S. Supreme Court (1980), p. 607.
17. See, for example, Schneiderman, M.A., "Expectation and limitation of human studies and risk assessment," in *Health Effects from Hazardous Waste Sites*, ed. by Andelman, J.B. and Underhill, D.W. (Chelsea MI: Lewis Publishers, 1987); Peto, R., "Epidemiologic reservations about risk assessment," in *Assessment of Risk from Low-Level Exposure to Radiation and Chemicals*, ed. by Woodhead, A.D., Shellebarger, C.J., Pond, V. and Hollaender, A., (New York: Plenum, 1985); Freedman, D.A. and Zeisel, H., "From mouse to man: the quantitative assessment of cancer risk" (unpublished manuscript, Statistics Department, University of California, Berkeley, 1986).
18. Ames, B.N., Magaw, R. and Gold, L.S. "Ranking possible carcinogenic hazards," *Science* 1987; 236:271–280. See correspondence in *Science* 1988; 240:1043–47.
19. Committee on the Biological Effects of Ionizing Radiation, *Health Risks of Radon and Other Internally Deposited Alpha-Emitters* (BEIR IV) (Washington: National Academy Press, 1988).
20. This issue is discussed in depth by a variety of authors. See, for example: Easlea, B., *Liberation and the Aims of Science* (London: Chatto & Windus, 1973); Rose, H. and Rose, S., "The myth of the neutrality of science," in *Science and Liberation*, ed. by Arditti, R., Brennan, P., and Cavrak, S. (Boston: South End Press, 1980); and a recent work focused on

public health, Tesh, S.N., *Hidden Arguments: Political Ideology and Disease Prevention Policy* (New Brunswick: Rutgers University Press, 1988).

21. See, for example, Brodeur P. *Outrageous Misconduct: The Asbestos Industry on Trial* (New York: Pantheon, 1985).

After reading: CONSOLIDATE INFORMATION

1. Throughout his article Professor Frumkin refers to "progressive scientists." What is your understanding of the term? To what group of scientists is Frumkin referring?
2. How does Frumkin analyze the political implications of occupational and environmental cancer rates?
3. How would you summarize Frumkin's major argument?

Low-Level Radioactive Waste: Gamma Rays in the Garbage
Scott Saleska

The following article appeared in The Bulletin of the Atomic Scientist, *a publication of the Educational Foundation for Nuclear Science. The audience for articles in the* Bulletin *is widely read and well-educated, and includes scientists and experts as well as non-experts. Scott Saleska is a scientist and scientific policy analyst.*

Before reading: FIRST THOUGHTS
    LOOK AHEAD

1. From Saleska's title, what can you predict about his article? What kind of reader do you think he is addressing?
2. What do you think the term *low-level radioactive waste* means? Is it dangerous?
3. What do you think is the source of most low-level radioactive waste in the United States?

During reading: REACT
    QUESTION
    SUMMARIZE

1. React to Saleska's suggestion that some low-level radioactive waste has been dumped in landfills that take the usual household garbage.
2. What kinds of problems have affected low-level waste sites in the United States?

THE U.S. GOVERNMENT in late 1989 admitted that it would have to revamp and delay its plans to build a dump for highly radioactive nuclear waste at Yucca Mountain, Nevada. The Nevada repository was to be the final resting place for spent fuel from commercial reactors, which has been stored temporarily on reactor sites since the advent of nuclear power, and for high-level waste left over from weapons production. The government's disposal scheme for another category of radioactive defense waste, the "transuranics," also ran into trouble due to environmental problems at the planned Carlsbad, New Mexico, dump site.

But the radioactive garbage issue that is attracting more and more public concern involves a third category—"low-level" radioactive waste. Under the federal Low-Level Radioactive Waste Policy Act, passed in 1980 and amended significantly in 1985, individual states are required to handle their own waste or join with other states to manage it collectively. So far, nine state associations, or "compacts," have been formed. At least three states—Texas, New York, and Massachusetts—have chosen to go it alone, however, and in early February New York's Governor Mario Cuomo announced a suit challenging the constitutionality of the law.

Citizens faced with radioactive dumps in their communities are beginning to realize that low-level waste, despite its benign description, does not necessarily mean low-level risk. Physicist and former nuclear weapons designer Ted Taylor, who lives in New York State, began looking into the waste issue about a year ago and discovered that the "low-level" category includes such intensely radioactive materials as reactor components that would deliver in a few minutes a lethal dose of gamma rays to anyone standing nearby.

"I was astonished," Taylor said. "And then I became angry—both at myself for not realizing the nature of the so-called low-level waste sooner and at the whole system that makes it all sound so innocuous."

Even as more questions are being raised about low-level radioactive waste, the federal government has drawn up plans to deregulate one-third or more of this category. Waste with such low levels of radioactivity as to be "below regulatory concern" (BRC) could then be disposed of in the same ways as other solid or liquid waste: through incineration, dumping in municipal landfills, or down the drain and into the sewer.

Diane D'Arrigo, a nuclear waste specialist at the Nuclear Information and Resource Service, a public interest group based in Washington, D.C., says that BRC serves only to help industry reduce its waste management costs. She calls it "a blatant subsidy to the nuclear industry at the expense of public health and worker safety."

MISCELLANEOUS RADIOACTIVE JUNK

Up to now, however, radioactive waste has been defined as nearly all waste material with any measurable amounts of radioactivity. The U.S. government recognizes four categories of radioactive waste, which are based more on how the waste was generated than on how dangerous it is or how it should be handled. As a result, some categories overlap, others must be subdivided, and the public is often confused.

- **Uranium mill tailings** are what is left over after uranium is extracted from raw uranium ore. The radioactivity of the gray, fine-grained material is relatively low but very long-lived, over 100,000 years. Mill tailings account for 96 percent of the volume of radioactive waste, although their radioactivity is a minuscule fraction of the total.
- **High-level waste** is intensely radioactive material that requires heavy shielding in order to protect those who handle it against its penetrating radiation and intense heat. There are two types: Defense high-level waste is mostly liquid, generated by the "reprocessing" of spent reactor fuel to extract plutonium for weapons. Disposing of this waste is the responsibility of the Energy Department. Commercial high-level waste consists of the used fuel rods from commercial nuclear power reactors. At the present all of these spent-fuel assemblies, which are more radioactive than any other kind of waste, are stored in ponds on reactor sites, awaiting a permanent disposal site.
- **Transuranic waste** is waste material generated during the production of nuclear weapons that is contaminated with significant amounts of elements such as plutonium, whose atomic numbers are greater than that of uranium. All transuranic elements are unstable, most of them are alpha-emitters, and many have very long half-lives. Because of the special disposal problems these materials present, transuranic waste was defined as a special category in 1970. Before that, much of it had been included in "low-level" waste, because it consists largely of equipment, clothes, and trash contaminated during reprocessing operations
- A better term for the last category, called **low-level waste,** might be "miscellaneous radioactive junk," because it is by definition everything that is not included in the other three categories.

The Low-Level Radioactive Waste Policy Act governs commercial low-level waste, which consists mostly of radioactively contaminated clothing and equipment from nuclear power plants, industry, medical applications, and research. (The Energy Department is responsible for low-level defense wastes.) It can include anything from intensely radioactive cooling-water filters from a power plant, to mops used to clean up a slightly radioactive spill, to obsolete instruments used to diagnose and treat cancer patients. Although much of this waste contains only low levels of radioactivity, some of it is highly radioactive, and it can include items contaminated with elements that remain radioactive for a very long time.

Recognizing this, government regulations establish four classes of low-level waste—A, B, C, and "greater than C"—and require different disposal standards for each. Strangely, "greater-than-class-C-low-level waste" might be as much as three times more radioactive than high-level waste generated during the production of nuclear weapons materials. The Nuclear Regulatory Commission (NRC) has recommended that greater-than-C waste be disposed of along with high-level wastes in a deep geologic repository. Under the low-level waste law, states do not have to deal with greater-than-C wastes, but they can do so if they wish.

Opponents of the new dumps worry that the term "low-level waste" conjures an image of mildly radioactive trash that does not pose much of a health risk. "The mere fact that this stuff is even called 'low level' is a major public relations coup by the nuclear industry," says Steve Meyers, chairman of the Concerned Citizens of Allegany County, a New York State group opposing a low-level waste dump that may be sited there.

Deregulating Nuclear Waste

No one knows exactly how much commercial low-level radioactive waste is generated each year in the United States, but the Energy Department keeps records on how much is disposed of. In 1988, about 1.4 million cubic feet of low-level waste, containing over a quarter of a million curies of radioactivity, was deposited in the country's three operating commercial low-level waste landfills. In all, about 45 million cubic feet of such waste has been deposited since commercial dumps began operating in the early 1960s. These amounts are not exceptionally large in terms of volume—by comparison, about 13 billion cubic feet of hazardous chemical waste was dumped in 1988—but their potential hazard is enormous.

Over two-thirds of the volume and over 80 percent of the radioactivity of commercial low-level waste disposed today comes from the nuclear power industry. This share will increase in the future, as decommissioning (the permanent shut-down and dismantlement) of nuclear plants generates huge amounts of radioactive waste which will fall into the low-level category. The Energy Department projects that between 1988 and 2020, nearly 80 percent of the volume and 97 percent of the radioactivity of low-level waste will come from nuclear power plants.[1]

The prospect of having to dispose of entire reactors has lent support to the little-known "below regulatory concern" (BRC) policy, which has been in the works since the early 1980s. It means that by late this year, one-third or more of what is now classified as low-level radioactive waste could be reclassified as regular garbage and sent, along with banana peels and coffee grounds, to local municipal garbage facilities.

The Energy Department considers BRC a prerequisite for a serious reactor decommissioning program.[2] The nuclear industry also favors the policy, and according to one utility think tank, deregulation could save the nuclear power industry about $1 billion over the next 20 years, largely by reducing the amount of waste from dismantled reactors that would require special disposal.[3] Another major area where waste deregulation could have sweeping implications is in the impending cleanup of the government's heavily contaminated nuclear weapons production complex. As one government official recently told Congress, "One of the biggest wildcards in determining the cost of cleanup at [Energy Department] facilities is the ... promulgation of BRC standards."[4]

Measures of Radioactivity and Exposure

THE CURIE, named after Marie and Pierre Curie, who discovered radium in 1898, is the basic unit of radioactivity. It is based on the amount of radioactivity in 1 gram of pure radium: the equivalent of the emission of 37 billion rays or particles per second. The more radioactive a substance is, the less of it is needed to make a curie. One curie of plutonium, for example, is 16 grams; a curie of strontium 90 is only one two-hundredth of a gram. A curie of thorium, which is very mildly radioactive, is 19,800 pounds.

A *megacurie* is a million curies. A millionth of a curie is a *microcurie*; a *nanocurie* is a billionth, and a *picocurie* is a trillionth. A large reactor core may contain over 10,000 megacuries. By contrast, there is about a nanocurie of radioactivity in common household smoke detectors. But small amounts can be biologically significant. The Washington University School of Medicine in Missouri, for example, requires decontamination if as little as 45 picocuries is found on a lab surface.

The time it takes for a radioactive substance to decay to a stable element is measured in terms of radioactive *half-life:* the average amount of time that it will take for half of the substance to decay. (After two half-lives, one fourth of the radionuclides remain, and so on.)

Exposure to radiation is discussed in terms of *rads* and *rems.* The rad ("radiation absorbed dose") is the amount of radiation that deposits 100 ergs of energy on a gram of material. The rem ("roentgen-equivalent man") is less precise. It is based on the rad but is modified to take into account the different biological effects of different kinds of ionizing radiation. For beta and gamma radiation, the dose in rads is generally about equal to the dose in rems, but radiation absorbed from alpha particles is more biologically damaging, so a one-rad dose from an alpha emitter is considered equal to 20 rems.

—S.S.

The NRC claims that the health risk associated with BRC is minimal and would be "of little concern to most members of society."[5] What the NRC claims is acceptable is an annual fatal cancer risk of one in 100,000 to the exposed population. Regardless of whether one considers this ask "acceptable," recent scientific data suggest radiation risks may be five or more times greater than the NRC's assumptions. Partly for this reason, even the Environmental Protection Agency, which is working on BRC standards of its own, referred to some provisions of the NRC policy as "totally inappropriate."[6]

But costs for low-level waste disposal have skyrocketed from about $2 per cubic foot ten years ago to about $40 per cubic foot today, and the cost is expected to be even higher at many of the planned new disposal sites. "It is not practical to dispose of BRC material in an engineered state-of-the-art low-level radioactive waste disposal facility when the material is equal to or slightly above background," says Donald Hughes, a Kentucky radiation control official. "Background" refers to the levels of radiation experienced every day from natural sources.

Critics point out that standard risk-benefit procedure would compare only the costs and benefits of the activity in question, not unrelated risks such as natural radiation. Thomas Cochran of the Natural Resources Defense Council says that by NRC logic "it is 'BRC' to randomly fire a bullet into a crowded Manhattan street on the basis that the individual risk to a person in New York City is less than one in several million."

The biggest practical problem with a general policy of deregulating radioactive waste is its potential for abuse. If large amounts of mildly radioactive waste are regularly allowed into the local garbage dump, abuses will be very difficult to detect. Since the NRC does not plan to monitor radiation levels at unregulated disposal sites, there will be no easy way to confirm that even the NRC's "acceptable" levels are not being exceeded.

So far, about four dozen counties and municipalities around the United States have passed resolutions opposing BRC. Maine has passed legislation prohibiting radioactive waste deregulation within its borders, and a similar bill is being considered in Massachusetts.

A History of Problems

Of the nation's original six low-level radioactive waste sites, only three are still operating, and two of these are slated to be closed in 1993 because they will be full.

Today, most commercial low-level wastes are buried a few feet below the surface in landfills. The history of shallow burial of radioactive waste in landfills is a checkered one, however. It began with the licensing of a site in Beatty, Nevada, in 1962, followed by Maxey Flats, Kentucky, and West Valley, New York, in 1963; Richland, Washington, next door to the nuclear weapons material production site, in 1965; Sheffield, Illinois, in 1967; and Barnwell, South Carolina, in 1971. Three of these sites—Maxey Flats, Sheffield, and West Valley—have been closed. Maxey Flats and West Valley were shut down because of environmental problems. Although Sheffield was originally closed when it was filled to capacity, similar environmental problems there subsequently have become apparent.

Maxey Flats's problems are particularly instructive. The site in northeast Kentucky is cut by tributaries of the Licking River, which feeds into the Ohio River—a major water supply for half a million people. Nine years after the site was opened, the Kentucky Radiation Control Branch discovered radionuclides escaping from the site, and two years later, plutonium contamination was detected beyond the site boundaries. The state finally closed the site in 1977, and the EPA declared it a Superfund site in 1986. But unless the burial trenches, which are up to 700 feet long, can be permanently capped to keep water out, Kentucky faces a problem that may never end, since plutonium has a 24,000-year half-life. Federal regulations now limit the burial of plutonium and other transuranics at low-level waste sites, but other long-lived radioactive elements continue to be allowed.

Management lapses have caused other serious problems. At the Beatty site, the Nevada government discovered that the disposal facility was known to local residents as "the store," because anyone who wished to could purchase from the site workers contaminated tools and materials that had been slated for burial. After the practice was discovered and halted in 1976, state health inspectors went door to door with radiation detectors, collecting thousands of radioactive items—clocks, watches, compasses, tools, electric motors—that should have been in the dump. In backyards and ranches outside of town, inspectors found 23 metal tanks that had once contained radioactive waste but had been converted to septic or water tanks. The cement floor behind the town's Sourdough saloon was found to be radioactive and had to be torn up.[7]

Officials closed Beatty for three months and fined the dump operator $10,000. The operator was the Nuclear Engineering Company (NECO), now U.S. Ecology—the same company that operated Maxey Flats and now plans to build and operate new sites slated for Nebraska and California. NECO fired the workers involved and promised to make sweeping changes in dump operations. Problems continued to plague the site for several years, however, and in 1979, shipping accidents and discoveries of waste buried outside the dump site prompted Gov. Robert List to close the site temporarily.

The Scramble for New Sites

The states will have their hands full meeting the stipulations of the Low-Level Radioactive Waste Policy Act, which requires them to find a place by 1996 to dump low-level waste generated within their borders, or else to accept full liability for it. Most states have joined one of the nine "compacts" which have been formed to share the responsibility. But as the states have banded together, local groups have quickly formed to raise serious questions about the plans, or oppose them outright. And some of the opposition has come from state officials as well.

Neighbors of proposed dumpsites are skeptical when waste disposal companies who are vying to build the next generation of nuclear dumps insist that leaking and mismanaged radioactive landfills are things of the past. In Illinois, Westinghouse Corp. won the waste disposal contract but confirmed residents' fears when it refused to take full liability for any accidents or leaks at the dump. When the state insisted, Westinghouse pulled out.

"On the one hand, they tell us there is nothing to worry about," says Eleanor Towns, spokeswoman for Wayne County's Individuals for a Clean Environment. "Yet on the other, they are unwilling to put their money where their mouth is and accept financial responsibility if something goes wrong. They're willing to ask our lives, but they won't risk their money."

Chem-Nuclear Systems, Inc., a Westinghouse competitor, stepped in, declaring its willingness to accept full liability. That is fine with the state of Illinois, which believes that liability will give Chem-Nuclear an incentive to operate the dump safely. "We're very pleased to have Chem-Nuclear on the project," says Tom Kerr, chief of the low-level waste division in Illinois's Department of Nuclear Safety. "Chem-Nuclear has the best track record in the field . . . and will use its assets to back its commitment to excellence."

But Hugh Kaufman, a maverick waste disposal expert at the EPA, describes Chem-Nuclear as a "smoke and mirrors corporation" with few assets. "If something goes wrong," Kaufman warns, "there'll be few damages to collect. The victims and the state will once again be left holding the bag." Chem-Nuclear operates the Barnwell site and has contracted to establish at least one other site besides the Illinois dump.

Inconsistencies in federal regulations governing the disposal of the waste raise other concerns. The NRC requires that access to a low-level disposal facility remain under institutional control for 100 years after it ceases to operate, during which period the radioactivity in most of the waste (classes A and B) will supposedly decay to acceptable levels. A small portion of the waste, class C, is defined as "500-year" waste and must be buried deeper.

Simple calculations show, however, that some mixtures of radioactive materials allowed in the "100-year" category will actually be hazardously radioactive, even according to NRC definitions, for hundreds of years. For example, the regulations allow 100-year class B waste to contain nickel 63 in concentrations of up to 70 curies per cubic meter. Because nickel 63 has a half-life of about 100 years, it will take well over 400 years to decay to class A levels of 3.5 curies per cubic meter—still hazardous enough to keep it buried for another 100 years. Some so-called 500-year waste will remain radioactive enough to be in that NRC category for over half a million years.

In January 1989, Gov. James Blanchard of Michigan halted the search for a disposal site in his state and threatened to pull Michigan out of the seven-state Midwest regional compact because he believed other states in the compact would not pay their fair share. A month later he backed down, after his neighbors assured him they would share the financial burden—and especially after the three states hosting existing dumps threatened to ban Michigan's waste from their dumps. But Blanchard's action illustrates the instability of the current situation. One state official said Blanchard "was in danger of bringing down a real house of cards."[8]

Losing access to existing dump sites is one of the stiff penalties that await any state failing to follow the provisions of the low-level waste law. The ultimate penalty, however, is liability: any state that has not made arrangements to dispose of low-level waste by 1996, at the latest, must accept title to all waste generated, and can be held liable for any damages resulting from failure to dispose of the waste. If a business that generates waste is forced to close because there is nowhere to put the waste, the state may be held accountable.

State organizations—the National Governors' Association and the National Council of State Legislatures—explicitly asked Congress in 1980 to give states responsibility for managing their waste. But some feel Congress may have gone too far. Partly because of the liability provision, and in response to pressure from citizens, Gov. Mario Cuomo and New York Attorney General Robert Abrams have brought suit challenging the constitutionality of the federal law. The action failed to appease protesters. "I think that by the time this lawsuit is settled someone will already have that dump in their backyard," said Sally Campbell, a member of the Allegany County Nonviolent Action Group.[9]

What is Ionizing Radiation?

GENERALLY, IN STABLE (NONRADIOACTIVE) ATOMS, the number of protons in the nucleus is about equal to the number of neutrons. If there is more of one particle than the other, the atom is likely to be unstable and therefore radioactive—it will at some point *decay* into a different atom, emitting a ray or particle of *ionizing radiation* in the process.

When a radioactive atom (often called a *radionuclide*) emits radiation, it decays into a different element, or a different isotope of the same element (same number of protons, different number of neutrons). The resulting atom may also be unstable, and decay into another. Radioactive uranium 238, for example, eventually decays into stable lead 206, but usually with 13 different radioactive isotopes as intermediate links.

The ray or particle emitted by a radionuclide is typically an *alpha particle*, a *beta particle*, or a *gamma ray*, depending on the physical characteristics of the radionuclide. Alpha particles (helium nuclei with two protons and two neutrons) are the heaviest and least penetrating type of radiation, gamma rays (similar to X-rays) are the lightest and most penetrating, while beta particles fall in between. Gamma rays are generally most hazardous when the source of radiation is outside the body: they may require inches or even feet of lead or concrete to stop them. Alpha particles, on the other hand, cannot even penetrate skin, but once an alpha-emitting substance such as plutonium is inhaled or ingested, the particles can cause far more damage than equivalent amounts of other radiation.

—S.S.

NEW POLICIES NEEDED

Low-level waste has raised a whole new set of hard questions about the need for nuclear power. The obvious solution to this problem is to phase out nuclear power. But even without eliminating nuclear power entirely, a number of steps can be taken to deal sensibly with the problem:

- Withdraw the current inconsistent NRC standards, draw up new standards, and begin treating low-level wastes as the dangerous wastes they are. Sweden and West Germany dispose of these wastes in deep underground repositories rather than allowing them to be buried in landfills a few feet underground. The same should be done in the United States. At a minimum, the more hazardous and long-lived class C and greater-than-C wastes should be slated for eventual disposal with high-level waste.
- In the meantime, store low-level waste retrievably at reactor sites. Nuclear plants are already de facto radioactive dumps, and they will be the source of most low-level waste over the next 30 years. It makes little sense to go through the divisive process of siting and contaminating a dozen new waste dumps that are not necessary in the first place.

Even the nuclear industry recognizes that low-level waste dumps now planned by the states are far more than is needed and could result in soaring disposal costs. Most analysts believe that three or four sites would probably be adequate. And if some already contaminated reactor sites were made into permanent disposal sites, no further sites would be needed.

- Halt all efforts to classify certain radioactive wastes as "below regulatory concern."

Low-level waste must be seen as another part of the larger, intractable problem of nuclear waste. Ted Taylor reflects: "I used to think that it was politically difficult because of the NIMBY [not in my backyard] syndrome, but that technically it was probably solvable. Well, I don't think that anymore. I don't see any evidence of a solution that we can say with certainty will get rid of this stuff safely."

Notes

1. U.S. Energy Department, *Integrated Database for 1989: Spent Fuel and Radioactive Waste Inventories, Projections, and Characteristics*, DOE/RW-0006, rev. 5 (1989).

2. U.S. Energy Department, *Integrated Database for 1988: Spent Fuel and Radioactive Waste Inventories, Projections, and Characteristics*, DOE/RW-0006, rev. 4 (Sept. 1988), p. 173.

3. Jonathan Simon, "Wasting Away," *Public Citizen* (Feb. 1989).

4. Leo Duffy, cited by Lynda Taylor, "DOE and BRC: Will the Military's 'Low-Level' Nukewaste Go Public Too?" *The Workbook*, vol. 14, no. 2 (Albuquerque: Southwest Research and Information Center, April-June 1989), p. 50.

5. U.S. Environmental Protection Agency, *Statement on the Nuclear Regulatory Commission's Proposed Policy for Exemptions from Regulatory Control* (Jan. 12, 1989).

6. U.S. Nuclear Regulatory commission, "Policy Statement on Exemptions from Regulatory Control," *Federal Register*, vol. 53, no. 238 (Dec. 12, 1988), p. 49889.

7. U.S. House of Representatives, *Low-Level Radioactive Waste Disposal*, hearings before a subcommittee of the Committee on Government Operations, 94th Cong., 2d sess. (1976); David Foster, "Nevada Town Sees Nuke Waste Dump as 'Good Neighbor,'" Associated Press, March 10, 1989.

8. "Michigan Governor Reverses Pull-Out from LLW Compact," *Nucleonics Week* (March 9, 1989), p. 4.

9. Sam Howe Verhovek, "New York to Fight Nuclear Dump Law," New York Times, Feb. 10, 1990.

After reading: CONSOLIDATE INFORMATION

1. What does a Below Regulatory Concern (BRC) policy mean?
2. What are the economic implications of a BRC policy?
3. Summarize Saleska's suggested solutions to the problem of disposing of low-level radioactive waste.

Catching Some Rays: Earth-Based Detectors Hunt for Violent Stellar Events

Ron Cowen

This article appeared in Science News, *a journalistic digest of reports on new research in science for an audience of non-specialists.*

Before reading: FIRST THOUGHTS
       LOOK AHEAD

1. Read the title and the first two paragraphs of this article. What predictions can you make about the rest of the report?
2. What are gamma rays?
3. Why do you think the task of searching for high-energy gamma rays now unites astronomers and cosmic physicists?

During reading: REACT
       QUESTION
       SUMMARIZE

1. Why would the discovery of particles at energies higher than accelerators can produce cause scientists to search for gamma rays?
2. What do you think scientists hope to learn from their collection of high-energy gamma rays?

It's A Moonless Night as dozens of garbage-can-shaped devices face the sky from a desert bluff in central Utah. Each of these mirrored sentinels waits to witness a dim blue flash—leftover energy from some of the most violent collisions in our galaxy and beyond.

This array of instruments is just one of many that search for the telltale fingerprints left by cosmic rays penetrating Earth's atmosphere. At energies of up to 100 billion billion electron-volts, cosmic rays rain upon our planet from the depths of the Milky Way and from stars hundreds of thousands of light-years beyond.

The rays come in two varieties. Most are charged particles (ions), while a tiny minority encompass energetic, uncharged particles of light—photons called gamma rays. Believed to be created during such cataclysmic events as supernova explosions and galactic collisions, both types of cosmic rays represent, quite simply, the most energetic particles in the universe.

Since the 1980s, several types of ground-based detectors—most of them surprisingly simple in design—have detected cosmic rays one million times more energetic than any generated by the world's most powerful atom smasher—the Fermi National Accelerator Laboratory's tevatron particle accelerator in Batavia, Ill. Indeed, notes University of Chicago physicist Leslie J. Rosenberg, searching for cosmic rays—particularly high-energy gamma rays—is now uniting astronomers and particle physicists in a common pursuit.

"The study of astrophysical sources has traditionally been the exclusive domain of astrophysics," he notes. "Particle production and decays have traditionally been the exclusive domain of particle physics ... [But] at sufficiently high energies, particle production and decays become prominent features of astrophysical sources, and the two fields of study intertwine."

In fact, since 1988 researchers have puzzled over observations that suggest very-high-energy gamma rays have properties similar to energetic ions. Findings from several independent research groups all suggest that new physical phenomena may emerge at high energies—either an elementary particle never before discovered or unexpected behavior by photons (SN: 10/29/88, p.276).

Gamma rays make up less than one-hundredth of 1 percent of all high-energy cosmic rays, particles associated primarily with such exotic objects as neutron stars, supernovas, quasars, exploding galaxies and the long-sought black holes. But scientists say that searching for gamma rays has a distinct advantage. Most charged cosmic rays form a diffuse, uniform background that offers few clues to the site of their stellar or galactic birthplaces. The straight-line path of gamma rays more readily indicates their precise origin (see box).

Cosmic-ray investigators caution that after nearly two decades of observations, they have pinpointed only a few possible sources of energetic gamma rays. "The field of ultra-high-energy gamma-ray astronomy is in its infancy," declares Jordan A. Goodman of the University of Maryland at College Park. But if new, more sensitive detectors can verify the 1988 reports from the Whipple Observatory near Amado, Ariz., the Haleakala Gamma Ray Observatory in Hawaii and the CYGNUS experiment at Los Alamos (N.M.) National Laboratory, scientists may find themselves grappling with a cosmic mystery: why high-energy gamma rays begin to masquerade as charged cosmic rays.

The Gamma Ray Observatory launched April 6, [1991] may further spark interest in ground-based gamma-ray studies. Carrying the four largest scientific instruments ever flown in space, this orbiting observatory promises to reveal a myriad of new findings over its anticipated four-year life. Its quest includes the search for telltale radiation from such exotic objects as pulsars, quasars and black holes (massive objects believed to exist but never yet detected). The orbiting laboratory will also attempt to measure the balance between matter and antimatter

Cosmic Rain Gauges

BENT, KICKED AND ACCELERATED by galactic magnetic fields, a typical charged cosmic ray travels a zig-zag path for millions of years before striking Earth's atmosphere. Such meandering particles—mostly hydrogen ions—have no "memory" of the violent, highly energetic collisions that spawned them.

Not so gamma rays. Born in the same violent reactions, these cosmic-ray photons carry no charge, and therefore cannot be deflected by magnetic or electric fields.

Traveling in a straight line from their source, the path of gamma rays indicates the nature and location of the cataclysmic events that created them. Physicists believe that many of the highest energy gammas derive from charged particles, such as energetic protons near a rapidly rotating star system. When these particles slam into other charged particles, another class of elementary particles—neutral pions—are born. Neutral pions rapidly decay into gamma rays.

Only space-borne detectors, such as those aboard NASA's Gamma Ray Observatory, can directly catch these photons, since any gammas able to penetrate the Earth's atmosphere rapidly self-destruct, forming other particles. However, space-borne instruments are usually limited to recording rays with energies smaller than about 10 billion electron volts (10 GeV). The dramatically lower abundance of gammas with higher energies allows most to elude the relatively small collecting area of orbiting detectors.

Fortunately, these higher energy gammas do penetrate Earth's atmosphere. Their interaction with gas molecules there generates charged secondary particles and an air shower of photons that can be detected with large, ground-based instruments.

In order of ascending energies, physicists classify gammas that penetrate the atmosphere into three categories: very-high-energy (100 to 100,000 GeV), ultra-high energy (10^5 to 10^7 GeV) and extremely high energy (10^8 to 10^{11} GeV).

As they die out in the atmosphere, extremely high-energy gamma rays (and similarly energetic charged cosmic rays) excite nitrogen atoms to fluoresce. Mirrored detectors trained on the night sky can infer the existence of such gammas from a telltale flash of blue light and attempt to pinpoint their source.

In contrast, ultra-high-energy gamma rays don't incite much fluorescence. But they do undergo fatal interactions with the atmosphere at an altitude of about 20 kilometers, generating a falling cascade of charged particles. These particles eventually fan out to shower a large pancake-shaped area of Earth's surface. With arrays of plastic scintillators on the ground, astronomers can not only "observe" the charged particles but also infer the location and incoming angle of their parent gamma rays.

For slightly less energetic gammas, those in the very-high-energy range, ground-based arrays of particle detectors prove useless, because the atmosphere absorbs all of the charged secondary particles. Before these

> secondaries vanish, however, the speedy particles emit a visible bluish-white light, known as Cerenkov radiation, along the direction of motion. Specially equipped ground-based telescopes seek out these Cerenkov flashes that signal the annihilation of very-high-energy gamma rays.
>
> —R. Cowen

in the universe. Moreover, the observatory's location above Earth's atmosphere enables its instruments to directly detect gamma rays, rather than having to infer their presence from secondary particles.

Like all space-borne technology, however, this observatory has limitations: It can study only "medium-energy" gamma rays—those with energies up to 10 billion electron-volts (10 GeV). Particles generated close to a neutron star, a rapidly spinning binary-star system, or other seat of celestial power may have even higher energies—a discriminating characteristic of the universe's most violent territories. But at energies greater than about 10 billion GeV the rain of photons and charged particles they emit slows to a trickle. The limited collecting area of space-orbiting devices therefore makes detection of them all but impossible.

Trevor C. Weekes of the Whipple Observatory and other researchers hope, however, that findings from the new orbiting observatory will uphold an old adage: Where there's smoke, there's fire. These scientists hope that the observatory's expected discovery of several hundred new medium-energy gamma ray sources may identify areas of the sky likely to emit higher-energy photons—gamma rays whose presence can be inferred only from Earth.

Observes Weekes: "By a happy accident of nature, just where space-borne detectors become impractical, ground-based techniques, which use Earth's atmosphere as the detection medium, become feasible."

Progress in cosmic-ray physics has proven slow since the field's birth in 1911. Nonetheless, for the first several decades, "catching some rays" proved a riveting adventure.

The quest for cosmic rays began in western Europe. Father Theodor Wulf, a Jesuit priest and amateur scientist in Paris, set up a pioneering experiment atop the Eiffel Tower. In Austria, a young physicist named Victor Hess ascended several miles in a hot air balloon. Working independently, both men succeeded in their goal: the first evidence for particles later dubbed cosmic rays.

Laboratory experiments had previously demonstrated that energetic radiation strips electrons from atoms in a gas, permitting these ionized atoms to conduct electricity. Relying on this phenomenon, Hess and Wulf probed the atmosphere with an electroscope, two thin gold leaves suspended from a common point inside a gas-filled, electrically insulated container. An electric charge initially stored on the surface of the leaves causes them to repel each other and move apart; but as incoming radiation ionizes gas inside the electroscope, the charge leaks away and the leaves come back together. The faster the leaves return to their original position, the stronger the radiation source.

Taking his electroscope aloft, Hess found that above 5,000 feet, the radiation steadily increased its intensity—to several times ground levels at 17,500 feet, the maximum altitude of the physicist's balloon. This "extra-terrestrial source of penetrating radiation," as Hess termed it, represented the first evidence of cosmic rays.

Throughout the 1930s and 1940s, scores of young physicists scaled mountaintops in an effort to record ever higher energy cosmic-ray showers striking Earth. Some of the scientists braved blizzards, and a few froze to death trying to capture the shower of high-speed atomic nuclei generated by cosmic rays. Their rewards included the discovery of a new zoo of elementary particles: kaons, pions and muons.

In the following decades, most high-energy physicists switched their allegiance from the heavens to the laboratory as particle accelerators—highly efficient generators of energetic particles—became standard research tools. Why study the unpredictable cosmic rain when a researcher could make as many high-energy particles as desired, and with just the right energy, inside a heated building?

Beginning in the 1970s, gamma-ray astronomy launched a comeback. The few diehards who had never abandoned their cosmic-ray studies reported finding many particles at energies far higher than accelerators could produce. Scientists once again turned skyward, searching for gamma rays.

These studies required several types of instruments. None directly detects the rays, since the photons self-destruct to form pairs of oppositely charged ions some 20 kilometers above Earth's surface. But the variety of devices, each tailored to track the activity of gamma rays of different energy share a common principle: They wait to see the light.

For example, 67 cylindrical detectors, each outfitted with a large mirror that focuses light onto several photomultiplier tubes, sit atop a hill at the Army's Dugway (Utah) Proving Ground. Every detector surveys a different portion of the night sky waiting for a faint bluish glow—the hallmark of 10^8 to 10^{11} GeV particles, the most energetic cosmic rays known. A fluorescence signals their collision with nitrogen atoms in the air.

Two miles away, a smaller array of identical detectors stands at attention, recording atmospheric fluorescence from atoms at up to 10 kilometers altitude. Designed at the University of Utah in Salt Lake City and known as Fly's Eye I and II, the multi-mirror arrays, which can operate only on dark, moonless nights, emulate the compound character of insect eyes. Together, the two detectors help distinguish signals produced by cosmic gamma rays from spurious light emitted by nearby sources.

Several other detectors at the Dugway site detect lower-energy gamma rays. A collection of 1,089 plastic scintillators surround Fly's Eye II. A project completed last month by the University of Chicago and known as the Chicago Air Shower Array, these detectors cover 250,000 square meters—the largest grouping of their kind in the world. Night and day, they record cosmic showers induced by gamma rays a few notches down in energy from those detected by Fly's Eye—about 10^5 to 10^7 GeV.

Though not energetic enough to make nitrogen glow, these gamma rays do induce a cylindrically shaped stream of charged secondary particles that induce a flash when they strike the plastic scintillators. The incoming angle and intensity of this shower helps astronomers pinpoint the celestial source of the gamma rays.

Buried three meters below the Dugway site lies yet another group of instruments, this set designed by researchers at the University of Michigan in Ann Arbor. The 16 underground detectors count muons—elementary particles that resemble heavier versions of the electron—during cosmic-ray showers. A relative paucity of muons indicates that a gamma ray likely induced the particle shower detected above ground; an abundance of muons suggests charged cosmic rays created the shower.

Surveying gamma rays at the same energies as the Chicago array, a set of 202 scintillators spreads over 85,000 square meters atop a plateau at Los Alamos National Laboratory. Known as CYGNUS, this joint venture of research groups from Los Alamos, Argonne (Ill.) National Laboratory, the University of Maryland at College Park, the University of California in Irvine and Santa Cruz, and George Mason University in Fairfax, Va., also includes muon detectors buried under six feet of concrete.

Goodman notes that the proximity of the University of Chicago scintillators in Utah to the CYGNUS experiment may have a special payoff: "If you have two experiments observing the same sky, the same source, at the same time, you can't attribute a finding to a mere statistical fluctuation."

About 880 kilometers away from Los Alamos, perched atop Mount Hopkins in southern Arizona, lies another type of detector, sensitive to the lowest-energy gamma rays that can be indirectly detected on Earth.

On clear, moonless nights, a 10-meter-wide dish of 248 mirrors on this mountaintop focuses incoming light onto a cluster of 109 photomultiplier tubes. This Whipple Observatory telescope, like several other similar instruments around the world, infers the presence of gamma rays at slightly lower energies—100 to 10,000 GeV—from a telltale, forward-directed beam of extremely faint light several hundred meters in diameter and about one meter thick.

Analogous to a shock wave, this light, called Cerenkov radiation, appears when the speed of particles exceeds that of light in the medium through which they're moving. Because the particles emit light along their direction of motion, scientists can trace their path and that of their parent gamma rays.

In fact, reconstructing the path of gamma rays has, not surprisingly, proven a primary focus of these studies. By determining the rapid time order—a matter of nanoseconds—in which detectors in a large array receive a signal, investigators can calculate the angle at which a cosmic ray collided with the atmosphere, as well as its point of origin.

Using such ground-based detectors, researchers have found several likely gamma-ray sources. The most convincing data, Rosenberg says, come from Whipple Observatory scans of the Crab pulsar, part of the Crab nebula. Using the Cerenkov telescope, Weekes and his colleagues identified a region near this isolated X-ray-pulsing neutron star three years ago that appears to emit 1,000 GeV gamma rays.

Rosenberg notes that the researchers found a steady gamma-ray signal from the Crab at widely separated times and no evidence that these emissions varied with the Crab's X-ray pulsing interval of 33 milliseconds. While these data suggest that gamma rays may not emanate from the pulsar itself, he says the Crab nonetheless represents the only undisputed source of high-energy gamma rays.

Goodman and other researchers have speculated about what type of violent collisions might trigger the production of these gamma rays. Physicists believe that high-energy gamma rays occur as a by-product of particularly violent collisions between protons and other charged particles. But in the isolated Crab—a single neutron star surrounded by nearly empty space—it's hard to see what other charged particles protons could collide with, Goodman says.

Instead, he suggests, a process called inverse Compton scattering may account for the gamma rays. In this scenario, a beam of high-energy electrons traveling at nearly the speed of light collides with ordinary X-rays emitted by the star. The electrons impart nearly all their energy to the photons, transforming the X-rays to gamma rays. Goodman says if his theory about the origin of these photons proves correct, the number of gammas above 100,000 GeV should begin to fall, since Compton scattering cannot produce photons at these higher energies.

Indications that gamma rays also emerge from Cygnus X-3, an X-ray-emitting binary star system, appear less compelling. In 1979, Soviet researchers at the Crimean Astrophysical Observatory in Nauchny reported finding that this star system—consisting of a neutron star and a lower-mass companion about 30,000 light-years from Earth—appear to emit 10,000 GeV gamma rays. Four years later, investigators using scintillation detectors at the University of Kiel in Germany also saw evidence for energetic gamma-ray bursts near this binary system.

Some researchers speculate that matter drawn from the lower-mass companion and falling onto a hot disk surrounding the neutron star may accelerate fast enough to produce very-high-energy protons and gamma rays. But more recent observations showed no excess of cosmic rays from this stellar pair. Though some investigators now question the validity of the earlier reports, Rosenberg notes that others interpret the data to suggest that Cygnus X-3's gamma emissions may be on the wane.

"If you're a pessimist, you say the previous results were a statistical fluctuation; if you're an optimist you say that previously the source was on, now the source is off," explains physicist Eugene C. Loh of the University of Utah, a researcher with the Fly's Eye experiments.

Cygnus X-3 observations at even higher energies offer similarly contradictory interpretations. For instance, while several decades of data collected by the Fly's Eye experiments and a similar airglow study at the Akeno (Japan) Cosmic Ray Observatory suggest X-3 may emit 10^9 GeV gamma rays, a 1989 air shower observed by detectors at Havarah Park, England, showed no such evidence.

The most controversial—and potentially exciting—observations involve Hercules X-1, another binary system possessing a neutron star. During 1986, separate teams of researchers working at the CYGNUS project, at the Whipple Observatory, and at the Haleakala Gamma Ray Observatory in Maui, Hawaii, independently reported signs of mysterious cosmic-ray bursts that maintained a period just slightly shorter than the neutron star's X-ray pulsing cycle.

Several lines of evidence suggested the pulses stemmed from high-energy gamma rays. For example, the tightly focused beam apparently had traveled in a straight line and carried no charge. But data from the underground detectors at

Los Alamos confounded this explanation: They showed the particle shower possessed far more muons than gamma rays normally create.

Several possibilities, none fitting accepted theories about matter, could explain the mystery Rosenberg says. Photons at high energies might behave more like protons or other particles with mass—interacting strongly with atomic nuclei in the upper atmosphere to produce muons. Alternatively the beam might have contained an unusual type of massive neutrino—neutral particles generally assumed to have no mass, but whose gravitational properties remain uncertain.

The debate over the data continues, involving both astronomers and particle physicists. "To be very candid, nobody understands what's going on and nobody is even convinced, at this stage, that they've observed these damn things," says Goodman. "There's enough controversy in the field now that people aren't 100 percent happy with anything."

While many issues remain unresolved, ground-based cosmic-ray astronomy continues to thrive. In addition to the recently completed Chicago Air Shower Array, other gamma-seeking arrays are planned at the Las Palmas Observatory in the Spanish Canary Islands, and near Lhasa, Tibet.

Cosmic-ray physics is also evolving into a fluid endeavor. Goodman says his CYGNUS group proposes to detect gamma rays with a pond in the Jemez mountains of northern New Mexico. The researchers plan to divide the pond, 8,700 feet above sea level, into two horizontal sections. Detectors submerged in the top half will search for cosmic rays, while devices lying near the bottom will record neutrinos in an attempt to help discriminate charged cosmic rays from gammas. Some 600 photomultiplier tubes immersed 1.5 meters below the pond's surface will act as Cerenkov detectors, recording any light that particles from cosmic air showers produce as they pass through the water.

Unlike Cerenkov detectors above water, these detectors can operate night and day, thanks to a light-tight cover that will blanket the pond. "To look for these [gamma-ray outburst] episodes, you need a powerful detector that's on all the time," Goodman says.

A series of round-the-clock muon detectors will operate under another light-tight cover, in the lower layer, eight meters beneath the pond's surface. Eventually says Goodman, his group hopes to move its CYGNUS project from Los Alamos to the perimeter of this pond.

His CYGNUS group has already begun to adopt aquatic technology with the purchase of several backyard swimming pools. One, filled with water and light detectors, now sits alongside CYGNUS at Los Alamos. Goodman says this pooling of detectors should improve the angular resolution of CYGNUS' scintillators, helping to better pinpoint the direction of cosmic gamma sources.

Researchers have also begun work on a new, triangular version of the Fly's Eye. Each of its three "eyes," spaced 15 kilometers apart, will contain a network of 54 mirrors two meters in diameter. Loh's team already has a working prototype and expects completion of the entire project within four years.

"The reason we're not frustrated is that we know cosmic rays are coming at a steady rate," Loh says. "It's not like somebody decides they're going to turn off your laboratory experiment before you're ready . . . If you're good at it, you're bound to catch them."

Loh adds that his group has plenty to do—including better characterization of extragalactic sources—even if the origin of cosmic rays remains a mystery for some time to come. Regardless of the pace of new discoveries, he says, radiation associated with the powerful collisions and violent accelerations of deep space will provide researchers with a continuing tale of adventure and suspense.

After reading: CONSOLIDATE INFORMATION

1. What is the major debate between astronomers and cosmic physicists about high-energy gamma rays?
2. What about this article indicates that it was written for a popular, non-specialist audience?
3. What inferences can you make about cosmic physics from Cowen's report?

A World of Difference
Evelyn Fox Keller

This essay appeared as a chapter in a book, Reflections on Gender and Science, *which was written for an audience of scientists and non-scientists. Professor Keller is a scientist and historian of science whose main research in recent years has been with issues of gender and science. Implicit in her writing is an analysis of science as a discipline conducted almost exclusively by men.*

Before reading: FIRST THOUGHTS
                   LOOK AHEAD

1. When you think of scientific research, do you think of career opportunities for women? Why or why not?
2. What can you predict about Keller's essay from reading the title?
3. Barbara McClintock won the Nobel Prize in 1983 at the age of 81. After reading Keller's essay, why do you think it took so long for the world of science to recognize McClintock's work?

During reading: REACT
              QUESTION
              SUMMARIZE

1. What do you think Keller means when she refers to Barbara McClintock as a philosophical and methodological maverick?
2. Do you think Barbara McClintock was justified in expecting to be rewarded on the same footing as her male colleagues? Why or why not?

IF WE WANT TO THINK about the ways in which science might be different, we could hardly find a more appropriate guide than Barbara McClintock. Known to her colleagues as a maverick and a visionary, McClintock occupies a place in the history of genetics at one and the same time central and peripheral—a place that, for all its eminence, is marked by difference at every turn.

Born in 1902, McClintock began in her twenties to make contributions to classical genetics and cytology that earned her a level of recognition few women of her generation could imagine. Encouraged and supported by many of the great men of classical genetics (including T. H. Morgan, R. A. Emerson, and Lewis Stadler), McClintock was given the laboratory space and fellowship stipends she needed to pursue what had quickly become the central goal of her life: understanding the secrets of plant genetics. She rejected the more conventional opportunities then available to women in science (such as a research assistantship or a teaching post at a woman's college)[1] and devoted herself to the life of pure research. By the mid 1930s, she had already made an indelible mark on the history of genetics. But the fellowships inevitably ran out. With no job on the horizon, McClintock thought she would have to leave science. Morgan and Emerson, arguing that "it would be a scientific tragedy if her work did not go forward" (quoted in Keller 1983, p. 74), prevailed upon the Rockefeller Foundation to provide two years interim support. Morgan described her as "the best person in the world" in her field but deplored her "personality difficulties": "She is sore at the world because of her conviction that she would have a much freer scientific opportunity if she were a man" (p. 73). Not until 1942 was McClintock's professional survival secured: at that time, a haven was provided for her at the Carnegie Institution of Washington at Cold Spring Harbor, where she has remained ever since. Two years later she was elected to the National Academy of Science; in 1945 she became president of the Genetics Society of America.

This dual theme of success and marginality that poignantly describes the first stage of McClintock's career continues as the leitmotif of her entire profes-

---

[1]For an excellent overview of the opportunities available to women scientists in the 1920s and 1930s, see Rossiter 1982.

sional life. Despite the ungrudging respect and admiration of her colleagues, her most important work has, until recently, gone largely unappreciated, uncomprehended, and almost entirely unintegrated into the growing corpus of biological thought. This was the work, begun in her forties, that led to her discovery that genetic elements can move, in an apparently coordinated way, from one chromosomal site to another—in short, her discovery of genetic transposition. Even today, as a Nobel laureate and deluged with other awards and prizes for this same work, McClintock regards herself as, in crucial respects, an outsider to the world of modern biology—not because she is a woman but because she is a philosophical and methodological deviant.

No doubt, McClintock's marginality and deviance is more visible—and seems more dramatic—to her than to others. During the many years when McClintock's professional survival seemed so precarious, even her most devoted colleagues seemed unaware that she had no proper job. "What do you mean?," many of them asked me. "She was so good! How could she not have had a job?" Indeed, as Morgan himself suggested, her expectation that she would be rewarded on the basis of merit, on the same footing as her male colleagues, was itself read as a mark of her ingratitude—of what he called her "personality difficulties."

When discussing the second stage of her career, during which her revolutionary work on genetic transposition earned her the reputation more of eccentricity than of greatness, her colleagues are likely to focus on the enduring admiration many of them continued to feel. She, of course, is more conscious of their lack of comprehension and of the dismissal of her work by other, less admiring, colleagues. She is conscious, above all, of the growing isolation that ensued.

Today, genetic transposition is no longer a dubious or isolated phenomenon. As one prominent biologist describes it, "[Transposable elements] are everywhere, in bacteria, yeast, *Drosophila*, and plants. Perhaps even in mice and men." (Marx 1981, quoted in Keller 1983, p. 193). But the significance of transposition remains in considerable dispute. McClintock saw transposable elements as a key to developmental regulation; molecular biologists today, although much more sympathetic to this possibility than they were twenty, or even ten, years ago, are still unsure. And in evolutionary terms, McClintock's view of transposition as a survival mechanism available to the organism in times of stress seems to most (although not to all) pure heresy.

My interest here, as it has been from the beginning, is less on who was "right" than on the differences in perceptions that underlay such a discordance of views. The vicissitudes of McClintock's career give those differences not only special poignancy but special importance. In *A Feeling for the Organism: The Life and Work of Barbara McClintock* (Keller 1983), I argued that it is precisely the duality of success and marginality that lends her career its significance to the history and philosophy of science. Her success indisputably affirms her legitimacy as a scientist, while her marginality provides an opportunity to examine the role and fate of dissent in the growth of scientific knowledge. This duality illustrates the diversity of values, methodological styles, and goals that, to varying degrees, always exists in science; at the same time, it illustrates the pressures that, to equally varying degrees, operate to contain that diversity.

In the preface to that book (p. xii), I wrote:

> The story of Barbara McClintock allows us to explore the condition under which dissent in science arises, the function it serves, and the plurality of values and goals it reflects. It makes us ask: What role do interests, individual and collective, play in the evolution of scientific knowledge? Do all scientists seek the same kinds of explanations? Are the kinds of questions they ask the same? Do differences in methodology between different subdisciplines even permit the same kinds of answers? And when significant differences do arise in questions asked, explanations sought, methodologies employed, how do they affect communication between scientists? In short, why could McClintock's discovery of transposition not be absorbed by her contemporaries? We can say that her vision of biological organization was too remote from the kinds of explanations her colleagues were seeking, but we need to understand what that distance is composed of, and how such divergences develop.

I chose, in effect, not to read the story of McClintock's career as a romance—neither as "a tale of dedication rewarded after years of neglect—of prejudice or indifference eventually routed by courage and truth" (p. xii), nor as a heroic story of the scientist, years "ahead of her time," stumbling on something approximating what we now know as "the truth." Instead, I read it as a story about the languages of science—about the process by which worlds of common scientific discourse become established, effectively bounded, and yet at the same time remain sufficiently permeable to allow a given piece of work to pass from incomprehensibility in one era to acceptance (if not full comprehensibility) in another.

In this essay, my focus is even more explicitly on difference itself. I want to isolate McClintock's views of nature, of science, and of the relation between mind and nature, in order to exhibit not only their departure from more conventional views but also their own internal coherence. If we can stand inside this world view, the questions she asks, the explanations she seeks, and the methods she employs in her pursuit of scientific knowledge will take on a degree of clarity and comprehensibility they lack from outside. And at the heart of this world view lies the same respect for difference that motivates us to examine it in the first place. I begin therefore with a discussion of the implications of respect for difference (and complexity) in the general philosophy expressed in McClintock's testimony, and continue by discussing its implications for cognition and perception, for her interests as a geneticist, and for the relation between her work and molecular biology. I conclude the essay with a brief analysis of the relevance of gender to any philosophy of difference, and to McClintock's in particular.

To McClintock, nature is characterized by an a priori complexity that vastly exceeds the capacities of the human imagination. Her recurrent remark, "Anything you can think of you will find,"[2] is a statement about the capacities not of mind but of nature. It is meant not as a description of our own ingenuity as discoverers

---

[2] All quotations from Barbara McClintock are taken from private interviews conducted between September 24, 1978, and February 25, 1979; most of them appear in Keller 1983.

but as a comment on the resourcefulness of natural order; in the sense not so much of adaptability as of largesse and prodigality. Organisms have a life and an order of their own that scientists can only begin to fathom. "Misrepresented, not appreciated, . . . [they] are beyond our wildest expectations. . . . They do everything we [can think of], they do it better, more efficiently, more marvelously." In comparison with the ingenuity of nature, our scientific intelligence seems pallid. It follows as a matter of course that "trying to make everything fit into set dogma won't work. . . . There's no such thing as a central dogma into which everything will fit."

In the context of McClintock's views of nature, attitudes about research that would otherwise sound romantic fall into logical place. The need to "listen to the material" follows from her sense of the order of things. Precisely because the complexity of nature exceeds our own imaginative possibilities, it becomes essential to "let the experiment tell you what to do." Her major criticism of contemporary research is based on what she sees as inadequate humility. She feels that "much of the work done is done because one wants to impose an answer on it—they have the answer ready, and they [know what] they want the material to tell them, so anything it doesn't tell them, they don't really recognize as there, or they think it's a mistake and throw it out. . . . If you'd only just let the material tell you."

Respect for complexity thus demands from observers of nature the same special attention to the exceptional case that McClintock's own example as a scientist demands from observers of science: "If the material tells you, 'It may be this,' allow that. Don't turn it aside and call it an exception, an aberration, a contaminant. . . . That's what's happened all the way along the line with so many good clues." Indeed, respect for individual difference lies at the very heart of McClintock's scientific passion. "The important thing is to develop the capacity to see one kernel [of maize] that is different, and make that understandable," she says. "If [something] doesn't fit, there's a reason, and you find out what it is." The prevailing focus on classes and numbers, McClintock believes, encourages researchers to overlook difference, to "call it an exception, an aberration, a contaminant." The consequences of this seem to her very costly. "Right and left," she says, they miss "what is going on."

She is, in fact, here describing the history of her own research. Her work on transposition in fact began with the observation of an aberrant pattern of pigmentation on a few kernels of a single corn plant. And her commitment to the significance of this singular pattern sustained her through six years of solitary and arduous investigation—all aimed at making the difference she saw understandable.

Making difference understandable does not mean making it disappear. In McClintock's world view, an understanding of nature can come to rest with difference. "Exceptions" are not there to "prove the rule"; they have meaning in and of themselves. In this respect, difference constitutes a principle for ordering the world radically unlike the principle of division or dichotomization (subject-object, mind–matter, feeling–reason, disorder–law). Whereas these oppositions are directed toward a cosmic unity typically excluding or devouring one of the pair, toward a unified, all-encompassing law, respect for difference remains content with multiplicity as an end in itself.

And just as the terminus of knowledge implied by difference can be distinguished from that implied by division, so the starting point of knowledge can also be distinguished. Above all, difference, in this world view, does not posit division as an epistemological prerequisite—it does not imply the necessity of hard and fast divisions in nature, or in mind, or in the relation between mind and nature. Division severs connection and imposes distance; the recognition of difference provides a starting point for relatedness. It serves both as a clue to new modes of connectedness in nature, and as an invitation to engagement with nature. For McClintock, certainly, respect for difference serves both these functions. Seeing something that does not appear to fit is, to her, a challenge to find the larger multidimensional pattern into which it does fit. Anomalous kernels of corn were evidence not of disorder or lawlessness, but or a larger system of order, one that cannot be reduced to a single law.

Difference thus invites a form of engagement and understanding that allows for the preservation of the individual. The integrity of each kernel (or chromosome or plant) survives all our own pattern-making attempts; the order of nature transcends our capacities for ordering. And this transcendence is manifested in the enduring uniqueness of each organism: "No two plants are exactly alike. They're all different, and as a consequence, you have to know that difference," she explains. "I start with the seedling, and I don't want to leave it. I don't feel I really know the story if I don't watch the plant all the way along. So I know every plant in the field. I know them intimately, and I find it a great pleasure to know them." From days, weeks, and years of patient observation comes what looks like privileged insight: "When I see things, I can interpret them right away." As one colleague described it, the result is an apparent ability to write the "autobiography" of every plant she works with.

McClintock is not here speaking of relations to other humans, but the parallels are nonetheless compelling. In the relationship she describes with plants, as in human relations, respect for difference constitutes a claim not only on our interest but on our capacity for empathy—in short on the highest form of love: love that allows for intimacy without the annihilation of difference. I use the word *love* neither loosely nor sentimentally, but out of fidelity to the language McClintock herself uses to describe a form of attention, indeed a form of thought. Her vocabulary is consistently a vocabulary of affection, of kinship, of empathy. Even with puzzles, she explains, "The thing was dear to you for a period of time, you really had an affection for it. Then after a while, it disappears and it doesn't bother you. But for a short time you feel strongly attached to that little toy." The crucial point for us is that McClintock can risk the suspension of boundaries between subject and object without jeopardy to science precisely because, to her, science is not premised on that division. Indeed, the intimacy she experiences with the objects she studies—intimacy born of a lifetime of cultivated attentiveness—is a wellspring of her powers as a scientist.

The most vivid illustration of this process comes from her own account of a breakthrough in one particularly recalcitrant piece of cytological analysis. She describes the state of mind accompanying the crucial shift in orientation that enabled her to identify chromosomes she had earlier not been able to distinguish: "I found that the more I worked with them, the bigger and bigger [the chromosomes] got, and when I was really working with them I wasn't outside, I was down there. I was part of the system. I was right down there with them, and everything got big. I even was able to see the internal parts of the chromosomes—actually everything was there. It surprised me because I actually felt as if I was right down there and these were my friends. . . . As you look at these things, they become part of you. And you forget yourself."

Cognition and Perception

In this world of difference, division is relinquished without generating chaos. Self and other, mind and nature survive not in mutual alienation, or in symbiotic fusion, but in structural integrity. The "feeling for the organism" that McClintock upholds as the sine qua non of good research need not be read as "participation mystique"; it is a mode of access—honored by time and human experience if not by prevailing conventions in science—to the reliable knowledge of the world around us that all scientists seek. It is a form of attention strongly reminiscent of the concept of "focal attention" developed by Ernest Schachtel to designate "man's [sic] capacity to *center* his attention on an object fully, so that he can perceive or understand it from *many* sides, as fully as possible" (p. 251). In Schachtel's language, "focal attention" is the principal tool that, in conjunction with our natural interest in objects per se, enables us to progress from mere wishing and wanting to thinking and knowing—that equips us for the fullest possible knowledge of reality in its own terms. Such "object-centered" perception (see chap. 6) presupposes "a temporary eclipse of all the perceiver's egocentric thoughts and strivings, of all preoccupation with self and self-esteem, and a full turning towards the object, . . . [which, in turn] leads not to a *loss* of self, but to a heightened feeling of aliveness" (p. 181). Object-centered perception, Schachtel goes on to argue, is in the service of a love "which wants to affirm others in their total and unique being . . . [which affirms objects as] "part of the same world of which man is a part" (p. 226). It requires

> an experiential realization of the kinship between oneself and the other . . . a realization [that] is made difficult by fear and by arrogance—by fear because then the need to protect oneself by flight, appeasement, or attack gets in the way; by arrogance because then the other is no longer experienced as akin, but as inferior to oneself. (p. 227)

The difference between Schachtel and McClintock is that what Schachtel grants to the poet's perceptual style in contrast to that of the scientist, McClintock claims equally for science. She enlists a "feeling for the organism"—not only for living organisms but for any object that fully claims our attention—in pursuit of the goal shared by all scientists: reliable (that is, shareable and reproducible) knowledge of natural order.

This difference is a direct reflection of the limitations of Schachtel's picture of science. It is drawn not from observation of scientists like McClintock but only from the more stereotypic scientist, who "looks at the object with one or more hypotheses . . . in mind and thus 'uses' the object to corroborate or disprove a hypothesis, but does not encounter the object as such, in its own fullness." For Schachtel,

> modern natural science has as its main goal prediction, i.e. the power to manipulate objects in such a way that certain predicted events will happen. . . . Hence, the scientist usually will tend to perceive the object merely from the perspective of [this] power. . . . That is to say that his view of the object will be determined by the ends which he pursues in his experimentation. . . . He may achieve a great deal in this way and add important data to our knowledge, but to the extent to which he remains within the framework of this perspective he will not perceive the object in its own right. (1959, p. 171)

To McClintock, science has a different goal: not prediction per se, but understanding; not the power to manipulate, but empowerment—the kind of power that results from an understanding of the world around us, that simultaneously reflects and affirms our connection to that world.

What Counts as Knowledge

At the root of this difference between McClintock and the stereotypic scientist lies that unexamined starting point of science: the naming of nature. Underlying every discussion of science, as well as every scientific discussion, there exists a larger assumption about the nature of the universe in which that discussion takes place. The power of this unseen ground is to be found not in its influence on any particular argument in science but in its framing of the very terms of argument—in its definition of the tacit aims and goals of science. As I noted in the introduction to this section, scientists may spend fruitful careers, building theories of nature that are astonishingly successful in their predictive power, without ever feeling the need to reflect on these fundamental philosophical issues. Yet if we want to ask questions about that success, about the value of alternative scientific descriptions of nature, even about the possibility of alternative criteria of success, we can do so only by examining those most basic assumptions that are normally not addressed.

We have to remind ourselves that, although all scientists share a common ambition for knowledge, it does not follow that what counts as knowledge is commonly agreed upon. The history of science reveals a wide diversity of questions asked, explanations sought, and methodologies employed in this common quest for knowledge of the natural world; this diversity is in turn reflected in the kinds of knowledge acquired, and indeed in what counts as knowledge. To a large degree, both the kinds of questions one asks and the explanations that one finds satisfying depend on one's a priori relation to the objects of study. In particular, I am suggesting that questions asked about objects with which one feels kinship are likely to differ from questions asked about objects one sees as unalterably alien. Similarly, explanations that satisfy us about a natural world that is seen as "blind, simple and dumb," ontologically inferior, may seem less self-evidently satisfying for a natural world seen as complex and, itself, resourceful. I suggest that individual and communal conceptions of nature need to be examined for their role in the history of science, not as causal determinants but as frameworks upon which all scientific programs are developed. More specifically, I am claiming that the difference between McClintock's conception of nature and that prevailing in the community around her is an essential key to our understanding of the history of her life and work.

It provides, for example, the context for examining the differences between McClintock's interests *as a geneticist* and what has historically been the defining focus of both classical and molecular genetics—differences crucial to the particular route her research took. To most geneticists, the problem of inheritance is solved by knowing the mechanism and structure of genes. To McClintock, however, as to many other biologists, mechanism and structure have never been adequate answers to the question "How do genes work?" Her focus was elsewhere: on function and organization. To her, an adequate understanding would, by definition, have to include an account of how they function in relation to the rest of the cell, and of course, to the organism as a whole.

In her language, the cell itself is an organism. Indeed, "Every component of the organism is as much an organism as every other part." When she says, therefore, that "one cannot consider the [gene] as such as being all important— more important is the overall organism," she means the genome as a whole, the cell, the ensemble of cells, the organism itself. Genes are neither "beads on a string" nor functionally disjoint pieces of DNA. They are organized functional units, whose very function is defined by their position in the organization as a whole. As she says, genes function "only with respect to the environment in which [they are] found."

Interests in function and in organization are historically and conceptually related to each other. By tradition, both are primary preoccupations of developmental biology, and McClintock's own interest in development followed from and supported these interests. By the same tradition, genetics and developmental biology have been two separate subjects. But for a geneticist for whom the answer to the question of how genes work must include function and organization, the problem of heredity becomes inseparable from the problem of development. The division that most geneticists felt they had to live with (happily or not) McClintock could not accept. To her, development, as the coordination of function, was an integral part of genetics.

McClintock's views today are clearly fed by her work on transposition. But her work on transposition was itself fed by these interests. Her own account (see Keller 1983, pp. 115–17) of how she came to this work and of how she followed the clues she saw vividly illustrates the ways in which her interests in function and organization—and in development—focused her attention on the patterns she saw and framed the questions she asked about the significance of these patterns. I suggest that they also defined the terms that a satisfying explanation had to meet.

Such an explanation had to account not so much for how transposition occurred, as for why it occurred. The patterns she saw indicated a programmatic disruption in normal developmental function. When she succeeded in linking this disruption to the location (and change in location) of particular genetic elements, that very link was what captured her interest. (She knew she was "on to something important.") The fact that transposition occurred—the fact that genetic sequences are not fixed—was of course interesting too, but only secondarily so. To her, the paramount interest lay in the meaning of its occurrence, in the clue that transposition provided for the relation between genetics and development. Necessarily, a satisfying account of this relation would have to take due note of the complexity of the regulation process.

Transposition and the Central Dogma

Just two years after McClintock's first public presentation of her work on transposition came the culminating event in the long search for the mechanism of inheritance. Watson and Crick's discovery of the structure of DNA enabled them to provide a compelling account of the essential genetic functions of replication and instruction. According to their account, the vital information of the cell is encoded in the DNA. From there it is copied onto the RNA, which, in turn, is used as a blueprint for the production of the proteins responsible for genetic traits. In the picture that emerged—DNA to RNA to protein (which Crick himself dubbed the "central dogma")—the DNA is posited as the central actor in the cell, the executive governor of cellular organization, itself remaining impervious to influence from the subordinate agents to which it dictates. Several years later, Watson and Crick's original model was emended by Jacques Monod and François Jacob to allow for environmental control of the rates of protein synthesis. But even with this modification, the essential autonomy of DNA remained unchallenged: information flowed one way, always from, and never to, the DNA.

Throughout the 1950s and 1960s, the successes of molecular genetics were dramatic. By the end of the 1960s, it was possible to say (as Jacques Monod did say), "The Secret of Life? But this is in large part known—in principle, if not in details" (quoted in Judson 1979, p. 216). A set of values and interests wholly different from McClintock's seemed to have been vindicated. The intricacies, and difficulties, of corn genetics held little fascination in comparison with the quick returns from research on the vastly simpler and seemingly more straightforward bacterium and bacteriophage. As a result, communication between McClintock and her colleagues grew steadily more difficult; fewer and fewer biologists had the expertise required even to begin to understand her results.

McClintock of course shared in the general excitement of this period, but she did not share in the general enthusiasm for the central dogma. The same model that seemed so immediately and overwhelmingly satisfying to so many of her colleagues did not satisfy her. Although duly impressed by its explanatory power, she remained at the same time acutely aware of what it did not explain. It neither addressed the questions that were of primary interest to her—bearing on the relation between genetics and development—nor began to take into account the complexity of genetic organization that she had always assumed, and that was now revealed to her by her work on transposition.

McClintock locates the critical flaw of the central dogma in its presumption: it claimed to explain too much. Baldly put, what was true of *E. coli* (the bacterium most commonly studied) was *not* true of the elephant, as Monod (and others) would have had it (Judson 1979, p. 613). Precisely because higher organisms are multicellular, she argued, they necessarily require a different kind of economy. The central dogma was without question inordinately successful as well as scientifically productive. Yet the fact that it ultimately proved inadequate even to the dynamics of *E. coli* suggests that its trouble lay deeper than just a too hasty generalization from the simple to the complex; its presumptuousness, I suggest, was built into its form of explanation.

The central dogma is a good example of what I have earlier called (following Nanney 1957) master-molecule theories (Keller 1982). In locating the seat of genetic control in a single molecule, it posits a structure of genetic organization that is essentially hierarchical, often illustrated in textbooks by organizational charts like those of corporate structures. In this model, genetic stability is ensured by the unidirectionality of information flow, much as political and social stability is assumed in many quarters to require the unidirectional exercise of authority.

To McClintock, transposition provided evidence that genetic organization is necessarily more complex, and in fact more globally interdependent, than such a model assumes. It showed that the DNA itself is subject to rearrangement and, by implication, to reprogramming. Although she did not make the suggestion explicit, the hidden heresy of her argument lay in the inference that such reorganization could be induced by signals external to the DNA—from the cell, the organism, even from the environment.

For more than fifty years, modern biologists had labored heroically to purge biological thought of the last vestiges of teleology, particularly as they surfaced in Lamarckian notions of adaptive evolution. But even though McClintock is not a Lamarckian, she sees in transposition a mechanism enabling genetic structures to respond to the needs of the organism. Since needs are relative to the environmental context and hence subject to change, transposition, by implication, indirectly allows for the possibility of environmentally induced and genetically transmitted change. To her, such a possibility is not heresy—it is not even surprising. On the contrary, it is in direct accord with her belief in the resourcefulness of natural order. Because she has no investment in the passivity of nature, the possibility of internally generated order does not, to her, threaten the foundations of science. The capacity of organisms to reprogram their own DNA implies neither vitalism, magic, nor a countermanding will. It merely confirms the existence of forms of order more complex than we have, at least thus far, been able to account for.

The renewed interest in McClintock's work today is a direct consequence of developments (beginning in the early 1970s) in the very research programs that had seemed so philosophically opposed to her position; genetic mobility was rediscovered within molecular biology itself. That this was so was crucial, perhaps even necessary, to establishing the legitimacy of McClintock's early work, precisely because the weight of scientific authority has now come to reside in molecular biology. As a by-product, this legitimization also lends McClintock's views of science and attitudes toward research somewhat more credibility among professional biologists. To observers of science, this same historical sequence serves as a sharp reminder that the languages of science, however self-contained they seem, are not closed. McClintock's eventual vindication demonstrates the capacity of science to overcome its own characteristic kinds of myopia, reminding us that its limitations do not reinforce themselves indefinitely. Their own methodology allows, even obliges, scientists to continually reencounter phenomena even their best theories cannot accommodate. Or—to look at it from the other side—however severely communication between science and nature may be impeded by the preconceptions of a particular time, some channels always remain open; and, through them, nature finds ways of reasserting itself. (Keller 1983, p. 197)

In this sense, the McClintock story is a happy one.

It is important, however, not to overestimate the degree of rapprochement that has taken place. McClintock has been abundantly vindicated: transposition is acknowledged, higher organisms and development have once again captured the interest of biologists, and almost everyone agrees that genetic organization is manifestly more complex than had previously been thought. But not everyone shares her conviction that we are in the midst of a revolution that "will reorganize the way we look at things, the way we do research." Many researchers remain confident that the phenomenon of transposition can somehow be incorporated, even if they do not yet see how, into an improved version of the central dogma. Their attachment to this faith is telling. Behind the continuing skepticism about McClintock's interpretation of the role of transposition in development and evolution, there remains a major gap between her underlying interests and commitments and those of most of her colleagues.

The Issue of Gender

How much of this enduring difference reflects the fact that McClintock is a woman in a field still dominated by men? To what extent are her views indicative of a vision of "what will happen to science," as Erik Erikson asked in 1964 (1965, p. 243), "if and when women are truly represented in it—not by a few glorious exceptions, but in the rank and file of the scientific elite?"

On the face of it, it would be tempting indeed to call McClintock's vision of science "a feminist science." Its emphasis on intuition, on feeling, on connection and relatedness, all seem to confirm our most familiar stereotypes of women. And to the extent that they do, we might expect that the sheer presence of more women in science would shift the balance of community sentiment and lead to the endorsement of that vision. However, there are both general and particular reasons that argue strongly against this simple view.

The general argument is essentially the same as that which I made against the notion of "a different science," in the introduction to part 3. To the extent that science is defined by its past and present practitioners, anyone who aspires to membership in that community must conform to its existing code. As a consequence, the inclusion of new members, even from a radically different culture, cannot induce immediate or direct change. To be a successful scientist, one must first be adequately socialized. For this reason, it is unreasonable to expect a sharp differentiation between women scientists and their male colleagues, and indeed, most women scientists would be appalled by such a suggestion.

McClintock is in this sense no exception. She would disclaim any analysis of her work as a woman's work, as well as any suggestion that her views represent a woman's perspective. To her, science is not a matter of gender, either male or female; it is, on the contrary, a place where (ideally at least) "the matter of gender drops away." Furthermore, her very commitment to science is of a piece with her lifelong wish to transcend gender altogether. Indeed, her adamant rejection of female stereotypes seems to have been a prerequisite for her becoming a scientist at all. (See Keller 1983, chaps. 2 and 3.) In her own image of herself, she is a maverick in all respects—as a woman, as a scientist, even as a woman scientist.

Finally, I want to reemphasize that it would be not only misleading but actually contradictory to suggest that McClintock's views of science were shared by none of her colleagues. Had that been so, she could not have had even marginal status as a scientist. It is essential to understand that, in practice, the scientific tradition is far more pluralistic than any particular description of it suggests, and certainly more pluralistic than its dominant ideology. For McClintock to be recognized as a scientist, the positions that she represents, however unrepresentative, had to be, and were, identifiable as belonging somewhere within that tradition.

But although McClintock is not a total outsider to science, she is equally clearly not an insider. And however atypical she is as a woman, what she is *not* is a man. Between these two facts lies a crucial connection—a connection signaled by the recognition that, as McClintock herself admits, the matter of gender never does drop away.

I suggest that the radical core of McClintock's stance can be located right here: Because she is not a man, in a world of men, her commitment to a gender-free science has been binding; because concepts of gender have so deeply influenced the basic categories of science, that commitment has been transformative. In short, the relevance of McClintock's gender in this story is to be found not in its role in her personal socialization but precisely in the role of gender in the construction of science.

Of course, not all scientists have embraced the conception of science as one of "putting nature on the rack and torturing the answers out of her." Nor have all men embraced a conception of masculinity that demands cool detachment and domination. Nor even have all scientists been men. But most have. And however variable the attitudes of individual male scientists toward science and toward masculinity, the metaphor of a marriage between mind and nature necessarily does not look the same to them as it does to women. And this is the point.

In a science constructed around the naming of object (nature) as female and the parallel naming of subject (mind) as male, any scientist who happens to be a woman is confronted with an a priori contradiction in terms. This poses a critical problem of identity: any scientist who is not a man walks a path bounded on one side by inauthenticity and on the other by subversion. Just as surely as inauthenticity is the cost a woman suffers by joining men in misogynist jokes, so it is, equally, the cost suffered by a woman who identifies with an image of the scientist modeled on the patriarchal husband. Only if she undergoes a radical disidentification from self can she share masculine pleasure in mastering a nature cast in the image of woman as passive, inert, and blind. Her alternative is to attempt a radical redefinition of terms. Nature must be renamed as not female, or, at least, as not an alienated object. By the same token, the mind, if the female scientist is to have one, must be renamed as not necessarily male, and accordingly recast with a more inclusive subjectivity. This is not to say that the male scientist cannot claim similar redefinition (certainly many have done so) but, by contrast to the woman scientist, his identity does not require it.

For McClintock, given her particular commitments to personal integrity, to be a scientist, and not a man, with a nonetheless intact identity, meant that she had to insist on a different meaning of mind, of nature, and of the relation between them. Her need to define for herself the relation between subject and object, even the very terms themselves, came not from a feminist consciousness, or even from a female consciousness. It came from her insistence on her right to be a scientist—from her determination to claim science as a human rather than a male endeavor. For such a claim, difference makes sense of the world in ways that division cannot. It allows for the kinship that she feels with other scientists, without at the same time obligating her to share all their assumptions.

Looked at in this way, McClintock's stance is, finally, a far more radical one than that implied in Erikson's question. It implies that what could happen to science "when women are truly represented in it" is not simply, or even, "the addition, to the male kind of creative vision, of women's vision" (p. 243), but, I suggest, a thoroughgoing transformation of the very possibilities of creative vision, for everyone. It implies that the kind of change we might hope for is not a direct or readily apparent one but rather an indirect and subterranean one. A first step toward such a transformation would be the undermining of the commitment of scientists to the masculinity of their profession that would be an inevitable concomitant of the participation of large numbers of women.

However, we need to remember that, as long as success in science does not require self-reflection, the undermining of masculinist or other ideological commitments is not a sufficient guarantee of change. But nature itself is an ally that can be relied upon to provide the impetus for real change: nature's responses recurrently invite reexamination of the terms in which our understanding of science is constructed. Paying attention to those responses—"listening to the material"—may help us to reconstruct our understanding of science in terms born out of the diverse spectrum of human experience rather than out of the narrow spectrum that our culture has labeled masculine.

References

ERIKSON, ERIK H. 1965. Concluding Remarks. In *Women in the Scientific Professions*, ed. J. Mattfield and C. van Aiken. Cambridge: MIT Press.

JUDSON, HORACE. 1979. *The Eighth Day of Creation: Makers of the Revolution in Biology.* New York: Simon and Schuster.

KELLER, EVELYN FOX. 1982. Feminism and Science. *Signs: A Journal of Women in Culture and Society* 7, no. 3, pp. 589–602.

KELLER, EVELYN FOX. 1983. *A Feeling for the Organism: The Life and Work of Barbara McClintock.* New York: Freeman.

MARX, JEAN L. 1981. A Movable Feast in the Eukaryotic Genome. *Science*, 211, p. 153.

NANNEY, DAVID L. 1957. The Role of Cytoplasm in Heredity. In *The Chemical Basis of Heredity*, ed. W.D. McElroy and H.B. Glass. Baltimore: Johns Hopkins University Press.

ROSSITER, MARGARET W. 1982. *Women Scientists in America*. Baltimore: Johns Hopkins University Press.

SCHACHTEL, ERNEST. *Metamorphosis*. New York: Basic Books.

After reading: CONSOLIDATE INFORMATION

1. Re-read Keller's title. How does it refer to McClintock as a scientist as well as to her place in the scientific community?
2. Summarize what Keller views as the significance of Barbara McClintock's story.
3. How do you evaluate Keller's conclusions about the relevance of McClintock's being a woman?

Biology's Moon Shot: The Human Genome Project
Tom Shoop

This article by Tom Shoop on the federal government's $3 billion project to create a biological map of human genetic structure was directed to a general audience of government employees. It appeared in 1991 in Government Executive.

Before reading: FIRST THOUGHTS
               LOOK AHEAD

1. Why does Shoop call the government's Genome Project "Biology's Moon Shot"?
2. What do you think the term *genome* means? Look it up in a dictionary.
3. Why do you think the federal government funds research in human genetics and biology?

During reading: REACT
               QUESTION
               SUMMARIZE

1. Why are biologists surprised when they find out that the Department of Energy helps fund the Genome project?
2. Who is James Watson and why is he so controversial?

THE MANHATTAN PROJECT. The Apollo Program. The Space Station. The Superconducting Supercollider. They are the essence of "big science," the kind of multibillion-dollar physics and engineering feats on which the United States has staked its scientific reputation since World War II.

Now biology has joined the fray. Its entry is the Human Genome Project, targeted to spend $3 billion over the next 15 years to identify and locate all of the genes in the human body (which, taken together, are known as the genome). The program holds out the hope for the early diagnosis and treatment of scores of diseases, ranging from heart disease to manic depression to alcoholism.

Some scientists, though, are asking whether it's worth all the "big science" fuss. Biology, especially biomedicine, has always been a bastion of "little science." Most of the money that the National Institutes of Health distributes for basic biomedical research is in the form of direct grants, averaging about $200,000 each, to individuals or small groups of scientists. But while the number of such grants has increased in the last decade to about 20,000 a year, the growth has been concentrated in renewals and extensions of existing grants. The number of new grants awarded has dropped steeply, from more than 6,000 in fiscal 1985 to 4,600 in 1990. In some disciplines, 85 percent of grant proposals go unfunded.

Meanwhile, the genome project has gone big time, building a budget of $135 million this year. That budget is expected to peak at $200 million a year, and half of it will go to government labs and large genome research centers. This, critics say, robs individual researchers of much-needed funds.

The genome project has also raised some administrative questions. It is co-administered by two federal agencies that have little in common, the Energy Department and NIH. One of them (Energy) has what some scientists consider a flimsy rationale for engaging in massive biological research. The other is led by a Nobel laureate whom a leading science journal has described as "something of a wild man," and whom one colleague calls a "loose cannon."

THREE BILLION LETTERS

The Human Genome Project is arguably the most important of any of the big science programs. There is no limit to the riddles it might solve: Besides diseases (cystic fibrosis, for example) that are known to be genetically transmitted, plenty of others, like cancer, may also turn out to have significant genetic components.

Then again, if, as the Nazis proved, a little knowledge of genetics can be a dangerous thing, the genome initiative may show that a lot of knowledge could be worse. Both NIH and DOE have committed 3 percent of their genome budgets to studying the ethical, legal and social questions surrounding the project, such as: What will employers and insurance companies do if they are able to determine, through simple tests, that certain people are much more susceptible to disease than others? What will parents do when they can predetermine the genetic destiny of their children?

As anyone who has taken high-school biology knows, that genetic destiny is determined by the 23 pairs of chromosomes we get from our parents. Within the chromosomes is DNA, containing the instructions for making the proteins that are the essence of life itself. Genes (of which there are about 100,000 in the human body, scientists estimate) are short snippets of DNA, each responsible for a different physical characteristic, like eye color. Finally, each gene is made up of a different combination of bases, which are probably best left represented by the first letters of their names: A, C, T and G.

To come up with a complete guide to human genetics, all you need to do is list all of the A's, C's, T's and G's in the order in which they are linked in the genome. All three billion of them, that is. It's a lot more than one scientist could do on an NIH grant in his or her lab.

Energy Steps In

Enter the Energy Department. In the mid-1980s, an enterprising biophysicist named Charles DeLisi, head of Energy's Office of Health and Environmental Research, was one of a small number of scientists around the country who more or less simultaneously came up with the idea that a diagram of the entire human genome could be a rather incredible research tool.

At this time, in the wake of the energy crisis of the 1970s, "DOE was casting about for imaginative new projects that could appeal to Congress and the public," say Jerry E. Bishop and Michael E. Waldholz in *Genome*, a history of the early stages of the genome effort (Simon and Schuster, 1990). Studying the genome, DeLisi argued, was a logical outgrowth of Energy's mission to study the biological effects of nuclear radiation. Besides, the department's four national laboratories, dating from the development of the atomic bomb, had both the brain and computer power to deal with the massive amount of information-gathering the genome project would entail.

Nevertheless, many in the scientific community wonder why DOE, essentially an organization of physicists, is consuming 35 percent of the budget for the biggest biology project around. In a letter to the Senate Energy and Natural Resources Subcommittee on Energy Research and Development last July, Bernard Davis, a professor at Harvard Medical School, noted that while he did not object to DOE's role, "the linkage to its mission seems a bit forced."

"It does seem to strike biologists [as strange]," admits David J. Galas, DeLisi's successor at Energy. "They're always surprised initially." But, he adds, "I think biology will be revolutionized in a major way by the genome project. So the fact that all aspects of it aren't directly down the line of DOE's mission is sort of irrelevant."

Mapping vs. Sequencing

Satisfied with DeLisi's rationale, Energy plowed ahead. By 1987, the department had shifted funds within its budget to get its national labs started on genome research.

Energy's initial goal was what scientists call "sequencing" the genome; that is, coming up with the complete list of all its lettered bases in order. "Unfortunately," Galas says, "it rapidly became clear that it was the consensus of the scientific community that this was not the thing to do."

That consensus developed because scientists believe that more than 90 percent of the genome is "junk" DNA, vast stretches of biologically meaningless bases between genes. So sequencing the genome would be a little bit like trying to understand the world by listing all of its cities and towns (or, to get a better idea of the actual amount of data involved, all of the world's people), without a map showing which were the most important and where they were located.

At some point, the entire sequence of the human genome could be a great research tool, enabling scientists to focus in on the bases that make up genes and even devise ways to repair defective genes. But in the meantime, they wouldn't be able to tell where an individual gene started or ended in the vast string of letters.

Then there was the issue of cost. Technology for sequencing the genome was (and still is) relatively primitive. At current costs, just paying for the long, meaningless sequence would cost more than has been estimated for the entire genome project.

So influential biologists began to argue in favor of "gene mapping," in which researchers break down chromosomes and try to plot the location of genes, especially disease-causing genes, within the chromosomes. Such mapping had been going on for years, much of it funded by NIH.

Even without sequencing, mapping can make great strides in the diagnosis of disease. For example, scientists using mapping techniques recently zeroed in on the region where a gene responsible for some forms of breast cancer is located. Once the mapping is completed and the gene's exact location is found, a blood test for the gene can be developed, and women can be forewarned if they are susceptible to the disease.

Eventually, scientists might be able to sequence many different genes, repair their defects, and stop genetically inherited diseases in their tracks.

In February 1988, the National Research Council of the National Academy of Sciences released a report recommending a 15-year, multibillion-dollar genome effort that would start with mapping and proceed to sequencing when the technology improved and the price went down. A later report from Congress' Office of Technology Assessment also endorsed the idea of a long-term genome project, with the sequencing aspect on the back burner.

The Watson Factor

On the heels of those reports, NIH set up its own office of human genome research, and NIH director James Wyngaarden began casting about for a high-profile scientist who could convince Congress that NIH ought to have an independent genome effort. He landed James Watson, who had helped change the course of biology—and captured the Nobel Prize—by co-discovering the double-heft structure of DNA in 1953.

For the 62-year-old Watson, unlocking the secrets of the genome would be the cap to a storied career that has included stints at major universities and research centers. Since 1968, he has directed the Cold Spring Harbor Laboratory in New York, one of the nation's leading biological research labs.

In the world of science, Watson is a heroic figure. But he has never run a government office, and he is hardly a typical administrator. He has, according to a lengthy profile in *The New Republic* last summer, "long kept colleagues wondering, if not about his actual sanity, then about just exactly what frequency he's on." The profile raised a number of questions about the scientist's "judgment and character," concluding there were "various grounds for labeling Watson a screwball...."

"It was an ad hominem attack," says one of Watson's colleagues, "but about 90 percent of it was true."

To be sure, diplomacy is not Watson's strong suit. For example, he has accused the Japanese of "freeloading" on the project and threatened to declare scientific war on them if they didn't increase their genome funding. He has also openly ridiculed DOE's physicists. Of his tactics, Watson told *Science* magazine, "I've found you never get anywhere in the world by being a wimp."

Watson has little patience with those who do not see the value of the genome project. At a hearing of the Senate Energy Research and Development subcommittee last July, Watson was asked what he thought of scientists who argued that the initiative was diverting money from individual research efforts. "I believe they cannot read," he snapped.

Much of Watson's impatience can be traced to the fact that the genome project continues to be widely perceived as a mind-numbing effort to simply sequence all the bases in the human genome. "Some of the early publicity stuck very well," says Elke Jordan, Watson's deputy at NIH's National Center for Human Genome Research. "Some people have not realized that the project looks quite different today."

In fact, NIH has always been more interested in mapping than sequencing, and almost all of its $87.4 million genome budget this year will go to mapping efforts. DOE is studying some of the technological aspects of sequencing, but it too will spend most of its $47.7 million budget this year on mapping research at its national labs. Concerted sequencing efforts are years away.

Nevertheless, the more vociferous critics of the program do not seem to be getting the message. Martin Rechsteiner of the University of Utah's biochemistry department spoke for such critics when he wrote during last year's budget battle, "The Human Genome Project now wants a 70 percent increase in budget for a crash program to sequence the entire human genome.... We see no reason to sequence this spacer DNA. It is simply a waste of money."

Some of the critics, though, are aware of the new focus on gene mapping. Such mapping may be very valuable, Harvard's Davis told the Senate energy research subcommittee in July, but "it is not self-evident to many people in the community that it is worth a very expensive crash program." He and other critics ask, why not let little science run its course?

LITTLE BIG SCIENCE

This question cuts to the heart of the controversy that has plagued the genome project since its beginning. In large measure, the project's proponents have no one but themselves to blame for the big science/little science rift. At first, they used the big science analogy very successfully in convincing Congress to fund the genome initiative. As recently as last April, Watson wrote in *Science* that the genome project was "similar to the 1961 decision made by President John F. Kennedy to send a man to the moon."

But after the congressional hearings last summer, and a letter-writing campaign against the project orchestrated by Rechsteiner and others, the big science label didn't look so attractive. In the fall, Watson changed his tune. In a letter to *The New York Times*, he wrote, "The project is nothing like the big science research and development initiatives with which it is continually compared."

In staking out his new position, Watson has a point. First of all, the $200 million a year that genome backers are seeking would be a drop in the bucket of a big-science agency like NASA. The genome project, even if it takes the full 15 years, will cost a lot less than the space station or the supercollider.

In addition, notes Jordan, "We are not trying to build any unique piece of machinery. You don't have to build the whole resource before it can be used." Unlike the research into the supercollider, much of which would be wasted if it were never built, most of the data gathered in the genome project will be of value to biologists, whether or not the whole genome is sequenced.

In biology, though, where half a million dollars is a huge grant, the genome project's budget is positively jaw-dropping. Its $200 million a year, Davis told Congress, is equal to 5 percent of all government funding of biomedical research, a sum he called "quite substantial for a single, general program."

Davis is hardly alone in criticizing the scope of the genome effort. A majority of his colleagues in the Harvard microbiology department have endorsed his views. At the University of Michigan, 80 scientists joined microbiologist David Friedman in criticizing the program. And at Texas A&M University, 45 scientists signed a petition to Sen. Phil Gramm, R-Texas, saying they were "united in concern about the potential effects of funding the Human Genome Project within NIH at a time when the resources available for non-targeted, investigator-initiated basic research are a a fraction of the NIH budget."

In December, Leon Rosenberg, dean of the Yale Medical School, told *Time* magazine, "If it is impossible to increase significantly the federal budget for health-sciences research in the near future, then I would favor reducing funding for the human genome initiative and even for AIDS."

BUDGET "RED HERRING"

Galas says he understands. "I absolutely agree with all the critics of the genome project in that part of their argument, that we really need strong support for individual research projects."

But he dismisses as a "red herring" the argument that the genome project is draining money from individual research. "The budget is the budget," Galas says, "and you can't say, 'If this weren't here, what would the budget be?' How can you possibly say what it would be like if this weren't here?"

It is simply a political reality, Galas argues, that Congress looks at the genome project in a different way from individual research grants. The genome initiative is the kind of large-scale, high-potential project for which Members of Congress love to earmark funds, especially if those funds go to their constituents. Sen. Pete Domenici, R-N.M., ranking minority member of the energy research and development subcommittee, waxes rhapsodic about the genome project's potential to "unlock the secrets to all kinds of illnesses," but he also knows that his strong support of the project brings $9 million a year in funding for genome research to Los Alamos National Laboratory in his state.

Jordan says that at NIH, the genome effort "is not trying to interfere with individual research in any way." Half of NIH's genome funding, she says, will always be disbursed to individual researchers.

The other half will go to multimillion-dollar "genome research centers" at universities around the country. Last September, the first four centers were set up at the University of California at San Francisco, Stanford University, the University of Michigan, and Washington University in St. Louis.

These large centers particularly annoy the genome project's critics. "It seems that a very small group of well-funded scientists will divide very large amounts of money," Rechsteiner told the Senate subcommittee. Indeed, last spring Jane Peterson, chief of NIH's research centers branch, told *Science* that it was going to be difficult to find scientists to review applications for the center grants because so few scientists were in the field. "It would be easier if everyone wasn't interrelated," Peterson said. "It's such a small community."

But NIH and DOE argue that the large centers and centralized administration are necessary to get full maps of the genome. Watson has told Congress that if he were forced to choose between more individual investigator grants and the genome project, he would take the latter. Of those who say that "little science" could provide a complete human genome map eventually, Jordan says, "In a sense they're probably right. But it would probably take many times as long, and maybe it would never be completed."

In the end, Galas says, those biologists who critize the genome program are just stuck in their ways. "They've seen the tremendous success of molecular biology over the last 50 years, and it's all been achieved by the way they've always done things. So why change? It's a pretty stupid argument, but it's just human nature."

Dual-Agency Effort

Despite the protests of dedicated "little scientists," the genome project's funding has been rising fast in recent years ... and the program is probably here to stay. Which still leaves the question of whether two agencies ought to be working on it at the same time.

Two years ago, in its report on the genome project, the Office of Technology Assessment looked at the issue of whether Congress should designate one agency to lead the genome project. Such a move, OTA said, might reduce duplication of effort, help focus the program, and give Congress one agency on which to concentrate oversight. But, the report concluded, "The choice of a lead agency would likely precipitate a protracted battle among agencies and congressional committees, which could only serve to delay projects." Since each agency has already established turf, the two-track genome project is likely to continue for the foreseeable future.

NIH and DOE argue that their efforts are complementary, not redundant. "In NIH," Galas says, "their tradition is all individual researchers doing their own things in their labs. Which is terrific for most biology. And we need some of that in the genome program, but we also need a focus, an ability to coordinate work so it's not redundant. It's much easier for us to manage a focused program than it is for NIH."

Jordan agrees that seeing how DOE operates in close cooperation with its national labs gives NIH a different perspective on its program. She says that DOE and NIH have worked out "a rather unusual relationship," and that it evolved naturally at the work level, rather than being imposed from above. "It's agreed by everyone that I'm aware of that this is a strength, even though it's a nuisance administratively," she says. "It prevents you from getting too narrow and too insular in how you look at things."

Galas acknowledges that NIH and DOE are "friendly rivals," and both he and Jordan clearly relish the competition. "Only time will tell what the relative contributions of the two agencies will be," Jordan says. "Those things are much easier to see with hindsight."

After reading: CONSOLIDATE INFORMATION

1. What is the big science/little science controversy?
2. Evaluate the position of critics of the Genome project who say that it is too big and too expensive.
3. Summarize Watson's justification for the Genome project and its funding requirements.

Memories Might Be Made of This: Closing in on the Biochemistry of Learning

Carole Ezzell

In this short journalistic report for the general audience of Science News, *Carole Ezzell summarizes some recent research on memory and its composition. Note that she summarizes the work of several collaborative pairs of scientists, not all of whom agree.*

Before reading: FIRST THOUGHTS
      LOOK AHEAD

1. How does Ezzell indicate that she is writing for a broad, non-specialist audience?
2. Read the first two paragraphs. Does the description in these paragraphs help you predict what the rest of the article will tell you?
3. Do you think that memory is primarily physiological or psychological?

During reading: REACT
      QUESTION
      SUMMARIZE

1. How did Alkon and Farley develop a hypothesis about the molecule PKC?
2. What elements of memory are the scientists discussed in this article focusing on?

A BLUE-AND-YELLOW SEA SNAIL sits complacently in its dark test chamber—a plastic trough atop an electronic shaker-table at the bottom of a jury-rigged refrigerator. Suddenly, bright light shines down on the snail and the chamber floor shakes mildly in a simulation of ocean turbulence. The snail instinctively anchors itself in place by tensing the muscular "foot" running along the underside of its body. Seconds later, the cycle of light and shaking repeats, once again prompting the snail to contract its foot.

After 150 such "training" cycles, the snail finds itself in a second refrigerated chamber, now with the eye of a video camera staring at it from below. This time, when bursts of light flash, an interesting thing happens behind the closed refrigerator door: The animal tenses its foot—without being shaken.

"Ordinarily, light alone would never cause that response," says Daniel L. Alkon, chief of neural systems at the National Institute of Neurological Disorders and Stroke (NINDS) in Bethesda, Md. But if the light appears repeatedly just before and during shaking, this snail, called *Hermissenda crassicornis*, eventually learns to contract its foot when light flashes, "just as Pavlov's dog would salivate when the bell occurred, as if the smell of meat were there," Alkon says.

For the past 20 years, Alkon and a number of other researchers have been studying the nervous systems of marine snails—and those of rats and rabbits—in a quest for the molecular mechanisms of memory. Their searches have led them to a molecule called protein kinase C (PKC) in the surface membranes of nerve cells.

PKC exists in all animal cells, where it plays a role in such diverse physiological processes as growth, blood clotting and the action of hormones. The molecule was first discovered in the early 1970s by a Japanese scientist; in 1979, researchers found that it acts by tacking a phosphate group onto specific sites on other molecules. The added phosphate changes the function of those molecules, increasing or decreasing their level of activity.

One of the first direct clues that PKC might underlie learning and memory came in 1986. Joseph Farley of Princeton (N.J.) University observed that injections of PKC, or of a chemical known to activate PKC, excite light-receptor nerve cells in the eyes of *H. crassicornis*. This excitation mimics that induced by the light-and-shake regimen: The nerve cells open pores in their membranes that absorb calcium, and close other pores that expel potassium. Using tiny electrodes to track this process, Farley observed that it reversed the normal negative charge inside the cells.

Six years earlier, Alkon had shown that the electrochemical current in neurons changes as an animal learns. He and Joseph Neary, now at the University of Miami, went on to demonstrate that a protein requiring calcium is involved in learning. Because chemicals like PKC mimic the cellular changes of learning, Alkon and Farley launched separate studies investigating PKC as the agent behind those learning-induced current alterations. They proposed that PKC contributes to learning by somehow closing potassium pores, priming the neurons to react more strongly to a new stimulus.

Alkon and Farley reasoned that if a single molecule was responsible for learning and memory, its appearance, disappearance and reappearance should coincide with learning, forgetting and remembering. The molecule might also bring about structural changes in neurons so that they branched to communicate with other neurons in different ways. Moreover, the learning agent would likely prove active in only one region of a neuron at a time, so that one neuron would have the capacity to hold multiple memories.

Over the past 18 months, evidence has piled up in support of the theory that PKC orchestrates neuronal functions necessary for learning and memory "I have no doubt PKC is central to learning and memory in the models we have looked at," says Alkon, because "we've used so many different measures, and have so many different pieces of evidence that are consistent" with PKC's important role.

Farley, now at Indiana University in Bloomington, agrees. The most compelling evidence, he says, comes from experiments with marine snails.

"I think it's reasonably clear you can mimic learning [in these snails] using PKC," Farley says, noting that "inhibitors of PKC will block those changes." Moreover, his data suggest that "ongoing PKC activation is also necessary for the maintenance of memory in *H. crassicornis*."

Terry J. Crow, who also works with the colorful marine snail, says the link between PKC and learning is gaining acceptance among other neuroscientists. "All of the things we have done here suggest that PKC is sufficient to get the neural changes involved in learning going," says Crow, a neurobiologist at the University of Texas Medical School at Houston.

A year ago, he reported studies demonstrating that a chemical that inhibits protein synthesis also prevents sea snails from remembering a training cycle for more than one hour. Crow's experiments differed from Alkon's because these snails received only one flash of light, immediately followed by an injection of serotonin—a neurotransmitter that Crow believes is also crucial to memory.

"These results indicate that synthesis of proteins during or shortly after training may be a critical step in the formation of long-term memory," write Crow and James Forrester, also from the University of Texas at Houston, in the June 1990 PROCEEDINGS of the NATIONAL ACADEMY OF SCIENCES (Vol.87, No. 12).

Crow has also shown that chemicals that block PKC prevent short-term, but not long-term, memory in *H. crassicornis*. He says this suggests PKC may only be important in linking two stimuli together for short periods—perhaps a few hours—and that another mechanism may be responsible for memories lasting days, months or years. In the March 1991 JOURNAL OF NEUROSCIENCE, Crow reports evidence that short-term and long-term memory involve excitation of two different light-receptor cells in the eyes of *H. crassicornis*.

Alkon interprets the findings differently. Even though Crow and Farley have evidence that the neurons feeding signals to the light receptors in the eyes of sea snails contain serotonin, Alkon remains unconvinced that serotonin plays a primary role in learning. He has never found serotonin in cells adjacent to sea-snail light receptors, and he contends that the serotonin detected by Crow and Farley must arise elsewhere in the brain.

Alkon suspects that a different neurotransmitter—called GABA, for gamma-aminobutyric acid—provides half of the one-two punch that causes *H. crassicornis* to link two events such as light and shaking.

Neurophysiologists Juan V. Sanchez-Andres and René Etcheberrigaray, working in Alkon's laboratory, have used two different techniques to measure the effects of GABA on light-receptor cells taken from *H. crassicornis* eyes. They found that GABA causes the receptor cells to close their potassium pores, exciting them in a manner that mimics the effects of learning.

Other researchers in Alkon's lab have detected GABA in the tiny, hair-bearing cells of statocysts—organs used by *H. crassicornis* to sense motions such as shaking. In addition, says Alkon, they have demonstrated that chemicals that inhibit PKC also block the memory-mimicking effects of GABA.

"A lot of people may be excited by this," says Alkon. In previous studies, he says, GABA had been shown to inhibit neurons, not to excite them. He and senior coauthor Louis Matzel will present the new results in BRAIN RESEARCH.

On the basis of his group's GABA findings, Alkon has constructed a theoretical model of the sequence of events occurring in the outer membranes of a snail's light-receptor nerve cells when the animal learns to connect light flashes with being shaken. According to his model, an incoming light flash triggers a series of impulses in the neuron, accompanied by an influx of calcium. Then the shaking causes the snail's statocyst to release GABA, which binds to the neuron. Both events cause PKC stored inside the cell to move to the cell membrane, where the PKC shuts down the potassium channels by acting through one member of a class of membrane agents called G proteins. When the potassium channels close, the neuron becomes more excitable, so that light later produces the same behavioral response as shaking.

Crow and Farley have developed a similar model to explain snail learning, except that it substitutes serotonin for GABA. They believe serotonin acts indirectly upon PKC, which in turn moves into the neuron membrane to shut down its potassium channels. With the potassium channels closed, the neuron becomes trigger-happy and fires after receiving another stimulus—be it light or a shot of serotonin. After the snail has learned, "the same light then gives you a different response" in the form of foot tensing, explains Crow.

Farley challenges Alkon's assertion that a G protein is necessary to help PKC close potassium channels and keep a neuron excited for learning. "In our model, PKC acts on the channels directly.... There's no need for a G protein," Farley says.

Crow, Farley and Alkon do agree, however, that PKC is responsible for the increased excitability of neurons that have learned—"The PKC-induced changes in learning last for many days, and sometimes even for weeks," notes Alkon.

But how do the relatively short-term effects of PKC get translated into long-term memories?

Alkon's team is tracing the longer-term effects of PKC to find out. In the January 1990 PROCEEDINGS OF THE NATIONAL ACADEMY OF SCIENCES (Vol.87, No. 1), Thomas J. Nelson from Alkon's lab reports that neurons from trained snails contain elevated levels of messenger RNA (mRNA), the chemical intermediary through which DNA makes protein. Alkon and Nelson also showed that the extra MRNA was the result of learning, and not just the experience of being under bright light or being shaken: Snails that experienced random shaking and lighting did not learn and did not show elevated amounts of mRNA.

More recently, Nelson has uncovered evidence that the G protein cited by Alkon exerts control over mRNA. "It turns out that this G protein regulates the turnover of mRNA or the readout of mRNA," Alkon says. "That's very exciting, because it suggests the G protein not only has effects on the [potassium] channels, but also affects the synthesis of proteins." Nelson and Alkon are now preparing to publish the finding.

What does protein synthesis have to do with learning?

Alkon thinks long-term memory depends upon "hard-wiring" changes that strengthen some connections between neurons while reducing others. These structural changes occur in the dendrites, the branching fingers through which neurons receive incoming electrical impulses. To change their branching pattern, neurons must manufacture new proteins.

In Alkon's scenario, learning activates a neuron's PKC, which in turn activates a G protein. The G protein then closes the potassium channels, keeping the neuron excited for short-term memory. The G protein also regulates protein synthesis, which "hard-wires" the memory over the long term by changing the neuron's branching structure.

Farley questions whether changes in neuron branching build long-term memories. "I'm a little skeptical about these changes in cell volume that are purported to be happening [as a result of learning]," he says.

Experiments at Alkon's laboratory back up this scenario, however. In the February 1990 PROCEEDINGS OF THE NATIONAL ACADEMY OF SCIENCES (Vol.87, No.4), Alkon and several coworkers report the results of injecting dye into light-receptor cells of trained and untrained snails. The dye revealed that the neurons of snails trained to associate light and shaking had fewer and more condensed branches than did those of untrained snails, suggesting that learning could reroute a nerve cell's branching.

Such rerouting should be reflected in fluctuations in the shipment of new cell membrane from the body of the cell to the branch tips, Alkon reasoned. Last year, Simon Moshiach from Alkon's lab, together with Nelson and Sanchez-Andres, demonstrated just such a change. With one squirt of G protein extracted from a snail, they slowed the flow of new protein globules along the axon—the long "arm" that transmits outgoing messages—of a large nerve cell taken from a crab.

Although Alkon contends that long-term memory probably requires changes in neuron structure, he also finds evidence that PKC is involved. Working with Matzel, now at Rutgers University in New Brunswick, N.J., he turned up evidence that PKC's effects can persist for weeks after *H. crassicornis* has learned.

Matzel trained the snails with just enough paired cycles of light and shaking that they learned to associate the two stimuli. He did not repeat the cycles over and over to reinforce the animals' memories, however. After about one week, the snails forgot the association: Light alone no longer caused their feet to tense. But when Matzel retrained the animals after waiting two weeks, he found that they could relearn the association after just a handful of trials.

"Even though they had forgotten, they retained some memory, because they relearned much more quickly," Alkon says.

To see if PKC had a hand in this effect, Matzel studied light-receptor cells taken from the eyes of snails that had forgotten their training. If he jolted the cells with a shot of calcium, they clamped down their potassium channels just as they would have if they had learned. But if he also added chemicals that blocked PKC, the potassium channels stayed open. "That's good evidence for long-lasting involvement of PKC in learning," Alkon argues.

With increasing evidence linking PKC to learning and memory in snails, Alkon's team began looking for a similar link in higher animals.

In 1988, Alkon's coworker Barry Bank, with colleagues from NINDS and Yale University, used a radioactive stain to trace the activation of PKC in rabbits. They found that rabbits trained to associate a particular tone with a mild electrical shock near their eyes eventually learned to drop a protective membrane over their eyes whenever they heard the tone. The stain revealed that the trained rabbits harbored increased levels of PKC in the hippocampus of the brain. Previous studies involving animals and humans with hippocampal injuries had shown that this area of the brain is crucial to maintaining memory for many days.

James L. Olds of NINDS went one step farther by precisely tracing the movement of PKC throughout nerve cells in the rabbit hippocampus. He found that PKC levels increased in the cell bodies of the neurons one day after the rabbits had undergone training, and that the PKC moved to the dendrite membranes three days after training. These results support the finding in sea snails that after learning, PKC moves from the body of a nerve cell and into its membrane.

Working with David Olton of Johns Hopkins University in Baltimore, Olds has also trained rats swimming through a tank of water to distinguish unstable platforms from those stable enough to allow the animals to climb out and dry off. Rats given cues about which platforms were stable had lower hippocampal levels of PKC than did rats that learned the difference through trial and error, the researchers report in the November 1990 JOURNAL OF NEUROSCIENCE.

Recently, Olds and Sanchez-Andres have begun to investigate the PKC changes that occur early in an animal's development. By staining brain slices from baby rabbits not yet old enough to have opened their eyes, they have discovered that most of the PKC in the hippocampal neurons resides in two tracks flanking the cell body. In contrast, the hippocampal neurons of older rabbits have a single, diffuse track of PKC situated around the dendrites. When the baby rabbits open their eyes and begin exploring their environment at about 10 days of age, their PKC moves into the dendrites, perhaps programming their memories, Olds says.

He speculates that very young rabbits hoard PKC near the cell bodies because they haven't yet had a chance to learn anything about their surroundings. Then, when they open their eyes, their brains are flooded with new information worth remembering—a change that kicks the PKC memory pathway into action.

Olds notes that many other researchers have now implicated PKC in the development of neurons. "I'm trying to figure out the role of PKC in learning and postnatal development," he says. "I'm convinced that similar molecular mechanisms are involved."

Others are investigating PKC's involvement in human disorders, such as Alzheimer's disease, that erode both memory and learning capacity. A group led by Tsunao Saitoh at the University of California, San Diego, reports in the July 1990 JOURNAL OF NEUROSCIENCE that the brains of 11 deceased Alzheimer's victims contained only half as much PKC as the brains of seven people who had died of other causes. The results confirm previous findings by Saitoh's team (based on a less specific method for measuring PKC), which had hinted that PKC levels drop in Alzheimer's patients.

Saitoh and his colleagues ruled out the possibility that the reductions in PKC resulted from the overall death of neurons in Alzheimer's patients by measuring the PKC levels of connective-tissue cells in the autopsied brains. These cells also showed lower-than-expected amounts of PKC, they found.

Researchers who are studying the humble sea snail find encouragement in the discovery that PKC is linked to human learning and memory. It proves they aren't chasing down blind alleys in their search for the molecular Holy Grail of memory. At the same time, they're cautious about attributing the entire orchestration of human learning to PKC.

"We don't know about other molecules, such as G proteins, that are likely to be involved in learning [in humans and other higher animals]," says Alkon. "Molecular pathways are very complex, and there are undoubtedly hosts of other actors in this drama that we haven't yet met."

Adds Farley, "There's little doubt that PKC is involved in an important way, but it's certainly not the entire story."

After reading: CONSOLIDATE INFORMATION
1. How is scientific knowledge formed when there are competing or different theories about the same thing?
2. Alkon's findings have led him to develop a model of what he hypothesizes about memory and learning; summarize that model.
3. How would you summarize what the scientists discussed here know about PKC and its role in memory?

Inhibition of Protein Synthesis Blocks Long-Term Enhancement of Generator Potentials Produced by One-Trial *in vivo* Conditioning in *Hermissenda*

Terry Crow and James Forrester

Neurobiologists Terry Crow and James Forrester collaborated on the research project described in this scientific article. In writing about their research for an audience of their scientific peers, scientists follow a prescribed sequence and format describing the methods, materials, results, and the significance of their results. This research report appeared in the Proceedings of the National Academy of Science.

Before reading: FIRST THOUGHTS
LOOK AHEAD

1. Read the abstract. What do you learn from the abstract that will help you understand the scientific experiments and the researchers' findings?
2. Make a list of terms you do not understand in the title and the abstract. Compare your list with that of another student in your class and collaborate on finding out what the terms mean.
3. The literature review in the first paragraph of this article surveys other research on the relation of protein synthesis to memory. What do you learn from this survey?

During reading: REACT
QUESTION
SUMMARIZE

1. Crow and Forrester focus on a very specific experiment concerning protein synthesis and how learning and recall may be blocked in snails. What is the experimental sequence they follow?
2. What do Crow and Forrester think is the most crucial element in the chemistry of memory?

ABSTRACT A one-trial *in vivo* conditioning procedure produces short- and long-term cellular changes that can be detected in identified sensory neurons of the pathway mediating the conditioned stimulus. The memory of the associative experience in the conditioned stimulus pathway is expressed by short- and long-term enhancement of light-evoked generator potentials recorded from identified lateral and medial type B photoreceptors within the eyes of *Hermissenda*. To identify mechanisms of the induction and expression of short- and long-term enhancement in identified photoreceptors, we have investigated the effects of inhibiting protein synthesis during the application of the one-trial *in vivo* conditioning procedure. Anisomycin (1 μM) present during and after the conditioning trial blocked long-term enhancement without affecting the induction or expression of short-term enhancement. Application of a control compound, deacetylanisomycin (1 μM), or delaying the application of anisomycin until 1 hr after the conditioning trial did not block either long- or short-term enhancement. These results indicate that synthesis of proteins during or shortly after training may be a critical step in the formation of long-term memory of the associative experience.

BEHAVIORAL AND CELLULAR NEUROPHYSIOLOGICAL STUDIES of memory have provided support for the hypothesis that protein synthesis during or shortly after an experience is a necessary step for the formation of enduring forms of memory called long-term memory (review in ref. 1). Support for the hypothesis that, for long-term memory to be formed, proteins must be synthesized is provided by learning and memory studies of vertebrates where inhibition of protein synthesis and/or RNA synthesis interferes with the formation of long-term memory while short-term memory remains relatively intact (2–5). Recently, studies of short- and long-term synaptic facilitation of monosynaptic connections between cultured sensory and motor neurons in *Aplysia* revealed that inhibitors of protein or RNA synthesis blocked long-term facilitation, while leaving short-term facilitation intact (6). Studies of short-term and long-term synaptic and cellular plasticity in invertebrate nervous systems are particularly attractive since such preparations provide for the opportunity of relating biochemical and molecular changes in identified neuronal cell types to learning and memory (6–11). The results of recent studies of *Hermissenda* have shown that a one-trial *in vivo* conditioning procedure produces a long-term change in phototactic behavior that depends upon pairing a conditioned stimulus (CS) with the direct application of serotonin (5-hydroxytryptamine, 5-HT) to the exposed nervous system of otherwise intact animals (12). One site for cellular changes that may contribute to the long-term behavioral modification is the sensory pathway mediating the CS. We recently reported that one-trial *in vivo* conditioning produces both a short-term nonassociative enhancement and a long-term associative enhancement of generator potentials recorded from identified lateral and medial B photoreceptors (13). The induction of short-term enhancement is due in part to activation of the Ca^{2+}/phospholipid-dependent kinase, protein kinase C (14–16). An essential role for protein kinase C in long-term enhancement has not been demonstrated; however, long-term enhancement can be produced by pairing the CS with activation of protein kinase C by diacylglycerol analogues or phorbol esters (14).

Although some progress has been made in understanding the events that may be critical for induction (i.e., the associative interaction between depolarization of photoreceptors and activation of protein kinases), the mechanisms responsible for the maintenance and expression of long-term enhancement are not understood. Here we report that the protein synthesis inhibitor anisomycin, when present during and after one-trial *in vivo* conditioning, blocks long-term enhancement without affecting the induction or expression of short-term enhancement. We found that the application of anisomycin 1 hr after *in vivo* conditioning was ineffective in blocking long-term enhancement, which is consistent with earlier reports from studies of vertebrates suggesting that a critical "time window" operates for macromolecular synthesis. The results of this study indicate that retention of the memory for the associative experience depends upon protein synthesis during or shortly after the presentation of the conditioning trial.

Abbreviations: 5-HT, 5-hydroxytryptamine (serotonin): CS, conditioned stimulus; ASW, artificial sea water.

MATERIALS AND METHODS

A total of 78 adult *Hermissenda* crassicornis was used in the experiments. *Hermissenda* were obtained from Sea Life Supply (Sand City, CA). The animals were fed small pieces of scallops each day during the experiment and housed in artificial sea water (ASW) aquaria at 14 ± 1 °C on a 12-hr light/dark cycle. The animals were prepared for the *in vivo* conditioning procedure as described (12). Before conditioning, animals were lightly anesthetized with 0.25-ml injections of isotonic $MgCl_2$, and a small dorsolateral incision was made to expose the circumesophageal nervous system. Surgically prepared animals were then transferred to a chamber containing 50 ml of normal ASW. The exposed nervous system was visualized in infrared illumination provided by a 45-W tungsten/halogen light source projected through an infrared filter (Schott model RG-850). A dissecting microscope formed an image of the nervous system upon a Dage MTi video camera connected to a video monitor and time-lapse video recorder.

In vivo **conditioning procedure.** The one-trial *in vivo* conditioning procedure consisted of presenting visible light (10×10^{-4} W/cm^2) paired with the injection of 0.5 ml of 5-HT to the region of the cerebropleural ganglion where previous immunocytochemistry revealed 5-HT-reactive processes near the optic nerve and photoreceptor terminals in the neuropil (17). The injection of 5-HT was applied to the desired region of the exposed nervous system by observing the image of the ganglion and injecting needle on a video monitor. The final concentration of 5-HT in the ASW was 0.1 mM. Anisomycin and deacetylanisomycin applications were adjusted to yield a final concentration in the ASW of 1 μM.

Measurement of protein synthesis. We used the reversible protein synthesis inhibitor anisomycin (18–20) at a concentration of 1 μM. The concentration of anisomycin and deacetylanisomycin used in the studies was based upon the results of experiments that examined the incorporation of [^{3}H]leucine (150 μCi/mi; 1 Ci = 37 GBq) into protein insoluble in trichloroacetic acid. The incorporation of [^{3}H]leucine into newly synthesized proteins was terminated after 40 min by washing and homogenizing each nervous system in cold (4 °C) phosphate-buffered saline, which was then adjusted to 10% (wt/vol) trichloroacetic acid and held on ice for 30 min. Solutions were centrifuged at $10,000 \times g$ for 10 min, and pellets were washed twice with 10% trichloroacetic acid by resuspension and centrifugation. Radioactivities were quantified by scintillation counting. We found that 1 μM anisomycin blocks protein synthesis by 86% in the *Hermissenda* circumesophageal nervous system. To address the problem of specificity of the inhibitor, we used a derivative of anisomycin, deacetylanisomycin (20), which produced 3% inhibition of protein synthesis at a concentration of 1 μM.

Experimental protocol. As shown in the diagram of the experimental protocol in Fig. 1. four different treatments were examined. The paired group received light (CS) paired with the injection of 5-HT in the presence of the protein synthesis inhibitor anisomycin or a derivative, deacetylanisomycin, that does not significantly inhibit protein synthesis at the concentration used in this study

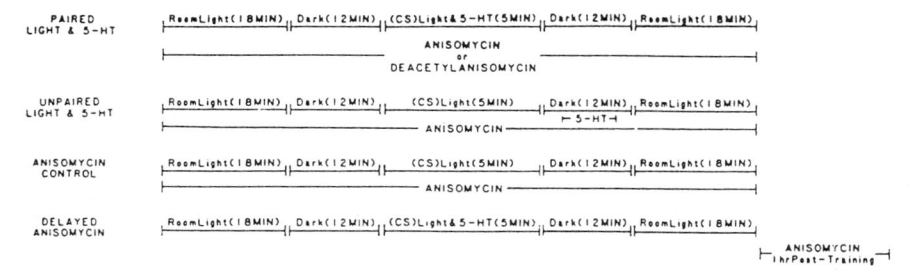

FIGURE 1 Experimental protocol for investigating the effects of protein synthesis inhibition produced by anisomycin on short- and long-term enhancement. Animals prepared for *in vivo* conditioning were assigned to one of four different treatment conditions. The paired light (CS) and 5-HT group received one 5-min trial of light paired simultaneously with the injection of 5-HT onto the exposed nervous system in the presence of either anisomycin or deacetylanisomycin. The unpaired control group received the CS (5 min) followed by a 5-min period in the dark before applying 5-HT (5 min) to the nervous system in the dark (infrared illumination). The anisomycin control group received only the 5-min CS in the presence of anisomycin. The delayed anisomycin group received the CS and 5-HT paired, and the anisomycin was applied 1 hr after the termination of one-trial *in vivo* conditioning.

(1 μM). The anisomycin or deacetylanisomycin was applied 30 min prior to the presentation of the conditioning trial and was present during the application of light and 5-HT. The anisomycin and deacetylanisomycin were washed out 30 min after the end of the one-trial conditioning procedure. An unpaired control group received light (CS) and 5-HT separated by 5 min in the presence of anisomycin. The 5-HT was applied in the dark (infrared illumination) and washed out at the end of the 5-min period (see Fig. 1). An anisomycin control group received only the 5-min light step (CS) in the presence of anisomycin. The final treatment group received light paired with 5-HT; however, the anisomycin was applied 1 hr after the end of the conditioning trial (1 hr posttraining). The anisomycin remained on the exposed nervous system for the same period (65 min) as was used for other treatment groups. After the various experimental treatments, the nervous systems were washed with ASW and the animals were returned to marked cages in the sea water aquaria.

Intracellular recording. One hour or 24 hr after the different experimental treatments, animals were prepared for intracellular recording from identified medial and lateral type B photoreceptors. Recordings of light-evoked generator potentials were collected either 1 hr after the end of the conditioning trial (short term) or 24 hr after the conditioning trial (long term). The animals were coded so that the experimenter collecting the electrophysiological data did not know the treatment condition that a given preparation had received. The nervous systems were removed, and B photoreceptors were isolated by axotomy of the optic nerve as described (11, 22). After 15 min of dark adaptation, generator potentials elicited by a 2-min light step (10×10^{-4} W/cm^2 at 510 nm) were recorded from visually identified B photoreceptors in the medial and lateral position in the eye by using standard procedures for intracellular recording and light stimulation. Microelectrodes used for intracellular recordings had a resistance between 40 and 60 MΩ when filled with 4 M potassium acetate. Prior to intracellular recordings, the isolated nervous systems received a mild incubation in a protease solution (type VIII, 0.67 mg/ml, 5 to 6 min; Sigma) to facilitate microelectrode penetration of identified B photoreceptors. Electrophysiological experiments were conducted in buffered ASW (10 mM Hepes/460 mM NaCl/10 mM KCl/10 mM CaCl$_2$/55 mM MgCl$_2$). The solution was brought to a final pH of 7.6 at 15 ± 0.5 °C with dilute NaOH. The temperature of the ASW in the recording chamber was maintained at 15 ± 0.5 °C. The sea water temperature was monitored by a thermistor inserted into the recording chamber.

Statistical analysis. A two-way analysis of variance with repeated measures (treatment × trials unweighted-means solution) was used to assess overall effects of the various treatments on the amplitude of generator potentials (21). Tests of significance of the peak and plateau phase of the generator potentials following a significant overall F test employed Newman-Keuls procedures (21). In cases where the interaction between treatment and trials was significant, the simple main effects were analyzed to determine significance. Within group comparisons of the change in amplitude of the peak and plateau phase of the generator potential following the application of 5-HT to animals that had previously received anisomycin pretreatment were made with difference scores using a t test for correlated means.

Results

Anisomycin does not block short-term enhancement. We previously reported that one-trial *in vivo* conditioning produces both a short-term and a long-term enhancement of light-evoked generator potentials recorded from identified medial and lateral B photoreceptors (13). Short-term enhancement of generator potentials recorded from medial and lateral B photoreceptors is not dependent upon pairing the CS with 5-HT, whereas long-term enhancement found only in lateral B photoreceptors is dependent upon pairing the CS with 5-HT (11, 13). Pretreatment with 1 μM anisomycin did not block the induction or the expression of enhanced generator potentials produced by light and 5-HT recorded from medial or lateral B photoreceptors 1 hr after the conditioning trial. Representative examples of generator potentials evoked by a 2-min light step are shown in Fig. 2A for preparations that received light paired with 5-HT (Fig. 2A1) or only the CS (light control) (Fig. 2A2).

Both preparations had received identical pretreatment with anisomycin. The enhanced generator potential shown in Fig. 2A1 as compared to the control in Fig. 2A2 indicates that anisomycin pretreatment did not block short-term enhancement produced by the light and 5-HT. This conclusion is supported by the analysis of the group data shown in the graph in Fig. 2B comparing the paired and unpaired groups to the anisomycin control group. The results of the treatment by trials

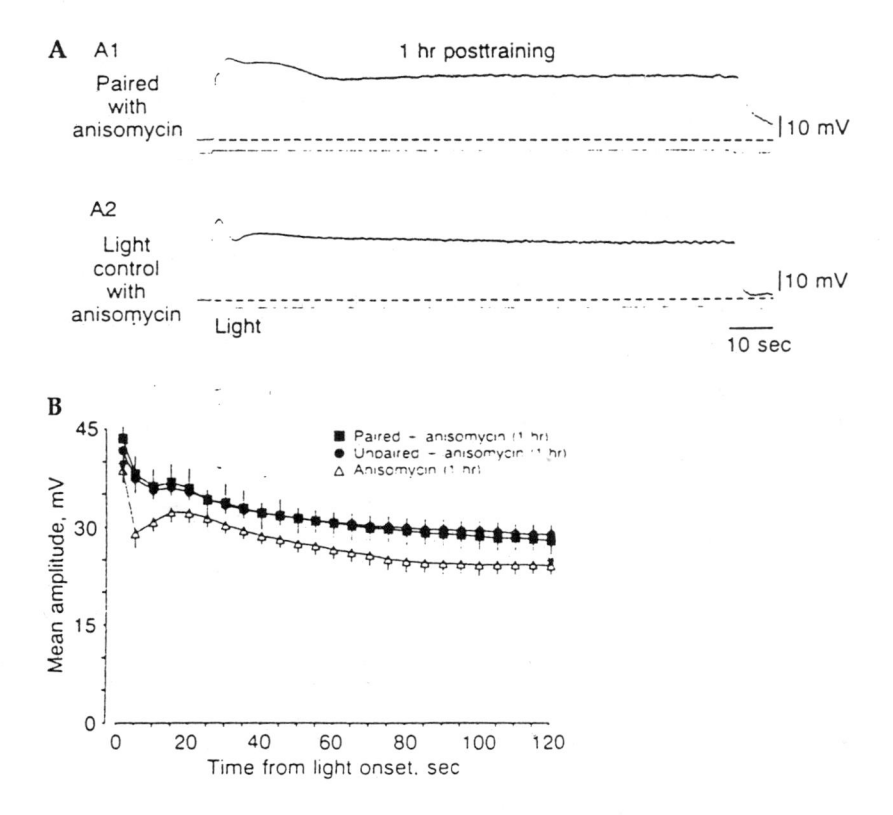

FIGURE 2 Anisomycin does not block short-term enhancement produced by light and 5-HT. (*A1*) Intracellular recording of a generator potential for an isolated medial B photoreceptor evoked by a 2-min light step (10×10^{-4} W/cm^2) 1 hr after the termination of one-trial *in vivo* conditioning. The conditioning trial was presented in the presence of 1 μM anisomycin. (*A2*) Generator potential evoked by the light step recorded from an isolated medial B photoreceptor 1 hr after the presentation of the light (CS) in the presence of 1 μM anisomycin. The dashed lines in *A1* and *A2* represent the dark-adapted resting membrane potential. Pretreatment with anisomycin failed to block the enhancement of the generator potential produced by light and 5-HT. (*B*) Group data showing the mean amplitude ± SEM (in MV) of the generator potential evoked by a 2-min light step for the groups that received the CS paired with 5-HT in the presence of anisomycin ($n = 10$), the unpaired CS and %-HT in the presence of anisomycin ($n = 11$), and only the CS in the presence of anisomycin ($n = 9$). The paired and unpaired groups were not signivicantly different from each other; however, the generator potentials from both groups were significantly larger as compared to the anisomycin control group ($P < 0.05$). The application of 1 μM anisomycin by itself does not produce a diminished generation potential since the transient peak and plateau phase at light offset is virtually identical to normal controls ($n = 10$), as indicated by the asterisks at time 0 and 120 sec after light onset.

analysis of variance revealed an overall significant difference between the groups ($F_{2,27} = 3.42$; $P < 0.05$). Short-term enhancement does not depend upon pairing light and 5-HT, which is consistent with previously reported results (13), since the generator potentials recorded from both the paired ($n = 10$) and unpaired groups ($n = 11$) exhibited significant enhancement. The statistical results revealed that, while the paired and unpaired groups were not significantly different from each other, both were significantly larger as compared to the anisomycin control group ($n = 9$), which received only the light (CS) ($P < 0.01$). The generator potentials recorded from the three groups exhibited adaptation, which was expressed by a significant reduction in the amplitude of the generator potential measured from peak onset to the end of the 2-min light step ($F_{24,648} = 63$; $P < 0.01$). A comparison of averaged generator potentials between the anisomycin control group and a normal control group that did not receive anisomycin ($n = 10$) revealed that anisomycin at the concentration used in this study (1 μM) does not significantly alter the amplitude of the generator potential (see data represented by asterisks in Fig. 2B). These results show that protein synthesis inhibition at the time of application of the CS and 5-HT does not block short-term enhancement produced by one-trial *in vivo* conditioning.

Anisomycin blocks long-term enhancement. After finding that short-term enhancement is not affected by inhibiting protein synthesis, we next examined the effect of anisomycin application upon long-term enhancement, which is detected in only lateral B photoreceptors. Previous results have shown that long-term enhancement is expressed in lateral B photoreceptors by a decrease in the rate of adaptation of the generator potential in response to a light step, which produces a larger plateau phase while the initial transient peak is not changed (11, 13). Presenting the *in vivo* conditioning trial during the period of protein synthesis inhibition blocks long-term enhancement. Representative examples of generator potentials are shown in Fig. 3A and the group data are shown in Fig. 3B. The results of the treatment × trials analysis of variance showed no significant overall effect of the different treatments. This is due to the observation that long-term enhancement is expressed during the plateau phase of the light step and not in the early part of the light response. Indeed, the mean amplitude of the generator potential was virtually identical during the first 40 sec of the light response for all of the treatment groups (see Fig. 3B). The significant differences between groups expressed during the plateau phase of the light response is supported statistically by the significant interaction between the treatments and trials (the time from light onset) ($F_{48,840} = 3.9$: $P < 0.01$). This means that there are overall significant differences in the later component (plateau phase) of the generator potential amplitude between the group that received *in vivo* conditioning in the presence of anisomycin ($n = 15$) and the groups that received either the control compound deacetylanisomycin ($n = 11$) or anisomycin application delayed by 1 hr ($n = 12$). The effect of light adaptation on the amplitude of the generator potential was significant for all groups ($F_{24,840} = 64.7$; $P < 0.01$). A separate statistical analysis of generator potential amplitudes for a group that received unpaired light and 5-ET in the presence of anisomycin ($n = 5$) and the paired light and 5-HT group ($n = 15$) in the presence of anisomycin revealed that there were no significant

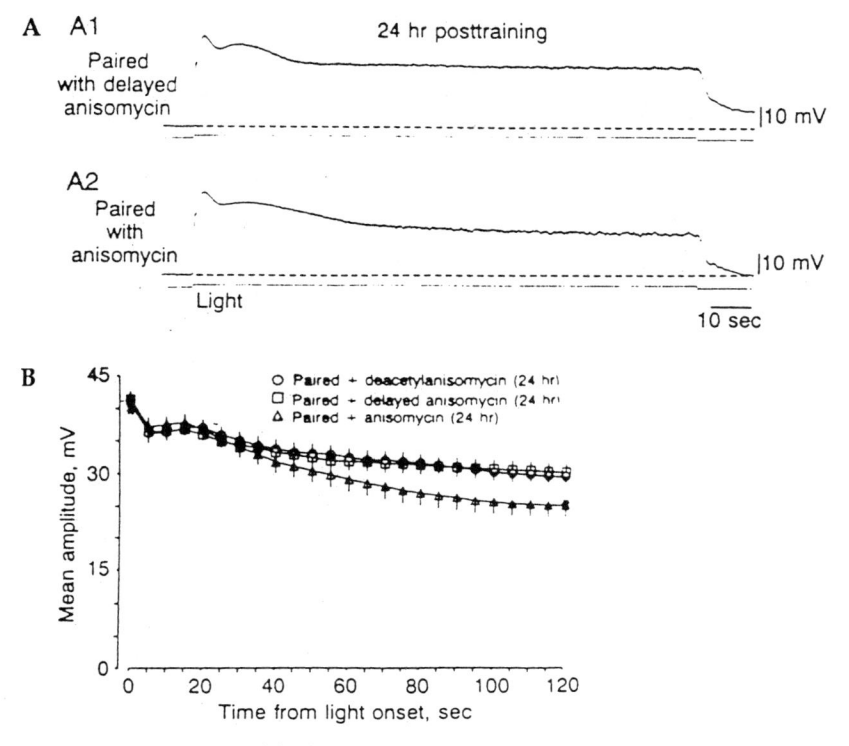

FIGURE 3 Anisomycin blocks long-term enhancement in lateral B photoreceptors produced by one-trial *in vivo* conditioning. (*A1*) Intracellular recording of a generator potential from an isolated lateral B photoreceptor evoked by a 2-min light step 24 hr after the termination of one-trial *in vivo* conditioning. The application of 1 μM anisomycin was delayed 1 hr after the conditioning trial. (*A2*) Generator potential evoked by the light step recorded from an isolated lateral B photoreceptor 24 hr after the termination of one-trial *in vivo* conditioning. The conditioning trial was presented in the presence of 1 μM anisomycin. The dashed lines in *A1* and *A2* represent the dark-adapted resting membrane potential. Delaying the application of anisomycin resulted in long-term enhancement of the generator potential while pretreatment with anisomycin blocked long-term enhancement. (*B*) Group data showing the mean amplitude of the generator potential ± SEM (in mV) evoked by a 2 min light step recorded 24 hr after the conditioning trial for the groups that received light paired with 5-HT in the presence of deacetylanisomycin ($n = 11$), light paired with 5-HT with anisomycin delayed 1 hr after one-trial conditioning ($n = 12$), or light paired with 5-HT in the presence of anisomycin ($n = 15$). The mean amplitude of the transient peak and plateau phase of the generator potential for an unpaired control group ($n = 5$) in the presence of anisomycin is denoted by the asterisks at time 0 and 120 sec from light onset. The plateau phase of the generator potential was significantly enhanced for both the paired with deacetylanisomycin and paired with delayed anisomycin groups as compared to the group that received the light paired with 5-HT or the unpaired light and 5-HT in the presence of anisomycin ($P < 0.01$). The amplitude of the transient peak and plateau phase of the generator potential was not significantly different from the paired and unpaired groups in the presence of anisomycin. Pretreatment with anisomycin blocked long-term enhancement (plateau phase of the generator potential) recorded from lateral B photoreceptors.

differences between the two groups. The average peak amplitude and average amplitude of generator potentials at the end of the 2-min light step for the unpaired control group in the presence of anisomycin is indicated by the asterisks in Fig. 3B.

Since previously published results have suggested that a time window must exist for protein synthesis inhibition to be effective in blocking long-term memory (see ref. 1), we examined the effect of delaying anisomycin application. We found that delaying the application of the anisomycin by 1 hr resulted in long-term enhancement that was identical to enhancement observed if the *in vivo* conditioning trial was presented in the presence of the control compound (deacetylanisomycin) (see Fig. 3B). Two examples of generator potentials recorded from lateral B photoreceptors in a preparation that received the anisomycin 1 hr after *in vivo* conditioning and a preparation that received conditioning in the presence of anisomycin are shown in Fig. 3A, and the group data are presented in Fig. 3B. These results show that anisomycin blocks the enhanced plateau phase of the generator potential if it is present during the presentation of the conditioning trial; however, inhibition of protein synthesis is ineffective if delayed 1 hr after conditioning.

Although the mechanisms for the expression of long-term enhancement are not known, it could be argued that anisomycin interferes with the expression of enhancement and not induction by interfering with second-messenger activation. To test this, preparations that received paired light and 5-HT with anisomycin pretreatment ($n = 5$) were tested at 24 hr to again verify that enhancement was blocked. After the light step, the preparations received an application of 5-HT to test if short-term enhancement could be induced. The analysis of the results showed that short-term enhancement could be induced by 5-HT application in preparations where anisomycin had been shown to block long-term enhancement. This is shown by the group data of average generator potential amplitudes before and after 5-HT application (Fig. 4). Both the peak amplitude ($t = 4.14$; $P < 0.01$) and plateau phase ($t = 5.89$; $P < 0.0025$) were enhanced following the application of 5-HT to the same preparations where anisomycin had blocked long-term enhancement. Our results indicate that inhibiting protein synthesis during the presentation of a one-trial *in vivo* conditioning procedure is sufficient to block long-term enhancement while leaving short-term enhancement intact. The effects of inhibiting protein synthesis show specificity since a derivative of anisomycin, deacetylanisomycin, which does not inhibit protein synthesis at the concentration used in this study (1 μM), does not block long-term enhancement. The results indicate that a time window must operate in which inhibiting protein synthesis will be effective in blocking long-term enhancement, since delaying the application of anisomycin by 1 hr results in normal long-term enhancement.

Discussion

We have found that inhibiting protein synthesis during one-trial *in vivo* conditioning blocks long-term enhancement but not short-term enhancement of light-evoked generator potentials recorded from identified B photoreceptors

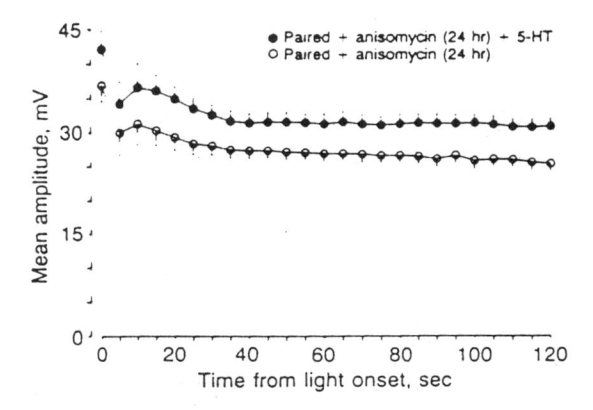

FIGURE 4 5-ht produces short-term enhancement in lateral B photoreceptors of preparations where long-term enhancement is blocked by anisomycin. ○, Average generator potential amplitude ± SEM (in mV) evoked by a 2-min light step 24 hr after one-trial *in vivo* conditioning ($n = 5$). The conditioning trial was presented in the presence of 1 μM anisomycin. Consistent with the data shown in Fig. 3, anisomycin blocks long-term enhancement. However, the same lateral B photoreceptors can express significant short-term enhancement of the peak ($P < 0.01$) and plateau phase of the generator potentials ($P < 0.0025$) after the application of 5-HT (●).

within the eyes of *Hermissenda*. In previous studies of *in vivo* conditioning, we showed that long-term enhancement in lateral B photoreceptors is expressed by a decrease in the rate of adaptation and/or accommodation of light-evoked generator potentials, which results in larger amplitudes of the steady-state or plateau phase of the generator potential (13). Our preliminary studies of intact B photoreceptors capable of generating action potentials indicate that the magnitude of enhancement of the amplitude of the plateau phases of generator potentials observed after *in vivo* conditioning would be sufficient to produce an increase in the frequency of action potentials recorded from intact photoreceptors during light stimulation. An increase in the light-elicited spike discharge rate of B photoreceptors could contribute to the reported suppression of normal phototactic behavior produced by *in vivo* conditioning (12) since *Hermissenda* are capable of behaviorally discriminating between light intensities that vary by as little as 1 logarithmic unit of attenuation (22).

Our results would indicate that inhibiting protein synthesis during the conditioning experience blocks the induction of events necessary for long-term enhancement, rather than interfering with receptor and/or second-messenger mediated steps that may be necessary for maintenance or expression of enhancement. This hypothesis is supported by our results demonstrating that 5-HT application is sufficient to produce short-term enhancement in the same identified photoreceptors where pretreatment with anisomycin blocked long-term enhancement. Moreover, the short-term enhancement that we observed 24 hr after anisomycin treatment was virtually identical to the enhancement detected at 1 hr (short-term enhancement) following 5-HT application.

The results showing that inhibition of protein synthesis after *in vivo* conditioning is ineffective in blocking long-term enhancement suggests that protein synthesis during or shortly after the conditioning trial is necessary for the formation of an enduring memory of the associative experience. This observation suggests that a critical time window must exist for protein synthesis and is consistent with studies in vertebrates where deficits of long-term memory were assessed by changes in behavior (1–5). Our results are consistent with the findings of recent studies of a 5-HT-induced short- and long-term facilitation in cultured *Aplysia* neurons (6). In *Aplysia*, protein synthesis inhibitors blocked long-term facilitation when given during 5-HT application but not when presented before or after the 5-HT application (6). More recently it was reported that inhibiting protein synthesis blocked both cAMP-evoked long-term facilitation (23) and long-term behavioral sensitization in the isolated gill-withdrawal reflex of *Aplysia* (8). Consistent with the results of studies of synaptic and cellular plasticity in invertebrates is the observation that maintenance of long-term potentiation in the rat dentate gyrus requires protein synthesis, which may be completed as soon as 15 min after tetanization (24).

As is the case with vertebrates, short-term memory for the conditioning experience in *Hermissenda* appears to be intact following the anisomycin treatment. Our results showing that inhibiting protein synthesis during and after one-trial *in vivo* conditioning does not affect the induction or expression of short-term enhancement indicates that the expression of gene products essential for long-term enhancement are not required for short-term enhancement. Long-term enhancement may operate through an independent and parallel signaling system, or alternately, both short-term enhancement and long-term enhancement could operate in series such that some of the same steps important for induction may be common to both. Recent work in *Aplysia* has shown that short- and long-term facilitation produced by 5-HT or cAMP (6, 23, 25–27) involves the phosphorylation of the same 17 substrate proteins (9). Although we do not know the cellular signaling systems essential for long-term enhancement, we have evidence that activation of protein kinase C may be an important step for induction of short-term enhancement (14–16). It is not known if the pathways essential for the induction of short- and long-term enhancement are independent; however, recent results have indicated that conditions that are sufficient to block short-term enhancement do not block long-term enhancement, which suggests that different and independent pathways may be involved (15).

Although we do not know which proteins may be involved in the induction and maintenance of long-term enhancement, the visual system of *Hermissenda* is attractive for such studies since it provides for the opportunity to identify proteins, in different identified neurons within the same structure, that may be involved in both a long-term associative change and a short-term nonassociative change.

Notes

1. Davis, H. P. & Squire, L. (1984) *Psychol. Bull.* **96**, 519–559.
2. Flexner, J. B., Flexner, L. B. & Stellar, E. (1963) *Science* **141**, 57–59.
3. Agranoff, B. W. (1970) in *Protein Metabolism of the Nervous System*, ed. Lajtha, A. (Plenum, New York), pp. 533–543.
4. Barondes, S. H. (1975) in *Short-term-Memory*, eds. Duetsch, D. & Duetsch, J. A. (Academic, New York), pp. 379–390.
5. Davis, H. P., Rosenzweig, M. R., Bennett, E. L. & Squire, L. R. (1980) *Behav. Neural. Biol.* **28**, 99–104.
6. Montarolo, P. G., Goelet, P., Castellucci, V. F., Morgan, J., Kandel, E. R. & Schacher, S. (1986) *Science* **234**, 1249–1254.
7. Castellucci, V. F., Kennedy, T. E., Kandel, E. R. & Goelet, P. (1988) *Neuron* **1**, 321–328.
8. Castellucci, V. F., Blumenfeld, H., Goelet, P. & Kandel, E. R. (1989) *J. Neurobiol.* **20**, 1–9.
9. Sweatt, J. D. & Kandel, E. R. (1989) *Nature (London)* **339**, 51–54.
10. Crow, T. & Forrester, J. (1987) *Soc. Neurosci. Abstr.* **13**, 389.
11. Crow, T. (1988) *Trends Neurosci.* **11**, 136–142.
12. Crow, T. & Forrester, J. (1986) *Proc. Natl. Acad. Sci. USA* **83**, 7975–7978.
13. Forrester, J. & Crow, T. (1987) *Soc. Neurosci. Abstr.* **13**, 618.
14. Crow, T. & Forrester, J. (1988) *Soc. Neurosci. Abstr.* **14**, 839.
15. Forrester, J. & Crow, T. (1988) *Soc. Neurosci. Abstr.* **14**, 839.
16. Crow, T., Forrester, J., Waxham, N. & Neary, J. (1989) *Soc. Neurosci. Abstr.* **15**, 1284.
17. Land, P. W. & Crow, T. (1985) *Neurosci. Lett.* **62**, 199–205.
18. Grollman, A. P. (1967) *J. Biol. Chem.* **242**, 3226–3233.
19. Vazquez, D. (1974) *FEBS Lett.* **40**, 63–84.
20. Jacklet, J. W. (1980) *J. Exp. Biol.* **85**, 33–42.
21. Winer, B. J. (1962) *Statistical Principles in Experimental Design* (McGraw-Hill, New York).
22. Crow, T. (1985) *J. Neurosci.* **5**, 209–214.
23. Schacher, S., Castellucci, V. F. & Kandel, E. R. (1988) *Science* **240**, 1667–1669.
24. Otani, S., Marshall, C. J., Tate, W. P., Goddard, G. V. & Abraham, W. C. (1989) *Neuroscience* **28**, 519–526.
25. Ocorr, K. A., Walters, E. T., & Byrne, J. H. (1985) *Proc. Natl. Acad. Sci. USA* **82**, 2548–2552.
26. Dale, N., Kandel, E. R. & Schacher, S. (1987) *J. Neurosci.* **7**, 2232–2238.
27. Scholz, K. P. & Byrne, J. H. (1988) *Science* **240**, 1664–1667.

After reading: CONSOLIDATE INFORMATION

1. What characteristics of this article tell you that the authors are addressing other scientists?
2. How do the authors interpret their findings?
3. How do the illustrations support the authors' findings?

Sex, Drugs, Disasters, and the Extinction of the Dinosaurs

Stephen Jay Gould

Stephen Jay Gould is a research biologist and professor at Harvard University, but he is also a widely published writer on scientific subjects for lay or non-scientific readers. He writes a regular column in the magazine, Natural History *and often writes articles for magazines such as* Discover, *in which the following article appeared in 1984. In this essay, he demonstrates the way scientists pose hypotheses to explain natural phenomena, but he also demonstrates his awareness of broad interests of a popular audience in his choice of a title that seems whimsical but also has a serious meaning.*

Before reading: FIRST THOUGHTS
                      LOOK AHEAD

1. React to Gould's title; why do you think he wrote such a title to a serious article?
2. What do you think the essence of science is? Read Gould's first paragraph; what does he think the essence of science is?
3. What is the scientific method?

During reading: REACT
                     QUESTION
                     SUMMARIZE

1. Read Gould's list of theories (paragraph 5) on the extinction of the dinosaurs. Before reading further, evaluate each theory for yourself.
2. In what ways besides direct statement does Gould let his readers know what he thinks of each theory?

SCIENCE, IN ITS MOST FUNDAMENTAL DEFINITION, is a fruitful mode of inquiry, not a list of enticing conclusions. The conclusions are the consequence, not the essence.

My greatest unhappiness with most popular presentations of science concerns their failure to separate fascinating claims from the methods that scientists use to establish the facts of nature. Journalists, and the public, thrive on controversial and stunning statements. But science is, basically, a way of knowing—in P. B. Medawar's apt words, "the art of the soluble." If the growing corps of popular science writers would focus on *how* scientists develop and defend those fascinating claims, they would make their greatest possible contribution to public understanding.

Consider three ideas, proposed in perfect seriousness to explain that greatest of all titillating puzzles—the extinction of dinosaurs. Since these three notions invoke the primally fascinating themes of our culture—sex, drugs, and violence—they surely reside in the category of fascinating claims. I want to show why two of them rank as silly speculation, while the other represents science at its grandest and most useful.

Science works with testable proposals. If, after much compilation and scrutiny of data, new information continues to affirm a hypothesis, we may accept it provisionally and gain confidence as further evidence mounts. We can never be completely sure that a hypothesis is right, though we may be able to show with confidence that it is wrong. The best scientific hypotheses are also generous and expansive: they suggest extensions and implications that enlighten related, and even far distant, subjects. Simply consider how the idea of evolution has influenced virtually every intellectual field.

Useless speculation, on the other hand, is restrictive. It generates no testable hypothesis, and offers no way to obtain potentially refuting evidence. Please note that I am not speaking of truth or falsity. The speculation may well be true; still, if it provides, in principle, no material for affirmation or rejection, we can make nothing of it. It must simply stand forever as an intriguing idea. Useless speculation turns in on itself and leads nowhere; good science, containing both seeds for its potential refutation and implications for more and different testable knowledge, reaches out. But, enough preaching. Let's move on to dinosaurs, and the three proposals for their extinction.

1. Sex: Testes function only in a narrow range of temperature (those of mammals hang externally in a scrotal sac because internal body temperatures are too high for their proper function). A worldwide rise in temperature at the close of the Cretaceous period caused the testes of dinosaurs to stop functioning and led to their extinction by sterilization of males.

2. Drugs: Angiosperms (flowering plants) first evolved toward the end of the dinosaurs' reign. Many of these plants contain psychoactive agents, avoided by mammals today as a result of their bitter taste. Dinosaurs had neither means to taste the bitterness nor livers effective enough to detoxify the substances. They died of massive overdoses.

3. Disasters: A large comet or asteroid struck the earth some 65 million years ago, lofting a cloud of dust into the sky and blocking sunlight, thereby suppressing photosynthesis and so drastically lowering world temperatures that dinosaurs and hosts of other creatures became extinct.

Before analyzing these three tantalizing statements, we must establish a basic ground rule often violated in proposals for the dinosaurs' demise. *There is no separate problem of the extinction of dinosaurs.* Too often we divorce specific events from their wider contexts and systems of cause and effect. The fundamental fact of dinosaur extinction is its synchrony with the demise of so many other groups across a wide range of habitats, from terrestrial to marine.

The history of life has been punctuated by brief episodes of mass extinction. A recent analysis by University of Chicago paleontologists Jack Sepkoski and Dave Raup, based on the best and most exhaustive tabulation of data ever assembled, shows clearly that five episodes of mass dying stand well above the "background" extinctions of normal times (when we consider all mass extinctions, large and small, they seem to fall in a regular 26-million-year cycle).... The Cretaceous debacle, occurring 65 million years ago and separating the Mesozoic and Cenozoic eras of our geological time scale, ranks prominently among the five. Nearly all the marine plankton (single-celled floating creatures) died with geological suddenness; among marine invertebrates, nearly 15 percent of all families perished, including many previously dominant groups, especially the ammonites (relatives of squids in coiled shells). On land, the dinosaurs disappeared after more than 100 million years of unchallenged domination.

In this context, speculations limited to dinosaurs alone ignore the larger phenomenon. We need a coordinated explanation for a system of events that includes the extinction of dinosaurs as one component. Thus it makes little sense, though it may fuel our desire to view mammals as inevitable inheritors of the earth, to guess that dinosaurs died because small mammals ate their eggs (a perennial favorite among untestable speculations). It seems most unlikely that some disaster peculiar to dinosaurs befell these massive beasts—and that the debacle happened to strike just when one of history's five great dyings had enveloped the earth for completely different reasons.

The testicular theory, an old favorite from the 1940s, had its root in an interesting and thoroughly respectable study of temperature tolerances in the American alligator, published in the staid *Bulletin of the American Museum of Natural History* in 1946 by three experts on living and fossil reptiles—E. H. Colbert, my own first teacher in paleontology; R. B. Cowles; and C. M. Bogert.

The first sentence of their summary reveals a purpose beyond alligators: "This report describes an attempt to infer the reactions of extinct reptiles, especially the dinosaurs, to high temperatures as based upon reactions observed in the modern alligator." They studied, by rectal thermometry, the body temperatures of alligators under changing conditions of heating and cooling. (Well, let's face it, you wouldn't want to try sticking a thermometer under a 'gator's tongue.) The predictions under test go way back to an old theory first stated by Galileo in the 1630s—the unequal scaling of surfaces and volumes. As an animal, or any object, grows (provided its shape doesn't change), surface areas must increase more slowly than volumes—since surfaces get larger as length squared, while volumes increase much more rapidly, as length cubed. Therefore, small animals have high ratios of surface to volume, while large animals cover themselves with relatively little surface.

Among cold-blooded animals lacking any physiological mechanism for keeping their temperatures constant, small creatures have a hell of a time keeping warm—because they lose so much heat through their relatively large surfaces. On the other hand, large animals, with their relatively small surfaces, may lose heat so slowly that, once warm, they may maintain effectively constant temperatures against ordinary fluctuations of climate. (In fact, the resolution of the "hot-blooded dinosaur" controversy that burned so brightly a few years back may simply be that, while large dinosaurs possessed no physiological mechanism for constant temperature, and were not therefore warm-blooded in the technical sense, their large size and relatively small surface area kept them warm.)

Colbert, Cowles, and Bogert compared the warming rates of small and large alligators. As predicted, the small fellows heated up (and cooled down) more quickly. When exposed to a warm sun, a tiny 50-gram (1.76-ounce) alligator heated up one degree Celsius every minute and a half, while a large alligator, 260 times bigger at 13,000 grams (28.7 pounds), took seven and a half-minutes to gain a degree. Extrapolating up to an adult 10-ton dinosaur, they concluded that a one-degree rise in body temperature would take eighty-six hours. If large animals absorb heat so slowly (through their relatively small surfaces), they will also be unable to shed any excess heat gained when temperatures rise above a favorable level.

The authors then guessed that large dinosaurs lived at or near their optimum temperatures; Cowles suggested that a rise in global temperatures just before the Cretaceous extinction caused the dinosaurs to heat up beyond their optimal tolerance—and, being so large, they couldn't shed the unwanted heat. (In a most unusual statement within a scientific paper, Colbert and Bogert then explicitly disavowed this speculative extension of their empirical work on alligators.) Cowles conceded that this excess heat probably wasn't enough to kill or even to enervate the great beasts, but since testes often function only within a narrow range of temperature, he proposed that this global rise might have sterilized all the males, causing extinction by natural contraception.

The overdose theory has recently been supported by UCLA psychiatrist Ronald K. Siegel. Siegel has gathered, he claims, more than 2,000 records of animals who, when given access, administer various drugs to themselves—from a mere swig of alcohol to massive doses of the big H. Elephants will swill the equivalent of twenty beers at a time, but do not like alcohol in concentrations greater than 7 percent. In a silly bit of anthropocentric speculation, Siegel states that "elephants drink, perhaps, to forget . . . the anxiety produced by shrinking rangeland and the competition for food."

Since fertile imaginations can apply almost any hot idea to the extinction of dinosaurs, Siegel found a way. Flowering plants did not evolve until late in the dinosaurs' reign. These plants also produced an array of aromatic, amino-acid-based alkaloids—the major group of psychoactive agents. Most mammals are "smart" enough to avoid these potential poisons. The alkaloids simply don't taste good (they are bitter); in any case, we mammals have livers happily supplied with the capacity to detoxify them. But, Siegel speculates, perhaps dinosaurs could neither taste the bitterness nor detoxify the substances once ingested. He recently told members of the American Psychological Association: "I'm not suggesting that all dinosaurs OD'd on plant drugs, but it certainly was a factor." He also argued that death by overdose may help explain why so many dinosaur fossils are found in contorted positions. (Do not go gentle into that good night.)

Extraterrestrial catastrophes have long pedigrees in the popular literature of extinction, but the subject exploded again in 1979, after a long lull, when the father-son, physicist-geologist team of Luis and Walter Alvarez proposed that an asteroid, some 10 km in diameter, struck the earth 65 million years ago (comets, rather than asteroids, have since gained favor. Good science is self-corrective).

The force of such a collision would be immense, greater by far than the megatonnage of all the world's nuclear weapons. In trying to reconstruct a scenario that would explain the simultaneous dying of dinosaurs on land and so many creatures in the sea, the Alvarezes proposed that a gigantic dust cloud, generated by particles blown aloft in the impact, would so darken the earth that photosynthesis would cease and temperatures drop precipitously. (Rage, rage against the dying of the light.) The single-celled photosynthetic oceanic plankton, with life cycles measured in weeks, would perish outright, but land plants might survive through the dormancy of their seeds (land plants were not much affected by the Cretaceous extinction, and any adequate theory must account for the curious pattern of differential survival). Dinosaurs would die by starvation and freezing; small, warm-blooded mammals, with more modest requirements for food and better regulation of body temperature, would squeak through. "Let the bastards freeze in the dark," as bumper stickers of our chauvinistic neighbors in sunbelt states proclaimed several years ago during the Northeast's winter oil crisis.

All three theories, testicular malfunction, psychoactive overdosing, and asteroidal zapping, grab our attention mightily. As pure phenomenology, they rank about equally high on any hit parade of primal fascination. Yet one represents expansive science, the others restrictive and untestable speculation. The proper criterion lies in evidence and methodology; we must probe behind the superficial fascination of particular claims.

How could we possibly decide whether the hypothesis of testicular frying is right or wrong? We would have to know things that the fossil record cannot provide. What temperatures were optimal for dinosaurs? Could they avoid the absorption of excess heat by staying in the shade, or in caves? At what temperatures did their testicles cease to function? Were late Cretaceous climates ever warm enough to drive the internal temperatures of dinosaurs close to this ceiling? Testicles simply don't fossilize, and how could we infer their temperature tolerances even if they did? In short, Cowles's hypothesis is only an intriguing speculation leading nowhere. The most damning statement against it appeared right in the conclusion of Colbert, Cowles, and Bogert's paper, when they admitted: "It is difficult to advance any definite arguments against this hypothesis." My statement may seem paradoxical—isn't a hypothesis really good if you can't devise any arguments against it? Quite the contrary. It is simply untestable and unusable.

Siegel's overdosing has even less going for it. At least Cowles extrapolated his conclusion from some good data on alligators. And he didn't completely violate the primary guideline of sitting dinosaur extinction in the context of a general mass dying—for rise in temperature could be the root cause of a general catastrophe, zapping dinosaurs by testicular malfunction and different groups for other reasons. But Siegel's speculation cannot touch the extinction of ammonites or oceanic plankton (diatoms make their own food with good sweet sunlight; they don't OD on the chemicals of terrestrial plants). It is simply a gratuitous, attention grabbing guess. It cannot be tested, for how can we know what dinosaurs tasted and what their livers could do? Livers don't fossilize any better than testicles.

The hypothesis doesn't even make any sense in its own context. Angiosperms were in full flower ten million years before dinosaurs went the way of all flesh. Why did it take so long? As for the pains of a chemical death recorded in contortions of fossils, I regret to say (or rather I'm pleased to note for the dinosaurs' sake) that Siegel's knowledge of geology must be a bit deficient: muscles contract after death and geological strata rise and fall with motions of the earth's crust after burial—more than enough reason to distort a fossil's pristine appearance.

The impact story, on the other hand, has a sound basis in evidence. It can be tested, extended, refined and, if wrong, disproved. The Alvarezes did not just construct an arresting guess for public consumption. They proposed their hypothesis after laborious geochemical studies with Frank Asaro and Helen Michael had revealed a massive increase of iridium in rocks deposited right at the time of extinction. Iridium, a rare metal of the platinum group, is virtually absent from indigenous rocks of the earth's crust; most of our iridium arrives on extraterrestrial objects that strike the earth.

The Alvarez hypothesis bore immediate fruit. Based originally on evidence from two European localities, it led geochemists throughout the world to examine other sediments of the same age. They found abnormally high amounts of iridium everywhere—from continental rocks of the western United States to deep sea cores from the South Atlantic.

Cowles proposed his testicular hypothesis in the mid-1940s. Where has it gone since then? Absolutely nowhere, because scientists can do nothing with it. The hypothesis must stand as a curious appendage to a solid study of alligators. Siegel's overdose scenario will also win a few press notices and fade into oblivion. The Alvarezes' asteroid falls into a different category altogether, and much of the popular commentary has missed this essential distinction by focusing on the impact and its attendant results, and forgetting what really matters to a scientist— the iridium. If you talk just about asteroids, dust, and darkness, you tell stories no better and no more entertaining than fried testicles or terminal trips. It is the iridium—the source of testable evidence—that counts and forges the crucial distinction between speculation and science.

The proof, to twist a phrase, lies in the doing. Cowles's hypothesis has generated nothing in thirty-five years. Since its proposal in 1979, the Alvarez hypothesis has spawned hundreds of studies, a major conference, and attendant publications. Geologists are fired up. They are looking for iridium at all other extinction boundaries. Every week exposes a new wrinkle in the scientific press. Further evidence that the Cretaceous iridium represents extraterrestrial impact and not indigenous volcanism continues to accumulate. As I revise this essay in November 1984... new data include chemical "signatures" of other isotopes indicating unearthly provenance, glass spherules of a size and sort produced by impact and not by volcanic eruptions, and high-pressure varieties of silica formed (so far as we know) only under the tremendous shock of impact.

My point is simply this: Whatever the eventual outcome (I suspect it will be positive), the Alvarez hypothesis is exciting, fruitful science because it generates tests, provides us with things to do, and expands outward. We are having fun, battling back and forth, moving toward a resolution, and extending the hypothesis beyond its original scope....

As just one example of the unexpected, distant cross-fertilization that good science engenders, the Alvarez hypothesis made a major contribution to a theme that has riveted public attention in the past few months—so-called nuclear winter. In a speech delivered in April 1982, Luis Alvarez calculated the energy that a ten kilometer asteroid would release on impact. He compared such an explosion with a full nuclear exchange and implied that all-out atomic war might unleash similar consequences.

This theme of impact leading to massive dust clouds and falling temperatures formed an important input to the decision of Carl Sagan and a group of colleagues to model the climatic consequences of nuclear holocaust. Full nuclear exchange would probably generate the same kind of dust cloud and darkening that may have wiped out the dinosaurs. Temperatures would drop precipitously and agriculture might become impossible. Avoidance of nuclear war is fundamentally an ethical and political imperative, but we must know the factual consequences to make firm judgments. I am heartened by a final link across disciplines and deep concerns—another criterion, by the way, of science at its best. A recognition of the very phenomenon that made our evolution possible by exterminating the previously dominant dinosaurs and clearing a way for the evolution of large mammals, including us, might actually help to save us from joining those magnificent beasts in contorted poses among the strata of the earth.

After Reading: CONSOLIDATE INFORMATION

1. Summarize Gould's criteria for good science.
2. Why does Gould think that the Alvarez theory is a good scientific theory?
3. Analyze the process by which Gould discounts the Cowles theory and the Siegel theory.

Indoor Radon in Northern Virginia: Seasonal Changes and Correlations with Geology

George W. Mushrush, Douglas G. Mose, and Charles E. Chrosinak

---

Three scientists collaborated on the research and writing of this report on the presence of indoor radon in northern Virginia. The three researchers studied the problem of radon in homes in a small geographic area, but their findings have significance for other scientists, as well as for non-experts who live in similar geological areas. This report appeared in Episodes, *the newsletter of the International Union of Geologists.*

Before reading: FIRST THOUGHTS
     LOOK AHEAD

1. What do you know about radon and its danger in homes?
2. Read the summary at the beginning of the article. What can you predict about the authors' research?
3. Where do you think radon originates?

During reading: REACT
     QUESTION
     SUMMARIZE

1. How do you react to the suggestion that many homes throughout the United States could be affected by radon and its dangers?
2. Why is radon such a serious problem?

Summary: Radon (Rn) in homes is a recently recognized hazard of geological origin, regarded by some as the second most important cause of lung cancer. In the U.S.A. where up to 20,000 deaths from Rn ingestion may now be taking place, it is estimated that 8–12% of American homes have average indoor Rn levels exceeding official guidelines. In the United Kingdom the "action level" is about twice as high as in the U.S.A. and in Sweden over four times higher, so that the degree of officially recognized risk is a matter of public policy and perception. The relationship between geology and radon levels is not obvious, for in some parts of the U.S.A. homes built on rocks high in Uranium (U) have indoor Rn concentrations much lower than expected. Elsewhere, Rn values have been shown to be influenced by fluctuations in the water table, by soil type, and even by time of day. In Virginia, where much of the research on Rn has taken place, it is probably more effective to use airborne radioactivity than geology at the surface to gauge regional and seasonal variations in Rn.

Introduction

THE RADIATION DOSE FROM INHALED DECAY PRODUCTS OF ^{222}Rn is the dominant component of natural radiation exposures to the general population (Steinhausler, et al., 1983; Nero, in Nazaross and Nero, 1988). The principal basis for present concern about exposures of radon decay products is the experience with the incidence of lung cancer in underground miners (George and Hinchliffe, 1972; NIOSH, 1985). High fatality rates observed for miners as early as the sixteenth century have been recently ascribed to lung cancer (Nero, 1988). The magnitude of natural radioactivity from radon was not realized until 1984 when the discovery of excessively high levels of radon gas in a home in Boyertown, Pennsylvania, aroused national concern (Lafavore, 1986). The U.S. National Research Council recently supported an earlier estimate by the U.S. Environmental Protection Agency (EPA) that radon exposure leads to 5,000 to 20,000 deaths annually (NRC, 1988).

Uranium in soil and rock is the source of most radon to which the public is exposed. The decay series beginning with ^{238}U is the major source of natural radiation exposure, with local high levels of uranium due mainly to the underlying rock type and its component minerals. Uranium is more soluble in an oxidizing environment and tends to precipitate in a reducing environment (Levinson, 1980). A significant uranium daughter is ^{226}Ra with a half-life of 1600 years. Radium follows the chemistry of other Group II elements in the environment. When dissolved in groundwater, radium is available for chemical reactions that lead to its wide incorporation as insoluble hydroxides and oxides. Radium's daughter, ^{222}Rn, is the only radioactive noble gas.

The potential for high radon concentrations depends on the radium and moisture content of the soil, permeability of the soil, the season and the weather. Radon gas enters the atmosphere by crossing the soil-air interface. It is estimated that the emanation rate from soil in the U.S.A. is 0.42 picoCuries (pCi) per m^2 per second (NCRP, 1984). The recognition of the importance of soil as a source of indoor radon, combined with the increasing evidence of unacceptably high radon concentrations in a significant number of houses, has raised the question of whether one might predict, on a geological basis, where high levels of indoor radon might be found.

Because of the long half-life of ^{226}Ra and its lack of chemical reactivity, ^{222}Rn itself acts much like a stable pollutant whose concentration can be determined by comparing the entry and ventilation rates of homes. The decay products are somewhat more complex, but in practical terms the decay product concentration is indicated approximately by the overall radon concentration.

THE FAIRFAX COUNTY SURVEY

The indoor radon situation as it existed in Fairfax County, Virginia, between November 1986 and November 1987 is described in this paper. This study is still underway, with the number of homes enrolled continually increasing. Data collected more recently confirm the 1986–1987 patterns. Approximately 1500 homes are now being monitored, with about 50 new homes added each month. The total now represents about 0.5% of the homes in Fairfax County, and the goal is to report on 1% of the homes in the area.

The test program requires the homeowner to participate in the entire four season testing period. The homeowner provides an exact location on a county map, so that the geological rock unit underlying the home can be identified and the house located on a map showing airborne radioactivity. A questionnaire requests information on home construction, the type of basement wall, the type of heating system, and many other factors. Specific instructions are given for placing the radon monitor.

The conclusions are based on indoor radon measurements over three month periods using alpha-track radon monitors provided by Tech/Ops Landauer Corporation of Illinois. After the exposure period in the houses, the monitors are returned to the company, where the film in the monitors is developed, the "tracks" produced by the decay of radon progeny near the film surface are measured, and the average amount of indoor radon recorded by the film is calculated. The accuracy of the radon monitors is tested by Tech/Ops Landauer through the EPA Proficiency Program: over the study interval, these tests revealed a ±25% accuracy at the 90% confidence level.

SEASONAL VARIATIONS

Table 1 is a summary of the observed indoor radon measurements without regard to the geological units under the homes. The comparison between seasons shows that winter is the time of greatest radon concentrations, probably because these houses are then normally closed to outside air. Conversely, summer is the time of lowest radon concentration, presumably reflecting the general increase in the rate of air exchange caused by open windows and doors. About 30% of the homes have an annual radon concentration above 4 picoCuries per litre (pCi/L), and spring or fall radon measurements tend to most closely approximate this percentage.

Table 1 also shows that indoor radon on the first floor above the ground is about 30% less concentrated than in the basement, where the walls are at least partly in contact with the surrounding soil, from which the indoor radon presumably originates. Radon enters the upper levels of a home by diffusion, and by air movement in homes with forced-air heating and cooling systems.

TABLE 1 Indoor Radon Measurements in Fairfax County, Virginia (In picocuries per litre—pCi/L)

Season	Median Radon pCi/L	% Over 4 pCi/L	% Over 10 pCi/L	Number of Homes
Basement Indoor Radon				
Winter 1986–87[1]	3.9	48	9	283
Spring 1987[2]	2.9	32	6	482
Summer 1987[3]	2.4	21	2	744
Fall 1987[4]	3.0	34	3	743
First Floor Indoor Radon				
Winter 1986–87[1]	2.4	21	5	39
Spring 1987[2]	1.6	16	4	75
Summer 1987[3]	1.6	11	1	127
Fall 1987[4]	2.3	21	0	109

1) From November 1, 1986 to February 1, 1987
2) From February 1 to May 1, 1987
3) From May 1 to August 1, 1987
4) From August 1 to November 1, 1987

RADON AND REGIONAL GEOLOGY

Figure I illustrates the three major geological provinces of the Appalachians that underlie Fairfax County (Froehlich, 1985). The Coastal Plain Province, located along the eastern edge of the study area, consists of poorly cemented clastic sediments mostly clay and sand, which were deposited during the opening of the modern Atlantic Ocean. These deposits were formed during the Early Cretaceous Period. The western margin of the county is part of the Culpeper Basin, a fault-bounded valley containing terrestrial clastic (siltstone, sandstone, conglomerate) along with extrusives and intrusives (diabase) all of mainly Jurassic age (190–150 Ma). Separating these two regions is the Piedmont Province, which extends from Maryland to Georgia, and which is composed of metamorphic and igneous rocks mainly of Paleozoic age (latest Precambrian to Devonian), formed when the Appalachian mountains were created.

Table 2 shows that the metamorphic and igneous rocks of the Piedmont correlate consistently with the highest percentage of homes with radon above 4 pCi/L, reaching a maximum of more than 50% of the Piedmont homes during the winter of 1986–1987. Presumably this is a consequence of uranium enhancement that is characteristic of rocks produced during mountain building events (Speer et al., 1981). The sedimentary strata of the Coastal Plain are associated with the lowest percentage of homes above 4 pCi/L: only about 10% of the homes have an annual indoor radon concentration above this level. This low percentage probably results because the fluvial and shallow marine sands that comprise most of the sedimentary strata were naturally depleted in uranium during their residence time in

TABLE 2 Indoor Radon in Fairfax County By Geological Privinces

Season	Geological Province	Median Radon (pCi/L)	% Over 4 pCi/L	% Over 10 pCi/L	Number of Homes
1986–87:					
Winter	Culpeper Basin	3.7	42	3	31
	Piedmont	4.1	53	11	224
	Coastal Plain	2.6	18	4	28
1987:					
Spring	Culpeper Basin	2.9	26	5	57
	Piedmont	3.1	36	7	376
	Coastal Plain	1.7	12	0	49
Summer	Culpeper Basin	2.0	11	4	72
	Piedmont	2.7	24	2	577
	Coastal Plain	1.7	6	0	95
Fall	Culpeper Basin	2.6	27	1	71
	Piedmont	3.4	37	4	577
	Coastal Plain	2.1	8	0	95

aqueous environments. The sedimentary rocks that make up most of the Culpeper Basin are composed of less weathered detritus, which could account for the somewhat elevated percentage of homes above 4 pCi/L here compared to the homes on the Coastal Plain.

Using Airborne Radiation

The radiation signal of the Earth's surface in our study area is rather better known than anywhere else in Virginia (Fig. 2). The total measurements of gamma-ray radioactivity were made during flights about 500 feet above ground along east-west flight lines, spaced 1/2 mile apart (Daniels, 1980). At this altitude the effective area of response of the scintillation equipment is approximately 1000 feet in diameter, and the signal is generated by the uppermost one foot of soil and rock cover. The combination of close flight lines and area of response is such that essentially all of the ground surface was examined for its radioactivity signal.

This type of survey is potentially very useful, though there are some disadvantages. One problem is that the total surface is examined, including water and man-made structures such as pavements and buildings. However, these comprise only a small percentage of the total land surface. Another consideration, at least for radon surveys, is that the measurements are of total gamma-ray radioactivity, derived from ^{214}Bi (a radioactive daughter of uranium, produced by the decay of ^{222}Rn), thorium and potassium. To a rough approximation, however, uranium, thorium and potassium tend to have a similar geochemical behaviour, with rocks rich in the latter tending to be enriched in uranium and thorium. Furthermore, as

Radon is a chemically inert radioactive gas produced by the decay of uranium in the ground, which in turn produces its own radioactive decay products. When we breathe, the radon decay products are deposited in the lungs and respiratory tracts. The main villains are the two polonium isotopes that emit alpha-particles—helium nuclei. They lose their energy in a very short distance, causing considerable damage to the cells they hit. These decay products all have short half-lives of up to 27 minutes before they decay to a long-lived isotope of lead, which is of no health significance in low concentrations.

Virtually any soil or broken rock has enough radon in its interstitial volume to cause a potential problem provided there is an easy pathway into the home. Radon measuring devices can monitor the concentration of radon by means of the alpha or gamma-ray emission of the radon daughters. However, there are problems associated with measuring the values in a house, because the radon concentrations can vary with time.

Figure A shows the daily variation of radon decay products found in a home near Ottawa, Canada (personal communication, Ian Thomson, 1988). A grab sample is thus not likely to be representative of the average levels present. There are also seasonal variations, the values generally being higher in the winter when the house is shut and the ventilation is lower. The difference between the inside and outside temperatures causes a lower pressure inside the house as compared to the outside; soil gases can thus be sucked in from the ground via small cracks and other openings in the basement walls and floors.

Public concern over radon in the United States started about four years ago in the Reading Prong of Pennsylvania, a basement complex containing several areas where uranium concentrations are unusually high. A worker in a local nuclear power station began to trigger the alarm on the plant's radiation detector. Close examination showed that his home was contaminated with unusually high concentrations of radon. It was estimated that he

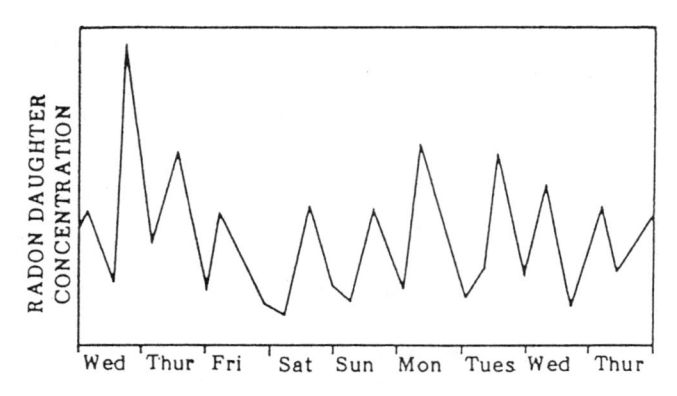

FIGURE A Daily variations of radon levels in a house near Ottawa, Canada.

was receiving a radiation dose equivalent to a chest X-ray every 20 seconds throughout the year. It has since been shown that his home, which had the highest radon level for any house found anywhere, and some houses nearby, also high in radon, are situated in an area of fractured and porous rock that is high in uranium.

In southwestern England radon levels are about ten times the national average in homes built on granites that are generally high in uranium, which is the source of the radon. And in Finland high radon levels are related to Rapakivi granites in the southeastern part of the country, though the incidences of lung cancer do not correlate with radon in the homes here.

—R.L. Grasty, Geological Survey of Canada, Ottawa

shown in Table 3, there is a good correlation between indoor radon and the total gamma-ray signal, suggesting that the component of the total signal due to ^{222}Rn is a relatively constant percentage of the total signal. The correlation persists through all seasons, even though the homes are typically tightly closed to outside air only during the winter.

Perhaps the most significant advantage of the Fairfax County airborne radioactivity surveys is that they cover most of the surface of the county. This

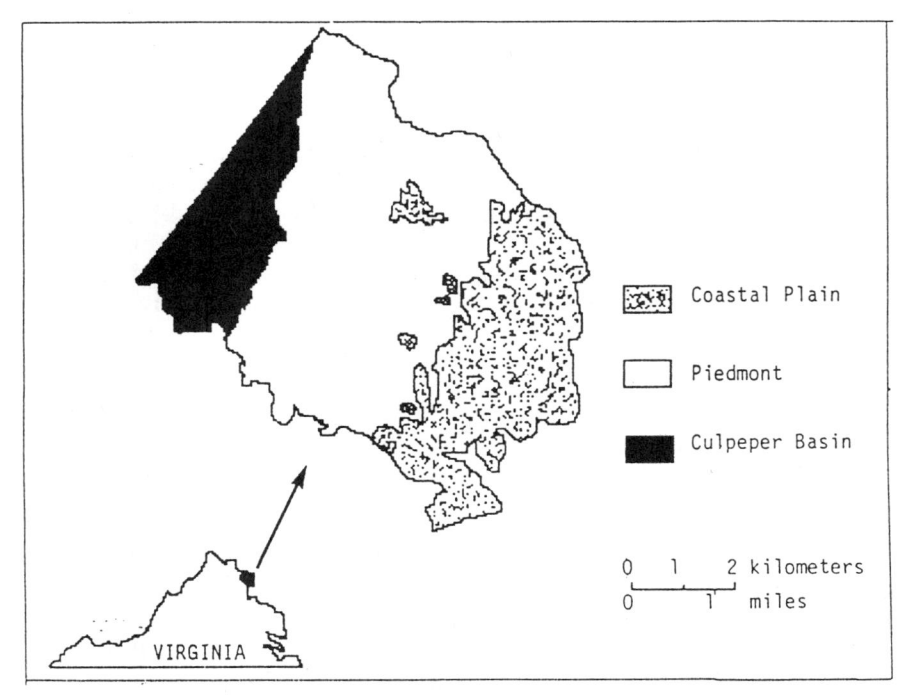

FIGURE 1 The three major geological provinces of Fairfax County, northern Virginia

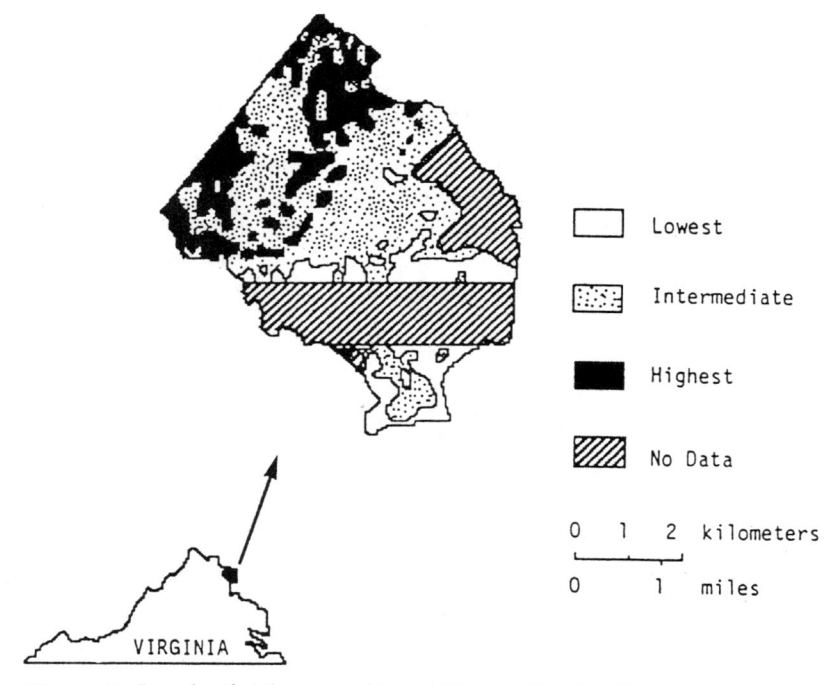

FIGURE 2 Levels of airborne radioactivity over Fairfax County.

makes such surveys a cost-effective improvement over an analogous land-based study in which a geologist would examine the radon emanation characteristics of all the area underlain by each geological unit. A comparable land-based study mainly on geological units and soil types would probably be less useful because, as can be demonstrated by comparing geological maps with aeroradioactivity maps for the study area (compare Fig. 1 and Fig. 2), most rock units vary in surface radioactivity.

Conclusions

Indoor radon and its progeny are a serious problem in northern Virginia, and elsewhere. In the present study, the indoor radon concentrations can be related to the season, the presence of a basement, the geology, and the aeroradioactivity of a region. Measurements in all areas were the highest in the winter, with about 45% of homes showing levels above 4 pCi/L, the EPA recommended action level. Spring and fall values were comparable, whereas the summer season showed the lowest values. The rocks of the Piedmont Province gave the highest median values for all four seasons. Homes in the Culpeper Basin Province yielded generally lower median radon values, and houses on the Coastal Plain had the lowest median level of indoor radon.

TABLE 3 Aeroradioactivity Versus Indoor Radon in Fairfax County

Aeroradioactivity	Total Homes	Median Rn In Homes (pCi/L)	% Over 4 pCi/L	Total Homes	Median Rn In Homes (pCi/L)	% Over 4 pCi/L
		Winter			Summer	
Less than 200 cps	10	2.2	10	55	2.1	16
200–300 cps	54	2.5	31	149	2.1	20
300–400 cps	106	4.2	55	266	2.6	22
400–500 cps	62	5.5	55	94	3.1	36
Above 500 cps	2	10.1	100	8	3.7	63
		Spring			Fall	
Less than 200 cps	32	2.3	16	51	2.5	24
200–300 cps	92	2.3	24	154	2.5	25
300–400 cps	171	3.2	37	267	3.4	38
400–500 cps	72	3.5	46	94	4.5	56
Above 500 cps	5	6.0	83	7	5.4	86

Typically indoor radon levels can be predicted using total-gamma aeroradioactivity. It is obvious that with some care a potential homebuyer can select a home with a climate and location compatible with low indoor radon concentration. It is also clear that current home owners can be alerted to a potential problem with indoor radon if the effects of climate and geology are understood.

References

DANIELS, D.L., 1980. Geophysical-geological analysis of Fairfax County, Virginia. U.S. Geological Survey, Report 80-1165, 64p.

FROELICH, A.J., 1985. Folio of geological and hydrologic maps for land use planning in the coastal plain of Fairfax County and vicinity, Virginia. U.S. Geological Survey Miscellaneous Investigations Series, Map I-1423.

GEORGE, A.C. and HINCHLIFFE, L., 1972. Measurement of uncombined radon daughters in uranium mines. Health Physics, v. 23, no. 6, p. 791–803.

LAFAVORE, M., 1986. Radon the Invisible Threat: What it is, Where it is, How to Keep Your House Safe. Rodale Press, Emmaus, Pa, 256p.

LEVINSON, A.A., 1980. Introduction to Exploration Geochemistry, Wilmette Illinois. Applied Publishing Ltd., 924p.

NAZAROSS, W.W. and NERO, A.V. Jr., 1988. Radon and its Decay Products in Indoor Air. John Wiley and Sons, New York, 518p.

NCRP (National Council on Radiation Protection and Measurements), 1984. Exposures from the Uranium Series with Emphasis on Radon and its Daughters. Report No. 77, 131p.

NOISH (National Institute for Occupational Safety and Health), 1985. Evaluation of Epidemiologic Studies Examining the Lung Cancer Mortality of Underground Miners. Cincinnati, Ohio, May 9, 1985, 80p.

NRC (National Research Council Committee on the Biological Effects of Ionizing Radiation), 1988. Health Risks of Radon and Other Internally Deposited Alpha-emitters. National Academy Press, Washington, D.C., 602p.

SPEER, J.A., SOLBERG, T.N. and BECKER, S.W., 1981. Petrography of the uranium-bearing minerals of the Liberty Hill Pluton, South Carolina, phase assemblages and migration of uranium in granitoid rocks. Economic Geology, v. 76, no. 8, p. 2162–2175.

STEINHAUSLER, F.W., HOFFMAN, W., POHL, E. and PHOL-RULING, J., 1983. Radiation exposure of the respiratory tract and associated carcinogenic risk due to inhaled radon daughters. Health Physics, v. 45, no. 2, p. 331–337.

After reading: CONSOLIDATE INFORMATION

1. The three researcher collaborators focused their research in northern Virginia, but there findings have implications for many other geographical areas in North America; summarize those implications.
2. Why is measuring airborne radioactivity more effective than measuring geological surface levels of radon?
3. Scientists frequently collaborate in doing their research and in writing up the results. Aside from the listing of three authors, what other devices do the authors use to signal their collaboration? How do you think collaboration influences the final product?

The International Geosphere/Biosphere Programme and Global Change: An Anthropocentric or an Ecocentric Future? A Personal View
W.S. Fyfe

Professor Fyfe is an internationally recognized geologist from New Zealand. This essay, which was written for other geologists and raises crucial questions about the fate of the earth, appeared in Episodes, *the newsletter of the International Union of*

Geologists. *In discussing the International Geosphere/Biosphere Programme, he is referring to a worldwide, interdisciplinary effort among scientists to develop initiatives to save the earth and its environment. Fyfe's audience—other geologists and scientists—would know the term immediately. Note that Fyfe subtitles this essay, "a personal view" so that his readers know that he is not writing about verifiable research.*

Before reading: FIRST THOUGHTS
                    LOOK AHEAD

1. What do the terms *anthropocentric* and *ecocentric* mean?
2. What do you think the International Geosphere/Biosphere Programme might accomplish?
3. What kinds of global changes do you think Fyfe means when he talks about "rapid life-threatening changes in the global life support system"?

During reading: REACT
                    QUESTION
                    SUMMARIZE

1. How has the technological progress developed by human beings affected the earth?
2. What does Fyfe mean when he refers to "the shock of the record"?

Summary: Rapid and life-threatening changes in the global life support system are accelerating and forcing the human species to decide between Nature itself or a totally anthropocentric view of the management of planet Earth. We have a very short time to decide this issue of ultimate values, but the results from an International Geosphere/Biosphere Programme are essential for rational choice. For security, we must protect and vastly expand the planet's biological reserves on land and at sea.

INTRODUCTION

We often hear that we live at a unique, critical time in the history of the human species. However, we are frequently suspicious of such statements, for our ancestors surely made similar statements—but this period of our history is unique. First, we possess a nuclear arsenal that, if used, could destroy, in a few days, our species and take many others with us. In addition, we have other technologies that could do the same. Second, because of a complex array of, for example, energy, medical, chemical, agricultural, and transport technologies, we have never before increased in population with such success. The last time we doubled our population took 37 years, compared to the 1,500 years it took after the birth of Christ. We know that what is happening now cannot continue.

The roots of the initiative for global change go very deep, and they were well summarized by Thomas Malone in 1984 (see Malone, 1985) during the general assembly of the International Council of Scientific Unions (ICSU) in Ottawa, Ontario, Canada. Charles Lyell said in 1872 (p. 451): "In reference to the extinction of species it is important to bear in mind, that when any region is stocked with as great a variety of animals and plants as its productive powers will enable it to support, the addition of any new species to the permanent numerical increase of one previously established, must always be attended either by the local extermination or the numerical decrease of some other species." Perhaps no better example could be given than that of what is now happening in the Amazon basin of South America as it is invaded by man. And this case may serve to show that a "local" event may have global consequences.

Then followed Vernadsky in 1929 (see Vernadsky, 1986), who had a clear appreciation of the fact that the biosphere was a critical part of the surface systems of our planet. After such champions, the social scientists perhaps led the game. I think of people like Aldous Huxley, who said in 1948 (see Bedford, 1987, p. 82):

> Industrialism is the systematic exploitation of wasting assets. In all too many cases, the thing we call progress is merely an acceleration in the rate of that exploitation. Such prosperity as we have known up to the present is the consequence of rapidly spending the planet's irreplaceable capital.
>
> Sooner or later mankind will be forced by the pressure of circumstances to take concerted action against its own destructive and suicidal tendencies. The longer such action is postponed, the worse it will be for all concerned.... Overpopulation and erosion constitute a Martian invasion of the planet....
>
> ... Treat Nature aggressively, with greed and violence and incomprehension: wounded Nature will turn and destroy you.... if, presumptuously imagining that we can "conquer" Nature, we continue to live on our planet like a swarm of destructive parasites—we condemn ourselves and our children to misery and deepening squalor and the despair that finds expression in the frenzies of collective violence.

In 1982 at the assembly of the ICSU in Cambridge, England, George Garland, geophysicist from Toronto, Ontario, Canada, suggested that it was time to look carefully at the influences of biological processes on our planet. Also, Herbert Friedman, who made major contributions to international science through the International Geophysical Year in 1957–58, suggested that it was time for a bold, holistic approach to the science of Earth. And in 1986 at the general assembly of the ICSU in Switzerland, the International Geosphere/Biosphere Programme (IGBP) was launched officially. Much of its philosophy and approach was taken from the report of the working group of the USA, which was chaired by Jack Eddy (see NRC, 1986). The focus of IGBP was clear: to understand the interactions in the global environment that involve the biosphere. Thus, it was seen to be a highly focused effort to fill the critical gaps in our knowledge of the surface interfaces of the planet or the system:

$$\text{Sun} \rightarrow \text{living cell} \leftarrow \text{Earth}$$

I always remember the wonderful words of Roger Revelle of the Scripps Institution of Oceanography at one of the early USA planning meetings. He said that the IGBP was urgent (for obvious reasons) and hard because it required observations and communication across all the geologic and biologic disciplines on a scale never seen before. The normal university research structures and programs were poorly prepared for a research program of this scope. However, the IGBP was clearly possible in the 1980s. For the first time in the history of the observation of natural systems, almost all the tools were available: satellites, submersibles, mass spectrometers, electron microscopes, and supercolliders, for example. The dynamics of the largest and smallest pieces of the puzzle can be described and the data managed by using the new and increasing power of computers.

In introducing the IGBP to the world, Sir John Kendrew (1988, p. 3), the president of ICSU, stated:

> The IGBP will certainly be the most ambitious, the most wide-ranging, and in its impacts on our understanding of the future possibilities for mankind the most important project that ICSU has ever undertaken. Its purpose is to study the progressive changes in the environment of the human species on this Earth, past and future; to identify their causes, natural or man-made; and to make informed predictions of the long-term future and thus of the dangers to our well being and even to our survival; and to investigate ways of minimizing those dangers that may be open to human intervention. From the point of view of fundamental science it is the extended study of the dynamics of the whole Earth system—its geology, its oceans, its atmosphere and its climate, and the thin green layer on its surface that we call the biosphere; a scientific enquiry offering immense intellectual challenges and rewards. So the programme will be scientifically exciting as well as immensely significant in charting the future of our species. It will necessarily continue for many years and will require the collection and analysis of huge amounts of data of all kinds using the most sophisticated techniques and the most powerful computers. It will be a major endeavor of the scientific community in every country of the world.

Part of the IGBP, a so-called underlying theme, was to understand human perturbations on the global system and to improve our ability to predict the state of the life-support system in the coming decades and centuries.

Words are often very important! By itself, the program named "IGBP" is focused, but when we use the words "global change," the concept is vast. In fact, global change has become what we might almost call a societal-scientific movement. Differences between various approaches and priorities are seen clearly in the programs that are expressed by the growing national efforts and national reports, and this is as it should be—and must be. We have truly global needs (for example, the study of the dynamics of the ocean, atmosphere, land surface, and biology), and we have equally valid local priorities, where local environmental changes influence local societies. However, I am always reminded of the words of Lyell (1872), who recognized that a special local advantage of a species can lead to a much longer term global perturbation. One need think only of the field of epidemiology (for example, AIDS) in order to appreciate Lyell's thoughts. And as the new work in genetic manipulation moves forward, we may see vast changes in the biosphere and we may face equally vast surprises.

The System

We surely live on the most remarkable object in the solar system (Mungall and McLaren, 1990). The geologic record shows that we have been almost covered by liquid water for 4 billion years, nearly 90 percent of the planet's history. In fact, the development of the geologic record may have started because of the hydrosphere and its moderating influence. The record also shows that, despite fluctuations in the Earth and Sun, we have never boiled dry or totally frozen. Planet Earth has a truly remarkable thermostat, and today we know that the biosphere plays a key role in the functioning of the thermostat.

Certainly, we must begin to understand the interactions, on all time scales, of the great nuclear power sources that drive the surface processes of the Earth. We must begin to understand their fluctuation on many time scales, as well as the mechanisms that link such changes to changes in the biomass. We do not really understand how small changes in solar input can be amplified through the atmosphere. At the other end of the power sources, we do not understand how changes in energy from the interior of Earth, expressed by such processes as volcanism and the water-cooling fluxes associated with such phenomena, influence the biosphere. We do know that these irregular processes can perturb the dust loading and chemistry of the atmosphere, as well as change the nutrient fluxes into the oceans (Groves, 1988; Fyfe, 1988). The development of the program on natural hazard reductions emphasizes the need to understand better (and prepare for) the short-term fluctuations that are driven from the Earth's interior or atmosphere.

We have also become aware of our lack of knowledge of the biosphere, which is full of surprises about the diversity of life in the deep oceans and in the canopies of the tropical forests. Is the Worldwatch Institute correct when it states that about 20 percent of this diversity will be destroyed in the next decade or so? We have an urgent need to know our present diversity and the unique interactions between the pieces of the geologic and biologic systems.

The Rise of Homo Sapiens

I think there is little doubt that the new scientific programs are with us because of the phenomenal increase in the human population. When Christ was born, the population was about 200 million. It then took about 1,500 years to double to 400 million. In 1900, the population was about 1.5 billion, and now it is over 5 billion and rising about 90 million per year, the last time doubling in 37 years! The population may well reach 10 billion toward the middle of next century, but the major increases will be in specific regions (for example, Nigeria may go from 105 to 300 million by 2025; Egypt, 51 to 100 million; India, 819 to 1,500 million). If this happens, the patterns of land use and industrialization must change dramatically and very fast.

The Shock of the Record

As the population of Homo sapiens has changed, so has our environment. We have been shocked by the record of gases, such as carbon dioxide, methane, and halogen organics, in the atmosphere. We have been shocked by the record of soil erosion and deforestation. In 1987, 8 million hectares of the Amazon was cleared; in 1989, 6.4 million hectares burned in Canada.

Studies of ice cores, ocean sediments, and terrestrial vegetation have shown us that the climate and atmosphere are tightly coupled and that major temperature changes can occur in periods of a century, or even less. Models of the future trends of temperature, precipitation, and the like, even if not very reliable, give cause for alarm. As we obtain better data over the next decades and produce better models, we will have even greater surprises. I am reminded of a speech by Mrs. Dahl, the Swedish Minister of Energy and Environment, who said that we cannot wait for scientists to be certain—we must prepare now!

Slowly, we see the growth of a new approach to the economics of development. In no area is this more apparent (and confused!) than in planning our global energy technologies for the future. The world, and particularly countries like the People's Republic of China and India, have great coal resources, enough for centuries. The developing world urgently needs more energy. While the New World, and particularly North America, must conserve (why do we use twice the energy per person compared to Europe?), the Old World and Third World need more energy. What will be the costs of using more fossil carbon if sea level rises a meter and if the cornlands and wheatlands of North America become much drier? What is the cost of hydroelectric power and its resulting loss of arable land at the time of a growing global food crisis?

Diversity

At present, we are alarmed by the reduction of biological diversity on this planet. As the opening quotation from Lyell states so clearly, one species cannot possibly expand without the accompanying reduction of others. And, for all our cleverness, the destruction of a species is irreversible. The French essayist Montaigne wrote 400 years ago that "the universal quality is diversity." The stability of our system also seems to require diversity. We must face squarely the reality that, if the human population continues to expand, an inevitable and massive loss of diversity will result. From this loss of diversity will come the potential for loss both in the stability of our own life-support system and in its ability to survive the changes caused by the fundamental systems of the planet.

In this context, the Bruntland Report (The World Commission on Environment and Development, 1987) has its fatal flaws. As given in the final statements, "General Principles, Rights, and Responsibilities, Number One, All human beings have the fundamental right to an environment adequate for their health and well-being." This is clearly an anthropocentric view of our planet. Why should we have this fundamental right if we do not use our knowledge with wisdom? As David Pimentel of Cornell (1987, p. 692) stated: "World resources and technology can support an abundance of humans, e.g., 10–15 billion humans living at or near poverty, or support approximately one billion humans with a relatively high standard of living."

Conclusion

We are entering a new period for the science of our planet. We must understand how our planet maintains its surface systems, which support all life. We can do this, as we have the tools for the necessary observations. Our programs related to global change must have the breadth and the dynamics to respond to the inevitable surprises that will come. I have great hope for the future because of the rapid changes that are occurring in social attitudes in many parts of the world, a changeover to what I would term an "ecocentric" view of the sustainable development of Earth.

We have a choice, a difficult, terrible choice. Bill McKibben eloquently described this choice in the New Yorker in September 1989 (p. 47–105; see also McKibben, 1989): Do we want to preserve Nature? It is now almost gone! Or do we want a totally anthropo-planned, anthropo-managed planet? Given the inevitable expansion of modern biotechnologies, it has never been so important for us to protect and expand the biological reserves in all of our planet's major regimes. Perhaps the most important features of life come from the unexpected. An anthropo-managed planet would be uniform, safe, predictable, and dead.

I remember a lecture at the University of California at Berkeley in the USA, long ago, by the great scientist and philosopher Michael Polanyi of Manchester, England. He said that if we knew exactly when the tulips would bloom, we would not bother to plant tulips.

References

BEDFORD, S., 1987, Aldous Huxley, a biography: London, Paladin Grafton Books, v. 2, 378 p.

FYFE, W.S., 1988, Deep earth fluxes and the biosphere: Bulletin of the Geological Institutions of the University of Uppasala, N.S. 14, p. 13–20.

GROVE, J.M. 1988, The little ice age: London, Methuen, 498 p.

KENDREW, JOHN, 1988, Foreword, *in* The International Geosphere-Biosphere Programme: A study of global change (IGBP): Stockholm, IGBP Global Change Report 4, 1988, p. 3–5.

LYELL, CHARLES, 1872, Principles of geology (11th edition): London, John Murray, v. 2, 652 p.

MCKIBBEN, BILL, 1989, The end of Nature: New York, Random House, 226 p.

MALONE, T.F., 1985, Preface, *in* Malone, T.F., and Roederer, J.G., eds., Global change: Cambridge, UK, Cambridge University Press, p. xi–xxi.

MUNGALL, C., and MCLAREN, D.J., eds., 1990, Planet under stress: The challenge of global change: Toronto, Oxford University Press and the Royal Society of Canada, 344 p.

NRC (National Research Council), 1986, Global change in the geosphere-biosphere: Initial priorities for an IGBP: Washington, D.C., National Academy Press, 91 p.

PIMENTEL, DAVID, 1987, Technology and natural resources, *in* McLaren, D.J., and Skinner, B.J., eds., Resources and world development, Dahlem workshop reports: New York, John Wiley, p. 679–696.

THE WORLD COMMISSION ON ENVIRONMENT AND DEVELOPMENT, 1987, Our common future: Oxford, Oxford University Press, 383 p.

VERNADSKY, V.I., 1986, The biosphere: Oxford, Synergetic Press, Inc., 82 p. [English language edition published in 1986 based on the 1929 edition in French].

After reading: CONSOLIDATE INFORMATION
1. Summarize Fyfe's major suggestions for saving the earth's environment.
2. Does Fyfe support an anthropocentric or an ecocentric view in order to save the planet? Why?
3. Why does Fyfe suggest that we are entering a new era for the science of the earth?

Effects, Countermeasures, and Implications of Muscle Atrophy Due to Weightlessness

Katherine Welch

Katherine Welch, a student at the University of Indianapolis, wrote this paper for an freshman seminar in Biology.

Before reading: FIRST THOUGHTS
           LOOK AHEAD
1. What kinds of medical research do you think the Space program has encouraged?
2. What do you think would be the effect on human muscles of weightlessness for long periods of time?
3. How does Welch's first paragraph prepare you for the rest of her paper?

During reading: REACT
           QUESTION
           SUMMARIZE
1. What kinds of changes occur in human muscles during weightlessness?
2. Why were the leg muscles and not the arm muscles of Skylab crew members affected?

Space Physiology Is a Facet of biology that has developed with the growth of the space program. Basically, it deals with the effects of space travel on the body. A major topic of concern is the effect of long-term existence in a zero-gravity environment on the muscular system, and how the debilitating effects can be countered. The results of these investigations carry some interesting implications about man's future in space.

In order to understand the after-effects of weightlessness, one first must understand what changes occur in the muscle. Many experiments involving hindlimb suspension in rats or head-down tilt have been done to study the effects on muscles in a simulated weightless environment. Astronauts are also studied during, before, and after missions in space.

Results from hindlimb suspension and other techniques have shown that muscle quickly atrophies without suitable resistance and that changes in muscle structure and composition occur. Weightlessness removes all antigravitational forces during standing and all counterbalance actions, as well as greatly decreases the weight load from all other muscle actions (Shaw et al 1987). The slow-twitch-dominant muscles, such as the soleus, provide the majority of antigravitational support. Experiments have shown that there is a significant decrease in size and number of slow-oxidative (type I) muscle fibers. There is also a shift in predominately slow-twitch muscles from mostly slow-oxidative fibers to a higher percentage of fast-oxidative (type IIa) fibers (Gardetto et al 1989). Therefore, in the absence of a weight load, these muscles suffer the most, and the ability and endurance to stand or walk (orthostatic tolerance) severely declines (Desplanches et al 1987; Gardetto et al 1989). A build-up of glucocortoids also has catabolic effects on muscle fiber. Glucocortoids tend to affect fast-twitch fibers more than slow-twitch fibers due to the greater flow to these fibers (Hickson et al 1986). An increase in glucocortiods in the blood can be tied to a decrease in exercise and an increase in stress. However, exercise increases androgen levels in the blood and "the growth-promoting effects of androgens reduce the effects of the muscle-wasting glucocortoids" (Hickson et al 1986). Although certain fibers may be affected in different ways, the net result is atrophy of the entire muscle and muscle groups.

The most debilitating effect of prolonged disuse is the loss of muscle mass, or atrophy. The crews from each of the Skylabs experienced a significant decrease in weight, leg volume, and leg strength (Thornton and Rummel 1977). A decrease in muscle mass results in an increase in leg compliance and orthostatic tolerance; it also causes a decrease in aerobic capacity and a greater susceptibility to injury. Force of contraction, endurance, and leg compliance all occur in direct proportion to muscle mass. Convertino et al found that a larger muscle mass will provide more support to the expansion of veins: "The most dominant contributing factor to the determination of leg compliance is muscle mass" (1989). It has been observed that returning astronauts have lost approximately two to three kilograms of body weight—most of which is muscle.

The Skylab examinations were very helpful in developing a suitable exercise program for future long-term space missions. In Skylab 2, only a bicycle ergometer was used for exercise during the mission. This provided excellent cardiovascular conditioning, but the leg muscles especially needed considerably more resistance and weight load to maintain enough strength to walk at earth's gravitational force. In Skylab 3 a "mini-gym" was implemented along with the cycle ergometer. However, the new exercises developed mainly the arms and trunk. Although forces to the legs were higher, they were still not even close to providing an adequate level of work, due to the nature of the device. On Skylab 4, an inclined treadmill was used in addition to the ergometer, the MK-1, and MK-2. For approximately 10 minutes per day the astronauts walked, jumped, and jogged on the treadmill, with bungee cords attached to a harness holding the astronaut down in order to simulate almost the full weight of the astronaut. After almost three months of weightlessness, these astronauts experienced a relatively small loss in weight leg volume, and leg strength compared to the previous Skylabs; and they also regained their pre-flight conditions more rapidly (Thornton and Rummel 1977).

The fact that the legs were the parts that were the most affected "illustrates a crucial point in muscle conditioning; to maintain the strength of the muscle, it must be stressed to or near the level at which it will have to function" (Thornton and Rummel 1977). The legs require forces equivalent to hundreds of pounds, while the arms require forces of only tens of pounds. Arm and hand muscle movement in space is still great, although great weight loads are absent. That is why Skylab 3 members retained or increased arm strength during the mission while they used the MK-1 and MK-2. However, these devices did not provide adequate levels of force to the leg muscles despite an increase in the level of ergometer exercise. The treadmill used on Skylab 4 was able to provide suitable exercise to significantly counter the atrophic effects of weightlessness (Thornton and Rummel 1977). Therefore, endurance training with resistive exercise components would be ideal for aeronautic in-flight training. This would increase aerobic fitness as well as muscle mass.

The human body is well made for life on earth, so weightlessness will have adverse effects on humans no matter what types of devices are employed. People in space for very long periods of time could experience great problems upon their return to earth. For muscles, much atrophy can be countered by including a suitable exercise program as part of the daily flight routine. Muscles do recover from atrophy over time, however, depending on the extent of the atrophy.

Along with the growing knowledge in space physiology come questions and implications about man's future in space. There has been one suggestion to send up leg amputees to work in long-term space stations. Legs in a zero gravity environment are not really used. In an environment where size and maneuverability are important, astronauts without the "extra baggage" should be considered. Less time would be spent exercising, and body fluid displacement would be more easily adapted. Perhaps these people would not be so restricted in space as they are on earth. Another possibility is the development of space stations with a controlled gravity environment. This would by far increase people's compatibility and availability to a sealed environment. These are only speculations, however, and the answers to them are still being researched. Perhaps, in time, great steps will be made towards providing devices to reduce or even end muscle atrophy that results from weightlessness.

List of Works Consulted

CONVERTINO, V.A. ET AL. 1988. Leg size and muscle functions associated with leg compliance. *J Appl Physiol.* 60:1017–21.

DESPLANCHES, D. ET AL. 1987. Structural and functional responses to prolonged hindlimb suspension in rat muscle. *J Appl Physiol.* 63:558–563.

GARDETTO, P.R. ET AL. 1989. Contractile function of single muscle fibers after hindlimb suspension. *J Appl Physiol.* 66:2739–49.

HICKSON, R.C. ET AL. 1986. Glucocorticoid cystol binding in exercise-induced sparing of muscle atrophy. *J Appl Physiol.* 60:1413–19.

SHAW, S.R. 1987. Mechanical, Morphological, and Biochemical Adaptations of Bone and Muscle to Hindlimb Suspension and Exercise. *J Biomech.* 20:225–234.

THORNTON, W.E. and RUMMEL, J.A. 1977. Muscular Deconditioning and Its Prevention in Space Flight. Johnston, R.S. and Dietlein, L.F. (Eds.) *Biomedical Results from Skylab.* pp. 191–197. Scientific and Technical Information Office NASA, Washington, D.C.

After reading: CONSOLIDATE INFORMATION

1. Summarize Welch's conclusions about research on the effects of space travel on muscles.
2. Evaluate the suggestion that people whose legs have been amputated should be considered likely candidates for space travel.
3. Do you think research on the effects of space travel on the human muscular system has implications for scientists and people who remain on earth?

Pikas: Ochotona Princeps
Amy Workman

Amy Workman, a student at Earlham College, wrote the following report for a Zoology class. Written for an upper-level course, this paper has a more technical tone than Katherine Welch's paper.

Before reading: FIRST THOUGHTS
LOOK AHEAD

1. Have you ever heard of or seen a pika? Read Workman's second paragraph; how do you visualize pikas after reading her description?

2. What is your understanding of the words *territorial* and *territoriality* as they refer to animals?

During reading: REACT
       QUESTION
       SUMMARIZE

1. Workman terms the social organization which pikas have developed "complex"; what do you think she means?
2. Why have pikas managed to reproduce in large numbers so rapidly?

IF YOU'VE EVER BEEN WANDERING in the mountains of western North America you may have noticed, as you entered an area of step rock fall, a small tailless creature with rounded ears, otherwise known as a pika, *Ochotona princeps*. These herbivorous mammals, once thought of as rodents, are classified under the order Lagomorpha, distinguished from other mammals by the extra set of incisors located directly behind the first set (Huntly, 1986). Originating in Asia, pikas spread to Europe in the Oligocene epoch and then to North America in the Pliocene epoch. Pika species reached their greatest diversity during the Miocene period whereas now sixteen genera are extinct and only one genus, Ochotona, with fifteen species, exists today (Southwick, 1986).

Reaching between 12 and 25 cm. in length and ranging in colors of greyish brown to red, in order to match their rocky habitat, pikas exhibit many unique behaviors relative to most other small, ground dwelling mammals (Huntly, 1987). Highly territorial and with a large range of vocals, *Ochotona princeps* have a very complex social organization. Because pikas live under harsh conditions, among the crevices of steep fallen rock and talus, they have a mating system and life development that denotes an original lifestyle which makes them truly fascinating creatures.

Pikas must obtain all their food for the winter during the short alpine summer months because they are not true hibernators and remain active in their dens all year (Golian, 1985). From May until June, they feed on grasses and flowering stalks and, towards the end of the growing season, partake in an activity called "haying." Wildflowers and shrubs are collected and stored in great piles within the pika den. This activity increases towards the season's end because such piles tend to decompose less rapidly in the fall than in the spring. *Ochotona* were found to hay farther from the dens than they would graze, the primary reason for this being predatory risk in more exposed areas associated with the amount of awareness needed for grazing versus haying (Huntly, 1986). Pikas with dens closer to optimal grazing and haying areas generally had better reproductive success than those pikas with less convenient sites (Brandt, 1989). Such situations have given rise to a strict establishment of territories and variety of behaviors that coincide with the maintenance of such territories.

Pika territories range from 30 to 100 meters in diameter and are thought to be food-based. In direct correlation with this, however, is the mate selection process that seems to be greatly influenced by the availability of food with respect to site location (Brandt, 1989). In choosing mates for the the breeding season, females preferred males who here heavier (160g compared to the normal 150g), had territories in optimal grazing locations and had den sites with one entrance only. Females that mated with males that occupied such territories produced more young than those females reproducing under lesser conditions (Brandt, 1989). It would reasonably follow that the defense of such territories would be to the male pika's advantage.

One study conducted by Andrew Smith gives more evidence showing how the mating process is related to the establishment of territories (1986). He found that pika sites were consistently set up in such a fashion so that each individual's territory was surrounded by territories of the opposite sex. It has been proposed that this arrangement was made so individuals would have better access to potential mates. Picas of the opposite sex frequently shared activity fields, where those of the same sex exhibited aggression when a territory was invaded. Because such acts of aggression often result in injury to one or both of the individuals involved, other means of establishing one's territory have developed among pikas.

The main forms of recognition used by pikas involve means of scent or vocalization. Scented secretions from glands in the cheeks of pikas can be found all over a given individual's territory and seem to convey sexual identify. Fecal matter and urine mark each site and are also thought to be used as a form of recognition (Meaney, 1987). Vocalizations, however, seem to be the most distinct form of territorial defense as well as a way of relaying messages between mates and mother and young.

Oftentimes, during a hike, one may spot a pika perched atop a boulder, head tilted back, uttering a long nasal twang of a call, only to quickly disappear amid the rocks and be heard in echoes along the valley walls. Though it may seem amusing or cute, such displays are not merely for human benefit. *Ochotona princeps* are the most vocal of all the Lagomorphs and adults possess a repertoire of nine different calls. Such calls were at first thought to be used solely for the purpose of attracting attention to a predator's approach. It was recently been determined, however, that these calls are used for a variety of different situations and are an essential form of communication among community and family members (Conner, 1985a).

Pikas are capable of vocalizing the moment they are born. These first calls are mostly associated with conditions of hunger, cold, injury and other uncomfortable circumstances. As pikas mature they develop a series of nine structurally distinct calls which have been categorized into two groups known as the short and long calls (Conner, 1985b). Short calls are fairly soft and rarely heard by the human ear. They consist of a combination of tooth chattering, 'coughing' and low trills and most commonly occur along territory boundaries and are sometimes followed by acts of physical aggression. Long calls vary in intensity, the loudest being a high nasal descending note often emitted upon spotting a potential predator. Other longs calls are often preceded by a soft twitter, are only used when potential mates are present and are therefore thought to be a form of mate advertisement (Conner, 1985a). Pikas seem to have developed such forms of vocalization so that the communications necessary for territorial establishment and mate choice could occur. From these findings it is evident that pika calls didn't evolve only because of the visually disruptive environment but also because of the development of the social organization unique to these small creatures (Conner, 1985b).

Another original characteristic of pikas is their incredibly fast rate of growth. Mating begins at the start of May and an average of two litters a year are produced. Although there is strong evidence for monogamy, males do not assist the females in rearing the young as is often the case in monogamous relationships (Brandt, 1989). Pika gestation periods last for 30 days followed by 30 days of weaning although young pikas are capable of ingesting solid food after only seven days. For the first few days out of the den, pikas remain within a few meters of the den entrance but by the end of the summer have travelled most of the surrounding talus areas. Quick growth rates are to the pika's advantage for the alpine summer months are short and the young must gather enough food in order to sustain themselves through the winter (Brandt, 1989).

Depending on the population density of a community, young sometimes inherit the activity areas of their parents and are not required to find new territories during their first season of life. The higher the population density the more likely parents are to drive their young away from the den and likewise, the lower the density, the more likely young are to become philopatric (Smith, 1987). Pikas have the most stable annual population densities of all small mammals with a fluctuation rate of less than 30% compared to most mammal fluctuations or 60 to 100%. This is thought to be due to the social organization and the consistent establishment of territories among pikas yet it is nonetheless a remarkable development considering the harsh environments, with such high annual and seasonal variations, in which these animals live (Southwick, 1986).

Though they share the same tooth configuration as other Lagomorphs, pikas could almost be put in a class by themselves. No other small mammals exhibit the unique characteristics of *Ochotona princeps*. Their original social, vocal and mating systems, not to mention their extremely rapid growth rate and life development processes, have, for many, made these creatures a topic of high interest. Although they seem to have passed their evolutionary peak, pikas will startle the wandering mountain traveler with their curious cries for many years to come.

Literature Cited

1. Brandt, Charles. 1989. Mate choice and reproductive success of pikas. Animal Behaviour: 118–32.

2. Conner, Douglas, 1985a. Analysis of the vocal repertoire of adult pikas: ecological and evolutionary perspectives. Animal Behaviour: 124–34.

3. Conner, Douglas, 1985b. The ontogeny of vocal communication in the pika. Journal of Mammology: 149–53.

4. Golian, Steven. 1985. Growth of pikas in Colorado. Journal of Mammology: 367–71.

5. Huntly, Nancy. 1986. Foraging behavior of the pika, with comparisons of grazing versus haying. Journal of Mammology: 139–48.

6. Huntly, Nancy. 1987. Influence of refuging consumers on subalpine meadow vegetation. Ecology: 274–83.

7. Meaney, Carron. 1987. Cheek-gland odors in pikas: discrimination of individual and sex differences. Journal of Mammology: 391–5.

8. Smith, Andrew. 1986. Territorial intrusions by pikas as a function of occupant activity. Animal Behaviour: 392–7.

9. Smith, Andrew. 1987. Temporal separation between philopatric juvenile pikas and their parents limits behavioural conflict. Animal Behavior: 1210–14.

10. Southwick, Charles. 1986. Population density and fluctuations of pikas in Colorado. Journal of Mammology: 149–53.

After reading: CONSOLIDATE INFORMATION

1. How do pikas provide an example of the adaptive processes of fauna?
2. Why does Workman suggest that pikas could almost be categorized in a scientific class by themselves?
3. What does Workman find so fascinating about pikas?

Marie-Sophie Germain, 18th Century Physicist
Carrie Masiello

Carrie Masiello, a Physics major at Earlham College, wrote the following paper for a History of Mathematics class. In her paper, Masiello raises some of the issues discussed by Evelyn Fox Keller in her essay "A World of Difference."

Before reading: FIRST THOUGHTS
LOOK AHEAD

1. How difficult do you think it would have been for a woman in the eighteenth century to become a scientists?
2. What is the significance of the two quotations from Gauss and Shakespeare at the beginning of Masiello's paper?
3. What are the advantages and disadvantages of being a self-taught scientist?

During reading: REACT
>QUESTION
>SUMMARIZE

1. What is your reaction to Gauss's evaluation of Sophie Germain's talent and his subsequent failure to help her win a place in the scientific community?
2. What were the kinds of obstacles Germain had to face in practicing mathematics?

"Mathematics is the queen of the sciences and arithmetic is the queen of mathematics."—Carl Freidrich Gauss

"Thou, nature, art my goddess; to thy laws
My services are bound." Shakespeare, *King Lear*; Gauss's motto[1]

MARIE-SOPHIE GERMAIN was born on April 1, 1776 in Paris into a wealthy family that was largely able to shelter her from the political chaos of the time; however, as a result she spent much of her childhood in solitude.[2] She found a biography of Archimedes in her father's library, and she was fascinated by the story of his death. She reasoned that if Archimedes found geometry so interesting that threatening soldiers did not break his concentration, then it might alleviate her boredom while cooped up in her home, and so she began to study math. By the time she was 18 she had taught herself differential calculus.[3]

She was not permitted to attend the Ecole Polytechnique in Paris, but she collected the lecture notes to a chemistry class and Joseph Lagrange's analysis class, and at the end of the term she submitted some of her original work to Joseph Lagrange under a pseudonym.[4] He reacted positively to her work, and after discovering who she was, he came to her home to praise her.

After mastering calculus, she acquired a copy of C. F. Gauss's *Disquitiones Arithmeticae*, a ground-breaking publication in number theory. As a result of reading *Disquitiones Arithmeticae*, she began a correspondence with Gauss, again under a masculine pseudonym. Gauss corresponded with her for three years before he found out who she was. His city in Germany was beseiged, and Sophie Germain, fearing for his safety, used connections in the French military to assure that he was not involved in the battles. Gauss was safe, but Sophie eventually had to identify herself.[5] Gauss's response to her was to praise her for overcoming so many of the barriers that prohibit women from studying math:

> But when a woman, because of her sex, our customs and prejudices, encounters infinitely more obstacles than men in familiarizing herself with the knotty problems [of number theory], yet overcomes these fetters and penetrates that which is most hidden, she doubtless has the most noble courage, extraordinary talent, and superior genius.[6]

He continued to correspond with her until 1808, and her work inspired some of his thinking; however, he did nothing toward forwarding her formal education.

Sophie Germain moved from number theory to mathematical physics after being inspired by a demonstration of a physical system for which no description had been found. Ernest Chaladni demonstrated the nodal patterns formed when an elastic surface was sprinkled with sand and then set vibrating with a bow. The French Academy established a prize of one kilogram of gold to the person who could analyze the different nodes formed. There is evidence that the competition was established by Pierre Laplace, who hoped that his student Simeon Dennis Poisson would be able to solve the problem.[7] Sophie Germain entered a solution after eight months of work, but was told by the judges (Laplace, Lagrange, and Legendre) that her principal equation was wrong. She worked for another year and produced a solution which was given an honorable mention. Meanwhile, the judging committee was enlarged to include Poisson, who soon after submitted a publication on elastic surfaces to the Academy which obviously reflected her work. Complaints were lodged, and Sophie Germain continued to work on the problem. Her third entry earned her the prize, although it was more for her experimental work than for her mathematical derivations.[8]

Her lack of formal education had not been a problem in her studies in number theory because it was such a new field. However, when she began to work in mathematical physics, it became a barrier.[9] She did not know the physical language that was in use at the time, and therefore some of her work was unacceptable in the academic community. After the Academy failed to respond to her later work in elastic surfaces, she went back to number theory. She spent the next few years working on the problem of Fermat's Last Theorem.

Pierre de Fermat wrote in the margin of one of his books,

> It is impossible for a cube to be written as a sum of two cubes or a fourth power to be written as the sum of two fourth powers or, in general, for any number which is a power greater than the second to be written as a sum of two like powers. I have a truly marvelous demonstration of this which this margin is too narrow to contain.[10]

Algebraically this becomes the statement that the equation $x^n + y^n = z^n$ has no solutions in the integers for $n > 2$. (For the case $n = 2$, the problem becomes one of finding Pythagorean triples). Initially Germain set out to prove the theorem, but Legendre encouraged her to limit her work to a specific case. She developed a theorem that verifies Fermat's statement for all prime numbers $n < 100$ if neither x, y, or z are divisible by n. Her work has been extended and improved by other mathematicians, but her method remains useful.

Fermat's Last Theorem is traditionally divided into two cases. Case I is the case in which none of the three numbers x, y, and z is divisible by n. In Case II, only one of the three numbers is divisible by n.[11] In this terminology, Sophie Germain's theorem becomes this:

> Theorem: Let n be an odd prime. If there is an auxiliary prime p with the properties that

(1) $x^n + y^n + z^n = 0 \mod p$ implies $x = 0$ or $y = 0$ or $z = 0 \mod p$, and
(2) $x^n = n \mod p$ is impossible
the case I of Fermat's Last Theorem is true for n.[12]

In words, this proof says that if n is an odd prime and there is some other prime p not equal to n, and p meets conditions (1) and (2), then $x^n + y^n + z^n = 0$ has no solutions if none of x, y, or z are divisible by n. This theorem allowed Sophie Germain to prove Fermat's Last Theorem for $n < 100$ (i.e., she found another p for every n.)[13] Her proof was a proof by contradiction: she assumed the conditions of the theorem are met and that x, y, and z are all integers which satisfy $x^n + y^n + z^n = 0$, and then she showed that this led to a contradiction.[14]

After her publications on elastic surfaces and Fermat's Last Theorem, Sophie Germain was invited into more frequent contact with members of the scientific community than she had enjoyed in her early career. She became friends with Joseph Fourier. Fourier eventually became the Permanent Secretary of the Academy of Sciences, and one of his first acts in that office was to insure that Sophie Germain could attend every session. However, she soon developed breast cancer and she spent the last few years of her life writing about philosophy.[15]

Sophie Germain was recognized during her lifetime as a mathematical genius, but was treated less as a mathematician than as a phenomenon.[16] Gauss, Legendre and Lagrange all encouraged her to continue working, but none of them did anything toward formalizing her education, the one vital ingredient that her genius lacked. Clearly this is because she was a woman, and they were unable to deal with women as intellectuals. Yet Gauss says that "Mathematics is the queen of the sciences, and arithmetic is the queen of mathematics." His motto also includes a reference to nature as a goddess. Surely his use of the feminine pronoun here is not accidental. In his language, Gauss equates women with what he studies: mathematics, nature. In both these cases woman is object here, and not subject. This use of language reflects the societal inability to take women seriously as subjects, independents in their own right. This is part of why Sophie Germain remained an untrained genius.

Endnotes

1. Howard Eves, *An Introduction to the History of Mathematics*, Philadelphia: Saunders College Publishing, 1983, p. 359.
2. Lynn M. Osen, *Women in Mathematics*, Cambridge, Massachusetts: The MIT Press, 1988, p. 84.
3. Osen, 85.
4. Margaret Alic, *Hypatia's Heritage: A History of Women in Science from Antiquity to the Nineteenth Century*, Boston: Beacon Press, 1986, p. 149.
5. Osen, 86.
6. Alic, 149–150.
7. Alic, 150–151.
8. Alic, 154–155.
9. Alic, 150.
10. Harold M. Edwards, *Fermat's Last Theorem: A Genetic Introduction to Algebraic Number Theory*, New York: Springer-Verlag, 1977, p. 1.

11. Edwards, 63.
12. Edwards, 64.
13. Edwards, 65.
14. Edwards, 65.
15. Alic, 156.
16. Alic, 156.

After reading: CONSOLIDATE INFORMATION

1. Summarize Masiello's conclusions about Marie Sophie Germain.
2. After reading Masiello's essay, what can you infer about women's professional roles in the eighteenth century?
3. Masiello wrote this paper for a History of Mathematics class. How do you think her audience (a professor and students in History of Mathematics) and context helped her decide how to focus the paper and what to include in it?

Further Explorations for Readings in the Sciences

1. Howard Frumkin, Scott Saleska, and Tom Shoop all address questions of scientific research and public policy. Review each essay and draw some conclusions about what you think the federal government's role in making science policy should be.
2. Review the essays by Carole Ezzell, Stephen Jay Gould, and Eveyln Fox Keller and write a short description of how scientific hypotheses are formed and then responded to, changed, modified, and accepted by the scientific community.
3. Much of the research described in Ron Cowen's article "Catching Some Rays," Tom Shoop's "Biology's Moon Shot" and Katherine Welch's essay "Effects, Countereffects and Implications of Muscle Atrophy Due to Weightlessness" is funded by the federal government. Do you think that the federal government should fund scientific research in all fields or should it restrict its funding to projects such as those directly connected to the Space program or defense? Defend your answer.
4. The research articles in this section co-authored by Terry Crow and James Forrester and by Mushrush, Mose, and Chrosinak, and the report written by Amy Workman address the authors' scientific colleagues. What characteristics of a formal research article can you infer from these articles?
5. In her conclusion about eighteenth century physicist Marie Sophie Germain, Carrie Masiello suggested that the scientific world was and is still dominated by men. Compare and contrast Masiello's conclusions about gender and science with those of Evelyn Fox Keller.
6. What kinds of questions do W.S. Fyfe's essay on the International Biosphere/Geosphere Programme and Scott Saleska's article on low-level radioactive waste raise about the destructive effects human technology has had on the earth's envi-

ronment? Does either author suggest any solutions for containing or reversing environmental damage?
7. The articles by Ron Cowen, Carole Ezzell, and Stephen Jay Gould address a broad range audience and would not be considered scholarly sources by scientists, yet these essays could point student researchers to questions which could be explored in scientific research literature. Choose one of these articles and list some of the issues and questions you might explore in an academic paper.

Credits continued

Page 29, Brian Henderson, "*The Civil War:* Did It Not Seem Real?" © 1991 by the Regents of the University of California. Reprinted from *Film Quarterly*, Vol. 44, No. 3 (Spring '91), pp. 2–14, by permission. **Page 42**, "Two Critical Views of *The Handmaid's Tale*" by Edd Doerr and Michael Calleri first appeared in the May/June issue of *The Humanist* and is reprinted with permission. **Page 50**, Richard Welch, "Rock 'n Roll and Social Change," *History Today*, February, 1990, pp. 32–39. **Page 60**, Thomas Fiddick, "Beyond the Domino Theory: The Vietnam War and Metaphors of Sport," *Journal of American Culture*, 1989, pp. 79–87. **Page 74**, James Kitfield, "Total Force," *Government Executive*, March 1991, pp. 10–15. Permission to reprint granted by *Government Executive* magazine (March 1991). **Page 82**, Anthony G. Amsterdam, "Capital Punishment." Originally published in *Stanford Magazine*, Fall/Winter 1977. **Page 95**, Christopher Meyers, "Racial Bias, the Death Penalty, and Desert." First published in *The Philosophical Forum*, Volume XXII, Number 2, Winter 1990–91. **Page 104**, Tracy Marschall, "An Exercise in Feminist Liberation Theology: Islam, Judaism, and Christianity." **Page 112**, Brian Handrigan, "The Way We Make Ethical Decisions: Understanding the Subjectivity of Values." **Page 117**, Lisa A. Jones, "Biblical Echoes in Margaret Atwood's *The Handmaid's Tale*." **Page 123**, B.F. Skinner, "Outlining a Science of Feeling." Reprinted from *The Times Literary Supplement*, 8 May 1987. (With permission of the B.F. Skinner Foundation.) **Page 132**, Hatfield, E., & Rapson, R. (1991). Emotions: A trinity. In E.A. Blechman (Ed.), *Emotions and the family: For better or for worse* (pp. 11–25). Hillsdale, NJ: Lawrence Erlbaum Associates, Inc. **Page 145**, Mary Field Belenky, Blythe McVicker Clinchy, Nancy Rule Goldberger, and Jill Mattuck Tarule, "Family Life and the Politics of Talk." Excerpt from *Women's Ways of Knowing* edited by Mary Field Belenky. Copyright © 1986 by Basic Books, Inc. Reprinted by permission of Basic Books, Inc., a division of HarperCollins Publishers. **Page 156**, Michael W. Tucker and Kevin O'Grady, "Effects of Physical Attractiveness, Intelligence, Age at Marriage, and Cohabitation on the Perception of Marital Satisfaction," *The Journal of Social Psychology*, 131(2), pp. 252–269, 1991. Reprinted with permission of the Helen Dwight Reid Educational Foundation. Published by Heldref Publications, 4000 Albemarle St., N.W., Washington, D.C. 20016. Copyright © 1991. **Page 171**, Margaret A. Eisenhart, "Learning to Romance: Cultural Acquisition in College." Reproduced by permission of the American Anthropological Association from *Anthropology and Education Quarterly* 21:1, March 1990. Not for further reproduction. **Page 191**, Steven A. Reiss, "Sport in the Black Urban Community." In Steven A. Reiss, *City Games: The evolution of American urban society and the rise of sports* (pp. 113–123). Urbana, IL: University of Illinois Press, 1989. Copyright ©

1989 by the University of Illinois Press. **Page 202**, Margaret Mead, *Coming of Age in Samoa*. New York: William Morrow & Company, Inc. Copyright © 1970 (1928) by Margaret Mead. Used by permission of William Morrow & Company, Inc./Publishers, New York. **Page 206**, Richard Feinberg, "Margaret Mead and Samoa: *Coming of Age* in Fact and Fiction." Reproduced by permission of the American Anthropological Association from *American Anthropologist* 90:3, September 1988. Not for further reproduction. **Page 217**, Wilson Carey McWilliams, "A Republic of Couch Potatoes: The Media Shrivel the Electorate." *Commonweal*, 10 March 1989, pp. 138–140. Copyright © 1989 Commonweal Foundation. **Page 222**, Christine F. Ridout, "The Role of Media Coverage of Iowa and New Hampshire in the 1988 Democratic Nomination," *American Politics Quarterly*, Vol. 19, No. 1 (January 1991), pp. 43–58, copyright © 1991 by Sage Publications, Inc. Reprinted by permission of Sage Publications, Inc. **Page 235**, Lori A. Rose, "Nonverbal Communication." **Page 240**, Richard Shea and Daniel Zona, "A Survey of Dating Violence on a University Campus." **Page 249**, Tamara S. Peters, "The Diagnosis and Treatment of *Bulimia Nervosa*." **Page 255**, Howard Frumkin, "Occupational and Environmental Cancer: Radical Chic and Mau-Mauing the Carcinogens," *Science for the People*, January/February 1989, pp. 12–17. **Page 263**, Scott Saleska, "Low-Level Radioactive Waste: Gamma Rays in the Garbage," April 1990. From the BULLETIN OF THE ATOMIC SCIENTISTS. Copyright © 1990 by the Educational Foundation for Nuclear Science, 6042 South Kimbark, Chicago, IL 60637 USA. A one-year subscription is $30. **Page 273**, Ron Cowen, "Catching Some Rays: Earth-Based Detectors Hunt for Violent Stellar Events," *Science News*, Vol. 139 (May 11, 1991), pp. 296–299. Reprinted with permission from SCIENCE NEWS, the weekly newsmagazine of science, copyright 1991 by Science Service, Inc. **Page 281**, Evelyn Fox Keller, "A World of Difference." In Evelyn Fox Keller, *Reflections on Gender and Science* (pp. 158–176). New Haven, CT: Yale University Press. Copyright © 1985 by Yale University Press. **Page 295**, Tom Shoop, "Biology's Moon Shot: The Human Genome Project." Permission to reprint granted by *Government Executive* magazine (February 1991). **Page 303**, Carole Ezzell, "Memories Might Be Made of This: Closing in on the Biochemistry of Learning." *Science News*, Vol. 139 (May 25, 1991), pp. 328–330. Reprinted with permission from SCIENCE NEWS, the weekly newsmagazine of science, copyright 1991 by Science Service, Inc. **Page 309**, Terry Crow and James Forrester, "Inhibition of Protein Synthesis Blocks Long-Term Enhancement of Generator Potentials Produced by One-Trial *in vivo* Conditioning in *Hermissenda*," *Proceedings of the National Academy of Science*, Vol. 87 (June 1990), pp. 4490–4494. **Page 322**, Stephen Jay Gould, "Sex, Drugs, Disasters, and the Extinction of the Dinosaurs," *Discover* (March 1984). **Page 329**, George W. Mushrush, Douglas G. Mose, and Charles E. Chrosinak, "Indoor Radon in Northern Virginia: Seasonal Changes and Correlations with Geology." Courtesy *Episodes*, Vol. 12, No. 1 (March 1989), pp. 6–9. **Page 338**, W.S. Fyfe, "The International Geosphere/Biosphere Programme and Global Change: An Anthropologic or Ecocentric Future? A Personal View." Courtesy *Episodes*, Vol. 13, No. 2 (June 1990), pp. 100–102. **Page 345**, Katherine Welch, "Effects, Countermeasures, and Implications of Muscle Atrophy Due to Weightlessness." **Page 348**, Amy Workman, "Pikas: *Ochotona princeps*." **Page 352**, Carrie Masiello, "Marie-Sophie Germain, 18th Century Physicist."